VALIANT YOUNG MEN

Heroes of Flight

BRYCE D. GIBBY

Valiant Young Men, Heroes of Flight, **1st Edition.**

Printed and bound in the United States of America.

ISBN 0-9741743-2-7

LCCN 2005909306

PERLYCROSS
PUBLISHERS
Wilmington, Delaware

Published by Perlycross Publishers
2711 Centerville Road, Suite 120, PMB 5544
Wilmington, Delaware 19808

Susan G. Hancock, Editor

"The Perle, as it flows on the north of the Churchyard, the bridge two or three hundred yards below, the vale, and the hills which shape it, are comprised in the parish of Perlycross." R.D. Blackmore

DEDICATED TO MY FATHER E. GRANT GIBBY —

That great aviator who now flies wingless towards his destiny as a Man, exalted and ennobled. He it was who first taught me of life's purpose, at times using the principles of flight to forge manhood. From his lips I first heard the name of two of the principal characters of this book, Antoine de Saint-Exupéry and Captain Eddie Rickenbacker. The third hero, Captain James Norman Hall, I discovered while doing research on the 94th Aero Squadron. A self-effacing man who shunned publicity, Hall is not as widely known as the other principals in *Valiant Young Men.* However, of the three protagonists Jimmy Hall is most like my own father in kindness, humility, and simplicity. Grant Gibby, much like Hall, thought of himself as a common man who, in truth, was anything but common. As Father greatly admired Rickenbacker and Saint-Exupéry, he would also have loved Hall had he known this man as I have come to know him.

Grant and Blanche Gibby – The author's father and mother

CONTENTS

Introduction

Bryce D. Gibby's book, *Valiant Young Men—Heroes of Flight,* is an exciting and informative comparison of three well known pioneers of aviation who shared common backgrounds, diversity, near death experiences, and a love for flying. It is filled with examples of the demanding challenges of flight during those early years. The lives, virtues, philosophical views, and experiences of Antoine de Saint-Exupéry, Captain Eddie Rickenbacker, and Captain James Hall are used to evaluate, define, and portray the development and measurement of manhood. Gibby's flowing writing style and special use of verse and quotation from these and other pioneers makes the book easy to read and relevant to life today. The stoic resolve of these heroes as they faced both everyday living and uncommon danger makes Gibby's theory on the development of young men credible and real. The growth of manhood or "man making" is a well-defined theme. Examining the personal history, values, faith, responsibility and self-reliance of each historic aviator reveals how they faced life threatening challenges and more—for these qualities learned and activated may likewise empower youth today.

As a former aviator, I found this book real, exciting, and appropriate to the theme of manhood. *Valiant Young Men—Heroes of Flight* is a book that I will read time and time again, for in it I come face to face with greatness. My compliments to Bryce Gibby for writing one of the best books on leadership and the development of young men that I have ever read.

N. Michael Bissell
Brigadier General U.S. Army (VA)
Commandant of Cadets
VWIL Corps of Cadets
Former Commander of the 17th Aviation Group

Former Commander of the Joint Republic of Korea Army Combined Aviation Force

Former Director of U.S. Army Flight Training

Former Deputy Chief of the Staff of the 101st Airborne Division (Air Assault)

Former Executive Officer to the Director of Operations at the Joint Chiefs of Staff

Two tours as a combat helicopter pilot in Vietnam where he received the Distinguished Service Cross, the Bronze Star, the Purple Heart and the Air Medal with "V" device and 24 Oak Leaf Clusters.

Foreword

To make this contribution to Bryce Gibby's inspirational book *Valiant Young Men—Heroes of Flight*, is undoubtedly one of the most intimidating, yet touching, requests that has ever been asked of me. As the grandson of James Norman Hall, one the three valiant young men whose lives are chronicled in this literary marvel, I know first hand how the lives of great men can influence and inspire youth to pursue paths of excellence. This is particularly true of aspiring aviators. Bryce Gibby has dedicated several years of his life merging the biographical histories of Captain Eddie Rickenbacker, James Norman Hall and Antoine de Saint-Exupéry into a work of literature that is truly one of a kind. This incredible volume will be an inspiration to the rising generation to follow in the wings of three of the most valiant, dedicated, adventurous and unique aviators in the history of aviation. It is an accomplishment of the highest order and is an invaluable contribution to our society—one that Bryce Gibby should be extremely proud of.

The aeronautical history of my family literally spans the history of military aviation. Grandfather Hall commenced this legacy with his service as one of the founding members of the Escadrille Lafayette and later as Captain Eddie Rickenbacker's wing commander in the famed 94th Pursuit Squadron of the First World War. My father served in World War Two as a Marine radio-gunner aboard the Grumman TBM Avenger. I fought and flew in Vietnam and am a former Commander of the UH-60 Blackhawk. My son defends our nation flying the F-15C in the present day War on Terrorism. Our sense of duty, our patriotism and pride in service to our country, no doubt has root in the values inherited from the sire of these four generations of the Hall/Rutgers family. A brief narrative of my family's unique involvement in the saga of aviation is included at the end of Chapter XVIII, *Roots and Branches,* and is written in tribute to the man we affectionately refer to as Papa Hall.

From the very young age of five I wrote to Santa Claus and asked for a model airplane—from that point on I was captivated with the desire to fly, which desire has never left me. I can remember sitting at my grandfather's desk a myriad of times during my childhood in Tahiti, a desk where Grandpa Hall wrote so many great works, such as *Mutiny on the Bounty.* I looked through Grandad's history of the Escadrille Lafayette and *Falcons of France,* aviation books that would inspire any impressionable young man. My Grandmother Lala often told me stories of Grandfather Hall's flying experiences during World War I. These true-life adventures left such an impression on my mind that they will stay with me forever. Many of the accounts are re-told in this narrative. Although I was only three when Papa Hall made his final flight Westbound, his presence in my life is so vivid that I have truly gotten to know this wonderful man. What is so remarkable about my valiant grandfather, is that in spite of the fact that he was one of the most decorated ace, fighter pilots of World War I, yet he never learned to drive a car, and thought that Tahiti in the 1920's was too commercialized. Jimmy Hall was also a man of such humility that none of his friends and neighbors ever knew of his stellar wartime heroism during the "War to end all wars" until his passing.

Most of us in the world of aviation are aware of the tremendous accomplishments of Captain Eddie Rickenbacker and Antoine de Saint-Exupéry. Yet Bryce Gibby has brought their lives to light, along with Grandfather Hall's, to a degree that is amazing—even to those of us who are related to these giants among men. These men lived and flew in the early, dangerous fledgling days of aviation; their astonishing experiences can never be replicated. In this era of fast-paced, high-tech aviation, it is sometimes hard to imagine what it must have been like in the beginning days of the flying machine. This book rolls back decades for the reader, placing him in the cockpits of biplanes made of wood and fabric, where through the eyes of these three young heroes he relives daring acts of courage and witnesses history-changing accomplishments of great valor. Not only do we visualize what they *did,* but we learn the values that made them what they *are.* This is a gift from Bryce Gibby to all of his fellow aviators.

By any literary measure, this latest work by Bryce Gibby will no doubt soar to great heights in the eyes of those of us in the aviation fraternity, past, present and future, and all others whose ideals and aspirations parallel the values we hold dear. A fellow aviator, Bryce Gibby, whose father learned to fly in the golden age of aviation prior to World War II and inspired him to follow in his contrail, has written a book so captivating and inspiring that young men of today who read this work, will aspire to follow in the footsteps of these most valiant aviation pioneers.

— Nicholas G. Rutgers III
Grandson of James Norman Hall
B-747-400 First Officer, United Airlines
CW4 (Ret) U.S. Army, Former Aircraft
Commander, UH-60 Blackhawk

Acknowledgments

This book is second in a series, preceded in 2003 by Valiant Young Women—Heroines. As in that volume, I acknowledge as instrumental in the development of this work a heroine of extraordinary vigor and virtue, my dear mother, Blanche Slater Gibby. I read every line of Valiant Young Men—Heroes of Flight to Mother as it was written, often in the late hours of the evening. Her comments, criticisms and suggestions were invaluable. The reader will notice on the dedicatory page a photograph of my father and mother. The aircraft is a "Fleet" Biplane, a total wreck two years earlier—restored to perfection by the craftsmanship of Dad, covered in "Grade A Linen" sewn by Mom. Her gaze is fixed on the eternal sky, the boundless dominion of father. His gaze is fixed on her, the partner of his dominion. As this book strives to teach unchanging truth, I am indebted to parents who lived in true unchanging love. The last time I saw my father look at my mother before he died, I saw the same devoted gaze as the one found in this 1936 photograph.

The tireless efforts of my editor and sister, Susan G. Hancock, were essential in this endeavor. Susan and I have always greatly enjoyed life and literature together. It was a particular pleasure to work with her on this labor of love as she shares equally an aviation heritage.

There are many others whose inputs and encouragements are much appreciated. Among these are Scott Cameron, Associate Dean of the J. Reuben Clark Law School, who graciously assisted in the final edit; Brigadier General N. Michael Bissell and Commander Nicholas G. Rutgers III wrote the introduction and foreward respectively; Nick and Nancy Rutgers opened their home and hearts to the author and provided first hand knowledge of the era of this work; the grandchildren of Eddie Rickenbacker, namely David Brian Rickenbacker, Nancy

Schindler, James Rickenbacker, Thomas Rickenbacker, and Marcie Rickenbacker willingly read the manuscript and provided valuable commentary on its accuracy; Ken Perich, a resolute advocate of aviation heritage and my tireless ally; my brothers, David and Roger Gibby and my good friend, Mel Kemp, were always available for content discussion.

Preface

The psalmist asked the question: "What is man, that thou art mindful of him? . . . [Thou] hast crowned him with glory and honour. Thou madest him to have dominion over the works of thy hands." The question is only partly answered by the psalmist as he recognized the kingly qualities of one who has attained valiant manhood. Man is greater than the sum of his years, his origin and destiny greater than the limits of mortality, his purpose greater than earthly dominion. A male is born, but a man is *made*—made through choice, sedulous effort, and through mastery of adversity. The best definition of manhood is not found in letters, but in life. This narrative puts before the reader three young men of valor who, in extreme circumstances, were exemplary to the principles of true manhood. They lived lives of tremendous challenge and adventure. Their life stories define the fundamentals of *man-making*. Edwin Markham wrote:

> We are all blind, until we see
> That in the human plan
> Nothing is worth the making if
> It does not make the man.
>
> Why build these cities glorious
> If man unbuilded goes?
> In vain we build the work, unless
> The builder also grows.[1]

There are cynics who loudly denounce all that is good and godly. With a wry smile on their lips and in their pseudo-sophistication they mock the great virtues as being unattainable. Being of low character it is inconceivable to their bent minds that any man could truly attain a life of greatness superior to their unremarkable existence. Believing only in the immensity of space and not in the omniscience of Heaven, thinking that they are the progeny of the fittest animals rather than sons of an omnipotent Heavenly Father, they adhere to an amoral code of conduct and seek to debunk God-given canons. In this effort such scoffers find it useful to debase the character of great men by exposing their real or pretended faults; believing that by pulling down they are raised up. In recent years it has become shockingly popular to seek to repudiate the integrity of such men as America's founding fathers or the leaders of great movements; to point out frailties and shortcomings, as if mortal greatness were dependent upon perfection. This indoctrination of our society has been so successful that, sadly, many young men no longer aspire to self-mastery, thinking it foolish and impossible to tame their so-called animal appetites. The immature predisposition of our nature is to find fault, but society builds upon this tendency by training our minds through humanistic education to suppress elevated thought and behavior. William George Jordan said:

> Most people study character as a proofreader pores over a great poem; his ears are dulled to the majesty and music of the lines, his eyes are darkened to the magic imagination of the genius of the author; that proofreader is busy watching for an inverted comma, a mis-spacing, or a wrong-font letter. He has an eye *trained* for the imperfections, the weaknesses. Men who pride themselves on being shrewd in discovering the weak points, the vanity, dishonesty, immorality, intrigue and pettiness of others, think they understand character. They know only part of character—they know only the depths to which some men many sink; they know not the heights to which some men may rise.[2]

There has lived only one Life that was flawless. Yet He has commanded: "Be ye therefore perfect . . ." Therefore greatness is a matter of *becoming*—to begin faulted and yet through persevering effort, rise above weakness, injury, sin and error. In this life a Hero cannot be perfect in all things, but can become nearly perfect in some things. When the greatest of men have breathed their last, there will remain in their character blemishes that can only be removed through the atonement of the Highest power. These pages will not dwell on those flaws that remained unconquered in our heroes' lives—but will focus on their incredible feats of character, that, if emulated, will establish in us the virtues of true manhood.

The subtitle of this book is simply Heroes of Flight. A Hero defined is a man of courage, often of divine ancestry, favored and inspired by the gods, willing to sacrifice all—even life itself—to accomplish a notable purpose. Certainly this denotes that he is heaven sent. Today's contemporary language has been corrupted and we violate the word hero when we commonly use it to describe the principal male character in a movie or novel—even if he is dissipated, weak willed or governed by carnal passion. We all tend to emulate those whom we regard as heroes, but this is especially true of young men. We see it in their fashion, speech, and mannerisms. Far more serious than these outward imitations is the insidious adoption by young men of the values of so-called celebrities. More than ever today, young men need to be exposed to the lives of noble role models. The narratives of the valiant young men found within these pages are true life stories of real Heroes, young men of profound faith and heroic accomplishment. In a concise manner this book examines the extraordinary lives of Eddie V. Rickenbacker, James Norman Hall and Antoine de Saint-Exupéry. All three of these young men were pioneer aviators. All three were accomplished authors. Each of these airmen played an essential role in our nation's history.

Rickenbacker, Hall and de Saint-Exupéry all belong to the past century. There are those who would therefore say the lives of these great men cannot be significantly relative to the world in which *we* live. Myopic minds extol contemporary intellectualism and eulogize all things modern while deprecating all things past, scorning the investigation of dead men's virtues. Bob Hope wrote of a young network executive who refused to consider WWII scripts, saying: "Nothing that happened before I was born could possibly have any relevance to my life." C. S. Lewis stated emphatically that the opposite is true:

> Most of all, perhaps, we need intimate knowledge of the past. Not that the past has any magic about it, but because we cannot study the future, and yet need something to set against the present, to remind us that the basic assumptions have been quite different in different periods and that much which seems certain to the uneducated is merely temporary fashion. A man who has lived in many places is not likely to be deceived by the local errors of his native village; the scholar has lived in many times and is therefore in some degree immune from the great cataract of nonsense that pours from the press and the microphone of his own age.[3]

This book is not about a particular denomination or a particular genre of religion. There is a God in Heaven who is Father to all the peoples of the earth. He grants light and truth to each person, society and nation according to their own desires to know and live truth. If they live that truth which they have received and in faith recognize Him as the Source of the truth they possess, God blesses them. These blessings come in the form of knowledge and increased power to do good. The more knowledge and wisdom we obtain by faith and diligence, the more knowledge and wisdom we are given; the more good we do, the more good we are able to do. We were designed to have ever increasing intelligence and ability.

The sphere of our influence is also designed to grow. Our first influence is over self. As we exercise authority over our own thoughts, through diligent study and meditation, we receive from God the energy and substance to influence others in ever widening circles. We, in fact, gather the raw materials from God. These are things we have not power to make, but organize them through our efforts of creativity into gifts that we give our fellowman. The more God sees that we rightly use the elements he gives us (whether they are physical, intellectual or spiritual) the more raw materials he makes available to us. Thus the more we possess of His goodness the more good we can give—and so the cycle continues.

At one time each of us left our Father in Heaven's presence with a mission to accomplish on earth, each to be born in a certain age or time, in a certain setting—cultural, political and religious. Some would be born in times and places with great advantage where truth and enlightenment would be easily available. Where much is given, God our Father, expects much. However, many others would be born in times of truth-void famines—times where it would be not only hard to obtain truth, but even extremely dangerous to seek it. Within the limitations of the individual setting in which each soul lives, a merciful Father adapts their life's mission accordingly. There have been great people in history who have been called of God to break limits and found new movements. Others have fulfilled their life's purpose by working within the limitations of their era to accomplish some great good.

In all times, ancient, medieval and modern, there have been only two kinds of people on this earth: one looks for answers and guidance horizontally, the other vertically. The first looks earthward, the second towards heaven. The first says that seeing is believing. The second knows that believing is seeing. The first believes in nothing that cannot be proven by the five senses. The second knows that there is a sixth sense that works in harmony with the five senses but supercedes them all. This sense is felt in the heart, heard softly in the mind, impressed upon the soul. Heroes possess a profound sixth sense.

The title of this book is *Valiant Young Men*, although their lives are here chronicled until their deaths. A young man of valor retains his youth throughout his life, and beyond. William Phelps wrote:

> There is no end to virtue;
> There is no end to might;
> There is no end to wisdom;
> There is no end to light.
> There is no end to union;
> There is no end to truth.
> There is no end to [power];
> *There is no end to youth.*

This work is not only about man-making. Additionally this book honors, through the exemplary lives of three men, all who have attained the high character of manhood. Like Rickenbacker, Hall and Saint-Exupéry, all true men have lived (or are living) perilous lives. The Enemy of Man will not be vanquished until the dawn of the Millennial Day. The war *he* wages is potentially more destructive to the individual than any physical conflict, for he aims to vanquish not only the body, but to devour the soul. When one rises to the rank of *man* he voluntarily leaves the ease of civilian existence and at the risk of all that he *is* joins the vanguard in the battle between good and evil. Of such men, Antoine de Saint-Exupéry wrote:

> They alone keep vigil with me who are fervent and suffer in their hearts; meanwhile let the others take their rest—all who have created in the day and are not called on to hold the front line against the powers of darkness.[4]

CHAPTER 1

THE TAIL SPIN

The key to every man is his thought. Sturdy and defying though he look, he has a helm which he obeys. The life of man is a self-evolving circle, which from a ring imperceptibly small, rushes on all sides outwards to new and larger circles. If the soul is quick and strong it bursts over the boundary on all sides . . . the heart refuses to be imprisoned; in its first and narrowest pulses it already tends outward with a vast force and to immense and innumerable expansions.[5]

—RALPH WALDO EMERSON

ON MAY 17, 1918, before daybreak Eddie Rickenbacker and Reed Chambers circled their fighters behind enemy lines, high above Nancy, France, at 18,000 feet altitude. Their strategy was simply that of the early bird. They were so high in the dimly lit sky that they could not be seen by anti-aircraft gunners, whose death dealing fire was known by the Allied aviators as "Archie" — and at that altitude they were out of range. In the open cockpit the air was so cold that Eddie said that the temperature at eighteen thousand feet "seemed about eighteen thousand degrees below zero." Their purpose was to maneuver out of sight and out of sound over enemy airfields and hunt their prey. Sooner or later a Boche reconnaissance aircraft would take off on so clear a morning and venture towards the front lines to photograph Allied positions. Eddie and Reed, would then swoop down with the goal to blow the Huns out of the sky. Aerial intelligence had become vital in the war and to permit such photographs to reach the German High Command was to give away the lives of countless infantry to the enemy. Yet time passed, precious fuel was being expended without any sign of prey. Eddie wrote:

> No other fool in the world was abroad at such an unearthly hour. But still, I had to admit to myself, Luf was right! It was just like going fishing. If there were no fish in the stream that certainly would be hard luck, but still one couldn't expect to catch any with his feet before his fire. I smiled to myself as I thought of the Alabama gentleman who spent the afternoon fishing in his water trough. [A passerby] watched him jerk his line out of the water half a dozen times. Finally he yelled:
>
> "You rascal! Don't you know there are no fish in that mud hole?"
>
> "Yes, boss! But it's close and handy!" replied the Alabaman.
>
> The old story gave me an idea. Perhaps I was selecting a poor fishing place whose only merit was that it was close and handy. I pulled up my machine and started towards Metz. I knew the fishing must be good there. It was twenty-five miles back of the lines and claimed one of the best of the German aerodromes.[6]

Eddie climbed to twenty thousand feet. Metz was coming into view ahead, beautiful in the light of dawn. He throttled his engine back and began a noiseless glide to overfly the city in complete silence. His plan would permit no warning of his presence. Should he be discovered, the enemy could quickly scramble a number of defensive fighters that would simply out gun him. Somewhere between Nancy and Metz he had lost sight of Chambers—he was alone. Eddie continued his stealthy glide until he was over the aerodrome at Thiaucourt when he saw three Albatros planes lift off, one after the other. These aircraft were single-seat fighters flying in a straight line towards the front. He brought his Nieuport to bear directly behind the last Albatros and began to narrow the intervening distance. This was not a hard task as they were climbing and he was descending, but nevertheless it

Eddie Rickenbacker and Nieuport

was a bold maneuver for one Nieuport to attack a flight of three Albatros fighters. The German pilots would not expect an attack from their rear as the skies behind them belonged to German fighters—or so they thought.

Just north of the village of Saint-Mihiel Eddie was three thousand feet in trail. He was now visible to the German anti-aircraft gunners below. These gunners had developed a way to signal to their own planes when Allied aircraft were hiding in the glare of the sun, or behind clouds, or attacking from a concealed position in any direction. They would send up anti-aircraft fire just ahead of the German aircraft fused to burst at the same altitude of the unseen enemy predator—the number of bursts and their configuration communicated all of the essential information to the

German pilots. On this occasion a black burst of Archie notified the three Albatros fighters to look behind. The pilot nearest Rickenbacker turned his head and Eddie distinctly saw the "sun glint off his glasses." The three German fighters pushed their sticks forward, diving for speed and distance.

Instantly Eddie went full throttle, also diving "headlong at the rearmost of the three Huns;" accelerating his speed to *two hundred miles per hour*—well in excess of the Nieuport's design maximum speed of one hundred twenty-two miles per hour. When Eddie was only two hundred yards behind the rearmost Albatros, the German flight leader banked sharply, intending to maneuver behind Rickenbacker; putting his guns on Eddie while the American was preoccupied with his intended target. This was the danger of attacking three fighters. The rear Albatros plunged steeply towards the earth without regard to the speed limitations of his aircraft, trying to out-dive Eddie. His plane could suffer structural failure in such an effort, but if he couldn't lose Rickenbacker he would *surely* die. Eddie nosed his Nieuport down in like manner, without "checking her speed." He never knew how fast he pushed his plane, but it is likely that he doubled its red line.

He was right on the German's tail and had closed the distance to a mere fifty yards when he opened fire. The burst from his machine guns was no more than ten seconds. He saw his tracer bullets perforate the Boche's fuselage; then, slightly adjusting the nose of his aircraft and drawing ever closer to his prey, he saw his tracers "piercing the back of the pilot's seat." The Albatros continued flying but its direction was erratic—no living hand grasped the control stick.

All the while Eddie was well aware of the vulnerability of his own position. By this time it was likely that both of the remaining fighters were now bearing down on *him*. At any moment enemy gunfire could rip through his plane. He knew that it was foolish to try to out-dive an enemy in a straight line. This was the mistake of his former antagonist, whose slumped and lifeless body was yet hurdling through the air in the Albatros, made drone. The only way to out wit an enemy fighter is to out maneuver him. Eddie pulled his control stick back, nearly full travel, abruptly converting his mighty descent into a steep climb. He would exchange his tremendous airspeed for altitude, throw his pursuers off track and try to get a visual on their proximity. But his speed was too great for such an immediate change of direction; the excessive flight load he imposed on the Nieuport exceeded its strength. Eddie wrote:

> A frightening crash that sounded like the crack of doom told me that the sudden strain had collapsed my right wing. The entire spread of canvas over the top wing was torn off by the wind and disappeared behind me. Deprived of any supporting surface on this framework, the Nieuport turned over on her right side. The tail was forced up despite all my efforts with joystick and rudder. Slowly at first, then faster and faster the tail began revolving around and around . . . I was caught in a tail spin, and with a machine as crippled as mine there seemed not a chance to come out of it.[7]

Out of control, Rickenbacker's plane fell, carving a shape in the air like an hour-glass, plummeting to earth. He saw the rapid approach of both enemy fighters, saw their tracer bullets find their bead on his Nieuport as they riddled his dying plane. Fortunately they missed his body and did not set his plane ablaze. He felt no animosity towards these Germans but felt "critical toward their bad judgment in thus wasting ammunition." Naturally the enemy wanted to be certain that Eddie was done for and not "playing possum."

The ground rushed towards Rickenbacker with incredible velocity. The two Albatros fighters broke off their attack, realizing that no biplane could fly with the fabric of one of its four wings completely gone, leaving spar and ribs naked. The damaged wing produced no lift, no control, and threw all flight surfaces out of balance. Looking down on the forest of Montsec Eddie wondered where he would crash; or at what moment his plane might simply break apart in flight and eject him "to the mercy of the four

Anti-Aircraft Guns

winds." He hoped his plane would hold together until impact, for other flyers had survived in such circumstances, however unlikely. He was still behind German lines. If he did survive he would assuredly be mangled and perhaps, worst of all, end up a prisoner of war. He wondered how an American fighter pilot, with a German name like Rickenbacker, would be treated as a POW. The tail spin continued, but oddly did not tighten or accelerate. What would his mother prefer, he thought, a dead son or the knowledge that her boy was in prison? This provoked his ire. In his mind's eye he saw his dear mother, widowed since he was twelve, who had so depended on him in their poverty, opening a cablegram from the war department, informing her of her son's death or capture. Instantly he was roused from defeatism. To save one's own life may not be sufficient motivation when perils overwhelm, but to save one's beloved from boundless anguish will empower the vanquished to efforts of faith and will. Eddie wrote:

> I began remembering all the major episodes of my life, the good things I had done and the bad things. The bad seemed to outnumber the good. And then I remembered the Lord above.
>
> "Oh, God," I prayed, "help me get out of this."[8]

Normally, to recover from a spin, the pilot closes the throttle to slow acceleration. He neutralizes his ailerons, as the wings are stalled, rendering the ailerons useless; therefore it is best to simply streamline these controls. Then the pilot puts his stick full forward to break the stall, while at the same time he applies full rudder pressure opposite the direction of rotation of the spin. This procedure Eddie, no doubt, attempted at the onset of his tail spin, but it failed to break the *vrille.* He tried other control combinations and even tried throwing his body weight this way and that way, but nothing altered in the least degree the steady and deadly spin. Eddie checked his altimeter and found he had fallen ten thousand feet—only three thousand feet and a few moments remained before he would strike the ground. He was now low enough to see *details.* Directly beneath him was a road lined with parked trucks and men—men whose faces were turned skyward gazing at the spectacle of his dramatic fall and imminent crash. As he drew nearer and nearer to these faces he could see that they were "exulting" in this life and death exhibition and would relish tearing souvenirs from his busted plane and body.

Only one thing he had not tried, the one thing that would normally exacerbate a tail spin. Angrily he opened his engine to full throttle. Wonder of wonders! The accelerating air over the tail was sufficient to once again make it a *control* surface. The rudder responded to his command and with literally no altitude to spare he recovered from the spin in a horizontal attitude. If he could only keep a semblance of control, just keep his Nieuport flying towards his own lines—not far away—maybe five minutes more! His enemies below, having been denied the pleasure of watching him crash, sought to remedy their loss immediately. Anti-aircraft fire saturated the sky surrounding him, but for Eddie, *Archie* held no terror. His recovery from the spin and his ability to fly, however "crippled," filled him with such gratitude that he had no fear of exploding airborne shells.

Soon he crossed the lines and made his way towards the 94th Aerodrome. He skimmed over the hangers and let his plane down

Rickenbacker's Nieuport with shorn upper wing.

onto the field with the throttle still "wide open." He wrote:

> The French pilots from an adjoining hangar came running out to see what novice was trying to make a landing with his engine on. Later they told me I resembled a bird alighting with a broken wing.
>
> I had passed through rather a harrowing experience, as I look back upon it now. Yet I do not recall that I felt anything unusual had happened . . . Rarely does a pilot betray much excitement over the day's work, no matter how extraordinary it is . . .[9]
>
> Reed came in for a landing a minute later. We walked in together. I felt perfectly calm. But, when I was alone in front of my bunk, suddenly my knees turned to water . . . And then I uttered a little prayer of gratitude to the Lord above for my deliverance.[10]

The following day the 94th squadron was notified by the French that they had not only witnessed Rickenbacker's inconceivable flight in his wounded Nieuport, "staggering homeward," but they had also witnessed the *landing* of the Albatros, confirming his fifth victory. Eddie was now an *ACE.* Regarding the landing of the Albatros when it should have crashed, Rickenbacker explained that the plane, with the dead German pilot slumped on his controls, incredibly continued to fly in a gradual descent, crossing the American lines and virtually "landed itself" a thousand feet or so inside Allied controlled territory.

CHAPTER 2

CHILD TO MAN

Truth forever on the scaffold, Wrong forever on the throne—
Yet that scaffold sways the future, and, behind the dim unknown,
Standeth God within the shadow, keeping watch above his own.
We see dimly in the Present what is small and what is great,
Slow of faith how weak an arm may turn the iron helm of fate! [11]

— JAMES RUSSELL LOWELL

EDWARD RICKENBACHER WAS BORN on October 8, 1890, in Columbus, Ohio. Eddie, was the third of nine children born to William and Elizabeth Rickenbacher. Mary, the eldest, was followed by Bill, a reliable youngster—but apt to lead his younger brother Eddie into boyish mischief. Bill was muscular and hardy, while four years younger Eddie was "skinny and wiry." To make matters worse, Eddie, although wanting to do whatever Bill did, resented his seniority and wanted to lead and *not* follow. This led to fights where Bill "beat the daylights" out of his competitive little brother. This was perhaps a blessing in disguise for their parents were immigrants from Switzerland and Eddie had inherited a pronounced German accent that earned him the nickname "Kraut"—requiring that he develop skills of self defense. Said Eddie:

> I had to fight my way into school in the morning, stand up for myself at recess and fight my way home again after school.[12]

Eddie's younger siblings were Emma, Louise (who died shortly after birth), Louis, Dewey and Albert. Their father was tall and physically powerful, of German ancestry, mustached, strict and earnest. Their beautiful mother was fair, of French extraction, "devoutly religious" and one who loved the arts. Eddie felt fortunate to belong to a family that combined the virtues of both the Old and New Worlds. William and Elizabeth instilled in their children the Germanic ethics of exactness, duty and diligence while creating in their hearts the love of America—a land of "fertile soil, opportunity, and promise."[13] As Eddie grew in stature, he likewise grew in his appreciation for his family who believed in God, country and each other.

When Eddie was three years of age, his father quit his job with the railroad and started his own small construction business, doing pavements and foundations. William's security was his self-confidence, empowered by faith, self-reliance and by his supportive young wife. With "his own two hands," very little money, and his hard earned credit he built their first home. It was a small house comprised of two rooms plus an attic, heated only by the kitchen stove—no electricity and no indoor plumbing. Nonetheless the Rickenbachers were proud of their new home. Just a few years earlier William and Elizabeth had landed on the shores of America with empty pockets and hopeful hearts. Now they were blessed with children, a small business, a little land, and a house—mortgaged, but deeded in their name. On their small lot they cultivated a wonderful vegetable garden, raised chickens, goats and occasionally a pig. The chickens and goats produced more eggs and milk than the Rickenbacher family needed and so they traded the surplus for sugar and flour. Eddie wrote:

> What a wonderful childhood we had! Of far greater value than mere riches was the opportunity to work together, play together, learn together and produce together, all under the loving guidance of our parents.
>
> How many children in America today, I wonder, are blessed

> with the opportunity to see the food they eat develop from tiny seeds placed in the moist spring earth? [14]

With permission the Rickenbachers gathered windfall apples from the ground of their neighbor's orchard. Mama, said Eddie, would take these apples, a little sugar and flour and "make the most delicious dessert in the world." Time and again Father and Mother asked their children, where else, but in America, could you begin with nothing and in a few short years, own your own home and business, till your own land, and give your children the luxury of fresh apple pie?

Elizabeth Rickenbacher deeply instilled in her family an abiding faith in God. Each evening she knelt in prayer, first with the girls in their bedroom, and then with the boys in theirs. The Rickenbacher children recognized Heavenly Father, Eddie explains, as "a friendly God . . . who was interested in our problems and sympathetic to them." Sundays found the Rickenbachers dressed in their very best and in attendance at Sunday School and worship services at St. John's Lutheran Church in South Columbus. However, Eddie recognized that the foremost influence in the development of his faith and knowledge of God was a "family ritual" that his dear mother lovingly administered each day. Eddie writes:

> After supper, when we had all helped to clear the dishes from the big kitchen table, Mother would ask one of us to bring in the Bible that she had brought with her from Switzerland. What an honor that was! It was big and heavy and bound in rich black leather. On the front, printed in gold in block capitals, were the words *"Heilige Bibel"*—Holy Bible. Mama would open it and begin to read. Her favorite passages were the Sermon on the Mount and the 23rd Psalm, and they are the ones I remember best. She would often stop reading to discuss the meanings behind the Scriptures and how we could apply the principles of Christianity to every day life.[15]

Eddie loved to work along side his father, growing vegetables, improving their home or working on mechanical projects. William Rickenbacher did not tolerate carelessness. To leave a tool or implement lying in neglect to gather rust brought swift and firm discipline. It was not just a matter of waste, even though money *was* scarce. It was a principle of life that the Eddie's father taught him—stewardship: to respect that which is entrusted into your care. William was a craftsman, one who loved excellence. He taught his sons to "do the job right to begin with . . . never to procrastinate [and] *to do it now*." When Eddie was only seven William taught him the art of sewing leather. Soon he was repairing all of the children's shoes in the family. What a feeling of satisfaction he felt when his brothers and sisters admired his workmanship in something so directly related to their own comfort and necessity. The sincere approval of his family prompted Eddie to search out new responsibilities. He considered work to be a privilege, even as a seven, eight, or nine year old.

Even before Eddie started school he began his "business career." Like Twain's fictional Tom Sawyer, real-life Eddie enlisted his buddies in his projects. Sam, the junk man, purchased bones to make fertilizer, rags and scrap metal to recycle. Eddie and his friends spent long hours pulling nails from discarded lumber, collecting bones which they soaked in water increasing their weight (bones were bought by the pound) and gathered clothing torn beyond repair for rags. When Eddie became suspicious of Sam's scales he purchased his own. Sam could scarcely believe being challenged by the skinny little Rickenbacher but knew he had been caught in the oldest scam of the trading business—unjust scales. Thereafter he respected the young entrepreneur all the more. A local paper, the *Columbus Dispatch,* hired ten year old Eddie and for the first time he had a job with dependable pay. Later he wrote that being a paper boy was as vital to his development as any position in business he ever held! He explained why in one word—duty, for, he said: "Without a sense of duty a man is nothing." He would leave the comfort of his bed at 2:00 a.m., walk two miles to the distribution office, collect his papers, then deliver the *Dispatch* to every home along his route regardless of wet or bitter cold weather.

One day a dirigible pilot named Roy Knabenshue came to town. As the airship sailed over Columbus, young Eddie was inspired with a vision of flight. How he wanted to fly like Roy! He lay awake many nights trying to figure out how to actually fly—and finally settled on a plan. His neighbor's barn roof would provide his bicycle with plenty of speed and send him hurling in space with altitude to spare. An umbrella, attached to his bike would provide a gentle landing. For extra insurance he piled up as much sand as he could haul to his proposed landing site for added cushion. On the appointed day of his first flight his friend Sam Wareham helped Eddie get his umbrella winged bike to the very top of the barn roof.[i]

On the apex of the barn roof, Sam held the bicycle while Eddie mounted the pilot's seat. The umbrella was fixed properly in its engineered place. Eddie writes:

> The ground looked mighty far away. But the promise of flight was greater than the fear of falling.
>
> "Okay, Sam," I said, "Let go!"
>
> Down the steep tin roof of the barn we went, bicycle, umbrella and Rickenbacher, gathering momentum. We left the roof. The umbrella gave a loud pop and turned completely inside out. The next thing I knew I hit the sand. Thanks to it and the good Lord, I was only stunned. The bike wasn't so lucky; it was demolished.[16]

---

i Someday this author would like to make a survey of professional pilots asking one question: "As a boy did you ever attempt to fly without the benefit of a real aircraft?" I believe that the majority would answer yes. My personal experience was from the east side of our one story home. I leaped from the top of the gable roof with a small war surplus parachute, a gift from my older brother Alan, attached lazily to my belt. Two things amazed me–how the stupid parachute failed to open and how short my flight was. Luckily small boys have bones like rubber.

This was not Eddie's only close encounter with death. As a three year old he had accidentally been struck in the head, his skull pierced by a pronged hoe, while his mother was gardening. Not long after he darted into the path of a street car and was consequently thrown headlong against a curb. Later he fell backward into a cistern. His neck took the blow and for a time he was "as limp as a broken toy" and all feared that his neck was broken. When he was six, he was playing with his brother Bill along the railroad tracks and jumped onto the *moving* coal tender car. Suddenly the train stopped, flinging Eddie to the tracks. The fall stunned the little boy—then to Bill's dismay, the train started backing up. Eddie was semiconscious and saw the huge and heavy train car moving towards him, but his shocked body would not respond. Bill was a hero that day, dashing to aid Eddie and dragging him free an instant before the Leviathan could crush his small frame. This episode did not end their days haunting the rails nor was it the end of Bill's heroism. Eddie wrote:

> Hurrying across the tracks in front of the switch engine, I stepped in an open switch. My foot was caught—and the engine was coming. Bill hurried up, and we yanked together. My foot came out of the shoe, and we both went back head over heels as the engine thundered by.[17]

One day gathering walnuts, Eddie climbed far into the thin boughs of the tree to shake down the luscious meat. More than one nut fell from the dizzying heights. When Eddie hit the ground he was knocked cold. Bill dutifully piled his brother into his cart and made for home where Eddie regained consciousness some time later.

The school the Rickenbacher's attended stood at the crossroads of Main Street and Miller Avenue. On one occasion, a fire broke out in the school basement and quickly rose through the wood structure. Fortunately a fire alarm sounded the emergency moments before fire engulfed the building. Children and teachers were quickly and safely evacuated. Outside Eddie was entranced by sights, smells and sounds—the building engulfed in flames, galloping horses, the cherry red fire wagon. Then it hit him—he had left his cap and coat in the school and felt he could not face his parents with such forgetfulness. He sprang into action, leaping through a sheet of flame as he dashed through a door which was alive with crimson heat, scorching his face and hair. Knowing right where he had hung his coat and cap, he grabbed them, turned on his heals and again lunged through the fire and ran for home. Only then did Eddie realize what he had done and the risk he had taken.

One day as the sun was setting, he heard the family goat cry for help; a dog was viciously dragging the animal down by the leg. Without thinking that such an act most likely meant the dog was rabid, Eddie ran to the rescue. He fought for "old Nanny," pulling the dog off with one hand and beating him on the head with the other. Just as the ferocious dog let go of the goat and turned toward Eddie, his Father suddenly entered the fray wielding a large stick. With great force William knocked the dog away from his son.

Few things in life are without purpose. In his youth Eddie recognized he had come close to losing his life on many occasions. He knew that God had preserved him time and again. These frequent encounters with, as he called it, "the Grim Reaper," taught him not to fear death. Not many years would pass before the boy would grow into a young man and take to the skies in defense of his country. As a combat pilot Eddie Rickenbacher would endure "one hundred and thirty four aerial encounters" in which the enemy would try to take his life.

When Eddie was thirteen and a half years old he engineered and built a perpetual-motion machine with ball weights, springs and gears. It served no purpose except to keep itself running. Proudly Eddie showed it to his father. William, in one glance, asked him what was its purpose—what could it accomplish? He put his arm on his boy's shoulder and spoke of the machines in the construction trade and in particular the pile driver. A relatively simple device, yet it was essential to the building of bridges. The machine lifted a massive weight which it then dropped headlong upon a pile, driving it deep into a riverbed. Upon these piles great bridges were constructed. He told his son to remember two things: there was no worth in a machine that could not accomplish a notable purpose and never try to run a machine that he did not know how to operate. William then spoke about the marvels of the future, the horseless carriage and the flying machine. William Richenbacher was not afraid of technology and possessed the gift of imagination. Many in that day thought the "Wright boys" of Dayton ridiculous in their efforts to attempt powered flight and felt they ought to stick to the bicycle trade; but not Eddie's father. As they walked, William told Eddie that he was fortunate to born in such an age of progress. He instructed Eddie to prepare himself for the great things that were soon to be. These were the last words that Eddie heard his father speak.

Later that night, while working the pile driver, an out of control timber struck William in the head. He did not die instantly but lingered in a coma for some time. On the night of August 26, 1904 William Rickenbacher died quietly at home. The day of the funeral Elizabeth gathered her large family around their papa's casket for a tender farewell. At that solemn moment she spoke of the coming years, warning that some would experience greater difficulties than others—yet they were a family and were to take care of each other. In those days there was no state welfare program and to be without life's necessities was to truly suffer. Along with his brothers and sisters Eddie promised his mother that he would shoulder family responsibilities. Never, he later wrote, had he meant anything more than that promise made before the lifeless body of his beloved father. After the services all of the exhausted Rickenbachers retired to bed early—all except two. Elizabeth sat at the kitchen table, head in hands, a young widow with a large family. She had lost not only her dear companion, but the *provider* of their life sustaining needs. Eddie sat down beside her and said: "Mama, I'll never make you cry again." Of course Elizabeth's tears had nothing to do with any boyish mistake Eddie had made—yet he resolved to never add to her sorrows but to live a life that would only bring his mother happiness and honor. He stayed with her the rest of the night, sitting there at the table, in silence. He wrote:

> Some time passed before I realized that I was sitting at the head of the table, where Papa had always sat. Mama knew where I was sitting, but she made no comment. Many years were to pass before I fully understood.[18]

The following morning Eddie skipped school and applied for work at the Federal Glass Factory. Child labor laws had recently come into being. To be employed Eddie had to lie about his age and state that he had finished the eighth grade. At the time he was short for his age, still skinny and could not fool anyone. Yet he was hired on the spot. Perhaps, Eddie thought, the man at Federal Glass saw the resolve in his eyes, and saw the necessity behind his determination—or perhaps he still was of the order of men who thought little of the laws outlawing the practice of exploiting children. He told Eddie that he would work a twelve hour shift, from six at night until six in the morning, and if he had any misgivings about such arduous conditions not to show up that night. Eddie excitedly ran the two miles home, to tell his mother that he would keep his promise and take care of her and the others—he had a job! His mother looked at him and tears began to fill her eyes. Eddie feared that he had he already broken his pledge not to make her cry. She told her son that he had to finish his schooling; but he responded that the needs of the family had to come first. He did all he could to ease her pain and dry her moist eyes with his willingness and optimism. Finally she gave her reluctant consent, for she knew as well as he—they "had to have the money."

The first night was the hardest. As Eddie could not afford the nickel for the streetcar fare, he walked the two miles to the Federal

Glass Company. Then all night long he continued walking, carrying heavy glass tumblers to the tempering ovens. After twelve hours of lifting and walking, he dragged his body back the two miles home and fell asleep eating breakfast. But he would not quit, and at the end of the week he proudly handed a plain brown envelope to his mother. She could scarcely believe it—inside were "three dollar bills and a silver half-dollar." It was to their family the *means of life* and her eyes beamed gratitude to her son that, although not the eldest, was nonetheless heir to his father's magnanimity. Eddie said it was the best day of his life.

Soon thereafter a truant officer paid a visit to the Rickenbacher home as Eddie had now an uninterrupted string of absences. Elizabeth made no apologies but simply led him up to Eddie's room, where exhausted he lay in a dead sleep. That sight was explanation enough, for the school official no doubt knew of William's death and the family's commensurate plight. The soiled clothes of the lad whose eyes were closed in slumberous weariness caused the man to shake his head and quietly leave the room—never to return. Eddie was also to never return to his formal education.

After some time young Rickenbacher realized that his job at the glass factory did not fit his aspirations. Also, he had to recognize that he simply could not keep up the pace without seriously injuring his health—for in addition to his twelve hour days he still had chores to do at home. Eddie's boss, a man named Crawford, was hard as nails, yet he had taken a liking to the boy who always gave his job his best effort. One night Eddie decided to simply quit, he felt so unbelievably tired. When he spoke with Mr. Crawford he found, to his surprise, that the boss was sympathetic and told him that if he couldn't find work elsewhere he could have his old job back. However, Eddie had never given a second thought to the notion that he might not be able to find better employment. By now he knew of his ability to apply himself enthusiastically to any task; as a quick learner he possessed the same confidence that was his father's hallmark. At 6:00 a.m. the following morning he applied for work at the Buckeye Steel Casting

Company. He told the man in charge of hiring that he was fourteen years of age, had finished school and was a good hand "in making molds and castings." Only the latter was true—at Federal Glass he had worked his way up from carrying tumblers to making glass molds. He started at Buckeye Steel an hour later making core steel castings. He nearly doubled his pay to six dollars a week, a small fortune to the Rickenbacher family. Best of all, he was working the day shift.

Still Eddie kept his eyes open for other opportunities. As he gave his employer a great deal more productivity than the average worker, he always felt square and never in the company's debt. Therefore, when he heard about an opening capping bottles with still better pay and hours, he quit Buckeye and was hired immediately at the bottling plant. His fourth job was one he could do at the same time—he earned a nickel a game setting up pins at the bowling alley on weekend evenings. After work during the week, Eddie spent his time beautifying the Rickenbacher home. To his mother's delight he hauled load after wheelbarrow load of top soil to the front yard and planted a lawn, as nice as any in the neighborhood. At this time an interesting thought occurred to him—the boyish pleasures of his old gang had now totally lost appeal. He recognized that although he was still only thirteen he "thought as a man," for he "worked as a man." This example inspired his younger siblings who now did the home chores under Eddie's direction. As summer came, Eddie found time for leisure activities. He especially loved to go swimming.

For years Eddie had been repairing his family's shoes and had become expert in working leather. This led to his fifth job at a shoe factory. Eddie also had always enjoyed art and drafting—so when Mr. Zenker, the stone cutter, came to their house hoping to sell Elizabeth a fine monument for William's grave, it occurred to Eddie that stone carving was art and something he could quickly learn. Right on the spot he asked Mr. Zenker for a job. It seems that no one could dismiss Eddie's enthusiasm. Within several months Eddie had learned nearly every aspect of cårving monuments and proved himself a skilled asset to his employer.

Horseless carriages were becoming more common in Columbus and Eddie had never forgotten his father's advice. Eddie felt it was time to hire on as an apprentice in a machine shop and learn the wonders of making machinery. Mr. Zenker did not want to lose Rickenbacher and offered to raise his salary from $1.50 a day to the unheard sum of $2.50 per day! However Eddie's mind was made up. He took a pay cut back to a dollar a day and went to work as a machinist for the Pennsylvania Railroad. Eddie loved the work and especially took great pleasure in creating on the lathe. During his work hours he made machined parts, but during his lunch hour he turned baseball bats for the enjoyment of his friends.

By the time Eddie turned fifteen he had amassed a considerable amount of skill as a craftsman in leather, stone, wood and steel. He also learned many of the wonders of the internal combustion engine. Richenbacher knew that progress was being made by leaps and bounds in this emerging technology, as well as advances in the machines these engines could propel. He felt it was time for yet another change of employment. On Chestnut Street was Evan's Garage—a bicycle repair shop that had recently moved into the automotive storage and service business. Mr. Evans was amenable to hiring Eddie for seventy-five cents a day. Again, Rickenbacher took a pay cut with no misgivings whatever. Working provided the opportunity of expanding his abilities and his knowledge. This new job represented the future to Eddie, more than any other he had yet obtained. Eddie cleaned the shop, repaired bikes, built batteries for electric cars, and of course whenever possible, learned all he could about automobiles. At first when Evans was out, Eddie often sat behind the wheel of a customer's car pretending to drive. It wasn't long, however, until he became brave enough to start the engine and move it several feet, back and forth, inside of the garage. In this manner he taught himself to drive—always careful to have the automobiles in their original positions before his boss's return.

Of all of his friends, Eddie was the only one who had even ridden in an automobile, and he couldn't help bragging a little. However, the kids in his neighborhood didn't believe him—after all, no one had ever seen him drive one of the new powerful horseless carriages. To them, he was still the undersized Rickenbacher, whom they seldom saw because he was always off working instead of spending time with them. Then one day Mr. Evans announced that he would be going to Toledo the following day; and Eddie would be responsible to tend the shop in his absence. Right then Eddie determined to put an end to the scoffing of his friends. After closing shop, Eddie opened the garage doors and backed out the shinny, sleek, Waverly Electric. The Waverly operated solely on battery power but Eddie had taken the precaution to be certain that it was fully charged. It was his first time driving on the streets, but he was already adept at handling the Waverly and quickly adapted himself to actual driving. Proudly he expertly parked the Waverly in front of his own home, swung down from the driver's seat and stepped lively up to his house. After her feeble protests Eddie then took his mother for her first ride in an automobile. She wore her finest hat, which she held with one hand, while she held on for dear life with the other. Never had she experienced such a rush of speed—imagine, ten miles per hour! Eddie rang the warning bell of the Waverly and all of their neighbors ran outside to see young Eddie behind the wheel with his lovely mother at his side, beaming with delight. Eddie said that it was better than a wonderful daydream. When they returned to their home, all of the kids in the area surrounded the young driver and the incredible machine. For some time Eddie demonstrated the Waverly to their entire satisfaction. Finally, he knew that he had to get the car back to the garage before his boss returned from Toledo. He had scarcely begun the short drive back to Evans Garage when the car began to slow down, then it stopped completely. With all of his driving he had depleted the batteries. It was getting dark and the garage was still a mile and a half away. What could he do? Then he remembered that a battery will recover a little current if allowed to remain inactive for a while. Eddie sat there, worried and impatient for an hour. He engaged the control lever and wonder of wonders, the Waverly moved down the road several blocks then once more came to a stop. He repeated this procedure, and although the automobile traveled less distance with each attempt, he finally birthed the Waverly safely in the garage at 3:00 a.m. Eddie connected the battery charger, dashed home and quickly ate breakfast, then hurried back to work. When Mr. Evans arrived he found the garage in perfect order and his attendant happier than he had a right to be. Said Eddie:

> I learned about automobiles and drove automobiles at an age when most boys still had many more years of dreaming to do.[19]

The more Eddie learned about automobiles, the more he realized how much he had yet to learn. Like the man who said, "The more I know, the more I know what I don't know." Without the resources to continue his formal education, he made a diligent search for correspondence courses in mechanical engineering. Though not an easy task in 1905, he found a course that perfectly suited his aspirations, The International Correspondence School in Scranton, Pennsylvania. Their course of study included engineering on the "automobile and internal-combustion engines." At first he found his studies extremely difficult. It had been a while since his mind had been inside a book and he had to re-teach himself to *think*. As there was no teacher, he had no one to clarify the often complex problems. Yet this very difficulty proved to be a benefit, for once he gained understanding of a subject the knowledge was indelibly his.

On weekends Eddie would hang out at the Frayer-Miller Company, an automobile manufacturer just down the street from Evans Garage, watching the building of cars with great interest. One day Lee Frayer, having become accustomed to seeing Rickenbacher at his plant, approached him, asked him his name and what he was doing. Eddie introduced himself, and with characteristic spunk, said he wanted to build automobiles. He then asked for a job. Frayer apologized and said there really wasn't anything for a kid to do in his shop. Eddie did not take "no" as an answer; he promised Mr. Frayer he would prove that the company needed services that he could provide. That was the end of his employment at Evans garage. Early Monday morning Eddie simply showed up at the Frayer-Miller plant, grabbed a broom and brush and began to clean. By the time Mr. Frayer arrived Eddie had meticulously cleaned one third of the shop, floor, benches and machines. Frayer could hardly believe the contrast and turned to Eddie saying, "You sure as hell meant it, didn't you?" He smiled and told Eddie to keep right on working, the job was his. After the cleaning was finished, he was assigned to assist a toolmaker build carburetors.

Whenever Eddie had a break, he pulled out his mechanical engineering correspondence course work and studied on the job. Frayer noticed and began moving Eddie around the plant from "spotting bearings" to "assembly of the chassis," until he became familiar with nearly every aspect of automobile construction. Then he assigned Rickenbacher to the engineering department where he actually assisted in the design of their product line. Eddie was still fifteen years of age.

His mentor continued to expand Eddie's horizons. In 1906 Frayer took Rickenbacher with him to race as his riding mechanic in the Vanderbilt Cup. Later, when the Frayer-Miller Company began to falter, Frayer was hired by the Firestone Automobile Company as their chief engineer and he offered Eddie the opportunity of going with him. At the age of seventeen Eddie was made the supervisor of the Firestone experimental department with the salary of twenty dollars a week, a tremendous sum for that day. In no time he learned "to speak the language of the internal-combustion engine." Just by listening to a faltering engine, Rickenbacher could correctly diagnosis the problem. Eddie had been without a father for years and began to realize that Mr. Frayer was filling that role in a wonderful manner. He was a *man* like his papa. Frayer was skilled, honest and determined—and one who took great interest in Eddie, as if he were his son.

One day the president of the company, Clinton D. Firestone, phoned Frayer that his personal car had simply quit along the road by the Scioto River Dam. Frayer sent Eddie to rescue the boss. Most likely Firestone had never seen Eddie and as he drove up he was met with a strong look of disapproval. Nonetheless Eddie greeted Firestone cordially and said he had been sent by Mr. Frayer to fix his car. Firestone briskly responded, "Hell, I asked for man, not a boy." Undeterred, Eddie went right to work. He turned the crank several times and felt no engine compression. Eddie knew that this engine had a flaw—the locks that held the spring of the intake valve would vibrate loose. In less than five minutes Eddie had replaced the locks, turned the crank and started Firestone's engine. When Eddie returned, Frayer called him into his office. "Say, what did you do for the old man? He thinks you're the seventh wonder of the world."

In no time Firestone was sending Rickenbacker around the country, working with dealers, designing field repairs for cars already delivered and demonstrating new cars to would-be clients. On one such demonstration the customer demanded that Eddie prove the automobile's superiority by climbing over a steep incline west of Dallas, known as Chalk Hill, in high gear. Normally, this was not a problem for the Firestone. But the prospect was "particularly heavy." As Eddie began the ascent he realized they would never make it without down shifting. Rather than lose the sale, Eddie again showed his ingenuity.

> Quickly I slammed on the brakes, and came to a dead stop. The customer turned to me, but before he could say a word I beamed at him with a proud smile. "How do you like those brakes?" I asked. "See how they hold us tight, right here on Chalk Hill."

He smiled back. "By Gad, they do hold, don't they?" He said. "Holy gee, that's great!"

He bought the car that afternoon, for cash.[20]

Eddie's salary was raised to one hundred and twenty-five dollars a week. Even though he was living out of town, still Eddie continued to support his family. Furthermore, by carefully watching every penny, and to the amazement of his mother, he paid off her mortgage. Elizabeth Rickenbacher owned her home and was in debt to no one. Eddie was eighteen.

For the next year Eddie continued to travel for Firestone, doing anything and everything, from improving the quality of service provided by their dealers to engineering field solutions. For example, an engine that ran perfectly at the factory would overheat in Arizona; so Eddie designed a fan belt driven water pump that provided coolant through the cylinder jacket.

During his time with Firestone, Eddie had not only grown in knowledge, but in physical stature. He left Columbus, Ohio standing five feet nine inches tall. When he returned to celebrate his nineteenth birthday he stood six feet two inches. While in Texas, with a little extra money, he purchased a present for his girl back home, Blanche Calhoun. It was just *meant* to be a very nice gift for a girl that he greatly admired. Trouble was his choice of gift—being of the type that to any girl would have but *one* meaning. Later he admitted he was "still pretty naïve about some things." When he presented Blanche with a beautiful diamond ring, she "accepted it graciously." Within two days the word had spread throughout Columbus that young Rickenbacher and the beautiful Calhoun girl were soon to be wed! He thought a great deal of Blanche, but the prospect of imminent marriage frightened Eddie out of his wits. What could he do? The only thing that came to his mind was to quickly leave town on business. Off he went to Omaha with no explanations. Gratefully he heard afterwards that Blanche married a local boy of good standing; and later when he happened to see her again she was as friendly as could be, holding no hard feelings whatever. However, he said that the next time he gave such a gift he "knew full well what it meant."

Eddie's first exposure to car racing had been with Frayer, years earlier. On that occasion he also experienced his first wreck. Their car left the track at about 70 miles per hour, traversed a ditch, then rolled when it struck a dune, flipping the vehicle and catapulting Rickenbacher through the air to a non-lethal landing in the soft sand. Now, as part of his efforts to promote the Firestone automobiles, he raced whenever the opportunity presented itself. He wrote that "some of the tracks amounted to invitations to commit suicide," and his brushes with death almost seemed routine. His winnings, at times, were fantastic, but the expenses for travel, equipment, drivers and mechanics could be nearly insurmountable. For example, when he arrived in Sioux City for a national race, he couldn't afford shelter for his crew or his cars. He parked his cars under the grandstand, provided cots for his crew, and found room and board for himself at a nearby farm on credit for $2.50 per week. But he finished the race in first place and with his team mate taking third, he won twelve thousand five hundred dollars—an absolute fortune in 1913!

One night he dreamed his car was involved in a terrific crash from which escape would have been impossible. He awoke shaking—it was so real! Then the impression came into his mind that the reason why he had lived through so many near death experiences was *not* due to any skill he possessed, but that God had preserved his life and had done so for some great purpose. Eddie had always prayed every evening before going to bed, but beginning that night he resolved to pray with "greater sincerity and gratitude." He also resolved to become more fit, physically and intellectually, with the feeling that his Father in Heaven was preparing him for something.

First he decided to improve his name, adding the middle initial "V," self-chosen for "Vernon." Then Eddie wrote a personal book of rules. In part it read:

> Always conduct yourself as a gentleman . . . don't go around with a long face [if you don't like your job] get another one somewhere else . . . Throw away false pride. No honest work is beneath you. Jump in and demonstrate your superiority . . . master everything about your own job, and get ready for the job at the top.[21]

Eddie continued his racing career, but introduced safety innovations such as reinforcing the engine cowling to make it more crashworthy, and wrapping his team drivers, including himself, mummy-like in a twenty foot length of burlap—likely the first protective padding and support gear worn by drivers. Not long after in a race at San Antonio, Eddie hit a soft spot in the track, catching his wheel and tumbling his car "like a barrel over Niagara Falls." He dove under the reinforced cowl and stayed with his machine until it came to rest, escaping with only a dislocated collarbone.

The winter and spring of 1914 belonged to a world that had changed little in centuries. The horse and buggy was still the primary conveyance, even in America. Wars had generally increased as the modern era approached, but were regional even in their grandest scale, and mainly spared civilian populations. However in the summer of 1914 Eddie Rickenbacher, with rest of humankind, was to see that traditional world die a fiery death.

CHAPTER 3

THE OATH

HADAD to TAMAR on Absalom's roof:
"The Tetragrammaton,—the powerful Name
Inscribed on Moses' rod, by which he wrought
Unheard of wonders, which constrains the Heavens
To part with blessings, shakes the earth, and rules
The strongest Spirits; or if God hath given
A delegated power, I cannot tell.
But 't was from him I learned their fate, their fall,
Who, erewhile, wore resplendent crowns in Heaven;
Now, scattered through the earth, the air, the sea . . ."
Tamar: "But did he tell it thee?"
Hadad: "He told me much,—more than I dare reveal;
For with a dreadful oath he sealed my lips." [22]

—JAMES ABRAHAM HILLHOUSE

ON THE BEAUTIFUL MORNING OF JUNE 28, 1914 a nineteen year old Serbian, Gavrilo Princip, stood near the front of a crowd that lined a street in Sarajevo. Hidden in his wool suit was a glass vial; its purpose was to seal in the secrecy of his own death his knowledge of *The Black Hand*. Concealed in his coat was a Browning revolver. In his heart he carried the passion of Slavic nationalism that inflamed and seared his powers of reason. What he would do he had never done before. He would spill blood; then before he could be apprehended, he would take to his lips the lethal dose of cyanide.

Heir to the throne of the Austro-Hungarian Empire, Archduke Franz Ferdinand and his wife Sophie, were returning from a reception in this capital city of Bosnia. The Royal Procession always drew large crowds as it wound its way among the subjects of the kingdom. Earlier in the day an attempt had been made on the life of the Archduke. Nedeljko Cabrinovic, also of the secret society of the Black Hand, had hurled a grenade at the royal car, but had missed his mark completely. The motorcade had then sped Franz and Sophie to the Town Hall for the ceremonies without further incident. Afterwards his regal convoy again traversed the Bosnian streets, lined, once more, with thousands of spectators. This time they traveled at a faster pace, until, they reached the bridge that crossed the River Nilgacka. A sharp turn at the entrance to the bridge forced the motorcade to slow considerably. The clever young assassin had foreseen this necessity and it was here that he waited. Scarcely could Gavrilo believe his good fortune when the Archduke's car not only decelerated as it neared his position, but came to a momentary stop, directly in front of him. Swiftly he pulled his gun from his coat. Two shots pierced the still air. One shot struck the Archduchess Sophie in the abdomen, a terrible wound for she was an expectant mother. According to Count Franz von Harrach, who was riding on the running board of the royal automobile, Sophie "slid off the seat and lay on the floor of the car, with her face between [her husbands] knees." He was wounded by the second shot but paid no heed to his dilemma. Count von Harrach clearly heard his majesty's plea, "Sofia, Sofia, don't die. Stay alive for the children!" She was already dead. The Archduke began to fall forward. Count von Harrach grasped his collar to keep him from collapsing on his wife. He asked if he was in pain, to which the Archduke replied, "It's nothing! It's nothing." This he repeated again and again, each time more feebly until at last he slipped into death.

Gavrilo, gun in hand, was immediately seized by members of the Royal Guard. So swift was his capture that he was not able to ingest the cyanide of potassium. His guilt was beyond question, but his young age legally prevented his execution. He died four years later, in prison, of tuberculosis.

Three weeks after the assassination of the Archduke and Archduchess, Austria-Hungary issued an ultimatum to Serbia. The ultimatum listed ten demands. Foremost was the stipulation that the Serbian government denounce on the front page if its newspaper any sentiments towards a "Greater Serbia;" that it condemn any "propaganda for the separation of any portion of imperial territory." Although Serbia was independent of Austria, there were many Slavs who resided in the Austria-Hungary Empire who fervently desired severing their lands from the Empire and enlarging the boundaries of Serbia. Austria insisted that the King of Serbia further censure such views in an order to his armies. The ultimatum also demanded the arrest and punishment of Serbians, including governmental officials, complicit in the assassination conspiracy. Finally, the Empire demanded that Austro-Hungarian officials participate in the Serbian tribunals to assure the conviction of the conspirators.

Serbia largely capitulated to the requirements of the ultimatum—except for the last demand. Austrian Prosecution of the conspirators, said Serbia, infringed upon its sovereignty. Nonetheless, on July 28, 1914, one month to the day of the tragedy, Emperor Franz Josef of Austria, in the sixty-sixth year of his reign, declared war on Serbia. The sequence of events that followed is nearly beyond belief. Russia was allied to Serbia and came to her defense against Austria-Hungary. Germany was allied to Austria-Hungary and on August 1, 1914, declared war against Russia. France was allied to Russia and declared war against Germany, and her allies, on August 3. Immediately Germany invaded Belgium so as to assault France more easily, although Belgium had announced her neutrality. Britain was bound by treaty to defend Belgium and so entered the fray on August 4. Along with Britain her dominions became involved in the war including South Africa, Australia, New Zealand, India and Canada. Japan soon followed suit, with her strong military ties to Great

Britain, and declared war against Germany on August 23. Turkey and the Ottoman Empire, along with Bulgaria, sided with Germany. For a time Italy avoided the awful conflict, although allied to both Austria-Hungary and Germany by stating that those nations were the aggressors and Italy was only bound by a "defensive" war. However the following May, Italy broke her alliance completely with the Germanic nations and entered the conflict on the side of France, Britain, the British colonies and dominions, Belgium, Japan, Russia and Serbia. Two years later, on April 6, 1917, the United States joined its forces with the Allies against the Central Powers. Thus for the first time in modern history nearly all of humankind was at war.

Gavrilo could have never imagined that his two shots would split the political atom of the world, commencing a chain reaction that would culminate, not in two deaths, but in the deaths of twenty million people!

CHAPTER 4

COVENANTS

And it came to pass that they formed a secret combination, even as they of old; which combination is most abominable and wicked above all, in the sight of God. . . For the Lord worketh not in secret combinations, neither doth he will that man should shed blood, but in all things hath forbidden it, from the beginning of man . . . And whatsoever nation shall uphold such secret combinations, to get power and gain, behold, they shall be destroyed . . .

—ETHER [23]

GAVRILO PRINCIP WAS A SLAVIC AUSTRIAN. In his heart he was Serbian, part of a Christian nation that had fought for centuries against the overlords of the Muslim Ottoman Empire. In 1813 Serbia won its independence and in 1913 acquired additional territory in the Balkans Wars. However, the Kingdom of Serbia did not govern all Serbs. There were many Austrian and Croatian Serbs, like Gavrilo, who still indignantly believed that justice had been miscarried, and would be until the vision of a Greater Serbia was realized. The more zealous and menacing of these Serbs had formed the secret society of *Union or Death,* commonly known as the *Black Hand.* Like all of the Black Hand initiates, Gavrilo had been received into the clandestine membership by taking a death oath.

Colonel Dragutin Dimitrijevic, the chief of the Serbian Army Intelligence General Staff, also commanded the Black Hand, under the code-name *Apis,* or *the Bull.* Dragutin had been involved in or directed many terrorist activities, including the assassination on June 10, 1903 of the King and Queen of Serbia, ending the Obrenovic dynasty, and the 1911 assassination attempt on the life of Austrian Emperor Franz Joseph. Apis had grown the Black Hand to an organization of some two thousand five hundred members that included officers in the Serbian Army, students, government officials, university professors, and was reportedly backed financially by the Crown Prince of Serbia himself. Gavrilo was among five Austrian Serbs selected by the Supreme Central Directorate of the Black Hand for the ominous mission they hoped would facilitate the "unification of Serbdom." Gavrilo and his fellow assassins were assigned to shed the blood of the heir to the Habsburg throne, the Archduke Franz Ferdinand. Ironically, the Archduke was sympathetic to the South Slavs and planned to grant concessions that would ease tensions between his Serbian and Germanic subjects. Apis, like many terrorists, was against peaceful solutions that would leave political power in the hands of his enemies. Instead, Apis desired to *increase* contentions between the Slavs and the non-Slavs; thereby increasing the zeal for Serbian Nationalism that could lead to a Greater Serbia. The appointed murderers were trained in Koπutnjak Park, Belgrade, in May 1914. They were armed for their lethal task and smuggled across the Austrian border by the *Narodna Odbrana*, the Serbian National Defense organization allied to the Black Hand.

The Black Hand was governed by a strict constitution. According to this constitution Gavrilo was bound to categorically obey all commands given by Apis, the Superior Directorate. Gavrilo was constrained by his oath to put the interests of this covert society above all else, to abandon all morals, to relinquish his agency, to accept the impossibility of ever resigning his membership in the society, and to keep secret all knowledge he possessed of the Black Hand—till death!

Gavrilo was the son of a peasant farmer. His father, who subsidized their meager family income by driving a mail coach, sent him to the Merchants Boarding School in Sarajevo when Gavrilo was thirteen. But Gavrilo had no inclination towards commerce;

his interests were intellectual, and he was particularly involved in student politics. It was his activism that caused his expulsion from school; although Gavrilo is often referred to as a "student," he was not, for he never re-enrolled. When the Balkan Wars were raging he volunteered for the Serbian Army; however, he was rejected due to his small stature, ill health, and lack of physical strength. Lacking in bodily prowess, Gavrilo nonetheless possessed steely nerves and the capacity for cruelty. Two of Gavrilo's Black Hand confederates were also in positions where they could have killed the Archduke. The first, an eighteen year old named Popovic, claimed to have not seen the royal car, but most likely could not go through with the murder. The second man, a nineteen year old by the name of Grabez, testified that he was afraid of hurting bystanders, and so did nothing when his opportunity came. But neither the successful trigger man Gavrilo, nor the mastermind behind the murderous plot, Colonel Dragutin Dimitrijevic, could have ever surmised the human catastrophe of global proportions their murders would precipitate. *That is always the way with evil when once it is unleashed.* When Gavrilo fired the fatal shot on June 28, 1914, he perhaps only envisioned the death of Archduke Franz Ferdinand and his suicidal demise. Dimitrijevic, a.k.a. Apis, as a mature terrorist, foresaw its consequences as leading to a regional war between Serbia and Austria, and in fact hoped for that eventuality. However, both of these men were powerless to stem the tide of the great deluge of war that flooded their home of Serbia along with the rest of mankind. Dimitrijevic was arrested in May of 1917 by the Serbian government and was executed on June 24, 1917 in an effort to suppress the Black Hand. On June 11, 1917 Dimitrijevic feebly acknowledged his guilt: "I may, without wishing to, have committed errors in my work as a patriot. I may even, unknowingly, have hurt Serbian interests."[24]

It is this author's opinion that neither Gavrilo or Dragutin, regardless of their terrible crime, desired anything more than a regional conflict—that neither could have been so evil as to desire world war. There were serious tensions between the European nations at the time of the assassination of Archduke Ferdinand, but it is fairly certain that the heads of state of those nations did not want a European war, let alone a global war. In fact, many of the monarchies were not just friendly one to another—they were *family*! King George of Great Britain was surnamed Saxe-Coburg-Gotha—that is, he was of German extraction. This obviously caused him difficulties during the war; which is why the royal family felt compelled to change their name to "Windsor." Michael Duffy explains:

> The First World War has sometimes been labeled, with reason, "a family affair." This is derived from the reality that many of the European monarchies—many of which fell during the war (including those of Russia, Germany and Austria-Hungary)—were inter-related.
>
> The British monarch George V's predecessor, Edward VII, was the German Kaiser's uncle and, via his wife's sister, uncle of the Russian Tsar as well. His niece, Alexandra, was the Tsar's wife. Edward's daughter, Maud, was the Norwegian Queen, and his niece, Ena, Queen of Spain; Marie, a further niece, was to become Queen of Romania.[25]

The correspondence between the Tsar and his cousin the Kaiser further exemplifies their personal opposition to a general war. At least ten telegrams were sent back and forth between these two cousin emperors from July 29, 1914 to August 1, 1914. Additionally these short epistles demonstrate the steady and deadly movement towards war by the two nations whose chief rulers attempted to prevent its commencement. Excerpts follow:

> Tsar to Kaiser
> 29 July 1914, 1 a.m.
>
> . . . In this serious moment, I appeal to you to help me. An ignoble war has been declared to a weak country. The indignation in Russia shared fully by me is enormous. I foresee that very soon I

shall be overwhelmed by the pressure forced upon me and be forced to take extreme measures which will lead to war. To try and avoid such a calamity as a European war I beg you in the name of our old friendship to do what you can to stop your allies from going too far.

Kaiser to Tsar
29 July 1914, 1:45 a.m.

It is with the gravest concern that I hear of the impression which the action of Austria against Serbia is creating in your country. The unscrupulous agitation that has been going on in Serbia for years has resulted in the outrageous crime, to which Archduke Francis Ferdinand fell a victim. The spirit that led Serbians to murder their own king and his wife still dominates the country . . . with regard to the hearty and tender friendship which binds us both from long ago with firm ties, I am exerting my utmost influence to induce the Austrians to deal straightly to arrive to a satisfactory understanding with you. I confidently hope that you will help me in my efforts to smooth over difficulties that may still arise.
Your very sincere and devoted friend and cousin
Willy

Kaiser to Tsar
29 July 1914, 6:30 p.m.

I think a direct understanding between your Government and Vienna possible and desirable, and as I already telegraphed to you, my Government is continuing its exercises to promote it. Of course military measures on the part of Russia would be looked upon by Austria as a calamity we both wish to avoid and jeopardize my position as mediator which I readily accepted on your appeal to my friendship and my help.
Willy

Tsar to Kaiser
29 July 1914, 8:20 p.m.

Thanks for your telegram conciliatory and friendly . . . It would be right to give over the Austro-Serbian problem to the Hague conference. Trust in your wisdom and friendship.
Your loving Nicky

Kaiser to Tsar
30 July 1914, 1:20 a.m.

Best thanks for telegram . . . If, as it is now the case, according to the communication by you and your Government, Russia mobilizes against Austria, my role as mediator you kindly entrusted me with, and which I accepted at your express prayer, will be endangered if not ruined. The whole weight of the decision lies solely on your shoulders now, who have to bear the responsibility for Peace or War.
Willy

Tsar to Kaiser
31 July 1914

I thank you heartily for your mediation which begins to give one hope that all may yet end peacefully.
It is *technically* impossible to stop our military preparations which were obligatory owing to Austria's mobilization. We are far from wishing war. As long as the negotiations with Austria on Serbia's account are taking place my troops shall not make any provocative action. I give you my solemn word for this. I put all my trust in Gods mercy and hope in your successful mediation in Vienna for the welfare of our countries and for the peace of Europe.
Your affectionate
Nicky

Kaiser to Tsar
1 August, 1914

Thanks for your telegram. I yesterday pointed out to your government the way by which alone war may be avoided.
Although I requested an answer for noon today, no telegram from my ambassador conveying an answer from your Government has reached me as yet. I therefore have been obliged to mobilize my army.[26]

Additionally, many nations including Italy and the United States demonstrated their reluctance to enter the Great War. If all of these key players did not want this catastrophe to commence, who did and what power controlled the rapid irreversible military engagement by nearly every nation in the world? This author would suggest a root cause that most narratives are reluctant to address, if not deny as impossible, because it involves the preternatural. To understand let us reflect on the man who fired the two shots that began it all and the death oath given him by the Black Hand. For the oath's sake Gavrilo's reason was blinded and his conscience seared. Was the author of this oath Apis the Bull? Or was there some intelligence greater than Dragutin, one who is a veteran wager of war, who foresaw with delight the consequences that his two pawns could have never envisioned? If the war began with the oath, is there inherent evil in oath taking or covenant making? The answer is simply that it depends on the inspiration behind the oath, the covenants contained within it, and the purpose for which it is administered.

For a *resolute* man, the making of a covenant is extremely powerful. The oath itself may very well determine his behavior in a crisis—when he has not time to ponder and weigh various considerations, or when his reason is obscured by compelling attractions or temptations. In such moments when he may otherwise waver, the decisive words of his covenant strengthen his resolve and simplify the choices and his commensurate actions. This truth is one reason why God fearing, or rather God *following* men, have always been covenant makers. A good man *knows* that under extreme duress he is capable of betraying that which he holds most dear. Ulysses of old commanded that his men's ears be stopped with wax and that he be bound fast to the ship's mast until far removed from the island of the Sirens. Likewise, a man who desires to do right will bind himself with vows of righteousness.

Two positive examples from the scriptures regarding the making of covenants may be of value. The first makes it clear that the covenant is self-enforced. The second example is a tribute to an ancient prophet king, a follower of Christ, who understood that when evil is spread by the power of the sword, it is altogether appropriate in self-defense, to protect, not only life, but faith and liberty.

> If a man vow a vow *unto the LORD* (note the vow in this case is made to God—*not* to a society), or swear an oath to bind his soul with a bond; he shall not break his word, he shall do according to all that proceedeth out of his mouth.[27]
>
> He was a man who was firm in the faith of Christ, and he had sworn with an oath to defend his people, his rights, and his country, and his religion, even to the loss of his blood.[28]

Eddie Rickenbacher was contemporary with Gavrilo. He felt passionately the desire to defend his country and he would take an oath as well. The oath that Rickenbacher was to take would *not* abdicate his agency or violate his God-given conscience. He would *not* be compelled to place the interests of a secret society *above all else*, including the laws of God, nor would his oath threaten to take his life should he resign after the fulfillment of his obligations. The oath that Rickenbacher would take would be nearly as follows:

> I, Edward V. Rickenbacher, do solemnly swear, or affirm, that I will support and defend the Constitution of the United States against all enemies, foreign and domestic; that I will bear true faith

> and allegiance to the same; that I take this obligation freely, without any mental reservation or purpose of evasion; and that I will well and faithfully discharge the duties of the office on which I am about to enter. So help me God.

Who then was the true mastermind behind the Black Hand? Who is behind all secret combinations and organizations of terror? Again the scriptures offer a clear explanation:

> Now those secret oaths and covenants did not come forth [from the ancient] records . . . but they were put into the heart of [the evil men] by that same being who did entice our first parents to partake of the forbidden fruit—Yea, that same being who did plot with Cain, that if he would murder his brother Abel it should not be known unto the world . . .[29]
>
> . . . Ye shall keep these secret plans of their oaths and their covenants from this people, and only their wickedness and their murders and their abominations shall ye make known unto them . . .[30]

The scriptures further explain who is behind destruction and ruin, and admonishes men to stand firm against his awful dictates:

> For we wrestle not against flesh and blood, but against principalities, against powers, against the rulers of the darkness of this world, against spiritual wickedness in high places.[31]
>
> Put on the whole armour of God, that ye may be able to stand against the wiles of the devil.[32]

Good and evil are not ethereal principles—they are realities. There is a Supreme Being who is the Author of good and likewise there is a fallen being of depravity who is the author of evil. Just as God understands the power of covenants to direct men, especially in dire circumstances, towards that which is right, honorable *and* merciful, the Enemy of God understands the power of covenants, of oaths, to direct those who would swear allegiance to darkness and secret combinations to malevolence and destruction. A *man* will make sacred covenants, in the light of day, in the company of nobles, increasing his agency and his power to do *good.* The very making of the covenant *assists in the keeping* of the promise. An individual who in the process of losing his manhood, takes an oath in secrecy and darkness, abandons his agency and joins a brotherhood of destroyers, will one day awaken to the awful reality that evil never supports her own, as did Gavrilo and Dimitrijevic of the Black Hand. Unfortunately, their oaths also assisted in the keeping of their vows that lead not only to the deaths of countless others, but to their own ruin.

Captain Eddie Rickenbacher, backed by his covenants and sense of duty, became a valiant warrior in defense of Country, family and faith. He fought openly and against armed enemies, yet without malice towards the men who opposed him. In our day, when terrorism has reached unprecedented proportions, it is vital that every man understand the difference between defending Godly law and liberty, and defending cleverly fashioned counterfeits of liberation that offer clichés of freedom, but in actuality deliver bondage or death. Men must not forsake the making of covenants and retreat to impotence, or take the liberal approach of skeptics who falsely claim that there are no *sides* to good or evil, that each should tolerate the other, and that the anti-terrorists, because they *must* use force, are no different from the terrorists themselves. When called upon by those holding righteous authority, a good man—like Rickenbacher—will fight even unto bloodshed, for evil does not retreat from reprisals of rhetoric. In the ready room of the 388th Wing at Hill Air Force Base, a banner bears these words: "Negotiate with your enemy with your knee in his chest and your knife at his throat." And as great God-fearing nations have proven in many instances, when the true enemy of man is subdued, the vanquished are made free.

CHAPTER 5

FIGHTER PILOT

As I descended the landscape widened, billowing into hills and folding into valleys. I landed and rolled down a long incline, and stopped not ten feet short of a small stream . . . The whole village came. I was mighty impressed by the haleness of the old men and women. As for the young girls [they] were exceptionally pretty. Someone pushed through the crowd. It was Monsieur the Mayor.

"Vous etes Anglais, monsieur?" with a smile of very real pleasure.

I said, "Non, monsieur, Americain."

That magic word. What potency it has, the more so at that time, perhaps, for America had placed herself definitely upon the side of the Allies only a short time before. I enjoyed that moment . . . for I felt the generous spirit of Uncle Sam prompting me to give those fathers and mothers, whose husbands and sons were at the front, the promise of our unqualified support. I wanted to tell them that we were with them now, not only in sympathy, but with all our resources in men and guns and ships and aircraft.[33]

—CAPTAIN JAMES HALL

PRIOR TO MAY, 1915, THE AMERICAN PUBLIC and particularly its President, Woodrow Wilson abhorred the idea of "entangling alliances." (In fact even after the United States entered the war U.S. officials preferred the term "associates" to that of "allies.") President Wilson sedulously avoided belligerency, but sought to mediate the confrontation between the Allied and Central Powers. However, in May of 1915 the nation's public opinion began a swift and irreversible swing in sympathy towards Britain, France

The Lusitania

and its allies. What caused America to abandon its neutrality? On May 1, 1915 the British luxury liner *Lusitania* left New York Harbor. On board were many Americans, including the wealthy Alfred Vanderbilt. On May 7, as the Lusitania neared the end of its voyage, and within sight of Ireland, two explosions rocked the ship. Incredibly, thirty year old Kapitan-Leutnant Walther Schwieger, commander of the German submarine U-20, had sent a torpedo ripping into the hull of the forty thousand ton steamer. Schwieger reportedly did not intend to sink the *Lusitania*, but wanted to see what damage a single torpedo would do to the largest ship in the world. The spectacular devastation certainly exceeded his expectations as the great vessel disappeared beneath the waves in eighteen minutes, killing eleven hundred and fifteen souls of which one hundred and twenty-four were Americans.

Miraculously, seven hundred and sixty-one people survived, including Alice Middleton. Alice believed that the man who placed a life belt around her was Vanderbilt; who had not time to secure his own life preserver before they were both swept off the deck.

President Wilson's response was directed to the German Ambassador Gerard. In part it reads:

> Department of State,
> Washington, May 13, 1915
>
> In view of recent acts of the German authorities in violation of American rights on the high seas which culminated in the torpedoing and sinking of the British steamship *Lusitania* on May 7, 1915, by which over 100 American citizens lost their lives, it is clearly wise and desirable that the Government of the United States and the Imperial German Government should come to a clear and full understanding as to the grave situation which has resulted.
>
> The sinking of the British passenger steamer *Falaba* by a German submarine on March 28, through which Leon C. Thrasher, an American citizen, was drowned; the attack on April 28 on the American vessel *Cushing* by a German aeroplane; the torpedoing on May 1 of the American vessel *Gulflight* by a German submarine, as a result of which two or more American citizens met their death and, finally, the torpedoing and sinking of the steamship *Lusitania*, constitute a series of events which the Government of the United States has observed with growing concern, distress, and amazement.
>
> Recalling the humane and enlightened attitude hitherto assumed by the Imperial German Government in matters of international right, and particularly with regard to the freedom of the seas; having learned to recognize the German views and the German influence in the field of international obligation as always engaged upon the side of justice and humanity . . . the Government of the United States was loath to believe — it cannot now bring itself to believe — that these acts . . .could have the countenance or sanction of that great Government . . .[34]

Over the next nineteen months, as atrocities mounted including the sinking of the French *Sussex* on March 24, 1916—killing twenty-five Americans, it became clear that Kapitan-Leutnant Schwieger had not acted as a renegade gun, but in accordance with Berlin policy. This was confirmed officially when in February 1917 Germany announced its doctrine of unrestricted submarine warfare. On April 6, 1917 the United States responded with a declaration of war.

By now Eddie Rickenbacher had firmly decided that he would join the battle against Germany. As he had always been drawn to the latest technologies and as he had become an expert in *speed* as a world class race car driver, it seemed natural that he would want to fight the enemy as a flyer. He recognized that his racing companions were "mature men of proven and swift reflexes." Eddie envisioned a flying squadron of competitive racers. His idea was met with quick approval by his friends in the business and they agreed to join the *Aero Reserves of America*. However, when Eddie met with Brigadier General George D. Squier, chief of the Signal Corps, and his officers, they dismissed Eddie and his racing flyers idea immediately. Condescendingly, they told Rickenbacher that it would be a mistake to make a pilot out of man who understood engines and mechanics. For, they said, as planes were always breaking down, such a man would be reluctant to engage the enemy in battle if he knew that his aircraft wasn't up to par. The same logic dictated the U.S. policy of *no parachutes*—the reasoning being that a pilot in the fray who couldn't possibly bail out would stay in the fight to the very last. Of course these policy makers were not pilots and the military's aviation war experience was nil. Still, Eddie could scarcely believe their stupidity. What was worse, Eddie was told that neither he, nor any of his colleagues could qualify for flight training as none were college graduates. Eddie explained that he had completed correspondence courses, was a competent engineer, and as such should qualify as having the equivalent of a college education. The officers thought that was some kind of joke.

Nothing had ever come easy to Eddie and the pompous dismissal by the Signal Corps of his proposal was only a temporary set back. An offer soon did come to Rickenbacher—but not to fly. Major Burgess Lewis, a friend and racing fan, invited Eddie to join up as a *staff driver* for the American Expeditionary Force. With scarcely a days notice, Eddie was in New York and was enlisted as a sergeant in the U.S. Army. Secretly the force, under General John J. Pershing, sailed for France two days later. In France, Eddie initially drove Colonel T. F. Dodd. Later, after he repaired Colonel Billy Mitchell's car, impressing the famous airman immediately, Eddie frequently chauffeured Mitchell around the French countryside. This was to prove to be a very opportune friendship, for when James Miller, commander of the flight school at Issoudun, requested Eddie as his engineering officer; Colonel Mitchell cut the red tape, turning his driver into a flight cadet.

Rickenbacher was transferred to Tours where he was trained by French instructors. Perhaps, using the word *trained* is an overstatement. Eddie was given a brief lecture—then was assigned to strap himself down, alone, in a French Morane-Saulnier, a plane with clipped wings so that it could not get airborne. He would start the engine, advance the throttle, practice steering with his feet, accelerate, push the control stick forward raising the tail skid off the ground, traverse the airfield, decelerate, reverse his direction, and repeat this procedure, again and again. Initially, he said that he "went down the field wobbling from side to side, with the tail bobbing up and down, like a frightened roadrunner." Within a couple of days he mastered ground handling a tail skid aircraft. Next he was given "two short flights with an instructor" in a French Caudron, a nine cylinder aircraft with a top airspeed of eighty miles per hour. He was then told it was time to *solo*. Eddie, the dare-devil race car driver, was frightened nearly half out of his mind by this command. Yet to refuse was to abandon his hopes of becoming a combat pilot.

To start with, the weather conditions were anything but ideal; it was a very blustery day. He began his takeoff fighting a crosswind. In trying to correct, he overcorrected and the plane skidded off his intended course and headed straight towards a hangar. Students and instructors who were on hand to observe Eddie's first solo flight scattered every which way, trying to dodge his ever changing ground path. To avoid colliding with the hangar he stomped on the opposite rudder swinging the aircraft back towards his original direction, narrowly missing the hangar by only a couple of feet. Despite his meanderings, his airspeed increased and as he eased the stick back, the Caudron took to the air. Once aloft everything seemed easy—that is until he brought the aircraft in to land. Eddie simply said, "I was scared stiff." He made his approach and when he neared the ground he raised his nose, lowering his tail to what he thought was a landing attitude. In such a position, with the aircraft nearly stalled, the nose is so high that a pilot cannot see over it and expertly uses his peripheral vision to guide his craft. But Eddie was no expert. He was anticipating the bump at touchdown, but there was no bump. He looked over the side and was shocked to see the ground still fifty feet below him. Fortunately the aircraft wasn't fully stalled and was still flying. Eddie stepped the aircraft down incrementally, until finally, and to his own wonder, he safely landed. By the time he finished his seventeen day flight course, basically self-taught, he had logged twenty-five hours and was promoted to the rank of first lieutenant in the American Signal Corps.

Rickenbacher reported to Issoudun in September, 1917, pilot and engineering officer. His first responsibilities were to requisition all of the equipment needed to mechanically operate his squadron. His duties were so demanding that he could only occasionally attend lecture sessions given to the new aviators who had just arrived from the states. These young men were all graduates of the finest universities, impeccably attired in tailored uniforms. These ivy-leaguers wouldn't take Eddie seriously. After all he hadn't finished the seventh grade; his grammar was coarse by their standards; and his German name seemed especially offensive. Behind his back they called him the "German spy."

Oddly enough, this was not the first time that Eddie had met personal prejudice. In England, during the early days of the war, Eddie had gone to Britain on racing business and was detained and interrogated. The British agents possessed a dossier that ridiculously traced his ancestry back to the aristocracy—he was, they said, a German Baron! Instead of responding with anger, he treated the whole affair good naturedly. Imagine, he thought, the poor fatherless kid from Columbus—a blue-blooded spy! He was released, but only into the company of agents who were to be with him wherever he went. The English agents checked into his hotel, each taking a room on either side of Eddie's room. Later that night, Rickenbacher felt it was time to stretch his feet and thought he would make a game of this fiasco. The moment he left his room, their doors opened and they followed him out into the dark fog. Suddenly Eddie bolted down the street, he abruptly turned into an alley and stopped, dead still. The Brits shot past him, running as fast as they could. Delighted, he stepped from the alley and yelled, "Here I am." Ordinarily they would have shot him, but he was already doubled over in laughter "enjoying the game immensely." His friendly manner, the sporting chase, his good humor, and the obvious fact that he really hadn't tried to "escape," caused the government agents to also break out in laughter. Eddie offered to buy a round of ale, to which they readily agreed.

Then later, when Eddie drove for Colonel Billy Mitchell, he was again reported to authorities as a spy for the Germans. The head of the Secret Service in Washington, William S. Nye, was a racing aficionado and a good enough friend to know the report was unfounded. He notified Rickenbacher that he was "under surveillance by counterintelligence." Forewarned, it wasn't long before Eddie surmised that the undercover agent assigned to him was his own tent-mate. For better or worse, he couldn't help himself and he incessantly teased the man, letting slip, on purpose, a comment that would quickly get his attention, only to say nothing more. Perhaps this U.S. agent, like the British agents, became familiar with his humor and soon recognized that he was a true American patriot, if ever there was one. The interesting thing is, Rickenbacher never railed accusations of discrimination against the authorities. Of course this was "profiling." There was a war on—the enemies were Germans, and although a citizen of the United States, he *was* the son of a Swiss-German immigrant. It would be strange indeed if he were not watched. Instead of reacting negatively to the precautions of the government, Eddie intensified his efforts and by his manner and merit earned the trust of his superiors. Instead of such a strict system impeding his progress he swiftly advanced, in a matter of months, from an enlisted man to an army officer.

When his resentful fellow aviators spoke of Rickenbacher disdainfully, sometimes right to his face, he did not respond in like manner. Rather, he determined for himself that they were basically good young men from excellent families that were simply a bit spoiled and had too much time on their hands. As squadron engineer, he observed that the airfield was besieged with rocks, that could seriously inflict FOD—foreign object damage. They were flying the French built Nieuport equipped with wooden propellers. Prop blast would often whirl these rocks into the blade, breaking the propeller. Rickenbacher requisitioned a hundred buckets and sent one hundred Ivy Leaguers out onto the muddy airfield to clear it of rocks. Their moans and groans, he said, were music to his ears. Not many months later, these same antagonists recommended Rickenbacher to their superiors to be their flight commander.

Gradually Eddie's flying proficiency improved as he practiced whenever he could break away from his never ending administrative responsibilities. In contrast, the other pilots devoted all of their time advancing their aviation skills. Rickenbacher taught himself spin recovery twenty miles from the airfield so no one would see his errors. When Eddie mastered this maneuver he entered a spin over a football game at Tours at just five hundred feet above ground level. He recovered so low, players and spectators alike, including army brass that were in attendance, dove for cover.

Although Rickenbacher was grounded for thirty days, nonetheless it was a tremendous demonstration of skill—regardless of how foolhardy. In early 1918 when the first class of pilots had completed their training at Issoudun they were sent to Cazeau to learn the art of aerial gunnery. And in March 1918 when the first American squadron, the 94th Aero Pursuit Squadron, was sent into battle on the western front, Lieutenant Eddie Rickenbacher was part of the new unit—a capable and eager fighter pilot.

The 94th Squadron was equipped with old Nieuport biplanes. The United States had yet to manufacture its own fleet of fighter aircraft and instead secured second hand planes from the French. The Nieuports were delivered to the 94th *without* guns. Nonetheless, on the morning of March 6, 1918, America's most experienced ace and veteran of the Lafayette Escadrille, Major Raoul Lufbery with seventeen kills to his credit, led a flight of three across enemy lines. The other two Nieuports were flown by Eddie Rickenbacher and Douglas Campbell. Without weapons it was strictly a training flight and would give the duo of inexperienced combat pilots their first taste of flying in adversarial skies. As Eddie followed the veteran Lufbery over Verdun, he was surprised by an acute physical reaction to the unstable air and anxiety of this first mission—he became suddenly and miserably airsick! Honored as the first to fly from the 94th alongside of America's Ace of Aces, he felt sure that he was about to "disgrace" himself and heave his breakfast over the side of his plane—the residue of which would be evidence to his comrades of a rookie's constitution. At the very moment when the nausea was about to overpower his stomach, Eddie's Nieuport pitched and rolled violently in the shock wave of anti-aircraft fire. Blooms of black smoke appeared near his ship as the Germans below let loose a barrage of eighteen pound shells. Instantly Eddie felt gratitude for two blessings: his Nieuport continued to respond to his command—the puffs of smoke were all below him, and secondly his stomach-churning distress had fled with the first explosion. As Eddie put it, "Archie had scared the nausea out of me."

As the anti-aircraft batteries persistently pounded the skies around Eddie, he quickly learned to emulate Lufbery's corkscrew pattern, making his plane a hard target to hit.

Nearly every combatant wonders how he will react when under fire. Of all life's disappointments, the greatest is to be disappointed in one's self. A truly honest man is most honest to himself. Such a man leans little on the approval of others. He also possesses the confidence to appropriately weigh the criticism of others. Of all life's joys, one of the greatest is to sincerely approve of one's own actions—to truly know that one is striving, without artifice, towards attaining the great virtues of life. It is a noble thing to never defraud another. It is nobler to never defraud oneself. No genuine person can experience the joy of a clear conscience unless he is not only true to his fellowman, but is also true to his own soul. Insincerity always is a result of a double-mind. Such a man can hardly *like* others, for he will never like his own company. Whereas the man who outwardly and inwardly *cultures* a single-mind, who looks for the good in himself as he does in mankind, who deals with others fairly and fairly deals with self—the only one over which he is sole master. Opposition is indispensable in the quest towards single-mindedness, for it grants a man the ability to measure the standing of his actions against the aspirations of his beliefs. In the face of approaching opposition every good man hopes he will not find himself lacking the requisite fortitude to stay his course, remain true to his God-received values, and fulfill his duty, whatever personal sacrifice may be required of him—even to the laying down of his life. In that he has developed the type of personality that can accept no self-accomplishment until it is *proven*, he will deprive his ego of false esteem. He hopes that he will be found worthy and capable; and when, in the midst of adversity he recognizes that *he is worthy*, he is given a commensurate blessing for this effort towards integrity—he is given happiness.

With anti-aircraft explosions all around him; with his Nieuport buffeted by the deadly blasts, his plane unarmed, Eddie discovered this and more. He writes:

> A rush of happiness came over me with the assurance that I was neither going to be sick nor was I any longer in terror of the bursting shells.
>
> A feeling of elation possessed me as I realized that my long dreamed and long dreaded novitiate was over. At last I knew clear down deep in my own heart that I was all right . . . I could go over enemy lines like the other boys who had seemed so wonderful to me! I forgot entirely my recent fear and terror. Only a deep feeling of satisfaction and gratitude remained that warmed me and delighted me, for not until that moment had I dared to hope that I possessed all the requisite characteristics for a successful war pilot. Though I had feared no enemy, yet I had feared that I myself might be lacking.
>
> This feeling of self-confidence that this first hour over the Suippe battery brought to me is perhaps the most precious memory of my life.[35]

As Eddie continued his flight, filled with joy, he reflected on his life and what had brought him to this moment in time, high above France and in harm's way. He had always been drawn to a life of excitement. He loved engines; he loved racing, and now, more than these passions, he loved flight! But this was completely different—this was flying and fighting. "The whole business of war," he said, "was ugly . . . the pleasure of shooting down another man was no more attractive to me than the chance of being shot down myself." Still he knew that in defense of liberty it would be necessary to withstand the cruelties of conflict and he must not flinch from what must be done. A firm resolve swelled within his breast—he would set himself decisively against the war-hardened German aviators, who had been at this horrific game for years, and "beat them at their own boasted prowess in air combat."

As his thoughts were engaged in these lofty aspirations he realized that Major Lufbery had turned their flight back towards the 94th squadron aerodrome. After Eddie had landed and was taxiing towards the hangars he could see that every pilot and mechanic had gathered, eagerly awaiting their return. They had been the first of their squadron to fly over German-held territory and all were anxious to hear of their adventure. Rickenbacher and Campbell proudly stepped down from their Nieuports and with a nonchalant manner told their crew-mates how the enemy had, to no avail, bombarded the skies around their planes with endless anti-aircraft fire—and how they "must have cost the Kaiser a year's income by [their] little jaunt into his lines." They had not seen, they said, any other aircraft, let alone German planes; no doubt they were reluctant to engage American aviators. About this time Major Lufbery chuckled under his breath and muttered that new pilots were always the same. This brought immediate questions from the two rookies. There, in front of their admiring audience, Lufbery explained. They had overflown a flight of five Spads as they crossed the lines. Yet another formation of Spads passed by them fifteen minutes later. Good thing, he said, they were not Boches. Lufbery factually stated that he turned their flight homeward when they approached four German Albatros fighters—not two miles distant and *armed* of course, while their little Nieuports were gun-less. Another enemy fighter passed by shortly afterwards. He admonished the two not to just look, but to *see*. Then he turned to Eddie, asking him how much of the shrapnel from Archie did he get? Of course, Rickenbacher knew that he had come through anti-aircraft barrage unscathed, and thought perhaps that Lufbery was trying to bolster him a little after the deflating comments he had just made. To his total dismay, the major walked over to his plane and poked his finger in one puncture in the tail. Then in quick succession and to Eddie's horror, he pointed to other shrapnel holes in the wings—one had missed him by a mere foot! Eddie realized that to beat the Germans at their own game, he would have to *learn* the game.

Eddie quickly gained more experience flying over the lines. Experienced French combat pilots would drop into the 94th Squadron and invite a number of the Americans to join them on patrol. The French aviators did not know the Americans were still awaiting the one essential piece of equipment that would turn their planes into fighters—guns! Unbelievably, the Americans didn't think to tell them. For the Yanks it was a new and exciting opportunity and they joined their French compatriots for these missions in such numbers that, fortunately, the enemy was kept at bay. Then one day, a Frenchman happened to notice the obvious, but unthinkable—the American flown Nieuports were not mounted with a solitary weapon. Said Eddie, "The French thought we had lost our minds."

In April, 1918, the 94th finally began to receive supplies and equipment—instruments, flying apparel, spare parts, and most importantly guns and ammunition! On April 29 Eddie departed Toul, France, along with another aircraft piloted by Captain Jimmy Hall. Just north of Pont-à-Mousson they spied a new German Pfalz fighter. Steadily the two Americans climbed into the sun's bright camouflage. When they were two thousand feet above their prey, Hall and Rickenbacher dove headlong towards the Pfalz. Hall was first to fire, but the German quickly saw his danger and maneuvered himself out of harm's way, trying to climb for the advantage. This offered temporary salvation but a far better move would have been simply to nose over and accelerate away from the Nieuports, whose fabric shedding tendencies at high speed were too well known. The Pfalz then tried to reverse the attack on Hall but, unable to gain the firing position, finally turned to flee. Rickenbacher had anticipated this eventuality and had placed his Nieuport above the path of his enemy's retreat. In an instant he was on the Hun's tail. The German then went for speed and a straight-line diving retreat. But it was too late. Eddie trained his sights on his enemy's aircraft and at one hundred and fifty yards,

Jimmy Hall Guides Eddie Rickenbacker To His First Victory
By Herb Kawainui Kane

pressed the trigger. His tracer bullets clearly marked the accuracy of his aim and cut a path through the narrowing distance into the German's tail. Like guiding a stream of water from a "garden hose" Eddie fine tuned the deadly flow of bullets and watched intently as they pounded into the aircraft. The flight path of the Pfalz suddenly became erratic, the left wing lowered as it gently banked earthward. The plane was still controllable—there had been no explosion, no in flight breakup, but there was no one alive to control it. A moment later the Pfalz crashed into a wood a mile from the lines. It was Rickenbacher's first victory.

Confirmation of the downed Boche reached the 94th Squadron HQ even before Eddie and Jimmy Hall landed. After they had shut down their aircraft engines, they ran to each other and embraced in a hardy handshake in celebration of their victory. Then they noticed that pilots and mechanics were running across the aerodrome, from the hangars, the staff buildings and barracks—all had heard the news and were eager to congratulate them. Their applause was worth more to Eddie than all the congratulations that would soon be received by telegraph from all over the world; for his comrades of the 94th shared the uncertainties, the aspirations, the ordeals and the perils of aerial combat. Eddie discovered that sincere praise is always positive and never led to conceit among successful fellow aviators. Said Eddie:

> The smallest amount of vanity is fatal in airplane fighting. Self-distrust rather is the quality to which many a pilot owes his protracted existence.[36]

Eddie's first promotion came a few weeks later when Captain Jimmy Hall was shot down behind enemy lines. Hall survived this calamity but was taken prisoner. His amazing adventures are included in *Part Two* of this book. With Hall held captive by the Germans, Eddie became Commander of Number 1 flight of the 94th Squadron. Rickenbacher took his new responsibilities very seriously. He knew that no matter how much native ability a pilot possessed, or how extensive his training had been, or how skilled he was in maneuvering his plane, his first missions over the lines and his first encounters with the Germans were extremely dangerous. The slightest mistake or the least manifestation of hauteur could prove fatal. Therefore, Eddie followed the example of Major Lufbery and always led the new pilots personally on their first few flights into enemy airspace. He watched over them like a mother hen to "assist them over that delicate period between the theory of the school and the hard practice of battle."

Despite the expertise and experience of the pilot, however, no one is exempt in war from the Grim Reaper. As mentioned earlier, America's high command did not believe in issuing parachutes to their pilots. Therefore, if a plane's fuel tank was pierced by a tracer bullet the fuselage was soon enveloped in flames and the pilot would have but two choices—either remain with his aircraft or jump. The aviator's greatest fear was to be burned to death, fueled not only by gasoline but by the highly combustible dope treated

American Aerodrome at Issoudon

fabric that burned with intense heat. To jump from the aircraft, without the benefit of a parachute, also meant certain death, but without the agony of enduring scorching flames. What to do in such a dire situation was a matter of frequent discussion in the 94th Squadron. Major Raoul Lufbery proffered this advice:

> I'd stay with the machine. If you jump you haven't got a chance. If you stay, you may be able to side-slip your plane down so that you fan the flames away from yourself. Perhaps you can even put the fire out before you reach the ground.[37]

One day in May, 1918, a German Albatros flew directly over the 94th Squadron Aerodrome. Of his seventeen victories, Lufbery had never brought down an enemy aircraft behind the Allied lines. Now a target was overhead in plain sight of his men. Lufbery's own plane was in the hangar for maintenance, so the Major fired up the first available aircraft on the line. This was critical in that each Nieuport was unique—flight and performance characteristics varied considerably from plane to plane. Nonetheless, in a matter of moments Lufbery was airborne in a frame of mind that Rickenbacher described as "impetuous abandon." In less than ten minutes the Major had engaged the Albatros. However, it appeared to those below that his guns had jammed, for he circled away evasively from his opponent. After a short time it seemed that he had cleared his guns for he took the offensive and swiftly advanced towards the Germans from their rear. As he closed the gap between his Nieuport and the Albatros, he obviously failed to evade the deadly sights of the rear gunner. In an instant Lufbery's plane erupted in a blazing inferno. He passed the Germans in nearly straight flight for a few seconds. Then to the terror of his friends below, they saw their Ace of Aces climb from the cockpit, straddle the fuselage and work his way precariously back towards the tail, trying to keep his body from the awful flames. Each second that passed seemed like an eternity as the airplane dropped closer and closer to the ground. Then, suddenly, at an altitude of only two hundred feet Major Lufbery leaped! Below him was a stream; to those who witnessed this tragedy, it appeared that he desperately tried to jump at the moment when he might direct his fall into the water below—a highly unlikely attempt but one that offered the only possibility of survival. He missed the stream and fell headlong onto a picket fence mercifully killing him instantly; for he had been burned terribly—his body was charred black.

Rickenbacher arrived at the scene only thirty minutes later. Thankfully Eddie was spared the sight of seeing his commanding officer, who had so carefully nurtured him through his first combat missions, impaled on that awful fence. Frenchmen from the nearby village had removed his body to their town hall. The villagers had covered his entire body with flowers from their gardens.

Rickenbacher continued to accumulate victory after victory until the first of June when he was stricken with a serious fever. He arrived in Paris on the morning of June 6, 1918 to convalesce. What he saw that morning he will never forget. The Germans were driving their war machine furiously towards the capital and were only thirty miles distant. Thousands upon thousands of refuges were pouring into the city. The Parisians themselves were completely disheartened but there was a "terror in the countenances of these homeless people . . . Old women, young women, all clothed in wretched garments and disheveled [wandering] blindly through the streets . . . with swarms of crying children clinging to their skirts." The plight of battle driven exiles is always horrible. The masses cannot purchase even the barest of

Fighter Pilot Eddie Rickenbacker
Photograph courtesy of the Lafayette Foundation
Photographic reproduction by Bryan Cox

necessities—they are penniless. By the time these starving souls fell under Rickenbacher's intense gaze there was no spirit left in them. Only the pangs of hunger "served to remind them that they must still live." Paris had already spent it resources. Without relief surely those desperate refugees would have broken out in riot, however the American Red Cross and YMCA came to their aid at the very brink of disaster.

Hospitalized in the midst of this pitiful turmoil Eddie became very introspective. The suffering that surrounded him and his own reoccurring fevers led to a self analysis that would prove to forever soften him towards humanity and toughen him towards himself. Lying in bed and shaking with chills, he was able to recall every maneuver of every combat. But there was a deeper chill than that of the fever which held him in its grip—for he realized then, as he analyzed the victories that had made him an ace pilot, he had committed many blunders along the way. He had made serious mistakes; the same errors which had cost other fliers their lives. He knew then that his success was only partly earned and that his deliverance from death was in fact due to the grace of God Almighty. There and then he offered a "fervent prayer" to his Heavenly Father in gratitude and asked that he might be blessed in like manner when again he took to the skies. Then the thought occurred to him that he was responsible to do as much as he could for his own salvation. What he could *not* do, he would trust to God; but what he could do, that he must do. For example, he could do something about the continual and infernal jamming of his guns. After all, guns are mechanical, and he knew a great deal about improving mechanical equipment. He vowed that he would improve the performance of his weapons and check every cartridge destined to be shot through his guns for proper fit. This would take considerable time before each sortie, but he knew it to be a matter of life or death. He vowed to be wary but never timid. Said Eddie:

> I recalled episodes in which boldness had been the most intelligent course of action and therefore the most cautious. It was said that I insisted upon getting close enough to my adversary to hit him with a baseball bat. I would continue to be bold but only at the right moment.[38]

Eddie vowed to know *himself* as well as he knew his aircraft. This would require constant self-examination. Never would he allow himself the luxury of excusing misbehavior by saying it was simply how he was. Rather he would chase down his faults and determine a course of action to eliminate them. Later he wrote:

> Only the man himself can make himself what he is, by taking full advantage of the excellent raw material supplied him by God.[39]

Eddie also decided to Americanize his German name and from then on he signed it Rickenbac*k*er, instead of Rickenba*ch*er.

A small thing perhaps, but he felt that great changes were derived from many small ones. This change was not missed by America whose populace closely followed the lives of its Aces. Newspapers across the United States printed the story: "Eddie Rickenbacker has taken the Hun out of his name!"

After nearly a month of hospitalization Eddie had recovered sufficiently to fly again. Just outside of Paris he stopped in at the American supply airport at Orly. What he saw he could scarcely believe. Three new Spads were on the flight line—assigned to the 94th Squadron! The Spad, an acronym for the Société pour Aviation et ses Dérivés, was the ultimate fighter aircraft of World War I—powerful, fast, highly maneuverable, and could withstand any "G force" without breaking up in flight—a plane vastly superior to the old Nieuport. Eddie felt that with continual aid from heaven above and with his hands on the controls of the mighty Spad, he could now truly accomplish his assigned mission and would be up to fighting even the great Flying Circus, the squadron of the Red Baron, Manfred von Richthofen. Without waiting for orders, and without even returning to Paris for his gear, Eddie strapped himself into Spad number "1" and took off for the 94th aerodrome. Far from the court marshal he could have received for informally requisitioning the Spad, his CO congratulated him and assigned that very plane to him.

Unfortunately Rickenbacker's medical problems returned. An abscess had formed in his right ear. The rapid changes of altitude required of a fighter pilot resulted in incredible pressure changes, causing Eddie's swollen ear to throb with pain. He returned to Paris and had the abscess lanced, which afforded him some relief. But in August Eddie's condition developed into mastoiditis, rendering him semiconscious and bed-bound. On one Sunday morning he felt particularly saddened by his situation. Eddie Green was leading a flight accompanied by Walter Smyth and a new flier, Alexander Bruce. Rickenbacker especially enjoyed flying with Smyth, a capable pilot, brave, "honest, wholesome, with a grand sense of humor." Eddie identified with this twenty year old aviator and felt closer to him than to any other of his friends of the 94th. Sometimes Smyth would become melancholy with a premonition that he would not live to see the war end. When this depression weighed heavily on Smyth, Rickenbacker would accompany him on long walks in the country to talk things out and cheer him up as best he could. As Rickenbacker lay in his bed he thought on these things, then fell into a deep sleep. He saw, as if in a dream, Walter Smyth's aircraft collide with the plane piloted by Alexander Bruce. He saw them in a cloud—they had lost sight of each other, when "their wings touched and fell off . . . both planes plummeting to earth." When he awoke Kenneth Marr was at his bedside. Before he could tell Rickenbacker the news Eddie said, "I know. Smyth and Bruce were killed. I saw it." Marr was amazed as he had just received the news by telephone only a minute before. The tragedy had happened just as Eddie had seen it in his dream.

As with Major Raoul Lufbery, the deaths of Smyth and Bruce were preventable. It angered Rickenbacker no end that the American Air Service would not supply their pilots with parachutes. Great flyers and great men had died needlessly. These men, and others like them, could have fled from their fiery flying coffins and lived to valuably serve the Allied cause—perhaps survive the war and return home to their country and their families. Eddie had experienced the wonder and "pleasure" of seeing his "enemy bail out of his plane and float to earth safely." He said, "I never wanted to kill men, only to destroy machines." It galled him to think that the Germans were more humane to their aviators than were the commanders of his own military.

Eddie postponed further medical treatment on his right ear for as long as he could consciously overpower the pain and returned to the 94th Aerodrome. He felt he could not take time off from the war when every mission could prove vital. Every night the squadron cook gave him a heated salt bag to afford some relief. But the next day, as he would swoop down from 22,000 feet, the piercing pain became unbearable. The infection finally penetrated into the mastoid bone of Eddie's skull, causing its honeycomb-like structure to begin to deteriorate. Of all pain, that of the bone is most excruciating. In the days before antibiotics, mastoiditis often led to death. Preliminary to this extreme the victim would become semi-comatose. Such was Eddie's current condition. This illness had robbed him of his flying status for three valuable months. Many soldiers considered themselves fortunate when removed from battle due to injury or illness. Not so with Rickenbacker; to him, time down represented lost opportunities. With far fewer fighting days than his fellow Americans, how, Eddie thought, could he prove himself in battle? In the early spring he could not fight because their planes were without guns. He flew hard in May, but his fevers began in June and seriously challenged him throughout the summer causing him to spend more time in bed than in the cockpit. Still, he had become an ace and had earned the respect of his formally antagonistic comrades—for when he was able to fly he was victorious! Finally, the last week in August surgeons in Paris operated on his right ear, draining the mastoid bone and removing the infected tissue and bone. This procedure proved successful and from that point on he had no further problems with ear pain.

While he was recovering from this second operation, some of the flyers from the 94th visited Rickenbacker in the hospital. They told him:

> We wish you were back, Rick . . . We not only want you back; we want you back as commanding officer. We want to go straight to Colonel Billy Mitchell and ask him to make you commanding officer of the 94th.[40]

Without the benefits of a high school and college education, handicapped by his German ancestry, faced with skepticism and scorn when he first applied to the Air Service, met with ridicule by the blue blood fledgling aviators when he joined their ranks, rarely able to participate in ground school and flight training and being

Eddie Rickenbacker after surgery

Photograph courtesy of Lafayette Foundation
Photographic reproduction by Bryan Cox

largely self-taught, tormented with debilitating head pain—Rickenbacker had nonetheless become such an able pilot and mentor that his entire squadron preferred his leadership, in matters of life and death, over any other man!

Ace Combat Pilot Eddie Rickenbacker

Photograph courtesy of Lafayette Foundation
Photographic reproduction by Bryan Cox

CHAPTER 6

LODESTAR

STAR of the North! though night winds drift
The fleecy drapery of the sky
Between thy lamp and me, I lift,
Yea, lift with hope, my sleepless eye
To the blue heights wherein thou dwellest,
And of a land of freedom tellest.

Star of the North! while blazing day
Pours round me its full tide of light,
And hides thy pale but faithful ray,
I, too, lie hid, and long for night:
For night;—I dare not walk at noon,
Nor dare I trust the faithless moon,—

Nor faithless man, whose burning lust
For gold hath riveted my chain;
Nor other leader can I trust,
But thee, of even the starry train;
For, all the host around thee burning,
Like faithless man, keep turning, turning.

And we are wise to follow thee!
I trust thy steady light alone:
Star of the North! thou seem'st to me
To burn before the Almighty's throne,
To guide me, through these forests dim
And vast, to liberty and HIM. [41]

—JOHN PIERPONT

RICKENBACKER RETURNED to the 94th Squadron on September 11, 1918, fit for duty after his operation. He arrived in the nick of time to participate in the "first great combined air-and-ground assault in the history of warfare"—the Saint-Mihiel Drive. Billy Mitchell commanded the operation consisting of one thousand five hundred aircraft—fighters, reconnaissance and bombers—supporting five hundred thousand Allied troops. At five o'clock on the morning of September 12, 1918 the attack began, announced loudly by the incredible din of thousands of explosions hailing from the big guns of the Americans upon the German forces. To the disappointment of the aviators a hard rain falling from extremely low clouds kept their planes grounded. Eddie waited impatiently for dawn to see if the ceiling would permit even skud running. By noon the cloud bases had risen somewhat but no pilots had yet taken off.

Eddie took Reed Chambers aside and suggested that they brave the rain and low clouds and "try a short flip over the lines to see what it was like." Chambers agreed and the duo launched their Spads, finding they were able to climb to a mere six hundred feet above ground level. They flew to Verdun, then east to Vigneulles, the objective of the massive offensive. South of Vigneulles the road to Metz was a flurry of activity as the enemy hastily withdrew their war machine to safer ground. Through the thick of the battle they continued their flight towards Saint-Mihiel where they observed the same phenomenon—guns, munitions and equipment being quickly relocated. Flying at only a few hundred feet of altitude along the road between Saint-Mihiel and Vigneulles Rickenbacker and Chambers dove their Spads below tree top level, strafing the transports at point blank range, creating utter chaos among the Germans. Again and again they rained their machine gun fire down upon the Huns, creating a bottleneck as "men fled, and horses stampeded." As soon as they landed back at the 94th, Rickenbacker provided the coordinates to the American ground artillery who successfully shelled the roadway, forcing the

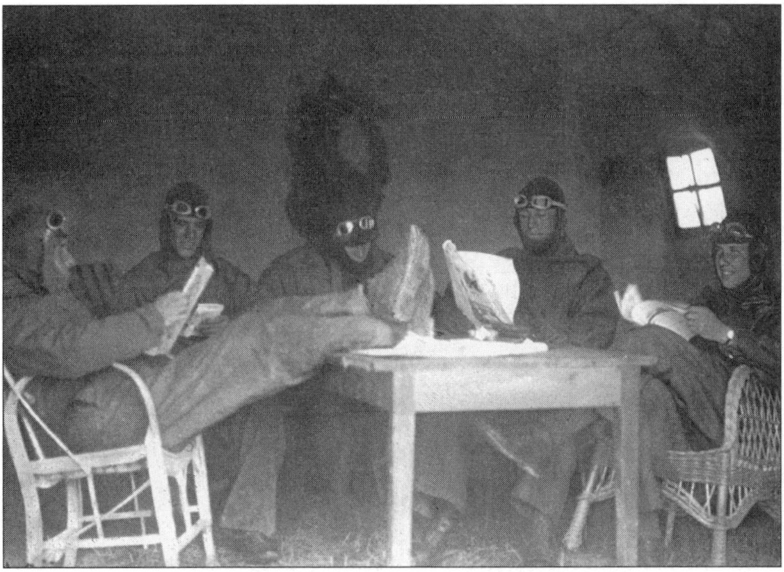

Rickenbacker with fellow pilots in the Ready Room

Photograph courtesy of Lafayette Foundation
Photographic reproduction by Bryan Cox

Germans to abandon huge quantities of armaments and equipment and flee on foot.

The following morning the weather broke and Eddie took off on a solo mission. Soon after he was airborne he saw American DH-4 bombers being overtaken by four Fokker D-7s. He emerged from the Sun's bright glare not fifty yards behind the rearmost Hun. A micro-burst of lead from Eddie's thunderous Spad and the Fokker fell to the earth in ruin. It was only then Rickenbacker saw the red cowlings of his antagonists. He had just successfully attacked the most skilled and deadly squadron of the war, von Richthofen's Flying Circus. Now he was outnumbered three to one and had to fly for all he was worth to stay alive. Never had he seen such aerial agility! Not for a moment could he lose sight of any one of the trio, as they performed their choreographed ballet of aerobatics for the sole purpose of training their machine guns on him. The four aircraft swiftly darted three dimensionally through space, twisting, rolling, looping. What Eddie needed was an opening below him where, for a brief moment, he could escape without exposing himself to crossfire. Suddenly he saw the required aperture appear and like a screaming eagle he dove his Spad, full throttle, straight for mother earth. He had worked with his mechanics to fine tune his engine to develop power well above what it was expected to deliver, and deliver it did. The Flying Circus could not overtake him as he rapidly slipped out of their lethal grasp.

Soon he was again aloft with Chambers on patrol. Thiaucourt and Montsec had been taken by the Americans. From their cockpits the two young flyers witnessed the "most spectacular free show that ever man gazed upon"—the Germans in retreat, the Americans advancing like Indian fighters, running fast and low, from stump to ditch to tree, the continual spray of automatic weapons fire kicking up dirt and debris. Eddie's flying speed would have been approximately 110 to 120 miles per hour. That is slow enough to see incredible detail. With perfect clarity they looked down upon the surreal scene, so close to the action that they could see the faces of the fighters, determined or desperate as to whether they were advancing or retreating. Rickenbacker could not help cheering for his fellow soldiers who were fearlessly and victoriously pursuing their enemies. Suddenly he was personally drawn into the unfolding drama as he heard the "rat-tat-tat" of a machine gun in deadly proximity and felt his Spad take several direct hits. In an instant he saw their source—three Germans nestled in the ruins of a building, machine gun sights locked on his plane, a stream of bullets connecting their position to his. His responded instinctively; the Spad banked, its nose swiftly lowered on target. So close was he to the ground that this attitude could be held for only a moment, otherwise he would crash headlong. But that moment was all that was needed. All this happened in the blink of an eye. The predators became the prey; without sufficient time to take cover Eddie's guns blazed a fiery path into their dead center. He saw his bullets riddle one man who dropped lifeless on the spot. The other two dived for a doorway as he zoomed over their heads.

On September 24, 1918 Major Hartney handed Rickenbacker the order that his fellow aviators had requested—Eddie was promoted to commander of the 94th Aero Squadron. He had continued to accumulate victories and was second only to Frank Luke of the 27th Squadron. However, it was not just his skill that the others admired—it was his sincere concern for the welfare of every pilot and his appreciation for every man, whether flyer or mechanic. Eddie's formula for leadership was straightforward and effective. In his own words he outlines this formula in five steps:

> 1. I should never ask any pilot to go on a mission that I myself would not undertake.
> 2. I would lead by example as well as by precept.
> 3. I would accompany the new pilots and watch their errors and help them to feel more confidence by sharing their dangers.
> 4. I would work harder than ever I did as a mere pilot.
> 5. I would stay in the air and lead patrols—all [the work of] making out reports, ordering materials, etc., would be [delegated] to competent men.[42]

One evening, not long after Eddie's promotion to Captain of the 94th Squadron, he was summoned immediately to headquarters by none other than General Billy Mitchell. Rickenbacker was ordered by Mitchell to select two of his men to fly an extremely dangerous night mission. Aircraft instrumentation of the era was primitive and basically consisted of a needle and ball indicator (which works on the same principal as a carpenter's level), airspeed indicator, compass and altimeter. Navigation was strictly a matter of pilotage and dead reckoning. Foul weather and darkness were potentially greater hazards than enemy aircraft. The home base was marked by a searchlight set at a particular angle, so as to allow the pilot to differentiate its beam from others that would be set against the night sky. It was a difficult task for the WWI aviator just to fly in his intended direction in low visibility conditions, especially after the sun had set. Today heading is maintained by directional gyros, often slaved to remote compass systems that constantly update the system's accuracy. In that day the only cockpit resource for heading reference was the compass set in a liquid sphere (still a fundamental backup in today's cockpit). This type of compass is fraught with problems, including acceleration, deceleration, variation, deviation and turning errors; it wobbles mercilessly in turbulence and the original variety was apt to stick. Attitude, the aircraft's position relative to the earth, is now controlled by an artificial horizon. The pilots in WWI had no such instrumentation and on a black night with few visual references an inexperienced pilot could easily become spatially disoriented and, in the clutches of vertigo, plunge to his death. Even a veteran aviator may have problems navigating to his mission destination and return in close enough proximity to find the search light of his home aerodrome. For these reasons even a practiced day pilot had very few hours of night flying.

General Mitchell explained to Captain Rickenbacker that several thousand American soldiers had been cut off from the main force beneath the ridge of Montfaucon. Intelligence reported that the elite Prussian Guard had been dispatched from Metz, traveling by rail to Montfaucon to attack this trapped infantry, already thirty-six hours without rations and ammunition. Confirmation of the rail cars bearing the Prussian Guard was vital to devise a plan of support and relief. The only way this information could be obtained in sufficient time to counter this threat was to send two airplanes down the rail lines and determine if a troop bearing train was on its way to Montfaucon. The pilots for this mission would have to know, by heart, all of the rail lines from Metz to the front. They would have to be extremely competent aviators, for their safe return with the necessary intelligence could mean the difference between life and death for thousands of starving American soldiers. Eddie asked for volunteers. Every pilot of the 94th Squadron stepped forward. He selected Coolidge and Cook, and faithful to his first rule of leadership determined that three reconnaissance flights were better than two. After he saw his two brave pilots aloft, Rickenbacker ordered his mechanics to ready his Spad for flight. Minutes later he was airborne in the ebony night.

At a mere five hundred feet above the ground he wound his way north. He looked back towards the airfield to fix in his mind's eye the angle of the brilliant column of light that rose from the 94th Aerodrome with inverse perspective into the infinite blackness of the heavens above. He noticed that this search light was one of several on both sides of the front. He saw other points of light that helped to fix the plane of the earth beneath him—village lights, a few scattered lights of vehicles moving along roadways, highways invisible to his eyes, and the quick flashes of heavy artillery that boomed across the abyss of no-mans land. Archie was asleep, for the anti-aircraft gunners never supposed that aircraft would venture from home base at this hour of night, when the sun had long since withdrawn even its faintest tresses of light. To the east Eddie picked up the dim reflection of starlight off the Meuse River. Above La Meuse he descended to only three hundred feet, and following its gentle shimmering, he flew ever deeper into the land of his enemies. This same river had likewise guided the young heroine, Joan of Arc, at the start of her mission of liberation five centuries before.

Forty miles behinds the lines he saw the dim lights of the engine of a train moving steadily down the tracks. To accurately discern what this engine was pulling he descended lower still, mindful that hidden in the cloak of darkness a slight elevation in terrain or an unseen tower could pluck his small craft from the sky and hurl him into the night of death. Flying low he readied his guns to strafe the train, should he sight troops through its car windows. Eddie swept swiftly down the length of the train and found it hauled only freight. He gained a little altitude and continued his quest. All the while he was flying he saw no sign of Coolidge or Cook. At one hundred and twenty miles per hour he traversed the tracks to Montemédy, then to Stenay and finally into Metz without sighting any rail transport of soldiers. He knew that no such train could have escaped his eye at the low level at which he flew.

This meant that the marooned men near Montfaucon were safe that evening. If, in the morning, the American forces could not get through to their rear, planes would drop relief supplies over the enemy artillery barricade. He hoped that his two pilots were, like himself, safe as yet. But as he could see no other plane in the dark sky, there was no aid he could render his comrades. It was now time to deliver the intelligence of his flight to General Mitchell.

Climbing, he turned his Spad towards Verdun, only five minutes away. However, the lights of the city did not appear below him as they should have. After twenty minutes not only had Verdun failed to come into view, but the Meuse River, his original guide, was nowhere in sight! As he continued straight ahead, he pounded on his compass. It whirled under the concussion of his blows, then settled on a course *opposite* to that marked only a moment before. Flying to Metz, Rickenbacker had followed the landmarks of the Meuse River, the tracks and cities that were so familiar to him. Each reference gave him a relative bearing to the next providing a fool proof course along his desired route. Bee-lining for home should have been a far simpler task. But he had flown some fifty miles in an unknown direction, far enough for all of the well known signposts to be lost in the nocturnal void. Again he shook the compass and again it settled on another heading, divergent from either of the formerly marked courses. His faulty compass had led him away from the one true course of safety. Eddie wrote:

> Never have I seen a compass—except those captured from Boche machines—that even pretended to disclose the direction of north! Mingled with my rage was a fear that was getting almost panicky . . . Thinking I might be in a ground mist I rose higher and circling about scanned the horizon and blackness below. Not even the flash of a gun that might direct me to the battlefront was visible![43]

There remained only forty-five minutes of fuel in his tanks. Rickenbacker knew that he was far behind enemy lines. Without guidance superior to his internal sense of direction (a pilot's directional sense can operate only when its bearings are fixed to something external, such as a known mountain range) Eddie would soon exhaust the life-blood of his Hispano-Suiza engine causing him to dead stick earthward to an inevitable crash. Far worse than his own suffering would be the loss of knowledge he possessed—as he had no guarantee that either Cook or Coolidge would fare any better than himself. Suddenly a thought flashed in his mind—look to the North Star. His eyes left off scanning the meager gauges of his cockpit and the erroneous man-made compass and began scanning the heavens. There, at the tail of the little dipper, shinned a star far less brilliant than most of the stars in the firmament; but of all the luminaries in the immensity of space, only this solitary point of light holds its position unwaveringly. Instantly the veteran navigator knew he had been flying west instead of south. He put the lodestar "behind his rudder" and confidently began his homeward trek. After a brief period of time he again saw the quiescent waters of La Meuse, this time far more beautiful to his eyes than before. Once again he followed her gentle curves, now sure of his position, until he reached Verdun. From Verdun he saw the beacon of the 94th Squadron searchlight and within ten minutes touched down safely on his home field with scarcely a drop of reserve fuel remaining. The other two pilots had already returned, but their intelligence was not as reliable as was Rickenbackers. General Mitchell gratefully received Eddie's report with a simple "Thank God" and dismissed the young captain to a well deserved evening's rest. Rickenbacker wrote:

> As I walked across the field to my bed I looked up and recognized my friend the North Star shining in my face. I raised my cap and waved her a salute and repeated most fervently, Thank God![44]

My father taught me simple, yet powerful principles of navigation. There is placed in man an internal guidance system that only operates correctly when it is used in relation to fixed standards of truth. A man learns to trust his sense of direction and uses this sense as a relative bearing—relative to something steadfast. For example, as a young boy my father taught me to use the long chain of the Wasatch Mountains, east of our home, as my reference point to enable me to always ascertain the cardinal points of north, south, east and west. My father also provided many other solid points of reference in my youth and he taught me that it was necessary to fine tune that inner sixth sense that would so vitally affect my life's direction. He lived the principle that the quintessence of a man's life is his home. From this point of reference, home, a man should depart and to this point he should return. Home must be a haven. In the midst of the blackest night a profound beacon of light must emanate from the home base to the outer reaches of heaven (as did the searchlight from the 94th Squadron). This light must be distinct from any other, and especially from the false beacon of the enemy. A man cannot always abide at home. In a world at war there are always those who are cut off from their homes; those who are besieged and desperate need the aid of a man who has empowered himself with wings—who can over-fly the artillery barrage of the adversary. To render aid to his brothers is to place one's self in common battle with the invader. Such a man knows the enemy is never satisfied with partial conquest; and when the enemy has destroyed or enslaved others, this adversary will seek to destroy *his* home base.

My father taught me that home is surrounded with other lights of familiarity, like the village lights over which Rickenbacker flew—that even when the horizon is lost at night, the light of friends provides a plane of reference so that a man might know where earth meets heaven. Father taught us that faith, like La Meuse, was a flowing, moving, living power that could be followed as a sure guide even when blackness veiled our existence and that in its benign depths we could always see reflected celestial light. Thus a man binds his internal direction, *not* to the frivolous occupations that would cowardly remove him not only from home but from the battle of life, rather he binds his purpose to those references that lead him to the front lines of the war.

Many times father said to me, "Are your hands green? No one needs green hands. No one needs inexperienced hands. Teach your hands to be skillful!" There is a time when a man must control his resources with deft agility, particularly as he prepares to confront his enemy (as did Rickenbacker when he flew low-level along the rail lines to Metz). At such times sudden death flanks a man on his left and right. If he descends just a little lower than necessary he will crash headlong in flames. He readies his powers, his feet on the rudders, and one hand on the stick, the other hand ready to trigger the weapons that will rain lead and horror on the evil forces that oppose him. There is no blood-lust in the godly warrior, and if his sights fall upon those who, although in the territory of the enemy, are discerned innocent, like the train near Montemédy, the man who is foremost master-of-self allows the guiltless to pass beneath his wings unmolested.

A man, my father said, is always accountable to his superiors, and when he completes his mission, he must provide a true report—where?—at his home base, as did Rickenbacker to Mitchell. There are also other points of references that, although they are temporal, are often of great value, like the man-made compass. These helps should be relied upon only if frequently cross checked for reliability, for they can fail at the very instant when they are most needed. When these fail, when panic begins to seize our minds, when the ebony abyss encompasses us, when darkness becomes so predominant that all of the former points of light have vanished, when we know we are deep in the territory of deadly opposing forces, when even our faith seems to have left us, when we have lost our bearings completely and destruction seems imminent, we must either abandoned ourselves to ruin or our minds must remember the Lodestar—the one point of light that never moves, that is changeless, eternal, fixed. Once we recognize the

North Star, immediately our sense of direction is restored and with assuredness we set our course for home. Rickenbacker knew the Star that was his salvation—"Thank God," he said, for his own safety and for the help he was able to give to thousands of his brothers.

The "American Ace of Aces" was Frank Luke, an incredibly skilled, courageous and confident fighter pilot. Reminiscent of Babe Ruth's legendary called shots in the 1928 World Series when he pointed beyond the right field wall, indicating accurately where he would place his forthcoming homerun, Luke had a way of calling his scores in advance. For example, on September 16, at twilight, while visiting the 94th Squadron, Luke pointed toward two German observations a couple of miles behind enemy lines, still plainly visible from the airfield. He told Eddie and a few others who were standing nearby to keep their eyes on the two Boche balloons telling them that the first would fall in flames at 7:15 p.m. and the second at 7:19 p.m. Observation balloons were very difficult to shoot down and very risky for the pilot who attempted the feat. The defense system surrounding balloons was intense, as these aerial platforms, set near the front lines, provided constant vital surveillance, defensively and offensively. Anti-aircraft guns surrounded the balloons and as the balloon height was known, the gunners could precisely preset their range to shoot down invading aircraft. It was extremely difficult for a pilot to penetrate the explosive barrage that circumscribed any approach to the balloon. Also, support fighters constantly over-flew their balloons, guarding them zealously. Therefore, an attacking aircraft had to run the gauntlet of deadly fire from earth and sky before he could claim his prize. It was far more likely that he would sustain a hit before he could drill his target. Even if he brought his guns within range of the balloon and was able to send his bullets tearing through the balloon's fabric, it was possible that he would fail to ignite the gas within. At such times the balloon would remain buoyant while the fighter pilot made his risky retreat. The probability of Frank Luke downing two balloons as predicted is immeasurably greater than Babe Ruth's three home runs and was infinitely more dangerous.

Nonetheless, as the 94th Squadron gathered in their open field, eyes riveted towards the distant specks that grew more difficult to discern in the darkening eastern sky, a simultaneous cheer rang through their ranks when a sudden blaze appeared where the first balloon had been. To add to their amazement the balloon fell at the precise time that Luke had specified. Could he do it again? Several minutes passed when another conflagration fired the sky. It was, said Rickenbacker, a most "spectacular exhibition!" Shortly after they heard the drone of Luke's aircraft returning safely to the 94th Squadron. It was now too dark to see the field and red Very lights were sent skyward to mark his landing site. Several minutes later Luke made a perfect landing directly in front of his admiring audience. When his Spad rolled to a stop the victorious ace jumped from his cockpit and, laughing, was hailed with congratulations. Balloons destroyed counted equally with downed aircraft, but most often their operators were able to parachute to safety. This added to the savor of triumph for the fighter pilot could score without taking life.

On September 27th Frank Luke did not return from patrol. Not until after the war was over did his comrades learn his fate. After three victories on that single sortie, Luke's engine took a direct hit and he was forced to land behind enemy lines. He made his escape from the landing site but was by an entire German platoon, ironically in a graveyard. He refused capture and made a desperate stand against his enemies armed only with a pistol. Luke was killed in the attempt. With Frank Luke's disappearance, Captain Eddie V. Rickenbacker became the "American Ace of Aces"—a dubious mark of distinction, as no one bearing that honored title had survived. Said Eddie:

> I had a strange feeling of dread. Four other flyers had held that title. All were dead. The honor carried the curse of death.[45]

On October 10, 1918 the 94th, 147th and 27th squadrons received orders to strafe two enemy balloons. The amount of airpower called for indicated that resistance was expected to be heavy. Rickenbacker positioned himself above the convoy, where nearing their destination he observed eleven Fokkers flying in from Stenay and another eight Fokkers inbound from Metz. Eddie set his course to intercept the Stenay aircraft, which he soon recognized, by their red cowling, to be the elite von Richthofen Flying Circus. As they passed underneath his Spad they held their formation tight—either Eddie was undiscovered or they felt invulnerable to a single Spad separated from his Squadron. Swiftly Eddie rolled his plane over, a maneuver commonly called the *split-ess*, and dove for the last Fokker of the formation. At close range Rickenbacker let loose a single burst and fire erupted from the Boche's fuel tank. The German aviator was unhurt from the gunfire and quickly unbuckled himself from his harness and leaped from his ill fated ship. Eddie was gratified to see the German's parachute blossom and begin a safe descent. He wished him luck but could not afford the luxury of watching him float earthward as an intense dogfight was forming around him. Eight other Spads had entered the fray. At that instant he saw Lieutenant White of the 147th Squadron execute a *renversement* to attack an aircraft bearing down on White's trailing man. The maneuver was so tight that White did not get off a shot but actually *rammed* the Fokker before he could bring down the Spad! The two machines collided at a combined speed of two hundred and fifty miles per hour, an incredible marriage of total destruction as wings and fuselages brutally wrapped round each other and chaotically tumbled through the air, smashing into a bank of the Meuse River below. Later Eddie wrote:

> For sheer nerve and bravery I believe this heroic feat has never been surpassed. No national honor too great could compensate Lieutenant White for this sacrifice for his comrade and his unparalleled example of heroism to his squadron.[46]

Unlike Rickenbacker and many of the pilots, White was married with two small children. This was to be his last flight before he was slated for leave to America to see his family. However, White was not to die un-avenged. Before this fight was over, another Fokker fell after being pummeled by Eddie's guns.

By late October Rickenbacker attained two more aerial conquests over the Flying Circus. On October 27, 1918 Hamilton Coolidge, one of the 94th Squadron's most skilled aces, was killed instantly when his Spad took a direct hit from Archie. Coolidge was a Harvard graduate. All of the flyers were well aware that the war would soon be won. Austria had buckled completely and the strength of German ground forces were obviously diminishing. Therefore the death of a comrade was bitter indeed and seemed senseless. Adding to the irony was the fact that Germany was concentrating their air forces in ever *increasing* numbers against the American Air Service, despite the inevitability of defeat. Therefore, as the Great War neared its end, its dangers greatly *increased.*

The Liberty bomber was no match for the deadly Fokker. On one flight alone, near Grand Pré, Rickenbacker saw three Liberty ships devoured by Fokkers that pounced on them from every side. In one of the dogfights that followed Rickenbacker discovered a red-nosed enemy on his tail, closing in for the kill. He looped his aircraft, positioning himself skillfully behind his foe and with a short burst sent his antagonist plummeting to the earth. Minutes later when, supposedly, the last Liberty had crossed over the American lines and Eddie had thought his work complete, he saw a straggling Liberty whose badly damaged engine barely sustained flight, still behind the lines, with a Fokker bearing down hard upon him. At full throttle Eddie came to his aid and the tables were soon turned. The Fokker, seeing Eddie's advance attempted to loop his aircraft, but his engine failed at that critical moment. Rickenbacker was shocked to see the Fokker, again from the Flying Circus, with a still propeller fall out of the loop in a hammerhead stall. He took his position behind the disabled German and with burst of gunfire guided the Fokker as his captive towards the American lines. Meanwhile the distressed Liberty bomber safely flew to its home base. Eddie almost succeeded in obtaining the most sought after prize of the Air Service—an intact scarlet-nosed Fokker! To his absolute disbelief as they neared an Allied field, another Spad, most likely French, spied the Fokker and thinking it fair game riddled it with bullets. Eddie dove towards the imprudent pilot who seeing Rickenbacker in trail of the Fokker, suddenly realized his error and broke off his attack. Nonetheless the Fokker crashed instead of landing safely. Miraculously the German pilot escaped injury. This was Rickenbacker's twenty-fourth victory.

On October 30, 1918 Captain Rickenbacker won his twenty-fifth and twenty-sixth victories. Lieutenant Kaye had departed with a flight of four and Eddie had decided to trail the Lieutenant and observe his tactics as a new flight leader. From a distance he saw Kaye's group skillfully encounter two Fokkers. Out numbered the Germans left the battle, flying westward towards Grand Pré. Eddie determined to swing wide and approach Grand Pré from Germany. Thus, Eddie reasoned, when the Fokkers first saw his approach they would be deceived into thinking that he was a Hun. His strategy worked perfectly. When their flights converged Eddie was well above the unsuspecting Germans. After they passed beneath him, Eddie dropped his wing, opened his engine to full throttle and plunged like a screaming eagle on the tail of the rear Fokker. A short burst of twenty rounds, placed with surgical exactness in the center of the fuselage, sent the enemy aircraft crashing to earth. At such close range Eddie saw the now familiar red markings and knew at once that he had "again outwitted a member of the von Richthofen crowd." The second member of the Flying Circus cut a fast trail homeward. As Eddie was low and inside of German lines he pulled his Spad up sharply to gain altitude before the inevitable barrage of anti-aircraft fire could riddle his plane at close range. He turned his plane towards France thinking his work was done for the day. As he passed the town of Saint George, scarcely two miles from the front, he was surprised to see a

German reconnaissance balloon, nestled in its bed, directly below him. As the balloon was harbored it had previously escaped his detection. Eddie wrote:

> On a sudden impulse I kicked over my rudder, pointed my nose at the huge target and pressed the triggers. I continued my dive to within a hundred feet of the sleeping Drachen, firing up and down its whole length by slightly shifting the angle of my airplane. Evidently the Huns thought they were quite safe in this spot, since this balloon had not yet been run up and its location could not be known to our side.[47]

Again Eddie applied max power to escape Archie, as he was so low that he could be hit by even small arms fire. However, his attack had been a complete surprise and his exit so swift that not a tracer bullet was sent his direction. Behind him the darkening sky was lit by the brilliant light of the soaring inferno of the downed balloon (his last conquest in the Great War). October had been an incredible month for the Ace—in one month Eddie had shot down fourteen German aircraft. Laughing to himself for his good fortune he again turned homeward. But something troubled him that, for a moment, escaped his understanding. He had been flying for quite a while when he saw his opportunity to attack the two Fokkers. The balloon had again diverted his attention when nearing the front. Both had proved to be profitable distractions, but he had allowed his attention to become too focused. He knew that he was overlooking something vital. In an instant he was stuck by the horrific answer. His Spad had fuel for two hours and ten minutes. One look at his watch told him that he had been flying for that exact time! Additionally he had, during the attacks, flown at gas guzzling full throttle. At any moment his engine would run dry. He was still very low and could not glide powerless for any distance. The terrain below was now quite indistinct, trees and meadows blurring together in blackness. Eddie throttled down to miser whatever fuel was left and crept unnervingly towards the 94th Aerodrome. All the while he expected his engine to cough, sputter and die. Of course it would happen—he was dumbfounded as to why he was still airborne.

Below him he could see the flash of gunfire as the Heinies took pot shots at his low and slow aircraft. He hoped he would at least crash on the American side of the lines. Minutes passed, each an eternity, but he continued to drone on. Within ten miles of his home base it was evident that no search light graced the sky. Why, he thought, couldn't those men be more attentive when they knew a pilot was yet out and would, if still aloft, be *desperate.* Eddie extracted his Very pistol and fired the red light to alert the airfield that his situation was critical. No response. Just as he fired a second shot his engine begin to lose its rhythm in sickening dissonance. Then it died and all, save the sound of the wind in his wings, was quiet.

He felt "cold chills" running up his spine. At that fateful moment a searchlight suddenly illumined the sky only a few hundred yards in front of him. He was nearly on top of the airfield! Still, without power he was rapidly descending. Could he make it? To his great relief he cleared the final obstructions and made the field with a thud. Wondrously he was safe, his Spad undamaged. Deadstick, he had landed in the dark of night without a drop of fuel and had come to a stop less than a hundred feet from his own hangar! However, Eddie was not jubilant but walked toward "mess with a chastened spirit." How in the world could he have forgotten something so crucial as his fuel reserves? Only a rookie could make such a mistake, not a veteran aviator, not America's Ace of Aces! Eternal vigilance, not only in regards to one's enemies, but over one's self, is the price that must be paid for true victory. How stupid to conquer his foes while allowing darkness to encompass him and surrender all *power* of escape? Perhaps these words of scripture came to his mind:

> What shall it profit a man, if he shall gain the whole world, and lose his own soul?[48]

Of the next ten days, three were spent by Eddie in Paris on leave, the other seven were hampered by inclement weather. On the evening of November 10, 1918 Rickenbacker received a momentous phone call. The caller's voice was frenzied with elation and announced that the war would end at precisely 11:00 a.m. the following day. Eddie shouted for joy. All the men of the 94th Squadron went "a little mad" with happiness and spontaneously commenced a 4th of July style celebration, igniting Very lights, parachute flares and rockets. Eddie wrote:

> For months these twenty combat pilots had been living at the peak of nervous energy, the total meaning of their lives to kill or be killed. Now this tension exploded like the guns blasting around us.[49]

November 11th dawned in a haze of fog. Headquarters had dispatched orders that all flyers should remain grounded for obvious reasons. War was war until the very last minute and a pilot could still lose his life until the clock struck that blessed hour when hostilities would end. However, Rickenbacker had never been one for convention and an hour before the cease-fire he had his Spad rolled out of the hangar and its engine warmed up. Tacitly he mounted his war-bird for the last time while officially the war still continued and took to the skies. From his unique perspective he was an eye-witness to the end of the First World War. He wrote:

> Flying over no-man's land . . . at less than five hundred feet . . . I could see both Germans and Americans crouching in their trenches, peering over with every intention of killing any man who revealed himself on the other side. From time to time ahead of me on the German side I saw a burst of flame, and I knew that they were firing at me. Back at the field later I found bullet holes in my ship.
>
> I glanced at my watch. One minute to 11:00, thirty-seconds,

> fifteen. And then it was 11:00 a.m., the eleventh hour of the eleventh day of the eleventh month. I was the only audience for the greatest show ever presented. On both sides of no-man's land, the trenches erupted. Brown-uniformed men poured out of the American trenches, gray-green uniforms out of the German. From my observer's seat overhead, I watched them throw their helmets in the air, discard their guns, wave their hands. Then all up and down the front, the two groups of men began edging toward each other across no-man's land. Seconds before they had been willing to shoot each other; now they came forward. Hesitantly at first, then more quickly, each group approached the other.
>
> Suddenly gray uniforms mixed with brown. I could see them hugging each other, dancing, jumping. . . .I flew up to the French sector. There it was even more incredible. After four years of slaughter and hatred, they were not only hugging each other but kissing each other on both cheeks as well. . . . I turned my ship toward the field. The war was over.[50]

No doubt until the dawning of the great millennial reign, there will be Evil in the world. There will be Dragutin Dimitrijevics, Gavrilo Princips and secret societies, like *The Black Hand*, that will plot destruction and death. There will be Rulers, Principalities and Powers who as ministers of Apollyon will continue to delight in covenants of abomination, in intrigue and murder. There will be hosts of men who will be deceived by dark intrigue and received into *these* ranks, who will likewise cry for war and bloodshed. There will be others, compelled to arms by their nation or by their conscience, to defend that which they hold most dear, their homes, their liberty, their faith. Of the latter, many will again be pitted against each other, all caught up in the deluge of universal war. Yet from the deceived war monger to the freedom fighter, the actuality of war sickens blood lust and universally chastens the heart and soul. Years of fighting bring a deep longing for peace. To the man in the trenches fighting fatigue and filth, malnutrition and malaise, bullets and bacteria, it seems that surviving the war is an impossibility. But ultimate Evil can never triumph. From the fox holes, to the cockpits, to the bombed out homes whose makers cleave to the ruin of their loves, prayers ascend to the Omnipotent Power, the Lodestar—He who gives meaning and reference and *life* in a war-torn world, begging for mercy, forgiveness and liberation. Then on the eleventh hour, those who have endured are liberated. Shackles fall from their eyes, hate gives way to humanity, and man embraces man, not as enemies, but as brothers. Is not the ending of World War I a type, a hope of that day when mankind, after having aligned itself more than ever to Apollyon, will be chastened with war more severely than ever before until it can never forget again the Fatherhood of God and the brotherhood of man. On that day there will begin a peace that will last one thousand years!

Rickenbacker "Super Sport" Coupe

CHAPTER 7

BETWEEN THE WARS

'Tis all a cheat,
Yet fooled, men favour the deceit;
Trust on and think, to-morrow will repay;
To-morrow's falser than the former day;
Lies more; and whilst it says we shall be blest
With some new joy, cuts off what we possessed.[51]

—DRYDEN

EDDIE RETURNED TO THE STATES A TRUE WAR HERO. America adored this down-to-earth, plain talking man who, ever cognizant of his tremendous influence on this nation's youth, would not endorse promoter's products; nor would he accept offers from Hollywood (one such offer came with an upfront certified check for $100,000—an unheard of sum for that day). Rickenbacker felt that to have his name associated with merchandise, from cigarettes to apparel, or to act in movies (even as himself) although an easy road to fortune, would require compromises that would cheapen his "own stature and the uniform" he had worn so valiantly. No, he thought, the appropriate manner to inspire the young men of America was through hard work and accomplishment. He determined that he would not be one of those men that went "from hero to zero." He set out developing the finest automobile yet built—the *Rickenbacker.* At the New York Automobile show of 1922 he debuted three models, a touring car, a coupé, and a sedan; priced from $1,485 to $1,995. The cars were an instant hit and within a year the Rickenbacker Motor Company had over one thousand distributors and dealers in America, and hundreds more overseas. Within two years this young aviator had sold 50,000 cars!

In California, before the war, Eddie had met a beautiful young lady, Adelaide Frost Durant. When he met her again it was in the early days of his automotive company. He had established direction and stability in life and felt the time was right to allow romance to blossom. He wrote that while escorting Adelaide to a New Year's Eve party in 1921 he was, for the first time, "shot down in flames"—not by the Germans, but by Cupid! Eddie and Adelaide were married on September 16, 1922 by Jacob Pister, the same pastor who had christened and confirmed Eddie as a child.

Shortly thereafter Eddie returned to France and Germany with Adelaide—his purpose vastly different from when he left home a few short years before as a soldier filled with the desire to become a fighter pilot. In that endeavor he had succeeded beyond his wildest dreams. And now, on his honeymoon, he was greeted as a returning hero by government officials and prominent business leaders. The reaction of the Germans to Rickenbacker was most surprising. They bore him no ill will whatever; in fact, quite the opposite—he was admired for his well known feats of bravery, even by former members of the Flying Circus. Of course, von Richthofen's squadron, along with all others, had been officially dismantled by the Treaty of Versailles. The fighting men of these units held no standing of importance in their country, as Germany was a nation without a military air force. The country itself was considered the lowliest in all of Europe, haggard by devastating inflation. Five days in a fine German hotel cost Eddie and Adelaide the equivalent of six American cents! Yet his former foes welcomed him "like a long-lost friend." While in Berlin three Hun aviators of the Great War called on Rickenbacker at the Hotel Adlon. All were now men without *apparent* power; two were formerly of the Flying Circus. They treated Eddie with great deference and, perhaps because he hailed from Germanic roots, they spoke frankly and without reservation. They discussed the causes that led to the defeat of their Fatherland and they disclosed to Eddie their vision of Germany's restoration to power. The very idea of a bankrupt, war ruined country reestablishing itself as a military world power within a few years would have seemed preposterous to nearly anyone but Rickenbacker. He had fought these men head on and knew that they were not braggarts, but men of skill, intelligence and determination. Their names were Ernst Udet, Erhardt Milch, and the foremost of the three—Hermann Goering. Goering told Rickenbacker:

> Our whole future is in the air. And it is by air power that we are going to recapture the German empire. To accomplish this we will do three things. First, we will teach gliding as a sport to all our young men. Then we will build up commercial aviation. Finally, we will create the skeleton of a military air force. When the time comes, we will put all three together—and the German empire will be reborn.[52]

At this time Göring was already associated with the infamous Hitler, then a little known mustached fanatic, as commander of the *Brownshirts.* Four years after Göring made these predictions to Rickenbacker, German high schools were offering glider training as part of their curriculum. When the Nazis came to power in 1933 Germany possessed an abundance of highly skilled glider pilots. Under Göring these young aviators formed the core of the Luftwaffe, the Air Force of Germany. A close friend of Göring, Willy Messerschmitt initially developed aircraft for "commercial" use but quickly adapted his award wining Messerschmitt 108, in 1935, to become the deadly ME-109 fighter. Incidentally, it was Göring who founded the Gestapo.

Blessings and challenges came quickly into the lives of the Rickenbackers. In 1925, Eddie began to build the first four-wheel brake system on a passenger car. At first his revolutionary design took the country by storm. However, the large automakers could not afford to allow the young company to leap so far ahead of their current inventory of hundreds of millions of dollars, so as to render their cars obsolete. They attacked the concept of four wheel brakes with full page ads—proclaiming that such a system was extremely dangerous. False accusations quickly spread across the country that a four-brake system could cause loss of control or that the car could stop so abruptly that the occupants would be slammed against the dashboard. The effect of this competitive propaganda caused the Rickenbacker Motor Company to quickly flounder and in a little over a year the "Car Worthy of its Name" went out of production.

Of course with their inventories saved and Rickenbacker out of the picture, the big companies gradually introduced four wheel brakes in their own lines, which over the next several years became the safety standard for all automobiles. Eddie was left "flat broke and $250,000 in debt." Yet he would not take out bankruptcy and eventually paid back every dime that he owed. Nor did he hold animosities towards the big car companies who, he said, simply could not afford being taken unawares by his innovation! It is an amazing thing when the little guy who is forced out of business has empathy for the giants who caused his ruin. But this attitude freed Eddie from cankerous misgivings that could have ruined more than his company—it could have destroyed him personally.

In the midst of these serious difficulties Eddie and Adelaide adopted two young boys. David Edward was born in 1925 and their second son, William Frost, in 1928.

It was fortunate that Eddie did not burn his bridges; under the circumstances most men would have. Ultimately these powerful industrialists became his allies. Later Rickenbacker would run Eastern Air Transport for General Motors, tripling its value and firmly establishing the airline's validity in the pioneering days of air transport. Ultimately he would outbid John Hertz, founder of Yellow Cab and Hertz "Drive-Your-Self" rental cars, in acquiring

Eastern Air Lines. He took the company public and formed a new corporation. As a principal stock holder and as its president, Rickenbacker built Eastern into one of the largest airlines in the world. Long before he enjoyed this success Eddie summed up the story of his failed automotive company by simply saying:

> The competition was too stiff for a newcomer; in a few years I lost the company and my shirt. Probably it was a lucky break for me. The disaster drove me back into aviation.[53]

In the interval between his automotive manufacturing days and Eastern Air Lines, Eddie accomplished incredible feats that are still very much a part of our American heritage. Although he had not raced cars since the war, Rickenbacker had kept in close contact with the sport. By 1927 the Indianapolis 500 Speedway was about to "pass out of existence." Eddie felt that this would not only be a nostalgic loss felt by the entire country, but that if the Indianapolis raceway was lost, the greatest "testing laboratory" of the automotive industry would also be lost. Eddie tried to raise the money to purchase the rack track in Indianapolis, but to no avail. However he was able to convince Frank Blair, of Union Guardian Trust Company, to arrange for a bond with the State of Michigan that raised the needed funds. Under Eddie the speedway flourished. He brought in NBC, put in an adjacent golf course, and resurfaced the dangerous brick pavers with Kentucky rock asphalt. When the depression hit in 1929, Rickenbacker's bond was the only one in Michigan that survived the crash and still continued to pay interest! He ran the raceway until 1941, when he closed the track to conserve the fuel, oil, rubber and other products for the vital war effort. After WWII he sold the Indy 500 to Anton Hulman who built upon the wonderful traditions of Rickenbacker making the track "the richest [racing] event in the world by far."

Also, for a short time Rickenbacker owned and operated Allison Engineering Company, arranging with the Department of

Navy to build an innovative 12-cylinder aviation engine. The Allison engine powered such notable WWII aircraft as the P-38 and the P-51. It was by developing and then selling Allison Engineering that Rickenbacker was able to pay off the $250,000 debt from the defunct Rickenbacker Motor Company.

Throughout the 20s and 30s Eddie continued to fly and promote the ever expanding capabilities of aviation. He made it his practice to speak at high schools, colleges, civic organizations and town halls on the destiny of aerospace. The world, he said, is surrounded by an ocean of air and every city on the planet could become a *port* on that ocean. And every city, he said, *should* have an air*port*. He asked his audience to look at the towns that refused to allow the railroad to pass through their communities during the time of the westward expansion; they are poor towns—while those that welcomed the railroad have prospered. He said:

> Transportation is life itself. Wherever you find rapid means of transportation and communication we find happiness, peace and prosperity. But where we do not find modern methods of transportation and communication, we find poverty and misery.[54]

Eddie encouraged our national governmental leaders to foster commercial and military aviation. He persuaded business and industry to utilize aviation as a tool that would prove instrumental in their progress. He encouraged cities and towns to build airfields and he convinced many young men to become *pilots.*

One of those young men who revered Eddie Rickenbacker was the father of this author, Grant Gibby. When I was thirteen years of age, my dad, seeing that his love of aviation had taken root in my life, allowed me to read his cherished manual *Flying and How To Do It.* Published in 1932, it offers a window through time back to the simplicity of post WWI aviation and the instruction manuals then in use. The basic principles taught in this text

book are still valid. Here the book illustrates the four forces that act upon an aircraft.

This second illustration shows the extent of aircraft instrumentation in that day.

INDICATES MOTOR REVOLUTIONS PER MINUTE

INDICATES PLANE'S SPEED IN RELATION TO THE AIR

INDICATES ALTITUDE

INDICATES STEERING DIRECTION OF PLANE

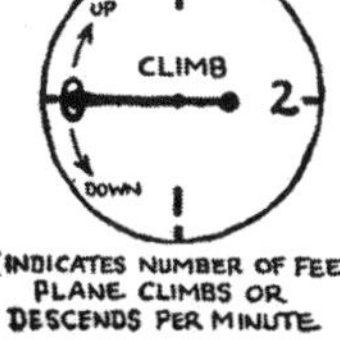

INDICATES NUMBER OF FEET PLANE CLIMBS OR DESCENDS PER MINUTE

INDICATES WHETHER PLANE IS CORRECTLY PILOTED

Illustrations by Larry Whittington

Today the Federal Aviation Regulations are voluminous. In 1932, only two pages were required to visually explain the rules of flight.

120

THOSE AIR RULES AND WHY

FIGS. 120 and 121. Air rules are equally necessary, even though some scatterbrains "wonder why" they have to exist when "there is so much room up there!" If it were not for air rules, landing fields would be literally peppered with wings and tails of planes and flyers would be popping out of the sky via parachutes one every two minutes!

That is why Uncle Sam sat down and wrote out a set of air rules. They

Excerpt from Flying and How To Do It
Illustrations by Larry Whittington

121

are not devised just to have more laws, or to annoy the carefree flyer, but to assure safety to you and to me.

They must be obeyed. Otherwise Uncle Sam can and will present you with a scolding, a suspension of flying license, a fine etc. Not a very different picture from the one you face if you get playful with your car on a highway.

Study the illustrations and notice how very wise and just these rules are.

Excerpt from Flying and How To Do It
Illustrations by Larry Whittington

Eddie continued to fly himself and worked closely with his old friend Donald Douglas in the development of the DC-1, forerunner of one the most successful transport aircraft in the history of aviation, the DC-3. Don Douglas had left Martin Aircraft to start his own company but lacked the necessary funds for the enterprise. Rickenbacker persuaded the publisher of the LA Times to raise the capital to put the Douglas Aircraft Company in business. After seven years of hard work Douglas rolled out the sleek, twin engine DC-1 that would change aviation forever. Together with Jack Fry of TWA, Rickenbacker flew the new Douglas aircraft from Los Angeles to Newark in thirteen hours and two minutes, setting a new record for commercial aviation. To say that this flight in this aircraft was a quantum leap is an understatement. The DC-3 and its military equivalent, the C47, proved to be the workhorse of WWII, transporting men and equipment safely to all parts of the world in all kinds of weather. Over ten thousand C47s were put into service during the war. After seventy years many of these grand old aircraft are *still* in service.

In 1935 Eddie and Adelaide returned to Europe. It had been thirteen years since their European honeymoon. They could scarcely believe the change of conditions in Germany. The formerly war-ruined nation was now vital and full of energy, although ruled by the dictator Adolph Hitler. Eddie wrote:

> Again I met the same four airmen. Göring, blazing with medals, had become Hitler's Number 2 man and chief of the new German Air Force. Milch was his deputy; Vandlent was in charge of highly secret research; Udet was in command of all aircraft production.
>
> "Herr Eddie," said Milch, "remember what we told you in 1922?"
>
> "Yes," I said, "I remember it vividly."
>
> "Well," said Milch, "come and see."
>
> I visited the Junkers factory where 20,000 men were working night and day building airplanes. Udet showed me the new

> Richthofen squadron, which we thought we had driven out of the air. Its headquarters were carefully hidden in the pine woods twenty miles or so from Berlin. I saw with amazement hangars made of concrete and repair shops that were bombproof. There were eighteen planes in the squadron, and it puzzled me that six were merely trainers. "But why trainers?" I asked.
>
> One of the fliers told me boastfully, "We use them to make our clerks, our mechanics, and our kitchen police into fliers. Every squadron in Germany is doing the same thing."
>
> That opened my eyes. The four derelicts of 1922 were assembling a striking force that would shake Europe to its foundations.[55]

On his way home to the states Rickenbacker stopped in London. There he met with several dignitaries, including the Undersecretary of State in the British Foreign Office, Sir Robert Vansittart and the publisher of the London Daily Express, Lord Beaverbrook. The Undersecretary asked Eddie when the Germans would be capable of an offensive war. Rickenbacker gave his frank opinion that they would be ready in three to five years. Vansittart agreed with this assessment but Lord Beaverbrook felt that Rickenbacker's assessment was absurd. Back in the states Eddie met with top U.S. government and military officials. He explained that he was an eyewitness to Germany's growing might and resolute purpose; while defensive preparations in England and France were far from adequate to meet this pending threat. American leaders were as dismissive as Lord Beaverbrook had been and labeled Rickenbacker as "an alarmist and warmonger." Of course they were proven dead wrong. Eddie's prediction was extremely accurate—four years later Germany attacked and conquered Poland, and the nations of the earth were once again thrust into world war.

CHAPTER 8

TWENTY-FOUR DAYS

It is the critical moment that shows the man. So when the crisis is upon you, remember that God, like a trainer of wrestlers, has matched you with a rough and stalwart antagonist. "To what end?" you ask. That you may prove the victor at the Great Games. [56]

—EPICTETUS

ON FEBRUARY 26, 1941, Eastern Air Lines Chief Executive Officer, Eddie Rickenbacker, boarded Flight 21 in New York. Shortly after seven in the evening, the beautiful new DC-3, dubbed *The Mexico Flyer*, lifted off gracefully and Captain James A. Perry turned to a heading of 246 degrees, the magnetic course for his first stop, Washington D.C., only one hour away. The landing and subsequent departure at Washington were routine. Flight 21 was scheduled to land next at Atlanta, a three hour flight from Washington, then at Birmingham, New Orleans, Houston, and Brownsville. *The Mexico Flyer* was configured with sleeping berths and a small lounge just aft of the cockpit. Rickenbacker was traveling to Birmingham to speak at a civic meeting. He took occupancy in the lounge where he busied himself with paper work. Flying over Spartanburg Captain Perry entered the sky lounge and advised his boss that the weather in Atlanta might make it "difficult getting in." Rickenbacker answered that Perry was pilot-in-command and should do what his judgment dictated. The Atlanta airfield was obscured with rain showers, poor visibility and a low ceiling. Perry commenced a low radio frequency guided instrument approach—state-of-the-art for its time. He followed the radio beam to the airport, then passed it, where he would reverse his course and begin his descent "on the beam" back to the airfield. It was approximately fifteen minutes to midnight when he began this *final* approach. When Perry began the 180 degree turn back to Atlanta airport it became tragically apparent to Rickenbacker that the young airline captain was flying at least one thousand feet too low; for from the left wing came an ominous scraping sound. The wing in fact had brushed against the tops of pine trees. Rickenbacker jumped from his seat and quickly moved towards the tail of the DC-3, the safest place to endure impact. He felt Perry immediately raise the left wing and felt the right wing drop just as abruptly. He was in the aisle when the right wing smashed into the pines and severed completely from the fuselage. Perry's last actions saved the lives of seven of the sixteen souls on board. Rickenbacker noted that the lights went out as Perry cut the master switch. A moment later the captain and copilot were killed instantly as the nose of the DC-3 struck with tremendous force. Of course the fuel tanks ruptured—surely, had Perry not cut the power all aboard would have been engulfed in flames. As it was, there was no explosion. The plane somersaulted back into the air then crashed again to the earth, this time on its tail. The DC-3 broke in two major pieces of wreckage. When the horrific tearing noises ceased Rickenbacker found that he was wedged between these two masses of metal, lying on the dead body of the steward. His left hip was crushed, his pelvis broken on both sides, his left knee was broken, his back was broken, his skull cut with a finger size groove, one eye was out of its socket and lay against his cheek. He was caught in the vise of the wreckage, drenched in high-octane fuel, and in terrible agony. Eddie determined that if fire should break out he would open his mouth and suck in the flames, for he said, "it's quicker that way."

Never during the ordeal did Rickenbacker allow himself to lose consciousness. It was obvious to him that although many had died, he, like others, had survived. In fact three men who had been seated in the tail escaped serious injury completely. From his immobile position Eddie took command of the awful situation. In addition to their injuries, all of the survivors, some who had been sleeping in their berths dressed only in night clothes, were exposed to the rain and cold. One of the men recommended they build a bonfire to get warm. Eddie quickly shouted, "For God's sake, *don't light a match.*"—then he explained the obvious—that such an action would set them all on fire. In a calm voice he gave comfort where he could and told them, on behalf of the airline, that *he was sorry.* He organized the three uninjured men into a communication line to aid in their rescue, placing one man away from the wreckage, but within the sound of his voice. The next man he positioned in a straight line from the first and within sound of that man's voice, and the third in like manner. Then he asked the men to rotate around the wreckage and see if they could find a house or roadway. It was a practical effort that, however, brought no results during the night. Finally as the sun rose in the cold and wet dawn, the search party found them. It took his rescuers an hour to free Rickenbacker from the grip of the twisted metal of the once spacious and comfortable *Mexico Flyer.* Those who could not walk, including Eddie, were placed on stretchers and carried across the rough terrain to a nearby highway. Every step of the bearers jolted his body with excruciating pain. An ambulance was on hand, but to their surprise left filled with those already dead. They waited roadside for a second ambulance to arrive. Finally, after nearly an hour, Eddie and the other survivors were transported to the emergency room of Piedmont Hospital. Rickenbacker learned from one of the medics the reason for this anomaly—ambulances were paid twenty dollars to transport a corpse while transporting an injured person brought only ten dollars.

At Piedmont Hospital Eddie came under the expert care of Doctor Floyd McRae. Initially he responded well to treatment but then his vital functions began to fail. Eddie knew that death was stealthy enveloping him, caressing him, removing from him all suffering, all care, all worry. The doctors quickly summoned his family to return to his bedside. In his room he clearly heard the voice of Walter Winchell on the radio. Winchell said: “Flash! It is confirmed that Eddie Rickenbacker is dying. He is not expected to live another hour.” At that moment Rickenbacker made a mental decision. He would not die! Later he wrote:

> I recognized that wonderful mellow sensation for what it was, death, and I fought it. I fought death . . . pushing away the rosy sweet blandishments and actually welcoming back the pain.[57]

His right hand had not been crushed in the accident, and with it he seized the water pitcher from a nearby table and flung it, smashing the radio to bits. Exhausted he lay back against the pillows while his wife, Adelaide, leaned close to his lips trying to make out his angry mutterings. Then she understood that Eddie wanted her to call the networks and tell them to cease such nonsense and tell them that he had determined that he was *not going to die!* Later Rickenbacker said that up to this point in his life this was the hardest battle he had ever fought. Recovery was hard and long and left him with “physical mementos.” A severed nerve in his leg gave him a permanent limp; his erect and manly carriage was altered; he was left with the marks of scars, the most noticeable was from the groove cut in his temple. Did this terrible accident also scar his mind? Eddie wrote:

> The crash, with all its immediate pain and permanent disabilities, did have a positive and beneficial result. It brought home to me once again the conviction that surely I was being permitted to continue living for some good purpose. I was being tested for some great opportunity to serve, a privilege that might come at any time. By early spring, I was ready—but for what?[58]

In March of 1942 Eddie received a phone call from the Chief of the Army Air Forces, General Hap Arnold. Subsequently they met in Washington where the General explained that he was concerned about the readiness of the pilot groups in training. He asked Rickenbacker, America's Ace of Aces of the last world war, to tour the Air Force training stations and impart his knowledge of aerial combat to these young flyers. General Arnold further told Eddie that he had the ability to inspire "these boys" and "put some fire in them." Within a week, although he was still lame from the Atlanta accident, Eddie began his nation-wide tour. In the next thirty-two days Rickenbacker visited forty-three bases, lecturing not only to fighter groups, but speaking also to light, medium and heavy bombardment units. The War Department was impressed; the impact was immediate, in terms of morale and practical instruction. Secretary of War Stimson asked Eddie if he would perform a similar mission overseas, first to England, Ireland and Iceland—then to the Pacific theatre. Additionally he was asked to evaluate the U.S. Air Force and compare American training techniques with those of our allies. Since Eddie was a civilian, his frank opinions were highly valued. He could not be censored as he might have been had he been military.

Eddie spent two delightful weeks in England where he had the opportunity of meeting with Prime Minister Winston Churchill. Then as planned, he traveled to Ireland and Iceland and on the way home, visited several units in Canada. Thereafter he reported his findings to the Secretary of War, along with long term recommendations to improve air force training and operations.

Richenbacker Instructing Pilots

On October 17, 1942, Rickenbacker departed New York to begin his tour of the bases in the Pacific. His planned route would take him from New York to Los Angeles, from there to Honolulu, Canton Island, Suva, New Caledonia, Brisbane, and to his final destination of Port Moresby. In his attaché he carried top secret papers. Also Rickenbacker had memorized a message to be given to General MacArthur, too sensitive to be entrusted to writing. At 10:30 p.m. on the evening of October 20, Rickenbacker, accompanied by Colonel Hans Adamson, boarded a "tactically obsolete Boeing Flying Fortress" at Hickam Field near Honolulu. They were bound for Canton Island (when Rickenbacker first wrote of this adventure his mission was still classified and he referred to the island as Island X). As the B-17 neared take-off speed, a hydraulic line on the brake system failed and the plane began to skid to the left. The pilot, Captain Cherry, by using asymmetrical thrust of the engines, was able to get the plane back on the runway. But stopping the plane before it ran out of runway and dropped into the Ocean was another matter. As his brakes were useless, Captain Cherry came down hard on his left rudder pedal, while simultaneously inducing power to the right engines, forcing a "violent ground loop." This is a skidding 180 degree turn where the plane nearly pivots on the inside landing gear. The maneuver was successful and when the plane came to a stop Cherry cheerfully announced to his VIP guest, "We got more of these planes, Captain. The crew and I will stand by until another plane is ready."

True to his word Cherry secured a replacement Flying Fortress and shortly after midnight on October 21 they lifted off on their 1,900 mile flight to Canton Island. Captain Cherry's crew consisted of First Lieutenant James Whittaker, copilot, First Lieutenant John De Angelis, navigator, Sergeant James Reynolds, radio operator, and Private John Bartek, mechanic. Besides Rickenbacker and Adamson, the B17 carried one other passenger, Alex Kaczmarczyk, making a total of eight souls on board.

All must have felt that the harrowing ground loop incident was but an anxious moment and would have no bearing on *this*

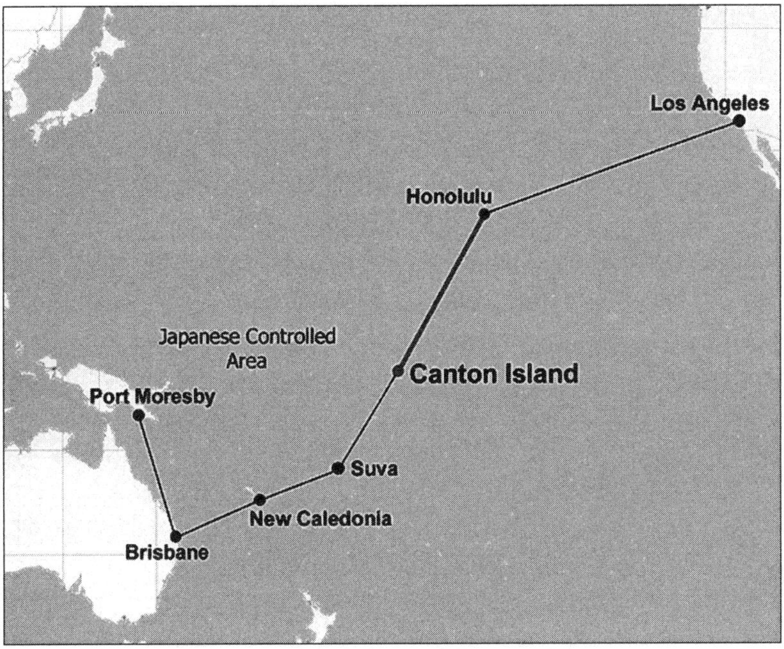

Rickenbacker's Intended Route

flight. No one was injured and they were in a different airplane, one that was perfectly sound. Climb out was beautiful; moonlight pierced a thin layer of clouds and spread soft light on the vast shimmering Pacific Ocean that seemed to extend to infinity. Captain Cherry announced to his seven comrades that he expected "an uneventful flight." Nonetheless, the ground loop had doomed their flight to Canton Island before Cherry had even started his engines. How? Navigator John De Angelis was dependent on his hand-held octant to take celestial readings to compensate for changes in wind direction and velocity; the octant is a delicate instrument that would enable the young navigator to make course corrections from the flight planned heading of 201 degrees. De Angelis's octant had been badly jarred during the ground loop episode, making every subsequent calculation erroneous. And the wind was not as forecast. At best, a *forecast* is only an educated guess. To make his destination a pilot must correct

Captain William Cherry

his bearings using outside references. Cherry would have no landmarks flying over the vast sea. There were no radio navaids along his route (although Canton Island had just received the equipment needed to take bearings on aircraft radio transmissions—however, this equipment had not yet be uncrated!) The only references available were the stars at night and the sun in the daytime. In this situation Cherry was dependent on his navigator, and his navigator was dependent on his faulty octant. Another plane departed Hickam Field that landed safely on Canton Island on the same night as Cherry's ill-fated flight. Its pilot reported the tailwind velocity at *31* miles per hour. This increase in wind speed should have shortened Cherry's flight by a full 50 minutes. Most of the flight to Canton Island was flown on top of a cloud layer that precluded the sighting of the island had they been within visual range. When Captain Cherry began his descent at the appointed time he had actually over-flown Canton Island by approximately 160 miles and was considerably west of course.

Aboard the flying fortress Rickenbacker had a fitful night. At nine thousand feet the cabin was cold and he suffered considerably from the after-effects of the Atlanta crash. He wore a suit, a leather jacket and covered himself with a blanket—but he couldn't get warm and was stiff all over. Little did he know that compared to what he was about to experience, he was in the lap of luxury. When the sun dawned bright and clear Eddie rose from his cot to the smell of hot coffee and sweet rolls.

Up in the cockpit Captain Cherry was relaxed and cheerful. He said their ETA for Canton Island was 9:30 a.m. At 8:30 a.m., when he was actually somewhere abeam the island, Cherry began a gradual descent, not to Canton, but to the open seas beyond. He leveled the Fortress beneath the clouds at 1,000 feet above the ocean. Nothing. Cherry held his course hoping to see the little island, only four miles wide, come into view. At 10:15 Rickenbacker again queried Cherry. They were now some three hundred miles southwest of Canton Island and drawing ever closer to the Japanese held Gilbert Islands. No one on board knew this of course. Their navigator was beside himself—nothing made sense. It was now horribly apparent to De Angelis that his octant was useless. Still the Flying Fortress had a full four hours of fuel remaining. There was considerable hope that within the next four hours they would make their destination. Ironically Reynolds was communicating with Canton Island on the radio; but could not fix their position by their transmission as Canton Island, as already stated, had not yet installed the equipment that would make this possible. Another American radio station at Palmyra Atoll was also on the air with Reynolds. Palmyra was able to take a bearing on their plane but without a cross-fix from another station, it was next to useless. A single bearing tells the Captain that he is flying somewhere along a line that stretches to infinity. He needs a second bearing to cross that line and fix his position.

Rickenbacker suggested to Cherry that he "box the compass." That is, fly west for one hour, then north for an hour, then east for an hour, then south for—well, for as long as they could until their fuel starved engines fell silent. Somewhere along this route they hoped to see an island or a ship at least. Time and again their eyes played cruel tricks on them. Off in the distance they would spy what appeared to be a

Navigator John DeAngelis

Private John Bartek

small haven of land. In each case it would prove to be only the shadow of a cloud. With one hour of fuel remaining Captain Cherry secured the two outboard engines to conserve his dwindling supply of fuel. By this time Reynolds was continually keying SOS, SOS, SOS . . . but now no response, not from Canton Island, not from Palmyra. Rickenbacker and the others were busy throwing virtually everything overboard, to lighten the B17's load and obtain another minute or two of flight. Perhaps, they hoped, that would be all they needed to reach some sandy beach where Cherry could safely put the big bird down. Eddie had with him a new Burberry coat from London, a beautiful suitcase presented to him by his friends at Eastern Air Lines, a spare bridge that his dentist had recently made him, his brief case, filled with vital papers. All went into the open air from the tail hatch. Eddie wrote:

> Let the moment come when nothing is left but life and you will find that you do not hesitate over the fate of material possessions, however deeply they may have been cherished.[59]

However, obeying a sudden thought that came into his mind Eddie kept a handful of handkerchiefs and sixty feet of rope which he tied about his person. He also stuffed a map into his shirt. Beneath the hatch where they proposed to make their exit they placed all of the emergency food rations they could garner, thermos bottles filled with water, and condensed milk. Each man wore a *Mae West* life preserver. Some of the men took off their shoes and pants so they would not be weighed down in the ocean.

Rickenbacker determined to stay fully clothed, including his shoes, and rely upon his life jacket to keep him afloat should he not make it to a raft.

The B17 was equipped with three life rafts. Two were larger, so called "five man rafts"—but inside they measured only *2 feet 4 inches wide by 6 feet 9 inches* in length. One raft was designated as a "two man raft" and could scarcely fit one man with any degree of comfort. Carefully the men rehearsed the forthcoming ditching—how they would abandon the Flying Fortress, who would occupy each raft, etc. The escape hatch was unlocked to prevent it from jamming when they hit the water. Having done all that could be done they sat quietly and braced for impact. Sergeant Bartek firmly grasped the raft release levers to enable quick deployment at the right moment.

Eddie felt Captain Cherry lower the nose of the B17. Making a forced landing in the ocean, or ditching as it is called, is always treacherous. Water does not compress and when hit at flying speed is as hard as concrete. The swells below them were at least twelve feet high. If they were to survive Cherry would have to land in a trough. Timing would be critical. If instead he hit a swell, it would be as disastrous as when *The Mexico Flyer* hit the pine hill outside of Atlanta. The plane would break up and go down like a rock to the bottom of the ocean. The men waited anxiously for the inevitable. Several of them asked repeatedly, "How much longer?" Cherry leveled the plane at fifty feet above the sea. The two inboard engines continued droning on. Would an island suddenly come into view? That hope was shattered when one engine began to sputter, and after only a few seconds, died. Rickenbacker yelled, "Hold on!

Radio Operator James Reynolds

Colonel Hans Adamson

Copilot James Whittaker

Here it comes!" Then of a sudden, the last remaining power-plant quit. The B17 continued to fly, to glide the last few feet down to what must be a precise crash landing. All was silent save for the sound of Reynolds, the radio operator, banging the keys, SOS, SOS, SOS, SOS. Then came a deafening clap of sound louder, said Eddie, than thunder; louder than the sound of the crash he had so recently experienced in Atlanta. It was a din of deafening proportions, made all the more terrible by the whining, whizzing sounds of shattered equipment, fractured from the bulkhead that ricocheted through the cabin like "shrapnel." For a fraction of a second the sound ceased. The Flying Fortress had only grazed the water and momentarily skipped back into the air; then came a second crash that clenched the mighty aircraft with such power that all forward motion ceased in an instant. Next to Eddie a window broke wide open—water, turbid and green, poured into the fuselage like a river. Reynolds' head had been dashed against the radio panel and his slashed nose was bleeding copiously. Admanson had been whipped around like a rag doll, wrenching his neck and back. For a moment all were simply stunned by the incredible impact, but Captain Cherry had wondrously put the huge glider down in a trough, tail first, then brought her to rest "against the waning

Sgt. Alex Kaczmarczyk

slope of a swell." The B17 was basically intact!

Sergeant Bartek quickly released the life rafts, severely injuring one of his hands on torn metal, and escaped through the forward hatch. Captain Cherry commanded that Rickenbacker be next out of the B-17. Eddie, still handicapped from the previous accident, stood on the arm of a seat and pulled himself out of the top hatch while the crew pushed from below. Adamson was almost incapable of helping himself and it was with great difficulty that he was pulled out of the hatch, onto the wing and into the raft. Whittaker, Cherry and Reynolds occupied the first raft, Adamson, Rickenbacker and Bartek the second, while Kaczmarczyk and De Angelis took possession of the tiny two man conveyance. The latter capsized when Kaczmarczyk tried to get in, but the two men were able to get the raft upright—unfortunately Kaczmarczyk swallowed a tremendous amount of ocean water in the process. It was a hasty exit as all of the men expected the Fortress to sink rapidly at any moment. All had been stunned by the impetus of the crash. Reynolds and Bartek were bleeding, Adamson had suffered serious internal injuries and Kaczmarczyk had swallowed buckets of seawater. As they pushed back from the B-17 someone shouted, "Who's got the water?" Each man looked at the others while all shook their heads. In the confusion no one had retrieved the water and rations.

In disbelief of this horrendous mistake the men briefly debated their next move. Should someone attempt to reenter the swamped, but still floating B17? Certainly those life-giving commodities would be scattered, buried somewhere underwater in the hull. Their aircraft had already stayed afloat for a remarkable three minutes—how much longer would it stay on the surface before it would lose buoyancy and dive for the ocean's bottom? Escape would be impossible for any poor soul trapped inside. However, their second mistake was not to risk the odds—the flying fortress remained floating for another three minutes, enough time, it was believed, to have secured their emergency supplies. Then of a sudden the tail rose, the nose sank, and the wreck disappeared forever beneath the foamy brine. The survivors pulled their rafts together and took inventory from their pockets. Captain Cherry possessed four small oranges. Kaczmarczyk and Rickenbacker had a few chocolate bars but they were saturated with salt water—useless, and were discarded overboard. Rickenbacker saw the wisdom in staying together and taking the rope from around his body secured the three rafts at twenty foot intervals. Surveying the survival gear stowed in the raft's compartments the castaways discovered two hand pumps to maintain inflation pressure, three patching kits, two bailing buckets, two knives, a compass, a Very pistol flare gun, a first-aid kit, two fishing lines with hooks, but sadly, no fish bait.

Save for Adamson, who was nearly incapacitated, Rickenbacker was the oldest of the group and far more experienced in facing likely death. He knew they were in horrible, but not hopeless circumstances. Some, he knew, would soon despair and he felt it would be up to him "to hold them together." Captain Cherry did not object when Rickenbacker began to take control of their situation. First he organized the men into two-hour watches and advised the watchman to be vigilant—they may only have a moment to fire the flares. Morale was improved for a time when Eddie told the men that he would pay a "hundred dollars for the first man to sight land, a plane or a ship." Of course he knew that his offer bordered on being ridiculous, as their lives were at stake, but he wanted to divert their focus from suffering and boost spirits as much as possible.

Evening came, the men were wet to the skin and very cold. But it was not only the black night that chilled Rickenbacker to the bone. It was a solitary bump that made him shudder. He lay on the raft's bottom with only a thin layer of rubber separating him from the ocean. The bump came from the underside of the raft and he felt its full force. A moment later he was hit again. There was the splashing sound of something large, at first unseen, which intensified the horror. But in the dim starlit night the vague shape of dorsal fins cut the water's surface as clean as a plane's air-foil cuts the wind. The three tiny rafts were surrounded by sharks! All night long these sea vultures circled their prey, scraping their rough scales against the rubber boats. Day was a long time coming, but when the dark mist finally gave way to the clarity of morning, Rickenbacker discerned that the ten foot long predators were bumping the rafts trying to rub free of leeches. In an odd way it was entertaining to watch these aquatic killers and Eddie thought how under other conditions he might sympathize with these voracious carnivores who were trying to rid themselves of parasites—grateful that for now, at least, the sharks were not trying to overturn the rafts to devour human cargo.

That morning a counsel was held and collectively the men decided to eat one orange, divided eight ways, every other day. In this manner the four oranges would last eight days. Eddie was selected to cut the precious fruit as all eyes watched carefully the fairness of his division. Such rations can only be called a taste, rather than a meal. Cherry and Rickenbacker saved their peel for fish bait. But the fish paid as little attention to such bait as they had to bare hooks and the two caught nothing. The cold of the night was quickly replaced by blistering heat. Those who had cast off much of their clothing before ditching, to make it easier to swim, now suffered the most. Exposed skin soon burned and blistered. The only thing more abundant than sun was salt. The saline water infiltrated every agonizing wound, cracked every sore, and flayed open the flesh to the scorching daystar whose exaggerated proximity led Rickenbacker to write:

> On the Pacific I was something being turned on a spit.[60]

However, he was better off than most, as he had kept all his clothes and wore a hat. Reynolds was pitiable, having stripped to his shorts in fear of drowning in the crash. He was now a "sodden red mass of hurt—even the soles of his feet were burned raw." A little cloth literally preserved life. Eddie passed around the handkerchiefs, which in that moment before impact he had intuitively kept. The men fell silent as the waves calmed into a glassy smooth sea, whose shining surface reflected the light of the sun like a mirror, attacking them like bristling barbs of searing light from all directions. The effect was stuporous and hypnotic. Silence was broken only by the occasional groan, or the whispered prayer, or the sound of the still water rippling in the wake of a shark's dorsal fin.

Temporary relief came at sunset before the broiling heat was replaced by awful cold. After another counsel the men decided to risk sending up a flare. As they did not know their position and feared that their error had taken them westward, towards the Japanese held Gilbert Islands, it was a potentially perilous action. The Japanese knew how to inflict more suffering upon prisoners than even the harsh elements of the open sea. Nonetheless Captain Cherry loaded the Very pistol and fired the first flare into the night sky. The first two attempts disheartened the men as the shells proved to be duds. But the third flare blossomed high above their heads, suddenly transforming the pitch of night into dazzling light. Slowly the parachute held red ball of brilliance descended, shrinking the circumference of illumination as it lost altitude, until at last it was snuffed out and disappeared beneath the waves. Rickenbacker, with his seven comrades, were amazed at the power of a single flare which had for a moment "illuminated [their] entire world." Morale soared as suddenly as did the light from the Very pistol. Surely such a light was seen by rescuers, and help, they thought, was even then on the way.

Everything is a matter of perspective. The light which had appeared so vast to these men lost at sea, was hid from all other eyes—for the flares ascent could not overcome the curvature of the earth. Had a sentinel on Canton Island been facing towards their precise location he would have seen no more light from Captain Cherry's flare gun than he would have seen from the great Sun which had set hours before. Search planes could have never supposed that the B17 to be so far from their intended destination and were likewise out of visual range of Cherry's beacon of distress. The night wore on, black, silent, and the spirits of the men slowly absorbed the essence of pervading gloom. This effort was repeated nightly until the flares were exhausted.

On the fourth day Eddie divided the second orange. The next, although scheduled as a fast day, he divided the third as the sick needed desperately the little refreshment and nourishment the shriveled fruit could provide. On the following day Eddie decided to proportion the last orange as it was beginning to rot anyway. Kaczmarczyk, whom the men now referred to simply as "Alex" was near death. Not only had he ingested saltwater when his raft capsized, but they had caught him in delirium drinking seawater, which only intensifies thirst and increases agony. In his hands he grasped a salt-washed photograph of the girl that he loved. Alex spoke to the photograph as if she were actually there beside him. These conversations often ended with Alex speaking not to his love, but to his God.

John Bartek, the mechanic, had kept on his person a little New Testament and would often silently read it. Eddie knew that the holy scriptures were undeniable sources of hope and faith. He knew that he had to keep the men believing that they would survive, otherwise they would surely succumb, abandon torturous life and surrender to anesthetic death. What Bartek held in his hands could very well keep the men alive. Eddie wrote:

> I've always been fully conscious of the existence of a Great Power above. I learned to pray at my mother's knee, and I had never gone to sleep at night without first getting on my knees and praying. But my religion had always been a quiet, personal thing. I had not worshiped formally since Sunday-school days. Now, for the first time in all those years, I realized that I should share my faith

with others and help them to find strength through God.

One morning I suggested that we pull the rafts together and have a prayer meeting. Some of us were religious, some not. Adamson and Whittaker made no secret of their lack of religion, but I insisted that they participate. Bartek read a passage from his New Testament, then passed it on. Each man read a passage. For some of us it was the first time, yet every man leafed through the little book to find something to fit the occasion . . . Under the baking sun on the limitless Pacific, I found a new meaning, a new beauty in its familiar words. [One passage really] struck home: "Therefore, take no thought, saying, What shall we eat? Or, What shall we drink? or, Wherewithall shall we be clothed? . . . For your Heavenly Father knoweth that ye have need of all these things. But seek ye first the kingdom of God, and his righteousness; and all these things shall be added unto you. Take therefore no thought for the morrow: for the morrow shall take thought for the things of itself. Sufficient unto the day *is* the evil thereof." [61]

The Ace of Aces, the man's man, presided over these prayer meetings twice everyday and would conclude with a hymn and prayer. One of their favorites was *Lead Kindly Light*, by John Henry Newman:

Lead, kindly Light, amid th'encircling gloom,
Lead Thou me on!
The night is dark, and I am far from home;
Lead Thou me on!
Keep Thou my feet; I do not ask to see
The distant scene; one step enough for me.
I was not ever thus, nor prayed that
Thou shouldst lead me on;
I loved to choose and see my path;
But now lead Thou me on!
I loved the garish day, and, spite of fears,

Pride ruled my will. Remember not past years!
So long Thy power hath blest me,
Sure it still will lead me on.
O'er moor and fen, o'er crag and torrent,
Till the night is gone,
And with the morn those angel faces smile, which I
Have loved long since, and lost awhile!
Meantime, along the narrow rugged path,
Thyself hast trod,
Lead, Savior, lead me home in childlike faith,
Home to my God.
To rest forever after earthly strife
In the calm light of everlasting life.

Although they didn't have a hymnal and didn't know all of the words, they did the best they could. The prayers were often halting and choked with emotion. The weaker the men became, the louder Eddie sang, beating time with his hand on the side of the raft. He said, "I never lost faith, not once, but it was sometimes necessary for me to rekindle the faith in others." He said for the first time in their lives some of the men began to seriously examine the way they had lived, how they had measured up to the test of life. All, including Eddie, felt they had fallen far short of what they should have been. What would it be like, they questioned, to actually meet God and give a report of their conduct? Their souls, in their extremity, were laid bare and they confessed to each other their mistakes and "*sins.*"

The seventh day was extremely difficult. As long as there were oranges, there was something to look forward to. Now that the last drop of nectar had been supped from the last orange the day before, this day passed without the slightest respite from torturous thirst, nor was there any sign on the clear horizon of rain or relief. Night came and the men huddled together to stay warm, even though the slightest touch aggravated their wounds and sores. The morning of the eighth day dawned and as the Sun warmed their cold bodies, it also, mercilessly, robbed them of precious moisture. They were not only in a state of extreme dehydration but were starving as well. In the afternoon, they pulled their rafts together for their worship service and once again "finished with a prayer for deliverance and a hymn of praise." They were beyond exhaustion, and simply lay quietly with the water lapping the sides of their rafts. Rickenbacker fell asleep with his hat protectively covering his eyes. He wrote:

> Something landed on my head. I knew that it was a sea gull. I don't know how I knew; I just knew.
>
> Everyone else knew too. No one said a word, but, peering out from under my hat brim without moving my head, I could see the expressions on their faces. They were staring at that gull. The gull meant food—if I could catch it.
>
> Slowly, gradually, a fraction of an inch at a time, I began moving my right hand up to my hat. Slowly, slowly. I felt that I was shaking all over, but it must have been my imagination, for the bird remained. My hand was up to the level of my hat brim. The temptation was great to make a sudden grab, but I couldn't take the chance. I didn't know just exactly where the bird was. I brought my open hand closer and closer to where I felt the bird should be, and then, when I sensed the presence of the gull, I closed my hand. The bird's legs were in it.[62]

There had been skeptics among these dying men, who had participated in the songs, the readings, and prayers, only because of Eddie's leadership. But at that moment there was no "unbeliever" among them. All knew that a miracle had occurred. In a snap he wrung the bird's neck and in a moment he plucked its feathers. The bird was divided equally, save for the intestines which Rickenbacker reserved for fish bait. The meat, though raw and tough, was "delicious" to their taste and was only a "first course" of what would be, to these famished men, a feast. The two fish lines with their gull bait dropped into the water. The first drew out a mackerel and Eddie's line drew in a sea bass. Moist, cool and rich in nutrients, the fish meat was indeed manna, given by the same Power that had preserved the people of Moses. Life came back into their bodies. In Eddie's words:

> There was not a one of us who was not aware of the fact that our gull had appeared just after we had finished our prayer service. Some may call it a coincidence. I call it a gift from heaven.[63]

At midnight Rickenbacker was awakened by a loud clap of thunder. The ocean was becoming wild with an approaching storm. However, no one was concerned with facing a squall in the open sea with boats the size of bathtubs—what they could smell in the air was *rain*. Soon a very light shower gave each man a taste of sweet pure water, and nothing, said Eddie "every tasted so good, before or since." When lightning illuminated the seascape, they saw they were only on the edge of the storm. Silhouetted by dazzling flashes of thunderbolts, they could see a microburst cascading as dense blackness from the heart of a cumulonimbus cell which spat darts of light. Blessings are often found in the midst of dreadful adversity. Buckets of pure, distilled water were pouring from that rain cloud, but to capture the smallest part of it would require the castaways paddle their little rafts through churning, perilous waves.

There was no hesitation. Above the tumult Rickenbacker yelled, "It's over there! Let's go to it. Grab your paddles." Those still possessed of strength exerted themselves manfully. While Rickenbacker strove with the muscles in his arms, his soul pled to God for help, not so much for safety, but to help them reach the furious core of the tempest! Soon their rafts were lifted by mountains of water, hurled against momentary acclivities, then dropped into the pits of swirling troughs. These ocean valleys channeled the resounding report of thunder, magnifying the horrific din echoless, until heaving skyward and breaking en masse upon their heads muffled the thunder under the noise of their own white capped cloaks. Then came a cry for help; Alex and De Angelis, in the small raft, had broken loose. Miraculously Bartek and Rickenbacker were able to reach the two and again fastened the rope securely. Soon thereafter Cherry's raft capsized. But determined, Cherry, Whittaker and Reynolds, aided again by Eddie and Bartek, righted the raft and somehow got back in.

Suddenly the rain fell, not "drop by drop," but "in sheets." For a moment all travail was forgotten. Salt deposits had encrusted their bodies, clothes, and rafts. All was swept away by the sweet deluge of pure water. The clear fluid was the Balm of Gilead, cleansing their wounds and hearts. Their prayers had been answered. Out of the sky, God had given them food, and now drink. Under Rickenbacker's insightful direction they removed their outer clothing. First they rinsed this clothing until it was free of all vestiges of salt, then allowed the cloth fibers to absorb clean water, and then wring it into their bailing buckets. When the storm subsided they pulled their rafts together for another counsel. Mutually it was decided that water would be rationed at the rate of one half jigger per man per day, save for Alex whose condition was critical—he was given two to three jiggers of water each day. Often tales are told of men and women in dire circumstances, who desert all values of decency in their extremities. Then we learn of men like Rickenbacker, who in the spirit of true Christianity, inspire their comrades-in-suffering to self-sacrifice. Imagine the love of brotherhood that existed between men who, themselves horribly dehydrated, willingly gave to one whom they knew already lay in the shadow of death. They gave him rations of water four to six times their own allotment.

Several days passed without additional rain and regretfully, they lost their fishing lines to sharks. Alex became semiconscious and the others transferred him to one of the larger rafts, hoping it would be a little more comfortable. Then one night as Eddie cuddled him, "as a mother would a child," his shivering stopped and the only sound that came forth from his parched throat was a long sigh. Alex's suffering was over. The next day his body was committed to the deep. However, the men had nothing to weigh down his body with and it simply floated on the surface. This was an unbearable sight to see, and as Alex's body would not leave them, they paddled away from the melancholy sight.

Their water supplies were replenished several times as other storms gave them drink. Ingeniously they stored water in the compartment of their life vests, to prevent evaporation. One more meal was given by God. The rafts drifted into a school of mackerel and sharks, who had been circling their vessels, began a feeding frenzy. In an effort to escape two of the mackerel leaped into Cherry and Eddie's rafts! Yet, despite these heaven-sent blessings, the days turned into weeks and a despair settled upon the men, nearly impossible to dispel. Every day the men continued with their prayer service and Rickenbacker and several others kept faith. But for men like Adamson, who had not been much better off than Alex, near-death seemed worse than death itself. One night, Adamson simply rolled out of the raft and quietly slipped into the sea. He had given up. Immediately Eddie was awakened—perhaps because Adamson was no longer pressing against him, or perhaps by the preternatural. He saw an object, darker than the water. He thrust in his hand and caught hold of Adamson's shoulder. Simultaneously he cried out for help. Cherry and Whittaker were there in a moment and the three hauled the suicidal man back into the raft. Adamson still breathed.

Nothing was said until dawn. Adamson, pensive, apologized to Eddie for what he had tried to do. Eddie wrote:

> He was sorry. In a brave, pathetic gesture, he pulled back his burned lips in what was meant to be a smile and stuck out his red, throbbing hand for me to shake.
>
> My response was one the most difficult actions I have ever taken in my life. It was doubly difficult because I really didn't know how much longer Hans had to live. He might die with this, his last memory of me. But I steeled myself. I had to get through to this man somehow.

> "I don't shake hands with your kind," I said, deliberately making my voice cold and harsh. "If you want to shake hands, you've got to prove yourself first."[64]

Adamson became angry with himself for this cowardly act. He knew that God alone should decide when our sufferings should cease. Hans Adamson would have to fight to live, and as he was so emaciated his fight continued long after he was rescued. But he did live and later he authored a fine biography on the life of the man who saved him with tough love, his dear friend, Eddie Rickenbacker.

Eddie later wrote that he felt God's purpose in preserving his life was so that he might keep his friends from giving up. To some of the men he was "soft and gentle as a mother." To the rest he gave "stronger medicine." A couple of the men swore they would live just long enough to bury Rickenbacker in the sea.

CHAPTER 9

REDEMPTION

But after the fires and the wrath,
But after searching and pain,
His Mercy opens us a path
To live with ourselves again.

In the Gates of Death rejoice!
We see and hold the good—
Bear witness, Earth, we have made our choice
For Freedom's brotherhood.

Then praise the Lord Most High
Whose Strength hath saved us whole,
Who bade us choose that the Flesh should die
And not the living Soul!

—RUDYARD KIPLING [65]

AFTER SEVERAL WEEKS CRAMPED in a tiny life raft in the midst of the eternal waters of the South Pacific it would seem a natural thing to forget that any other world existed than one of sun, and salt, and sea. Most men would become conditioned to the monotony of unchanging vistas and having lost the *memory* of green earth with its multitude of blessings that for the most part are esteemed little until lost, they are incapable of hoping for more than a rainstorm to wash away the saline crust and momentarily quench their unquenchable thirst. However, Rickenbacker suffered from no such delusional amnesia. In that he never lost faith in Heaven,

Heaven presaged his deliverance by revealing to him that he would again eat and drink the good things of life. In his dreams, early one morning, Eddie found himself on an island of beauty and bounty. He was given a most extraordinary breakfast that was accompanied by "large frosty pitchers of orange juice, grapefruit juice, pineapple juice, apple juice and grape juice." He dreamed that after he finished his meal he called Secretary Stimson. The dream came to him again and again and was a daily reminder that the desolate world that surrounded him would soon be a past existence.

On the afternoon of the nineteenth day a squall could be seen some five miles to the southeast of their position. Captain Cherry gazed at the squall intently, his head cocked as if straining to hear. He suddenly said that he could hear a plane! At that moment Rickenbacker heard it too. At the next instant a single-engine pontoon plane emerged from the storm. No one thought it might be a Japanese aircraft for all were shouting and waving. But the plane passed by without sighting the string of small rafts. With the disappearance of the aircraft some of the men nearly broke emotionally. A few openly cried. Rickenbacker came down hard on them, telling them to knock it off—that this was the first sign they had seen of the outside world, and that where there was one plane surely there must be more. The men recognized the truth in what he said. The following day this was in fact verified—two more planes were spotted. However, the desperate men were not seen by these aircraft.

Several days passed without further sightings. Cherry announced that he would strike out alone in the small raft. Rickenbacker tried to dissuade him, saying that three rafts were easier to spot than one. But Cherry was adamant and Rickenbacker simply wished him good luck. After Cherry's departure, De Angelis and Whittaker saw the wisdom of setting out in a different direction as well. With Reynolds, now unconscious, lying in the bottom of their raft, they removed the rope that secured their vessel to Rickenbacker's raft and were also soon out of sight.

The following day was November 13, the twenty-fourth day since their Flying Fortress had sunk in the green waters of the Pacific. Late in the afternoon Eddie was awakened by Bartek who announced that he could hear planes. Two aircraft came so close to their raft that they all felt they could not miss being seen. Eddie waved his hat frantically to attract attention, but the planes held to their course and were soon gone from sight. Even Eddie began to despair when the drone of planes was no longer heard.

The sun was low when aircraft reappeared. One airplane flew so low and so near their position that Eddie could see the smiling face of its pilot. In response to their frenzied waving he waved back. On the side of the silver bird was painted the bold insignia of the U.S. Navy! The pilot circled the raft and then joined formation with the higher plane; then the two simply left. Nearly an hour passed in silence. It was unnerving to say the least, but once again joyfully the planes returned. One aircraft established itself in a holding pattern above their position, while the other aircraft continued on to parts unknown. For three hours this saga continued with Eddie waving nonstop to show they were still alive while the plane overhead continued to orbit. Eddie did not understand what the circling plane was doing until he saw the lights of a boat in the distance and realized the pilot was guiding the boat to their position. Suddenly the Navy airship fired flares that illumined the dusky night. The skilled aviator dropped from the sky and remarkably touched down on the fairly rough sea. It should be noted that seaplanes normally land in protected waters, such as are found in harbors. An open ocean landing is extremely perilous. Nonetheless Lieutenant William Eadie did so safely and taxied within a short distance of Rickenbacker's raft. It took only a moment for Eddie to paddle up to the pontoon and was greeted warmly by the "finest-looking young men [Rickenbacker] had ever seen."

The Lieutenant quickly explained that they were in waters that were patrolled by the Japanese. His aircraft was too small to airlift all three men; which was why he had summoned the PT boat. The pilot, with the help of his radioman, lifted the critically ill Adamson inside the plane. Bartek and Rickenbacker were then *tied on the wings*! Lt. Eadie explained that it was forty miles back to their base, and if need be they would taxi all the way. He didn't dare, he said, show another light for fear of their enemies. Off they went, briskly. The seawater spray felt wonderful to Rickenbacker—they were moving and he repeated joyfully to himself, "Thank God" and "God bless the Navy!" However, it wasn't long until the plane and the PT boat rendezvoused successfully. Eddie and Bartek then transferred to the boat where they were wrapped in blankets and given hot broth, water and pineapple juice. Soon they were on the shore of a beautiful island, placed on stretchers and carried to the hospital. Eddie was overcome by the palm trees, radiant moonlight, and the night air—the night air that had always been so cold in the wet-soaked raft was actually warm and delightful. Inside the hospital, as the kind staff began undressing the men, their rotted clothing actually crumbled to pieces. The rescued were cleansed, their wounds dressed and then they were placed between heavenly sheets of clean linen. Adamson fell quickly to sleep, while Eddie, ignoring doctor's orders, drank an entire jug of water in less than one hour.

The following day Cherry, who likewise had been found alive, was brought to the hospital. Meanwhile Whittaker, De Angelis and Reynolds had made it to a small island. Risking extremely dangerous surf, compounded by treacherous reefs, De Angelis and Whittaker rowed with their remaining strength into the breakers. Having done all they were capable of doing, they trusted to God, who having preserved them for so long on the mighty deep, would not now abandon them to perish upon razor sharp reefs. The swift and violent surf swept their rubber raft past all treachery and deposited them safely on the beach. The two men, though near complete exhaustion, literally dragged Reynolds ashore. Their first food was a rat, which they clubbed to death and ate raw. Fortuitously, they were found by sympathetic natives who carried them by canoe to an island where an English missionary

DeAngelis and Whittaker after rescue

looked after them until Naval medical personnel arrived and transported them to the hospital.

The seven survivors had drifted to the Ellice Islands and were hospitalized at the Navy base on Funafuti, 739 miles southwest of their original destination of Canton Island! They had traveled approximately 450 miles in their three small rafts. After an astonishing twenty-four days from the day their B-17 crashed into the Pacific Ocean they were all liberated from this hell. Eddie had gone from 180 pounds down to 126. Yet he was better off than his comrades. Reynolds and Adamson were "emaciated wrecks." In comparative luxurious surroundings, with wholesome food and fresh juices, Rickenbacker rapidly recovered his strength. He was in fact, as he had foreseen in his dream, able to send a message to Secretary Stimson. Incredibly Eddie announced that he would be up to completing his mission in ten days to two weeks!

True to his word, on December first Eddie boarded a B-24. He visited several bases on the way to Australia where he spoke to the men, expressing appreciation for their brotherhood in the vital cause of freedom. He learned of their condition and challenges,

Rickenbacker arriving in Pago Pago after rescue

and in turn made recommendations to the Secretary of War. Also in this report he strongly suggested improving life rafts by increasing size and providing sea-tight compartments inside the rafts containing rations, potable water, improved first-aid supplies, jackknife, flare gun, radio transmitter, salt-water distiller, steel signal mirror, better fishing tackle ***and bait.*** Rickenbacker's advice was largely followed, resulting in tremendous reforms of life-saving benefits. In Australia Eddie boarded a heavily armed B-17 Fortress and was flown to Port Moresby. As he stepped from the plane Rickenbacker was greeted by General MacArthur himself, who threw his arms around Eddie saying how glad he was to see him alive. Dutifully, and at the first opportune moment, Eddie conveyed to the General the oral message from Secretary Stimson that, again, was so important and secret that it could not be written. What it was will never be known; Rickenbacker wrote:

> Though I remember every word of it to this day, I shall not repeat it. Stimson and MacArthur took it with them to the grave, and so shall I.[66]

The fact that Rickenbacker and his companions lived is amazing, but more astounding is how they reacted to the extreme adversity in which they were literally plunged. As conditions steadily deteriorated, instead of abandoning values as godless men are apt to do, their goodness and humanity to each other *increased*. When Alex died there was no thought of the unspeakable, of defiling his remains, for all the sufferers, even those who were formally agnostic, had been focusing through scripture study and prayer, on eternity. Their minds became fixed that their flesh should not be preserved at the sacrifice of their souls. Every man was brought to the tribunal of his own conscience; each one examined his past and found he had fallen short of those truths which he knew to be God-given; each had confessed to his friends, his mistakes, his sins. A friend is someone who sees the same truths, and shares the same sufferings as his comrades. All had paid the price of this noble fellowship. In their extremity the men had become determined (especially Adamson after nearly succumbing to cowardice) that they would not repeat past mistakes. They became much more concerned with the death of their souls rather than the death of their bodies. With such a spirit of truth fixed in their minds, such men are *saved* from self-destructive humanism whether or not their mortal bodies are *rescued*. Such men are conquerors, whether they live or die.

In this age of continual war and rumors of war we ought to reflect on Rickenbacker and his seven brothers, who in a time of world war had already committed their lives to the cause of freedom, but who additionally during an agonizing trial of twenty-four days, dedicated their lives to everlasting truths. We ought to fix our minds on the whole of life, not just on mortality—which is but a dot on the eternal line of our existence. The Secretary of Agriculture under President Dwight Eisenhower, Ezra Taft Benson, wrote:

> There are those who act as though they do not believe in

eternity or a resurrection. They cower at the thought of war, and to save their own bodies they would have peace at any price. Yet the best assurance of peace and life is to be strong morally and militarily. But they want life at the sacrifice of principles. Rather than choose liberty or death, they prefer life with slavery. But they overlook a crucial scripture: "Fear not them which kill the body but are not able to kill the soul; but rather fear him which is able to destroy both soul and body in hell (Matthew 10:28)."[67]

Rickenbacker no sooner returned from this mission to Port Moresby than he embarked on similar missions to the West Indies, Brazil, Dakar, Algiers, Cairo, Egypt, Tehran, India, Russia and China. In this cause he traveled over fifty-five thousand miles, inspected hundreds of Allied military installations, and personally addressed approximately three hundred thousand American troops, most of them aviators like himself. Lest the reader think that there is hyperbole in this incredible summary, it is altogether fitting to quote the whole of a citation which accompanied the Medal of Merit, given to Eddie Rickenbacker by President Harry Truman, on December 18, 1946. It reads:

EDWARD VERNON RICKENBACKER, for exceptionally meritorious conduct in the performance of outstanding services to the United States from December, 1941 to December, 1944. Mr. Rickenbacker, as Special Representative of the Secretary of War and Commanding General, Army Air Forces, made numerous tours of inspection of air bases and air units in theaters of operations throughout the world, and brought to the Air Command plans and recommendations based on his observations that contributed substantially to the fund of knowledge which ultimately brought about the defeat of the enemy. He directed the full facilities of Eastern Air Lines, Inc., of which he was president, to the prosecution of the war, and made available to the Command its air knowledge and experience as well as its operational facilities. Mr. Rickenbacker's great courage and fortitude in the face of the most harrowing physical experiences, and the unflagging zeal and devotion to the cause of his country which he displayed throughout the entire period of hostilities mark him as pre-eminent in the roster of those who rose to their Nation's defense, reflecting the greatest credit on him and the Government and people of the United States.[68]

After the war Eddie Rickenbacker continued his life of productivity and faith; proving that the two principles are intimately connected. His airline, Eastern, became the wonder of the industry. His old companies including Allison and the Indy 500 Speedway became post-war marvels. He assisted the Douglas and Lockheed aircraft companies develop jet-age commercial airliners that exceeded the wildest dreams of the most visionary of the pioneer aviators with whom he had flown in WWI. Always he continued as an Ambassador of Freedom and Free Enterprise, working with many governments to expand non-stop American routes into their nations. He was involved in many charitable organizations, which under his direction, provided millions of dollars of assistance to war-widows and others in need.

Always, Eddie gave the same love and attention to his beloved wife and family as his father and mother had given to him and each other. One lasting evidence of this is a compilation of letters to his son William; they are tremendous reading offering tender and tough-love insights into the personal life of this great man and those whom he loved above all else. It is important to know that William himself published these letters in his book *From Father to Son*. Several of these are included here in part.

Fatherhood is a sacred stewardship. When a man is blessed with sons or daughters he is not given autocratic authority over his children; they are not his property; rather he receives them for a time in trust. Each child comes into this world truly unique, inheriting some traits from progenitors, but *retaining* a profound individuality. A noble father is a great leader, not a powerful dictator. He understands his responsibility to firmly, especially in the

David and William Rickenbacker in their teens

formative years, curb ungodly and rebellious tendencies while at the same time granting *agency*, increasing freedom of choice commensurate with maturity. Such a man teaches *consequences*, sometimes in the form of punishments, for he will never coddle his child inappropriately—however, he will only discipline in love. To paraphrase a scriptural tenant: "No power or influence can or ought to be maintained by virtue of fatherhood, only by persuasion, patience, by gentleness and meekness, and by genuine love; By kindness, and knowledge, without hypocrisy or deception—admonishing promptly and firmly when inspired to do so, then showing forth afterwards an increase of love towards his child whom he hast chastened, lest his son or daughter misunderstand and think him an enemy; That he or she may know that their father's faithfulness is stronger than the cords of death." Certainly, like all fathers, Eddie Rickenbacker made mistakes, but he valiantly strove towards these God-given ideals. His manner of dealing with extreme difficulties, especially regarding humanistic sophistry that perhaps crept into his son's thinking while receiving an education away from home, is exemplary and beneficial to every man who bears this same responsibility. It is clear from these letters that Eddie is ever a friend as well as a father.

October 21, 1941

My dear Bill:

It was nice to have a chance to talk to you the other night and to know you are getting along so well with your studies at school but, very frankly . . . I know you are entirely too keen and sympathetic to mean what you said about your brother . . . Instead of criticizing you should be out promoting his welfare. Learn to fight for him as I know he would fight for you in a pinch. He has proven that often . . . You two boys have got to learn to have mutual respect and admiration for each other . . .

I know you are qualified to do what I recommend. It is all up to you because frankly, if you cannot change your way of thinking, then I am going to have to change it for you, which I do not want to do. In other words, I mean if you cannot learn to love and respect [your brother] for what he really is, as well as your fellow students, you probably would be much better off in a military school, which is not an easy life and where they teach you these traits by compulsion instead of persuasion. That, I do not want to do, only as a last resort, and I know you will help me to prevent it.

Love and best wishes,

As always,

Daddy[69]

February 6, 1948

My dear Pal Bill:

Your letter of February 3 was a real inspiration to read, and I want you to know how happy I am for your two A's and the wonderful compliment of Professor Miller on your essay . . . How can I refuse to send along a check to one who always dangles the sugar and honey in the first few paragraphs of his communication? Consequently, I am attaching a check for $500.00 . . .[70]

February 8, 1948

My dear Pal Bill:

Here I am at the office Sunday a.m. after . . . what might have been the greatest air transport disaster in the history of air transportation. Fortunately, however, it was not, and I thank God in Heaven for His help in making it possible for the crew to get back to Mother Earth with sixty-three passengers. One of the six crew members, unfortunately, was killed when a propeller blade let go on the right hand inboard motor and went through the galley, killing the Flight Steward instantly . . . one of our New-Type Constellations had developed serious engine trouble about 130 miles off the coast of Jacksonville, Florida, while flying at around 20,000 feet and [were] preparing to 'ditch' the ship.

Naturally, I couldn't believe that they could get down from that altitude, if they were on fire, without resulting in a deadly crash to all . . . to our great relief, we heard the ship was down at Bunnell, Florida . . .

Now for your letter of January 14 . . . Surely, I shall not try to change your hopes and ambitions for a long and useful life, for my one ambition for both you and Dave was to first help you get a sound physical foundation to weather the ruggedness of a long lifetime and, secondly, to be able to give you the best in an education that would expand and balance your mentality to the point where you would learn and be able to serve . . .

Now for your statement that you think there is no God or Supreme Being or Power and that anything that has a religious origin may just as easily be derived from pragmatic, practical thinking and, further, that confidence and faith in the Power Above is useless.

Frankly, only life and its many experiences—good and bad—will bring you to the conclusion sooner or later that there is a God in Heaven.

My own life and experiences should be ample evidence that there is a Supreme Being, because with all the things I have gone through, I must confess it wasn't my knowledge or intelligence that brought me through. It was my faith in God that my life's work had not been completed and that I wanted to continue to live in order to render the maximum service in keeping with my knowledge and ability.

The experience in Atlanta, the Pacific experience, and dozens of other examples . . . I wouldn't be here, and without my faith in that Power, my life would have been more or less meaningless . . .

Our experience yesterday with the Constellation is further evidence of that Power, because from all practical knowledge, and knowing mechanics, the boys should have lost control of the ship which would have crashed at sea . . .

On the raft in the Pacific, we had two men on board who were atheists—Lt. Whittaker and Col. Adamson. Neither of them believed in God; in fact, Whittaker had never been in a church or chapel or listened to a sermon until we arrived at the hospital in the Samoa Islands where they had a small chapel and I took him to his first sermon at his request . . . Since his return to this country, he has given a great amount of his time to the service of God.

And I shall never forget the letter from Colonel Adamson after I had brought him home and placed him in Walter Reed Hospital in which he stated "not only did you save a man, but saved a lost soul."

Take your own life and ours. Surely, [God] brought us together and thus made possible a happier and fuller life for Mother and myself, and we hope, a happy, pleasant, comfortable, long and useful life for you.

I know you will read and re-read this letter and take it seriously . . . Now I have to dash over to the NBC building for a couple of minute's tribute on the radio . . .

Love and best wishes.
As always,
Daddy[71]

Christmas, 1948
My dear Pal Bill:

Christmas and the Holiday Season are again with us, and I am happy, as is your Mother, that both of you boys will be with us during your Holiday vacation . . .

The future, as always, has it black spots, as well as its bright ones, but unless you are qualified to judge the difference between the two, and take advantage of the opportunities offered by the bright spots, you will fall victim to the evils of the black spots as millions have and always will.

The black spots in the future, as I see them, consist primarily of a trend on the part of the majority of our people to expect something for nothing, or more for less, or to think in terms of the world owing them a living.

Frankly, the world never has, and never will, owe anyone who is mentally and physically fit a living, unless they are willing to work and work hard for it.

The world is your oyster and it lies within your power and yours alone to succeed or fail in proportion to your experience, knowledge, and the judgment will come from both.

Consequently, may I again implore you to always remember that God helps those who help themselves . . .[72]

January 11, 1951
My dear Son and Pal:

. . . Always remember that a million friends are worth more than a million dollars . . . Always be respectful to your superiors and elders as it is an acknowledgement of your capacity to appreciate the benefits acquired from experience . . . Never worry about protecting my name or my reputation. But always remember that it is your name you must protect and live with the balance of your life . . . Never try to impress other people with your knowledge . . . Never fail to remember that to have a strong and healthy mind you must first have a strong and healthy body . . . Protect your body by limiting the abuses that go with every day life and you will automatically protect your mentality . . .

To become a good pilot and remain one never forget that an airplane is like a rattlesnake, you must keep your mind and eye on it constantly or it will bite you when you least expect it which could prove fatal . . .

For your peace of mind and emotional stability, play the piano . . .

Always keep in mind that men at the head of the Kremlin only respect force and power . . .There is no doubt that this country and our civilization are on trial and the problems of the future may be God's way of making us suffer for our lack of appreciation of the blessings bestowed on us by the Supreme Power . . . when the hour looks darkest never lose faith in the Power Above. With faith in the Power Above you will have faith in yourself. And because of your faith your call to God in Heaven for help will never go unheeded, and will bring you back to us, your family . . .

Love as always,

Daddy[73]

December 22, 1952

My dear Pal Bill:

We were all delighted to receive your letter of December 8th and glad to know that you have been checked out and are now in command. Heartiest congratulations on a well deserved honor for which you have worked so hard. Your description of your first flight as commanding officer of the ship is fascinating . . . the experience with the hydraulic system and landing gear is something that you must always remember can happen . . . I am also happy to note that your knowledge of the mechanics of the ship helped you in this emergency . . . Your decision to let the co-pilot, even though a greenhorn, fly the ship while you [resolved the emergency] shows that you have the faculty . . . to think under trying circumstances. Again, my congratulations on the good judgment.[74]

July 6, 1955
My dear Pal Bill:

It was nice of you to call us the other evening . . . Of course, I agree further with you that the public do not want to think of their own welfare or plan it. They want more and more of it to be done by the government or industry, and someday they will wake up and find themselves with a planned economy that practically equals a dictatorship . . . Of course, all politicians want to be in office and the only way for them to get into power is to promise everything under the sun from the cradle to the grave to get the great majority of the common people's vote . . . Unfortunately, people never learn without suffering. They do not go to church until they are either sick, broke or in some other misery. Then all human beings start crying for help, but when things are going good and they are riding the crest of the waves, as they are today in this country, the Power Above means nothing to them because the great majority are enjoying their blessings but have never earned them. Generations previously laid a foundation and made it possible for them to have what they do . . . someday [they must] pay a heavy penalty . . .
Love to Sandy and yourself.
As Always, Daddy[75]

Christmas, 1960
My dear Pal Bill:

. . . I realize that we Americans, above all other peoples, have been blessed with freedoms, opportunities and in the individual dignity of man. We Americans have an abundance of all the necessities of life, and when we think of the many peoples throughout the world, who are hungry on this blessed day, we should give thanks to the good Lord for having been born in this land where our brilliant forefathers had the courage and ability to write these blessings and freedoms into the Declaration of Independence and the Constitution of these United States which, unfortunately, too many have never read or remembered.

> I think of the birth of Christ who brought to earth the realization and understanding that all men should be free—free to worship as they see fit—free to work where they see fit—free to own their own homes—free to vote for whom they please . . . Then I realize that without the birth of Christ there never would have been the birth of our nation—a free America—whose moral obligation is to stand as a living example to the rest of the world of what a freedom-loving people can accomplish . . .
>
> Most sincerely,
>
> Daddy[76]

The principles addressed in these letters are timeless and could well be utilized to help all young men come of age. There is direct correlation between faith in God and patriotic convictions. Today the false dogmas associated with the word *liberal* are far removed from the truths interconnected with the doctrine of *liberty.* In all of his correspondence with his son, Eddie never condemned—rather he trained, he taught, and he testified.

Rickenbacker was a formidable adversary to the socialist and communist, abroad and at home. He used the bully pulpit, whenever opportunity presented itself, to instill faith in God, country and the inspired constitution of our nation. Although he ultimately attained fourteen doctoral degrees Eddie Rickenbacker never held a pilot's certificate or an automobile driver's license. He said that he was "both pilot and driver before they started issuing certificates" and what government bureaucrat would ever challenge a legendary world class race car driver or America's Ace of Aces? In 1967, six years before his death, Eddie left this challenge, which rings as true today as it did thirty-seven years ago:

> Our survival as a free people and the freedom of generations to come depend upon our ability to re-establish the eternal truths and principles upon which our beloved country was founded—and upon our willingness to demonstrate them in our personal and political lives and in our relations with the peoples of all nations.

To give the world the leadership it needs, to lead the world out of the current chaos and confusion, the United States does not need any new world-shaking discoveries in political science . . . To create harmony among nations and restore dignity to man, we need only to rediscover for ourselves the principles of the American way of life that have been tried and proved over nearly two tumultuous centuries . . .

The release of initiative and enterprise made possible by popular self-government *ultimately generates disintegrating forces from within.* Again and again, after freedom has brought opportunity and some degree of plenty, the competent become selfish, luxury-loving and complacent; the incompetent and the unfortunate grow envious and covetous, and all three groups turn aside from the hard road to freedom to worship the golden calf of economic security.

The historical cycle seems to move from bondage to spiritual faith, from spiritual faith to courage, from courage to liberty, from liberty to abundance, from abundance to selfishness, from selfishness to apathy, from apathy to dependence and from dependence back to bondage once more. But we are not yet in bondage. We still have some liberty left. We are at war to preserve that liberty.

It is not old-fashioned to wave and love the flag of our country or to worship God in heaven. Let us acknowledge and be grateful for the blessings of freedom that God has given us. Let us dedicate our lives to the perpetuation of the American principles of freedom with confidence. Let us stop and analyze ourselves to find out what life means to us.

I want nothing further in material value or personal prestige—no power, no wealth, no political plums. But I do pray that this exhortation in the name of freedom and liberty will spread into every nook and cranny of this land of ours for the benefit of future generations.

Let us therefore pray every night for the strength and guidance to inspire in others the gratitude, the love, the dedication that we owe our beloved country for the sake of our posterity.

Then, and only then, can we say when the candle of life burns low—Thank God, I have given my best to the land that has given so much to me.[77]

By including this exhortation, nearly in its fullness, this author is doing what he can to further Rickenbacker's prayer that his inspired words, backed by a life that was worthy of the truths he spoke, will spread to a new generation and deeper into the hearts of true Americans.

In 1973, nearly a year after Eddie and Adelaide celebrated their golden wedding anniversary, they returned to Europe for the last time. Eddie wanted to visit the ancestral homes of his father and mother. But this was not to be. Shortly after their arrival in Zurich, on July 12, Adelaide became seriously ill. Eddie had been subjected to great physical stresses, having only recently recovered from a series of life threatening maladies, including stroke, kidney failure and pneumonia. Perhaps the added anxiety of his wife's sudden illness induced the fatal blow. In the early morning hours of July 23, 1973 Captain Eddie Rickenbacker suffered a heart attack and died in the land in which his parents had been born. He was a valiant man of godly covenants—a faithful son, soldier, husband, leader, friend, and father. He was a man's man, self-reliant but never self-sufficient, for always he acknowledged that he was dependent on the Power Above, and because he never failed in placing his faith in God, God never failed Eddie Rickenbacker.

Bibliography – Book 1

Primary Sources

Keegan, John: *The First World War* (Vintage Books, A division of Random House, Inc., New York)

Strachan, Hew (Editor): *The Oxford Illustrated History of the First World War* (Oxford University Press, Oxford, New York)

Rickenbacker, Edward V.: *Rickenbacker—An Autobiography* (Prentice-Hall, Inc., Englewood Cliffs, New Jersey)

Rickenbacker, Edward V: *Fighting the Flying Circus* (Doubleday and Company, Inc., New York)

Rickenbacker, Edward V.: *Seven Came Through* (Doubleday, Doran and Company, Inc., Garden City, New York)

Rickenbacker, Edward V.: *We Prayed* (a pamphlet published under the auspices of the War Service Committee of American Viewpoint Incorporated, New York, New York)

Duffy, Michael: *First World War.com—The War to End all Wars*

Jordanhoff, Assen: *Flying and How To Do It!* (Grossset & Dunlap, Inc., New York, 1932)

Rickenbacker, William F.: *From Father to Son: the letters of Captain Eddie Rickenbacker to his son William, from boyhood to manhood* (Walker and Company, New York 1970)

CHAPTER 10

ECOLE D' AVIATION

An aviator, and a fledgling aviator in particular, often runs the whole gamut of human feeling during a single flight. I did in the course of half an hour, reaching the high C of acute panic as I came tumbling out of the first cloud of my aerial experience. [78]

— CAPTAIN JIMMY HALL

TODAY'S STUDENT PILOT WOULD FIND his training remarkably similar to that of the student pilot in France, 1916, learning to fly transport aircraft. Their biplane trainers were "double command" where the new aviator was accompanied by a "*moniteur*" with "his own set of controls" to "immediately correct any mistakes in handling." However, the training of "*pilots de chasse*," or fighter pilots, was a totally different matter. Incredibly, in those pioneering days of aviation, the French believed:

> Single command training is preferred for the airman who is to be a combat pilot. Certain it is that men have greater confidence in themselves when they learn to *fly alone from the beginning* . . . [such] offers excellent preliminary schooling for the Nieuport and Spad, the fast and high-powered biplanes which are the *avions de chasse* above the French lines.[79]

One can only imagine what it must have been like to *never* have an instructor at your side in a dual-control aircraft! It gives a whole new connotation to the term "solo"—for every lesson, from the first to the last, was flown solo. The combat student pilot did have his *"moniteur,"* but he was what we call today a ground instructor, or a classroom teacher. What syllabus was utilized to transform the would-be airman to a skilled flyer? The student pilot was to "grow his wings gradually" by advancing through various classes.

The first was appropriately called the Penguin Class where the novice strapped himself into a low-powered Blériot monoplane with clipped wings which, like its namesake, was incapable of becoming airborne. This procedure was not without merit. Planes of that era were all "taildraggers"—aircraft without a nose wheel. The weight of this type of plane on the ground is primarily supported by main landing gear, which at slower speeds, or at rest, is also supported by a tail skid or a tail wheel. Steering left and right is controlled by the pilot using his feet on the rudder pedals, or bar, as it was called then. If a taildragger is allowed to oscillate in the least degree on the takeoff or landing roll, the outcome is immediate and disconcerting—the plane ground-loops, or swings rapidly in an arc, pivoting on one landing gear and often striking the ground with the outward wing. Requiring the student pilot to master ground taxi technique *solo* was fairly safe and very useful.

Next came the Rolling Class, which was still of the order of the Penguin, but the Blériot's in this class had more horsepower and could attain far greater speed. The idea was to have enough power and wing surface to allow the trainee to lift the tail skid off the ground and *roll* the plane down the field on the main gear, but not achieve actual flight. However, the right combination of wing and power to get the tail up and yet stay flightless was not an exact science. It was not unusual for one of the "rolling machines" to suddenly become airborne. When this happened the hapless pilot would of course be taken completely by surprise and would have no knowledge or skill in returning his aircraft safely to earth.

Jimmy Hall, a U.S. citizen who had enlisted in the Franco-American Corps, was as excited as a kid in a circus. He had been assigned to attend *Ecole d' Aviation,* as a combat pilot trainee. His first lesson was to observe from the sidelines his classmates in action. He could scarcely believe his eyes when a penguin pilot left the ground in "an alarming manner." Jimmy wrote:

> [He] was working the controls erratically. First he swooped upward, then dived, tipping dangerously on one wing. I wondered what I would do in such a strait, when one must think with the quickness and sureness of instinct. My heart was in my mouth, for I felt certain that the man would be killed. As for the others who were watching, no one appeared to be excited. A *moniteur* near me said, "Oh, là là! Il est perdu!"[ii] in a mild voice. At the last, the machine made a quick swoop downward, from a height of about fifty meters (164 feet), then careened upward, tipped again, and diving sidewise, struck the ground with a sickening rending crash, the motor going at full speed. For a moment it stood, tail in air, then slowly the balance was lost, and it fell, bottom up, and lay silent.
>
> An enterprising moving-picture company would have given a great deal of money to film that accident. Civilian audiences would have watched in breathless, awe-struck silence; but at a military school of aviation it was a different matter. 'Oh, là là! Il est perdu!' adequately gauges the degree of emotional interest taken in the incident. At the time I was surprised at this apparent callousness, but I understood it better when I had seen scores of such accidents occur, and had watched the pilots, as in this case, crawl out from the wreckage, and walk sheepishly, and a little shaken back to their classes.[80]

There were other spectators who watched the student pilots with keen interest.

> Crows would watch us from afar, holding noisy indignation meetings in a row of weather-beaten trees at the far side of the

---

[ii] Translation: "Oh well, it is ruined."

Jimmy Hall

> field. And when some inexperienced pilot lost control of his machine and came crashing to earth, they would take the air in a body, circling over the wreckage, cawing and jeering with the most evident delight.[81]

When the trainee mastered the Penguin he was advanced to the First Flying Class where he was placed in an underpowered real airplane. Airmen of the First Flying Class were instructed to fly straight and make "short hops across the field at an altitude of two or three meters" (around 10 feet). Once the pilot became proficient in this endeavor he graduated to the Second Flying Class. In this class he was told he should not ascend higher than 160 feet and was to *teach himself* to "make landings without the use of the motor"—or full stall landings. The old adage, "fly low and slow" is a most dangerous admonishment, yet that was exactly what the French curriculum required of student pilots. Hall writes that as "many as eleven machines were wrecked in the course of one working day, and rarely less than two or three!"

If a pilot survived the Second Flying Class he went on to master the *Tour-de-Piste* Class. Here, for the first time, he was to actually *turn* the aircraft by flying the five mile circumference of the aerodrome at an altitude of 400 feet, then land without "cracking up." The pilot reader will, of course, be amused at this evolution in training, for in actuality one cannot be *taught* to fly straight and level, and then be *taught* to turn—for straight and level flying is accomplished by making continually corrections, or *turns*. Knowing how to execute a coordinated turn is key to flying straight. A direct course is maintained by constantly correcting away from adverse currents; the sooner the correction is made, the smoother the flight—much like life itself.

Next the airman was promoted to the Spiral Class. He was told to fly to an altitude of 3,000 feet and cut his engine directly above his intended landing site—then enter a steep spiraling descent, pivoting around the point down to a spot landing. This procedure is very similar to the power off 1080 spiral to a landing that was required of this author in his commercial training. However, the big difference again, is that the student *pilote de chasse* received ground instruction only from his moniteur and in the air learned the entire procedure solo. The last class given at the *Ecole d' Aviation* was the Brevet. To graduate with the honor of brevet de pilote, or to be a military licensed pilot, the airman was to successfully complete two short cross-country flights of sixty kilometers each, one longer flight of two hundred kilometers and a final cross-country flight of three hundred kilometers at a minimum altitude of two thousand meters.

Jimmy Hall wrote of the day when he and his compatriot, Drew, began their aviation instruction:

> Never have I seen a stranger sight than that of a swarm of Penguins at work. They looked like a brood of prehistoric birds of enormous size, with wings too short for flight. Most unwieldy birds they were, driven by, or more accurately, driving beginners in the art of flying; but they ran along the ground at an amazing speed, zig-zagged this way and that, and whirled about as if trying to catch their own tails. As we stood watching them, an accident occurred which would have been laughable had we not been too nervous to enjoy it. In a distant part of the field two machines were rushing wildly about. There were acres of room in which they might pass, but after a moment of uncertainty, they rushed headlong for each other as though driven by the hand of fate, and met head-on, with a great rending of propellers. The onlookers along the side of the field howled and pounded each other in an ecstasy of delight, but Drew and I walked apart for a hasty consultation, for it was our turn next. We kept rehearsing the points which we were to remember in driving a Penguin.[82]

When his turn arrived, Jimmy fastened himself in his seat and secured his helmet. Early aircraft had no battery or starter. The magnetos sparked to life when the propeller was manually swung or "propped." A mechanic stood directly in front of the Penguin.

"Coupe, plein gaz," or "Gas On?" he said. Jimmy responded in the affirmative. Next he spun the prop, priming the engine. "Contact, reduisez," the mechanic barked—meaning to switch on the magnetos. Jimmy confirmed, "Contact." With one swift pull the engine roared to life and the mechanic hastily moved to the side of the Blériot. Jimmy pulled the throttle full open and was off like a thoroughbred out of the gate. He wrote:

> Off I went at what seemed to me then breakneck speed. Remembering instructions, I pushed forward on the lever which governs the elevating planes, and up went my tail so quickly and at such an angle that almost instinctively I cut off my contact. Down dropped my tail again, and I whirled around in a circle—my first *cheval do bois* (or ground-loop). I had forgotten that I had a rudder. I was like a man learning to swim, and could not yet coordinate the movements of my hands and feet. My bird was purring gently, with the propeller turning slowly . . . Before starting again I looked about me, and there was Drew racing all over the field. Suddenly he started in my direction as if the whole force of his will was turned to the business of running me down. Luckily he shut off his motor, and by the grace of the law of inertia came to a halt when he was within a dozen paces of me.
>
> We turned our machines tail to tail and started in opposite directions, but in a moment I was following hard after him. Almost it seemed that those evil birds had wills of their own. Drew's turned as though it were angry at the indignity of being pursued. We missed each other, but it was a near thing, and, not being able to think fast enough, I stalled my motor, and had to await helplessly the assistance of a mechanic. Far away, at our starting point, I could see the Americans waving their arms and embracing each other in huge delight.[83]

After a good deal of practice Jimmy proudly conquered his little Penguin. When he had successfully made an entire dash across the field, without making a single ground-loop, he was eager to receive the praise of his *moniteur* and his peers. But as he triumphantly taxied back to the point of beginning, he realized that no one had seen his astounding accomplishment for not a soul was paying the least attention to *his* maneuvers. Every eye was fixed high in the heavens. When Jimmy followed their gaze with his own he saw a magnificent *avion de chasse,* a fighter aircraft, silhouetted against a billowy cumulus cloud. Obviously the plane had just leveled from a swift descent for it was flying at incredible speed. Suddenly, and with deft agility the aircraft zoomed straight up perpendicular to the earth. As the plane's airspeed fell off, rapidly approaching a vertical stall, the wings began to waver, as if hesitant to its future course. But the pilot was in complete control, even though his aircraft was on the ragged edge of a stall. The pursuit plane rolled "slowly on one wing, and fell, nose-down, turning round and round as it fell in a *vrille.*" The French word *vrille* literally means *auger,* which is perhaps more accurate than the term we use for this maneuver, which is *tail-spin*. Down the aircraft went for eight complete revolutions, plunging dramatically earthward, when suddenly, the pilot recovered instantly in a straight and level attitude. Just as the *vrille* was checked with precision, the aircraft again nosed over, accelerating at full throttle. Two perfect loops followed in quick succession ending in a split-s, exactly reversing course, then skillfully the pilot spiraled the *avion de chasse* down within fifty feet of the spectators, landing ever so lightly just beyond Jimmy's Penguin. Hall wrote:

> He had left the front, this birdman, only an hour before! I was incredulous at first, for I still thought of distances in the old way. But I was soon convinced. Mounted on the hood was the competent-looking Vickers machine gun, with a long belt of cartridges in place, and on the side of the fuselage were painted the insignia of an escadrille . . . Those of us who had never before seen this latest type of French avion de chasse, crowded round, examining and admiring with feelings of awe. It was a marvelous piece of aero-craftsmanship . . . It was hard to think of it as an inanimate thing, once having

> seen it in the air. It seemed living, intelligent, almost human . . .
>
> Drew and I examined it line by line, talking in low tones which seemed fitting in so splendid a presence. We climbed the step and looked down into the compact little car, where the pilot sat in a luxuriously upholstered seat. There were his compass, his altimeter, his revolution-counter, his map in its roller case, with a course pricked out on it in a red line . . .
>
> It was with a chastened spirit that I looked back from the splendid fighting plane, back to my little three-cylinder Penguin, with its absurd clipped wings and its impudent tail. A moment ago it had seemed a thing of speed, and the mastery of it a glorious achievement . . .
>
> Half an hour later, we stood watching the biplane climbing into the evening sky . . . Higher and higher it mounted, now and then catching the sun on its silver wings in a flash of light, growing smaller and smaller, until it vanished in a golden haze, far to the north.[84]

It seemed to Jimmy that his early training would never come to an end. Even when he was advanced to the flying classes and actually became airborne, albeit only a few meters above the ground, there was little in his exercises to excite his spirit of adventure. Rather it seemed to him to be the epitome of monotony. Up and down the field, whether in high speed taxi or a few feet above the ground, it was always the same. In no way could this compare to what he had seen and felt as he had watched the *avion de chasse,* looping, rolling, spinning, guided by the skilled touch of what he aspired to be—a pursuit pilot. However, the day came that in Jimmy's mind, marked the commencement of his career as an aviator. It was the day he flew his first traffic pattern, the *tour de piste*, his first flight around the field. This same genesis is experienced today when a pilot makes his first solo flight—when he commands the aircraft without the benefit of his flight instructor's presence. Again, however, in Jimmy's training there were no flight instructors and he had maneuvered each of his sorties solo.

However, never had he flown to an altitude of 400 feet, never had he banked the aircraft to substantially change his course, never had he flown a complete circuit around the aerodrome. The first *tour de piste* for an airman was always a well attended event. The pilot who was about to make this quantum leap was, of course, nervous, to say the least. His fellow classmates came out in droves in anticipation of a highly entertaining spectacle. Those airman who were only slightly more advanced, and had recently achieved the status of living through their *tour de piste*, were there to "offer gratuitous advice."

> Not too much rudder on the turns. Remember how that Frenchman [crashed into] the hangars when he tried to bank . . .
>
> You'll find it pretty rotten when you go over the woods. The air currents there are something scandalous!
>
> Believe me, it's a lot worse over the fort. Rough? Oh, là là!
>
> And that's where you have to cut your motor and dive, if you're going to make a landing without hanging up in the telephone wires.
>
> When you come down, don't be afraid to stick her nose forward. Scare the life out of you, that drop will, but you may as well get used to it.
>
> Pan-caking isn't too bad. Not in a Blériot. Just like falling through a shingle roof. Can't hurt yourself much.
>
> If you do spill, make it a good one. There hasn't been a decent smash-up today . . . Where's the Oriental Wrecking Gang?[85]

Whenever there was a crash on the air field, a wrecking crew of Oriental migrants ran to the site of the accident. Like a scene from a Charley Chaplin movie, they would quickly remove the debris and scurry off the field, dodging Penguins or landing aircraft, as the case might be.

Later Hall wrote that there was "enough truth in the warnings to make us uneasy." In the midst of all this advice, Jimmy's moniteur turned to him and announced, "*Allez! en route!*" The time had come for Hall's first *tour de piste*. Jimmy aligned his aircraft directly into the wind and opened his engine to full throttle. For a young man raised in the horse and buggy era, it seemed incredulous that the simple movement of a lever could unleash such muscle. Although his plane was equipped with only a forty-five horsepower Anzani engine, still the roar of it, coupled with the hurricane blast from the propeller and the swift acceleration of his aircraft "struck awe" into his soul. His lift off was smooth and for the first time he allowed his aircraft to really *climb*. Beneath his wings passed his classmates, the aircraft hangars, the glittering lake and the forest green. Time and again he had heard how thermal conditions vary with the terrain; how when flying over water the air can be as silky as the quiescent surface of blue below, but instantly the air can disrupt into significant up and down drafts the moment you cross over the foreboding woods. Jimmy gripped his controls firmly—watched his wings and nose in anticipation of a sudden change in pitch that would require his immediate corrective action. However, the day was perfect and the air as stable as a road. He relaxed a little and thought how his fellow airman had exaggerated for effect. It was not nearly as difficult flying this first real flight has he had supposed it to be. He glanced over the side of the aircraft at the beautiful countryside that spread out beneath him in the perfection that can only be seen from an aerial perspective. In no time at all he reached the half-way point and his thoughts quickly turned from exuberance to anxiety once again—in just a moment he would have to get this flying machine back on the ground without killing himself. In his own words he writes:

> I knew well enough how the descent was to be made. It was very simple. I had only to shut off my motor, push forward with my "broom-stick," — the control connected with the elevating planes, — and redress gradually, beginning at from six to eight meters from the ground. The descent would be exciting, a little more rapid than *Shooting the Chutes*. Only one could not safely hold on to the sides of the car and await the splash. That sort of thing had sometimes

> been done in aeroplanes, by over-excited pilots. The results were disastrous, without exception.
>
> The moment for the decision came. I was above the fort, otherwise I should not have known when to dive. At first the sensation was, I imagine, exactly that of falling, feet foremost; but after pulling back slightly on the controls, I felt the machine answer to them, and the uncomfortable feeling passed. I brought up on the ground in the usual bumpy manner of the beginner. Nothing gave way, however, so this did not spoil the fine rapture of a rare moment.[86]

Shortly after Jimmy landed, a fellow student aviator successfully completed his circuit as well. As they considered this to be the end of their apprenticeship they celebrated over dinner—now they were truly pilots! However, this celebration was a quiet one. They hardly spoke to each other for they were "under an enchantment which words would have broken."

Jimmy's next grand adventure was to be his "triangles"—his cross-country flights. Among his dispatch papers was a document that today we would consider highly unusual. In our era forced landings are extremely unlikely whereas in Jimmy's day it was a planned for eventuality. The text of this official declaration was addressed to the un-named mayor of the city or village in which the pilot made an emergency landing. It cited the law of France regarding military pilots and the obligations and "duty" of local officials to facilitate their needs. The document concluded with the procedure for recovering damages done by a forced landing, specifying how much a farmer would be reimbursed for each type of affected crop.

On a beautiful April morning Jimmy flew over a small village which he had often visited. He had strolled through its narrow, angular streets and rested along the banks of its beautiful canal. Jimmy especially loved the centuries old cathedral. He wrote:

> The cathedral was a favorite haunt. Looking down on it now, it seemed no larger than a toy cathedral in a toy town, such as one

sees in the shops of Paris . . . A toy train, which I could have put nicely into my fountain-pen case, was pulling into a station no larger than a wren's house. The Greeks called their gods "derisive." No doubt they realized how small they looked to them, and how insignificant this little world of affairs must have appeared from high Olympus.[87]

Jimmy continued to climb enroute. When he reached two thousand meters he was struck with the thought that he was over a mile high! In the clear air of this new day he could see dozens of villages, great expanses of primeval forests, and picturesque fields laid out like the patterns of an immense patchwork quilt. The earth below him was perfect, without the slightest hint of the terrible war that was raging just beyond the horizon. Jimmy was filled with joy and realized that he was seeing sights that men had dreamed of from the beginning of time, a pleasure that only the winged creations of God had experienced. Small wonder, he said, that birds *sing*. The day was so benign that his biplane seemed to fly itself and Jimmy thought it "the simplest thing in the world." Soon he approached his first destination and began his descent. He wrote:

Checker board patterns of brown and green grew larger and larger. Shining threads of silver became rivers and canals, tiny green shrubs became trees . . . Soon I could see people going about the streets and laundry-maids hanging out the family washing in the back gardens. I even came low enough to witness a minor household tragedy—a mother vigorously spanking a small boy. Hearing the whir of my motor, she stopped in the midst of the process, whereupon the youngster very naturally took advantage of his opportunity to cut and run for it. Drew doubted my veracity when I told him about this. He called me an aerial eavesdropper and said that I ought to be ashamed to go buzzing over towns at such low altitudes . . . disorganizing domestic penal institutions . . . But I was unrepentant, for I knew that one small boy in France was thinking of me with joy. To have escaped maternal justice with the assistance of an aviator would be an event of glorious memory to him.[88]

Soon Jimmy refueled his aircraft and was on to his next destination seventy kilometers away. For the first time he learned in a practical manner the difference between *course* and *heading*. As he flew due north he perceived that he was heading northwest. At first this puzzled him until it dawned on him that he was being blown off course by the wind. He recalled being taught something about this phenomenon from his moniteur and chastened himself for forgetting such vital information. Jimmy corrected his heading to the northeast to hold his intended course and began to search for landmarks that would confirm he was on the right track. However, the east wind was only the beginning of this vital lesson in meteorology.

As Jimmy attempted to get his bearings the weather was rapidly deteriorating. Thin clouds began to obscure his sight of the towns, rivers and roads below. At this point, at his altitude and above, the sky was still a brilliant blue. As a student pilot qualified to fly only in visual conditions he should have reversed course, or immediately found a suitable field in which to land. However, Jimmy was still exuberant, even as the scattered clouds under him formed into a solid floor, without breaks, as far as his eyes could see. His poetic mind romanticized the beauty of the welkin above in contrast to earth, hidden in shadow beneath. The lower layer of clouds formed in masse parallel to the horizon, which was all he needed to maneuver visually. He continued with the heading he estimated would take him, despite the winds, to his destination. The rest, he said, he "left to Chance, the godfather of all adventures." This was a fine sentiment for a poet, but not a pilot. Aviation is a science and navigation, then as now, an exact discipline. An airman cannot reach his destination if he is off course by a few small degrees of the compass.

Jimmy had an even more pressing problem than finding his intended aerodrome, he would have to find mother earth, and meet up with her gradually with his plane in one piece. Hall had thought his apprenticeship over—such is the universal nature of man when he has only acquired a little knowledge. This truth is expressed by the familiar words of Alexander Pope:

> A little learning is a dangerous thing;
> Drink deep, or taste not the Pierian Spring:
> There shallow draughts intoxicate the brain,
> And drinking largely sobers us again.[89]

The Pierian Spring of Macedonia was to the Greeks the sacred fountain of knowledge. Pope taught that to drink just a little from this spring was to intoxicate our thinking with destructive overconfidence. However, to drink in knowledge deeply is to gain an understanding that the more we know, the more we know how little we know compared to what there is to know.

As Jimmy continued to fly northward, the floor of clouds began to *accumulate* vertically, that is with convection currents they were maturing swiftly into cumulous clouds. Jimmy wrote:

> They were scattered at first and offered splendid opportunities for aerial steeple chasing. Then, almost before I was aware of it, they surrounded me on all sides. For a few minutes I avoided them by flying in curves and circles in rapidly vanishing pools of blue sky. I feared to take my first plunge into a cloud, for I knew, by report, what an alarming experience it is to the new pilot.
>
> The wind was no longer blowing steadily out of the east. It came in gusts from all points of the compass. I made a hasty revision of my opinion as to the calm and tranquil joys of aviation, thinking what fools men are who willingly leave the good green earth and trust themselves to all the winds of heaven in a frail box of cloth-covered sticks.
>
> The last space grew smaller and smaller. I searched for an outlet, but the clouds closed in a moment. I was hopelessly lost in a blanket of cold drenching mist.

> I could hardly see the outlines of my machine and had no idea of my position with reference to the earth. In the excitement of this new adventure I forgot the speed-dial, and it was not until I heard the air screaming through the wires that I remembered it. The indicator had leaped up fifty kilometers an hour above safety speed, and I realized that I must be traveling earthward at a terrific pace.[90]

Amazingly many pioneer pilots with rudimentary gauges learned the skill of flying with virtually no instrument references. Certainly they were greatly limited without the guidance systems of today's aircraft, but such an aviator could maintain his upright orientation with respect to the earth, fly straight and level, climb, turn, and descend. These pilots did fly in the clouds *enroute*, or would traverse a cloud layer to get above or below the obscuration. However, takeoff and landings were visual operations only. Remarkably they obtained this ability without instruction and typically acquired their skill incrementally by venturing into isolated clouds, where they could "fall out" with plenty of room to recover. Why is flying by instrument reference so difficult to the uninitiated? A visual pilot learns to "fly by the seat of his pants"—to trust the same basic senses he uses while walking on the ground, however attuned to the skies. But when a pilot loses sight reference to the horizon he must *not* trust those same senses that heretofore were his salvation. If he does, and the novice aviator *always* will, the result is a condition known as *spatial disorientation (SD)*, or simply said, vertigo.[iii]

[iii] Spatial disorientation is insidious and progressive. The Air Force Research Laboratory describes SD as follows:

"The pilot is oblivious to his or her disorientation, and controls the aircraft completely in accord with and in response to a false orientational percept. [Next] the pilot may experience a conflict between what they feel the aircraft is doing and what the flight instruments show that it is doing. [Finally] the pilot experiences an overwhelming — i.e., incapacitating – physiologic response to physical or emotional stimuli associated with the disorientation event."

Jimmy Hall knew that he "must be traveling earthward" and he recognized that he was dangerously above what is now called "redline," where the structural failure of the aircraft is likely. Hall had fallen victim to spatial disorientation—without being able to *see* the ground or horizon, there was absolutely nothing Jimmy could do to recover. Then of a sudden he fell from the clouds. Fortunately the hard earth was separated sufficiently from the overcast sky for Hall to recover his senses. Of the dramatic moment Jimmy wrote:

> I saw the earth jauntily titled up on one rim, looking like a gigantic enlargement of a page out of a 'Slant Book.' I expected to see

---

FAA Advisory Circular 61-27C explains that spatial disorientation often results from continuing a visual flight (VFR) into adverse weather conditions. This official circular further states that SD renders the pilot incapable of determining the attitude or motion of the aircraft in relation to the earth's surface. Illusions or false impressions occur when information provided by sensory organs is misinterpreted by the pilot causing him to maneuver the aircraft into a dangerous attitude in an attempt to correct this illusory movement. The Advisory Circular concludes that SD is regularly near the top of the cause/factor list in annual statistics on fatal aircraft accidents.

One of the most famous SD accidents occurred on July 16, 1999, when a Piper Saratoga, N9253N, was destroyed when it crashed into the Atlantic Ocean approximately 7 1/2 miles southwest of Gay Head, Martha's Vineyard, Massachusetts. The pilot, John F. Kennedy, Jr., and passengers Carolyn Bessette Kennedy and Lauren Bessette were killed. On that black night John Kennedy, Jr. might just as well been in the bowels of dense clouds for he lost all visual cues outside his cockpit. The National Transportation Safety Board determined the probable cause of this accident as follows:

"The pilot's failure to maintain control of the airplane during a descent over water at night, which was a result of spatial disorientation. Factors in the accident were haze, and the dark night."

The National Transportation Safety Board states that *today* the fatality rate is 87% for SD related accidents. Hence the FAA now requires even a private pilot, who initially is certified strictly for visual flight, to receive some instrument flight training in aircraft equipped far superior to Jimmy's biplane—yet the majority of pilots who still succumb to vertigo die. Therefore, in Hall's era the certainty of death in such circumstances was absolute, *unless* the pilot tumbled from the clouds with his plane still intact and had space and time enough to recover his senses before the fatal impact.

dogs and dishpans, baby carriages and barrels roll out of every house in France, and go clattering off into space . . .

An aviator, and a fledgling aviator in particular, often runs the whole gamut of human feeling during a single flight. I did in the course of half an hour, reaching the high C of acute panic as I came tumbling out of the first cloud of my aerial experience.

After some desperate handling of my "broom-stick," as the control is called which governs ailerons and elevating planes, I soon had the horizons nicely adjusted again. What a relief it was! I shut down my motor and commenced a more gradual descent, for I was lost, of course, and it seemed wiser to land and make inquires . . .

After leisurely deliberation I selected one surrounded by wide fields which appeared to be as level as a floor. But as I descended the landscape widened, billowing into hills and folding into valleys. By sheer good luck, nothing more, I made a landing without accident. My Caudron barely missed colliding with a hedge of fruit trees, rolled down a long incline, and stopped not ten feet short of a small stream. The experience taught me the folly of choosing landing-ground from high altitude.[91]

Soon the entire village, young and old surrounded the young pilot. Jimmy said they were "curious, but equally courteous." Patiently they stood, respectfully waiting for the airman, most likely the first pilot that any of them had ever seen, to make his purpose known. Hall was quite aware of the sensation he was making, but rather than feeling arrogance, he felt shy and somewhat embarrassed. While mustering courage and trying to decide how to explain to these anxious attendants that he was actually *lost,* Jimmy feigned that he was busily engaged with the his cockpit instruments. The crowd parted as Monsieur the Mayor stepped forward and, to Jimmy's relief, kindly addressed him. At first neither understood the other, but then the Mayor said:

"Vous etes Anglais, monsieur?" with a smile of very real pleasure.

> I said, "Non, monsieur, Americain."
>
> That magic word. What potency it has, the more so at that time, perhaps, for America had placed herself definitely upon the side of the Allies only a short time before. I enjoyed that moment. I might have had the village for the asking. I willingly accepted the role of ambassador of the American people. Had it not been for the language barrier, I think I would have made a speech for I felt the generous spirit of Uncle Sam prompting me to give those fathers and mothers, whose husbands and sons were at the front, the promise of our unqualified support. I wanted to tell them that we were with them now, not only in sympathy, but with all our resources in men and guns and ships and aircraft . . . Alas! This was impossible. Instead I gave each one of an army of small boys the privilege of sitting in the pilot's seat, and showed them how to manage the controls . . .
>
> To have an American aviator drop down upon them was an event even in the history of that ancient village. To have been that aviator,—well, it was an unforgettable experience, coming as it did so opportunely with America's entry into the war . . . one day it will be among the pleasantest tales which I shall have in store for my grandchildren.[92]

After discovering where he was and with the help of boys from the village he pushed his aeroplane to a nearby site more suited for a safe departure. He could hear the cheer of these lads above the roar of his engine and a moment later lifted his Caudron gracefully above their homes. The obvious adoration of these French boys brought to Jimmy's mind a scene from his own youth, when he had been privileged to be one of the youth who had held a "world famous" balloonist's guy-rope. The hero had yelled, "Let 'er go, boys!" and then had ascended into the sky and into the heart of young Jimmy Hall. He said:

> I kept his memory green until I had passed the first age of hero worship. I know that every youngster in a small village in central

France will so keep mine. Such fame is the only kind worth having.[93]

The rest of Hall's training at *Ecole d' Aviation* was without incident and he soon graduated a *brevets militaries.* The next aircraft Jimmy flew would be the powerful *avions de chasse.*

James Norman Hall — Brevets Militaries

CHAPTER 11

QUEST FOR THE ELYSIAN FIELDS

[In Typee] there were none of those thousand sources of irritation that the ingenuity of civilized man has created to mar his own felicity. There were no foreclosures of mortgages, no bills payable in Typee; no attorneys, to foment discord, backing their clients up to a quarrel, and then knocking their heads together . . . no destitute widows with their children starving on the cold charities of the world; no beggars; no debtor's prisons in Typee . . . no cross old women, no love-sick maidens, no sour old bachelors, no inattentive husbands, no melancholy young men . . .

Here you would see a parcel of children frolicking together the livelong day, and no quarrelling. [In Typee you would see] a throng of young females, not filled with envyings of each other's charms, nor displaying the ridiculous affectations of gentility, nor yet moving in whalebone corsets, but free, happy and unconstrained . . . With the young men there seemed almost always some matter of diversion or business on hand, that afforded a constant variety of enjoyment. But whether fishing, or carving canoes, or polishing their ornaments, never was there exhibited the least sign of strife or contention among them.

– HERMAN MELVILLE FROM TYPEE

JAMES NORMAN HALL WAS BORN ON APRIL 22, 1887, four years before John Lambert invented America's first gasoline-powered automobile and twenty years before Henry Ford's first Model T rolled off the assembly line. Throughout his life Jimmy Hall would mourn the passing of the horse and buggy era, proclaiming that the identity and simple charm of arcadian America "have been sacrificed to that worst of abominations, the automobile." It may seem paradoxical to the reader (but not to this author) that while Jimmy abhorred the changes wrought by mechanization, he loved trains and airplanes. He acknowledged these contradictory sentiments when he wrote:

> I was born a yea-sayer toward life . . . though a nay-sayer toward the trend of it in the U.S.A. I felt that we had taken a wrong turning somewhere . . . I vented my bitterness against the whole of our Industrial Civilization, and my particular spleen upon machines with internal-combustion engines, *inconsistently excepting those with wings [or on rails]*. I deplored the vast changes that motorcars were making in the tempo of life. The good roads they demanded, slashed through the green hills and graded up over the valleys . . . I loathed them.[94]

I have found this mental disposition among other aviators, most notably Saint-Exupéry. And personally, long before I had read anything written by Hall, I came to certain similar conclusions. I recall the exact moment when like thoughts crystallized in my mind. It was soon after spending some weeks in the timeless villages of Bavaria, Tirol and Provence. It occurred to me that what I loved so much of these far-away places was the immense individuality of each hamlet; I marveled how its citizens had resisted so well the homogenization of the last century. Such was my thinking as I was driving down Interstate 65, north of Mobile, Alabama. I was also hungry and as I had recently found an acceptable meal at a roadside restaurant somewhere along this stretch of freeway, I intended to return. On second thought, was the diner anywhere near here? Was it near Aurora or just outside Minneapolis? Or perhaps it was by Wiley Post Airport? In my aviation business travels I had been in Illinois, Minnesota, Oklahoma, Florida, Mississippi, Georgia and now in Alabama, all within the past few days. Simply said, I could not remember where I had eaten—why? The thought troubled me. Why could I not remember such a simple thing? The answer came to me like a thunderbolt—the appearance of the freeway, the franchised hotels and restaurants greeting my view, the service stations, the Walmart just ahead and adjacent strip mall, the *entire* panorama was nearly the same here as it was in all those places. The epiphenomenon of my memory lapse was a result of the modern proliferation of mass produced vistas. Gone, I lamented, is the provincial, the singular.

Our Creator fashioned a world of infinite variety and man was given lordship to replenish the earth, to continue the creative process. He was not commissioned to destroy the diversity that abounds in nature. It is not only certain species that thoughtless man has brought to extinction. The vivisection of village, town and countryside; the coalescence then formed of its remnants, a sterile genesis of concrete and steel so fashioned, is the antithesis of his lordly commission.

In the past, man used the resources of the living earth with discretion and in harmony with her. His building was art and designed to last for centuries. Today structures are fabricated to obsolescence in less than a generation. Archaic roadways followed the contours of the land and were as ever-changing as the landscapes they crossed. These byways hugged the hillside to preserve contiguous farmland or they followed rivers, those natural thoroughfares through the mountains. Bridges were so designed as to allow the eye to gaze wondrously down into the chasms or wistfully upon the rivers they spanned. Now super viaducts are built that hem one in with blinding concrete walls that *safely and speedily* allow passage from one side to the other. In former times a person knew where he was along a certain highway, so individual was each twist and turn. Now, the freeways and turnpikes are engineered to perfection, the radius of each turn so gradual, the ascent of each climb so precise as to permit unimpeded velocity. Of what point is the journey? A *traveler* enjoys the aesthetics of the pathway, while a *commuter* cares for not, but speed. Picturesque crossroads have become "spaghetti junctions"—monuments to this monomania.

In boyhood, James Norman Hall lived at such a time as he said of himself, to literally step from one age to another. Jimmy was born in quiescent times, in the middle of America's history and her continent, in Colfax, Iowa. As a young man he was thrust into the industrial age and, with the heart of a poet mourned the dehumanization and the *loss* of civilization that accompanied the commencement of the twentieth century. Jimmy was by no means a pessimist. However, at a time when such broodings disturbed him deeply, he wrote a poem entitled *Brother Jonathan, A Composite Portrait—1620-1919:*

> Behold this sharp and predatory face
> Made softer by unmerited reward.
> How little joy is written there, or grace!
> The fingers, talon-like, are clutching hard
> A ruined land: the forests, prairies, gone;
> Slums measureless, the rivers foul with slime.
> Three hundred years ago he chanced upon
> A very heaven, and this so brief a time
> Sufficed him, and he wrought the change we see,
> Driven by greed to conquer and destroy
> The heritage of millions yet to be.
>
> Our brother? Our? This old, half-witted boy?
> Then let us guard him well in years to come
> Or he will make a continent a slum.[95]

Although at an early age Jimmy recognized evil and ever after accepted responsibility to personally make a difference, he was not a pessimist. Rather he was, as he had said, a yea-sayer toward life. He loved living and enjoyed the simple blessings of home, the comradeship of true friends, the loveliness of music, the beauty of dirt roads that traversed his hometown and the little river that marked the boundary of the world of his childhood. But James

Hall was not destined to live his life within narrow confines, for his mother, Ellen Young Hall, read to her son while still upon her knee. Together they enjoyed the writings of James Fenimore Cooper, Charles Dickens and other great writers and poets. His favorite books were *The Last of the Mohicans, The Deerslayer, The Pathfinder, Oliver Twist, Nicholas Nickleby* and *David Copperfield.* With such accounts Ellen infused her son not only with a love for literature, but instilled within him a desire for godly adventure. Of this period in his life Jimmy wrote:

> There were no wealthy residents in the town, nor were there any poor. Modern conveniences were few. During my boyhood I remember only two houses furnished with bathrooms and indoor toilets. All dwellings were heated either by wood stoves or hard-coal burners. Furnaces were then unknown . . .
>
> Our house, on its exposed hilltop where it took the buffetings of the bitter midwinter winds sweeping down from Canada, was a story-and-a-half frame building with a porch eight feet wide, trimmed with gingerbread scrollwork. The only water faucet in the house was in the cellar . . . But that old frame house was a home in the best sense of the word. Comforts and conveniences there were none, but they were not missed because we had never known them. What amazes me now, as I think of boyhood days, is how our mother managed to raise five children, three boys and two younger girls, doing practically all of the work herself when we were little . . .
>
> Around my tenth year when I began my literary career, my model was James Whitcomb Riley, the Hoosier Poet, and my secret ambition was to be called, some day, the Hawkeye Poet.[96]

Jimmy devoured book after book. Herman Melville's *Typee* left a profound impression on his young mind and greatly influenced his later life and literary career. Although a self-declared introvert, the aspiring Hawkeye Poet was by no means a frail, shut-in, bookworm—quite the contrary! Jimmy more than emulated his boyhood heroes! Mark Twain's *Adventures of Tom Sawyer and Huckleberry Finn* inspired Jimmy to temerarious actions that are simply incredible. On summer nights, when his father and mother, his brothers and sisters had succumbed to deep sleep, Jimmy would stealthily creep, carrying his shoes, downstairs and outside. Soon he would be joined by his nocturnal confederates, Buller Sharpe and Preacher Stahl—the latter being the son of a Methodist minister. The three boys quietly crept to the very heart of Colfax, the Railway Station of the C.R.I. & P. Railroad. At 10:40 p.m. the lights of "Number Six" could be seen six miles away as the train cleared the top of the Mitchellville grade. To the three boys that light was glorious and together with the magical sound of the distant whistle, it permeated the summer night with spine-tingling excitement—for these three were not to be spectators only! At 10:45 p.m. the Number Six steam-powered locomotive took on water at Colfax, and it was underneath the water tank the young rogues waited, their ears attuned to every significant sound. First came the sound of the fireman pulling down the great iron spout, then the liquid tones of splashing water. When the great engine's reservoir had been serviced, two grand blasts of the whistle signaled the impending departure and then came the great "hough" and tons of steel began to heave forward, gathering momentum. At that tremendous resonance of leviathan's first sigh, Jimmy, Buller and Preacher would dexterously leap from the platform, catlike, and land upon the "cowcatcher"—the slanted ironwork that forms the very prow of the locomotive! Inches above the tracks and below the headlight the young men sat, or rather hung on. Later Jimmy wrote:

> What were the adventures of later years, compared with those summer-night rides on the [cowcatcher] of Number Six? There was happiness almost too great for the hearts of boyhood to contain. The deep toned whistle echoed among the sharp curves along the serpentine stretch of track skirting the hills, communicated the keen thrill of excitement from its own huge body to those of the twelve-

> and thirteen-year-olds who felt themselves a part of it. The head-light threw shafts of glory into the wooded land along the river; then, the curves passed, we felt sharp nudges from behind as the train gathered speed . . .
>
> A great part of our enjoyment came from being so close to the bosom of Mother Earth, which gave us the keen sense of traveling at enormous speed and with effortless power. All the odors of the summer night were ours: the cool dank fragrance of bottom lands along the river, mingled with that of skunk, one of the healthiest of all smells; the perfume of drying clover hay: the pungent odors of weeds and field flowers lying in swathes . . . [97]

On horse back or by carriage it was nearly a two day journey to travel the thirty-two miles from Colfax to Grinnell. Most of the boys in Colfax had never ventured so great a distance from home. Yet riding upon the fleet steel hoofs of Pegasus Number Six, Jimmy and his friends made the trek in less than one hour. Before the town clocks struck the bewitching hour of midnight the vagabonds dismounted from their iron horse to harmlessly prowl the empty streets of the sleepy town, careful to avoid the constable. Hall's favorite haunt was Grinnell College, seen by him for the first time illumined by moonlight. Scarcely could he then have realized the profound spell that was cast upon him by Grinnell campus, charmed by the light of stars and the greater light of learning. The *shade* of this love would ultimately direct his course far beyond confines of rail-spanned spaces.

Before the break of day, Hall, Sharpe, and Stahl would hearken to the siren call of the westbound train. In that growing light which hails the approach of dawn they perched atop the boxcar to better view the magnificent fields, forests and farms of Iowa. So as not to be seen disembarking at Colfax Station, they rode on until the freight train was subjugated by the steep Mitchellville grade. There the big engine slowed sufficiently for the three rascals to make their escape, returning to their homes to feign waking before the first direct rays of sun lightened their rooms.

Having completed many successful night rides to Grinnell, the boys graduated to longer day-journeys, sitting in open door box-cars, feet dangling and swaying in the summer air, viewing the ever changing vistas that greeted their eyes wondrously. Escapades of this sort, no matter how magical, by their very nature, cannot long endure. Jimmy wrote:

> Parents of those days should have known the value to boys of this kind of education, that "riding the rods" was not as hazardous at is seemed to be . . . [that such] was worth a month of geography lessons. But parents are often deficient in understanding a boy's point of view, and ours were bound to note absences, sometimes overnight because, in our love of travel, we journeyed too far. Furthermore, the great C.R.I. & P. Railroad System itself took notice of the fact, reported by various train officials, that three boys from a small town in central Iowa had become confirmed riders of trains. A letter was received by the 'Mayor, Colfax, Iowa,' reporting the matter. The identity of the boys was discovered and reported, in turn, to the parents, and there was an end to those wonderful journeys.[98]

As Jimmy matured his love of the arts increased. In his community were many families of Welch and African extraction who universally possessed the gift of song. Especially on cold winter days they gathered at H. G. Gould's clothing store where Hall worked. There, along with the Davis boys who managed the store, they would vocalize and harmonize in the warmth of stove-fire and friendship, singing such songs as "Oft in the Stilly Night," "Come Where the Lilies Bloom," "A Canadian Boat-Song," and "There's Music in the Air."

Hall continued writing, especially in verse. As a twelve year old he had posted on the woodshed wall this poem:

> Look to the northward, Stranger,
> Just over the barn roof, there.
> Have you in your travels seen
> A land more passing fair.[99]

These few lines foreshadowed his later life. However, as a high school graduate he re-wrote them as a parody for his younger brother Harvey. Jimmy had been selected to give the commencement oration of the Colfax High School Graduation Exercises held in the packed chapel of the Methodist Church. Writing and public speaking are two very different gifts. The former Hall embraced with vigor, the latter frightened him to death. As he sat upon the speaker's platform, awaiting the dreadful moment when he would stand before his peers and the seemingly infinite crowd of townspeople, his eyes scanned the pews for Harvey. His mother had *promised* Jimmy that she would keep Harvey sequestered far to the rear of the church so that the pint size scamp could not irritate, disturb, frustrate and annoy his big brother at the grand moment.

As the program advanced Bessie Wood played a violin solo of giddy notes that filled the air, Jimmy felt, with further anxiety. Next stood Hazel Swihart, whose flawless recitation was given with confidence and grace. The high school superintendent announced the oration to be given by Norman Hall and all eyes turned to the trembling graduate who rose hoping to follow the faultless examples of Bessie and Hazel in the grace and ease of public performance. He seemed to gather self-assurance until, of a sudden, his eyes met those of Harvey, who had miraculously appeared on the front row. Harvey, though not a poet of his own making, was completely familiar with his brother's woodshed writing and had on many occasions "quoted them for his own purposes." And Jimmy "had given him two or three bloody noses for this brotherly devotion." Harvey looked up at the distinguished speaker, knowing full well the power he then possessed to blank the mind of a brother, already in shock with stage fright, and began to mouth the words, "Look to the Northward, Stranger." Amidst all the scores of spectators, Jimmy's eyes could see only the little devil in the front pew, who did nothing further but wait in gleeful anticipation. The first line of Jimmy's address rolled mechanically from his mouth. The second line vanished from all memory! Silence filled the chapel—that terrible stillness pregnant with sympathy of parents and teachers and at the same time, that silence which seems enormously funny to peers, especially to kid brothers. One thought, and one alone, filtered through the depths of the *nothing* in Jimmy's mind and provoked his ire to "heroic effort"—he would not go down in "defeat before this imp of a kid brother." Hall raised his eyes gallantly and met those of the church janitor who stood at the rear of the building, and not allowing his gaze to stray whatever from this august person, he started his oration over. Victoriously he addressed the class of 1904 without further incident.

His father rewarded Jimmy's effort and graduation with a wonderful week-long trip, accompanied by no one, except his classmate, Elmer Black, to the great Exposition in St. Louis. Harvey was morose with jealousy, but Jimmy exacted further revenge when he left him at the kitchen door with this adaptation of the familiar poem:

> Look to the northward, Harvey!
> The dear old barn is there.
> All next week you can do my chores
> While I am at the Fair.[100]

After graduation Jimmy continued working at Gould's Clothing store in Colfax. His integrity had not escaped the notice of the store's owner. Mr. Gould had made his fortune in the cattle business and had a keen eye for good stock. One wintry day Gould paid a visit to his Colfax store and shaking the snow from his overcoat took a seat near the store furnace. In his kind, but commanding voice, he told Jimmy to leave his work for a while and take a seat beside him. After a bit of small talk, the familiarity of which puzzled Hall, Gould explained that he had purchased another clothing store in Belle Fourche and wanted Jimmy to be the store manager. Jimmy, who had not yet turned eighteen, was simply flabbergasted. Gould added to his astonishment, telling him that he intended on retiring in several years and would make it possible for Jimmy to own the store himself! He went on to say that Hall could pay for the store from the store's profit—and that Jimmy need not worry for the terms would not be demanding. Gould concluded his offer by telling Jimmy that he genuinely liked him, wanted to help him get a great start in life and make it possible for Hall to settle down in a fine Iowan town, get married and have a "thrivin' business" to support his family. Jimmy was overwhelmed by Gould's proposition and expressed sincere gratitude.

However, as the weeks passed he grew uneasy, for he felt he was too near the beginning of his life to be "settled for life." His reminiscence of boyhood nocturnal adventures on Number Six, walking in the moonlight shade across Grinnell campus, and particularly a singular memory where he had witnessed the Grinnell Men's Glee Club, marching with linked arms and singing robustly, filling the late night air with a wondrous feeling of brotherhood, made him realize that he could not accept security over *hope*. Ever since his early boyhood he had longed to *become*—something—something not yet defined in his own mind. He wanted to write like the great poets and authors. Not only did Jimmy want to be a writer, but he aspired to another intangible. The Grinnell Glee Club had been the catalyst for this desire—it was a conception, "an ideal conception of comradeship." He knew full well that these ambitions were impractical and vague.

To the astonishment of all, Jimmy declined the privilege of managing Gould's new store. Perhaps the most disappointed in this turn of events was his own father, who felt strongly that his son was passing over the opportunity of his life by not accepting Gould's generosity. Furthermore, he simply could not pay for his son's education. Jimmy, however, possessed an amazing confidence and though his ambitions were centered in developing his *mind*, his *hands* knew how to work. The same day he entered Grinnell College Jimmy found two jobs. The first was raking leaves and the second was peeling potatoes in a small downtown restaurant.

Hall found that he was ideally suited for college life. He found kindred spirits among classmates and teachers—men with whom he could discover and share the same truths. Professor Payne introduced Jimmy to Mathew Arnold and in particular his poem, *Sohrab and Rustum.* He told Jimmy that although he might be a little young for Arnold at the present, the day would come when he would want to read all of Arnold's works. Payne also recommended Tennyson's *The Idylls of the King* and *The Passing of Arthur.* From that moment, Hall declared, he "was lost to the world of reality." At every opportunity he read the soul building writings of the great poets. And when his body was busily engaged in earning his keep peeling potatoes, his mind was free to peruse the pages of eloquence he had stored there. Jimmy worked along side old Abbie, whose teeth had long decayed away, and whose voice was scarcely a whisper. Nonetheless she could peal four potatoes to Jimmy's one. The boss of Grinnell kitchen was a surly, loud, foul-mouthed oaf who delighted in berating Hall's lack of culinary aptitude. Yet the hours in the kitchen passed quickly and delightedly for scenes of grandeur rolled before his mind's eye continually, such as:

> So all day long the noise of battle rolled
> Among the mountains by the winter sea;
> Until King Arthur's Table, man by man,
> Had fallen in Lyonnesse about their lord,
> King Arthur. Then, because his wound was deep,
> The bold Sir Bedivere uplifted him,
> And bore him to a chapel nigh the field,
> A broken chancel with a broken cross,
> That stood on a dark strait of barren land:
> On one side lay the Ocean, and on one
> Lay a great water, and the moon was full.
> Then spake King Arthur to Sir Bedivere:
> 'The sequel of today unsoldiers all
> The goodliest fellowship of famous knights

> Whereof this world holds record. Such a sleep
> They sleep—the men I loved. I think that we
> Shall never more, at any future time,
> Delight our souls with talk of knightly deeds,
> Walking about the gardens and the halls
> Of Camelot, as in the days that were.[101]

Some of the greatest thoughts ever penned passed through the mind of Jimmy Hall. Each left an indelible imprint. As the poet Ella Wheeler Wilcox wrote, "I hold it true that thoughts are things, they're endowed with bodies and breath and wings . . ." James Hall had discovered these truths taught by John Ruskin. :

> Now books . . . have been written in all ages by their greatest men: - by great readers, great statesmen, and great thinkers. These are all at your choice; and life is short. You have heard as much before; - yet have you measured and mapped out this short life and its possibilities? Do you know, if you read this, that you cannot read that - that what you lose to-day you cannot gain to-morrow? Will you go and gossip with your housemaid, or your stable-boy, when you may talk with queens and kings; . . . when this eternal court is open to you, with its society, wide as the world, multitudinous as its days, the chosen, and the mighty, of every place and time?
>
> The place you desire [is] the place you fit yourself for, I must observe, this court of the past differs from all living aristocracy in this: —it is open to labor and to merit, but to nothing else. No wealth will bribe, no name overawe, no artifice deceive, the guardian of those Elysian gates. In the deep sense, no vile or vulgar person ever enters there. At the [portals]. . . there is but brief question: — "Do you deserve to enter? Pass. Do you ask to be the companion of nobles? Make yourself noble, and you shall be. Do you long for the conversation of the wise? Learn to understand it, and you shall hear it. But on other terms? — no. If you will not rise to us, we cannot stoop to you."[102]

Jimmy observed an interesting development in his character due to the association between *literature* and *life*; the former being a tremendous aid to the latter. Because his thoughts were pleasant and uplifted, despite his environs, there was a kind of transference of good will and tolerance to those with whom he worked. Instead of harboring ill feeling toward his boss who rebuked him daily, he actually grew to like him in a "left-handed" sort of way. He improved his abilities as a potato peeler, learning to leave "more and more of the potato intact" and finally increased his peeling speed to at least half that of old Abbie.

Jimmy tried out for the men's glee club and to his satisfaction was elected to fill a vacancy in the second-tenors. The combined men and women's glee clubs formed the vesper choir. Although Jimmy did not affiliate with a particular denomination he loved to worship through his singing in the Sunday vesper service. He had been raised in Colfax singing such religious folk songs as "When the Roll is Called Up Yonder," and "Leaning On Jesus." However, the hymns he sang at Grinnell seemed to Jimmy to be of a higher inspirational order and were to him "true spontaneous worship." He said that being a member of the glee club was his "heaven on earth." Hall, in his modesty, rarely revealed his own heart-felt faith. The hymns he revered spoke his avowal in the poetic form he most dearly loved. With sincerity he blended his voice with those of his friends singing these verses from George Matheson's *O, Love that Wilt Not Let Me Go:*

O Love that wilt not let me go,
I rest my weary soul in thee;
I give thee back the life I owe,
That in thine ocean depths its flow
May richer, fuller be.

O Light that followest all my way,
I yield my flickering torch to thee;
My heart restores its borrowed ray,

That in thy sunshine's blaze its day
May brighter, fairer be.

O Joy that seekest me through pain,
I cannot close my heart to thee;
I trace the rainbow through the rain,
And feel the promise is not vain,
That morn shall tearless be.

O Cross that liftest up my head,
I dare not ask to fly from thee;
I lay in dust life's glory dead,
And from the ground there blossoms red
Life that shall endless be.

Not many years hence, in the front-line trenches of World War, this prayer would find literal fulfillment. Hall would indeed trace the rainbow through the rain, would find the good amidst the ghastly. Courageously, and in the spirit of that brotherhood that is welded fast in battle fires, he did not flee his cross; but in the dirt and dust, blood-stained red, he persevered—a light to his comrades, and later through the power of his pen his words enlightened his own nation.

Again he lifted his voice with his fellows, singing these stanzas from Reginald Heber's *By Cool Siloam's Shady Rill:*

By cool Siloam's shady rill
How fair the lily grows!
How sweet the breath, beneath the hill,
Of Sharon's dewy rose!

Lo! such the child whose early feet
The paths of peace have trod,
Whose secret heart, with influence sweet,
Is upward drawn to God.

By cool Siloam's shady rill
The lily must decay;
The rose that blooms beneath the hill
Must shortly fade away.

And soon, too soon, the wintry hour
Of man's maturer age
Will shake the soul with sorrow's power
And stormy passion's rage.

O Thou Whose infant feet were found
Within Thy Father's shrine,
Whose years with changeless virtue crowned,
Were all alike divine.

Dependent on Thy bounteous breath,
We seek Thy grace alone,
In childhood, manhood, age, and death
To keep us still Thine own.

Jimmy sought to emulate the perfect Son of Peace who grew from grace to grace, the Only Begotten of the Father, who, from Child to Man, was crowned with changeless virtue and omnipotent divinity. Hall was devoted to peace and liberty, and this may appear contradictory (but it is not), as principles worth fighting for. Always, Jimmy sensed the brevity of mortality that like a flower springs forth in youth, blossoms in maturity, and all too soon fades with advancing age. These words teach that never is man self-sufficient—through all seasons of life he is dependent upon the bounteous breath of his Maker; and his prayer should ever be "To keep us still Thine own."

And finally Hall loved to sing Washington Gladden's *O Master, let me walk with Thee.*

O Master, let me walk with Thee,
In lowly paths of service free;
Tell me Thy secret; help me bear
The strain of toil, the fret of care.

Help me the slow of heart to move
By some clear, winning word of love;
Teach me the wayward feet to stay,
And guide them in the homeward way.

O Master, let me walk with Thee,
Before the taunting Pharisee;
Help me to bear the sting of spite,
The hate of men who hide Thy light.

The sore distrust of souls sincere
Who cannot read Thy judgments clear,
The dullness of the multitude,
Who dimly guess that Thou art good.

Teach me Thy patience; still with Thee
In closer, dearer, company,
In work that keeps faith sweet and strong,
In trust that triumphs over wrong.

In hope that sends a shining ray
Far down the future's broadening way,
In peace that only Thou canst give,
With Thee, O Master, let me live.

This hymn was also a harbinger of Hall's life. Soon after graduation Jimmy would make *service* his profession. He aspired to give guidance to the wayward and move those who were slow, wayward, and home-lost toward a greater good. Hall was to personally face the grim results of Pharisaic governments that were soon to thrust the nations into global conflict. There he would bear the sting of spite and see first hand the judgments of Heaven upon the faith-dulled multitudes of the world who only dimly perceived the goodness of God. Jimmy was to learn patience, as he had never known this virtue before, in war-labor. He would see the triumph of good over evil and was to experience that hope—whose rays penetrate the future, and prefigure the lasting peace found only in *living* eternally with the Master of our existence.

Jimmy returned home for summer vacation and spent many hours contemplating how he should spend the rest of his life. In youthful confidence he decided that he would roam the earth! He would first visit Somerset, Scotland where Coleridge had written his epic poem, *The Ancient Mariner.* Ultimately he planned to scale the Himalayas, swim in the lagoons of the islands of the Pacific, sail the Straits of Magellan and witness first hand the Northern Lights from the Arctic Circle. He determined to let nothing interfere with his wanderings. He would see the "glories of the earth," abide only for a short time in any particular place and always remain a stranger to those he met. Far away places beckoned his youthful spirit. He would be a traveler, a discoverer, a seeker of Shangri-La. It was a wonderful dream that would influence, but not direct his future.

Returning to school in the fall, Jimmy found a job working for two late-middle-age spinsters (known affectionately in Grinnell as the "Davis girls") who were both school principals. It wasn't long before Jimmy regarded them as maiden aunts and loved them as if they were indeed family. Extremely generous to their many dinner guests, the two delighted in fine food. This was reflected, as Jimmy delicately said, in their "amplitude of body." He took care of household chores, working as a gardener and a caretaker of their spacious residence. In his small, cozy room, when his time was his own, Hall enjoyed the poems of Shelley, Wordsworth, Keats and Francis Thompson.

Unfortunately, Jimmy did not enjoy the study of trigonometry nearly as much as his studies in literature. His failing grades in math forced him to enroll, the following summer, at the University of Chicago. There, he said, he experienced "the worst form of loneliness, the solitude of multitude." Attending school in Chicago was the antithesis of his experience at Grinnell—the city and the University seemed equally inhuman to Hall. However, he accomplished his goal and returned to Grinnell to complete his college education. One evening Jimmy rested from his studies on the south campus lawn, secluded somewhat by shrubbery. As he lay upon the grass, marveling at the wonders of the star-filled sky, he heard the voices of two of his professors. His interest peaked when he heard them discussing none other than himself. Stoops, Professor of Philosophy, said that Jimmy Hall was:

> . . . an example of the exasperating type of student—They seem to have the ability in the abstract . . . You hope it will crystallize so that you can see what it is composed of, but it remains in solution.

Professor Peck responded that for such types:

> Their promise is always better than their performance.[103]

The two continued conversing, discussing the purpose of liberal arts colleges and the practical pressures working against their survival. Professor Stoops then made a comment that Jimmy took sincerely to heart. Stoops said the purpose of liberal arts was to "teach young men and women that the bird in the bush is worth two in the hand." Rather than discouraging Hall, this critical observation empowered him. In fact it gave to Jimmy the name of his intangible quest—"The Pursuit of the Bird in the Bush." He would not attempt to capture the practical bird in hand—rather he would pursue the unseen, the elusive. In 1910 James Norman Hall graduated from Grinnell a bachelor of philosophy and was anxious to engage himself with vigor in this most unusual vocation.

CHAPTER 12

SERVICE AND SELF-DENIAL

O blessed Lord! how much I need
Thy light to guide me on my way!
So many hands, that, without heed,
Still touch thy wounds, and make them bleed! [104]

—HENRY WADSWORTH LONGFELLOW

THE APOSTLE PAUL ONCE SAID THAT "all things work together for good to them that love God."[105] Hall had learned more than trigonometry during his disillusioned stay in Chicago. Among the thousands on the great campus of the University of Chicago he had not found a single friend. This isolation and its commensurate unhappiness had, like most sufferings endured by the good and kind, produced a *beneficial* end in the character of Hall. A short time earlier he had dreamed of a future that was completely self-centered; albeit one which promised world-class adventure. He had imagined that he would roam the earth, always a stranger, always a *guest.* Hall wrote:

> The most valuable part of my education during this summer was the discovery of the slums of Chicago. At the University, Sunday was my one day off, and, although I sometimes visited the parks, art galleries and the like, *most* of the time was spent in wandering through those grim districts . . . It seemed necessary to do this, to atone for my ignorance of such places . . . [106]

The following summer Jimmy indeed commenced his earth wandering—but with a different purpose than that which had motivated his freshman daydreams. In London and Glasgow Jimmy saw that which was beautiful—the inspiration of his hero poets. He also saw the ant-hills reminiscent of the Chicago slums. The effect of these experiences, said Jimmy, awakened his "social consciousness." Paul also wrote, "When I was a child, I spake as a child, I understood as a child, I thought as a child: but when I became a man, I put away childish things." Hall was acutely aware that he was becoming a *man* and the delightful self-serving vagabond images of his youth were losing luster. A door was forever closing, he said, upon his childhood. He still aspired to adventure, however not as a guest, but as one who would *serve.*

Grinnell's Professor of Applied Christianity, Dr. Steiner, arranged for Jimmy to interview with C. C. Carstens, a former graduate of Hall's alma mater and the current Director of the Massachusetts Society for the Prevention of Cruelty to Children in Boston. Carsten was impressed with young Jimmy Hall and offered him an immediate position with the M.S.P.C.C. He accepted. Here was an opportunity, as Hall so modestly put it, "to be of some use."

Boston proved to nourish Jimmy in the two directions his life was taking. Life in the city provided invaluable experience into understanding humanity while Boston also fostered his literary aspirations. Hall could not believe his good fortune when he found lodging in the quaint home of elderly Mrs. Atherton at number 91 Pinckney Street, off Louisburg Square. His upper floor window looked down on the grand old brownstones, the cobblestone streets and the prestigious Square, where it is said the tradition of door-to-door Christmas caroling had its birth. This enchanting Square has been the home of the Vanderbilt and Heinz families, as well as authors such as Louisa May Alcott.

In Jimmy's mind Boston was more like the London of which Charles Dickens had written than the real London. Boston's twisted alleyways and quaint shops of red brick seemed right out

James Norman Hall
Photograph by Mrs. Lewis Chase
May 1916

of *The Old Curiosity Shop.* Although at times a little homesick for the open spaces of the Midwest, Hall loved his new life. Often he thought of how the shadows of Oliver Wendell Holmes and Henry Wadsworth Longfellow had fallen upon the same cobblestones over which he now trod. Indeed their ghosts seemed still to nobly haunt the colonial corridors through which Jimmy daily walked. Whenever leisure hours were his Hall would retreat to one of two places. In inclement weather or when the sun had set, he would retire to his wonderful room off Louisburg Square to read and to write. A fine day, however, found Jimmy seated on a particular park bench in Boston Common near Beacon Street. Many a book he read from cover to cover on that bench while enjoying, with the peripheral senses, the genial sea scented air and the quiet sounds of strollers upon the green.

The offices of the Massachusetts Society for the Prevention of Cruelty to Children were located in a building that had once been a palatial residence situated at 43 Mt. Vernon Street. The Street symbolically represented Jimmy's two-fold mission in Boston—not only was it home to the M.S.P.C.C. but also another stately mansion which housed The Atlantic Monthly, the periodical that published the poems of Longfellow in the 1870s and 80s. In the not distant future The Atlantic Monthly would publish a series of articles written by a new author from Colfax, Iowa. Upon completion the series would again be published as a hard-bound book, subtitled *The Adventures of an American in the British Army.*

In sharp contrast to Hall's residence and office were the dwellings in which he actually *worked.* Typically Jimmy would receive a case from Miss Butler, the complaint secretary of the M.S.P.C.C. He then left his office and walked south, along Tremont Street, Springfield Street and ultimately Ruggles Street. An incredible transformation occurred along this relatively short walk, becoming more pronounced as he progressed in the southerly direction. At first the buildings were only slightly less illustrious than those which lined Mt. Vernon. By the time he reached Ruggles Street, however, the buildings were horribly neglected and dilapidated. The grievances which Hall, and the other agents of the society, investigated mirrored these surroundings, and dealt with the harsh realities of the slums—"cases of beatings and maimings, incest, infanticide, poisoning, death by deliberate starvation" and so forth. Not all complaints were founded in truth and some situations of seeming neglect were in reality hardships cases. When the facts were known, Jimmy often felt tremendous empathy for the parent as well as the child. An unwed mother was not always a prostitute, but oft times a poor woman, discarded by her so called man, and possessed only meager job skills. Such a mother was unwilling to abandon her child and did the best she could to both *work* and *nurture.* Therefore, before the facts were known, it was extremely difficult for Jimmy to inform a parent that he had to investigate her for possible child abuse. However, there were reports of maltreatment to the society that proved to be understatements. Jimmy wrote:

> Sometimes the evidence in proof of neglect was evident at first glance—as in one case where I found a mother in a drunken stupor, lying upon the body of her two-weeks-old child which she had crushed to death, while another child, a little ghost of a famine and neglect, stared at her mother from a chair nearby.[107]

For James Hall, in his early twenties, the service he rendered in the rat infested tenements of Boston was an adventure in humanity. Having been raised in the purity of the country, and being by nature a man of innocence, abhorring guile, this experience was a baptism of fire. The effect of this work did not harden the poetic heart of Jimmy. Although he witnessed life, at times, in the most deplorable of circumstances and became a realist at facing *what is*, still he stayed true to his utopian quest—seeing what is, but seeking the ideal. The decadent and disgraceful is readily apparent and easily found, but even in conditions most grim *good* can found—by the seeker of th*e bird in the bush.*

Jimmy received a report accusing a Mrs. Moriarty "of being unfit to raise her three children because of lewd conduct [harboring] men." The compliant went on to denounce Mrs. Moriarty on the grounds that she often did not return to her apartment until the wee hours of the morning, leaving her likely illegitimate children unattended. However, when Jimmy met with the informer he began to have suspicions as to the informant's character—for she could not say enough good about herself or enough bad about her "riffraff" neighbors. She spoke in generalities and when Jimmy required her to focus on specifics she admitted knowing of only one male caller who came in the daytime. He was, it turned out, an Italian image-maker, a man who made effigies of those saints honored by devout Catholics. The complainant was, by her admission, a Protestant. She spiced up this harboring men allegation, saying:

> He stays with her for as long as an hour. She ain't buyin' plaster dolls fixed up to look like saints all that time. But don't you let on I made the complaint. She's an awful woman, and strong too. She might murder me.[108]

It appeared true that Mrs. Moriarty did keep late hours, for her room was on the floor directly above the accuser's. When

Jimmy asked if she had attempted to talk with her upstairs neighbor about these suspicions she responded abruptly that she would never speak to the likes of her, that she had a foul mouth and continually fought with other women in the tenements.

The building in which these women lived looked down upon a narrow courtyard. Sanitation was deplorable as there were no proper garbage receptacles. Clotheslines on pulleys crisscrossed the brick-paved yard while women, from open windows, yelled at one another, disputing "washing" rights. They shrieked in the many accents and languages of the immigrant, but, Hall observed, the Irish could out-yell the best of them. At that moment Mrs. Moriarty appeared at her window and:

> Hurled threats, curses, and anathemas so varied and so vividly pictorial that [Hall] marveled at her versatility . . . the words of the answering blasts seemed to burn the stagnant air.[109]

Somewhat timidly Jimmy climbed the stairs and knocked on the Irish woman's door. It opened revealing a middle-aged woman with graying hair, a strongly built frame, and possessing a "careworn face." Her Irish ire had her in a mood fit for skirmishing. Mrs. Moriarty was ready and willing to change fronts from clothes-line battle to fighting off bill collectors, which she supposed, was the occupation of the man whom she now faced. When Hall relieved her anxiety on that account she calmed a little and with the cordiality for which the Irish are also known, invited him to take a seat in her humble, but *clean* quarters. On a small shelf on the wall Jimmy noticed two little plaster-of-Paris statues of catholic saints. A four year old emerged from his bedroom, looked kindly at Jimmy, then at his mother. Hall could not help but notice the immediate affection by which the little boy was greeted. Here was a mother who obviously loved her son and he ran to her embrace. As she looked back at Jimmy her stern features softened and Hall saw an "honest Irish face." Although he had explained that he was not a "collector of dues" he had not yet announced his purpose or whom he represented. Sensing that despite her Irish flare, this woman was head and shoulders above her accuser, it was with great difficulty that Hall told Mrs. Moriarty that he was an agent for the M.S.P.C.C. and that he was required to investigate allegations that she was guilty of child abuse. She listened with "an air of ominous quiet," almost unable to comprehend the serious nature of the charges. Even in that day, a neglectful parent would lose custody, often permanently. Respectfully she listened until Hall had finished speaking. Then Mrs. Moriarty simply said:

> 'D'ye see anything amiss with my Timmy? Does he look like I starved him or abused him? And I've two more, studyin' their lessons at St. Joesph's School at the very minute. Don't I walk the floors of the courthouse on my knees, night after night, scrubbin' the marble steps after the dirty feet of them asleep in their beds that pays me ten dollars a week to house and feed three healthy, hungry boys? And don't I do it in spite of 'em, and pay me dues, up to three weeks ago when I was lamed past bearin', for a decent burial when I'm a worn-out old woman at rest in the peace of God? But I'm not that yet, blessed be Mary and Joseph that stands on the shelf above the stove where I've got a fine stew cookin' . . .[110]

The rest of Jimmy's investigation proved the truth of what she had said. She was employed at the courthouse and had been working on crippled knees. The police officer on the beat, knew Mrs. Moriarty well and spoke highly of her. Naturally, the officer explained she came home late for she scrubbed floors after hours. As for the Italian image maker, he was a fat jolly man who occupied the Moriarty children with stories to give their mother an hours rest. Her neighbors that knew her also held Mrs. Moriarty in high regard. True some women exchanged verbal volleys regarding the washing rights to the clotheslines, but when it came to her motherhood, they staunchly defended her character. Mrs. Moriarty *was* a Mrs., and her children had been born honorably. Her husband and their father had left his family, without support, two years previously. Even in this matter she honestly shouldered a portion of the blame, for she said, it was partly her fault as one who had "the divil's own temper." This trait once again surfaced when it occurred to Mrs. Moriarty to ask the identity of the "foul-mouthed" liar who had reported her to the Cruelty Society. Although required to keep the names of complainants anonymous, Jimmy sincerely wished he could have told her it was the "Old Hatchet-Face who lives just below you."

This was not the end of Jimmy's investigation. He tracked down Mr. Moriarty and hauled him into court. The judge ordered him to pay his wife twenty-four dollars a month in child support. This he readily agreed to do, "provided that he should not be compelled to return to her."

Of course, not all children that Hall worked with were as fortunate as Mrs. Moriarty's little ones. Working with families he learned more than ever the importance of parenthood and blood ties—and how vital it was, when possible, to preserve the family. One of his co-workers told him:

> Take the kind of children we have to do with: there ain't one in a hundred that wouldn't ruther be in his own home, no matter how bad it is, than be in any Home, no matter how good it is.

Jimmy's own experience bore this out. He wrote:

> More than once I had a case before Judge Baker, in the Juvenile Court, in which the evidence showed the most gross and palpable neglect, moral and physical, on the part of fathers and mothers who were a disgrace to parenthood. And yet, when the moment came to decide what was to be done with the children, there was no doubt as to their wishes; they wanted to stay with the parents. I realize that this is no valid reason for permitting them to remain. Nevertheless, when the bonds of love between parents and children were unmistakable, it was disturbing, to say the least, to see them broken.[111]

There were other factors which Jimmy had to deal with as a social worker. Domestic violence has always been of the explosive, extremely dangerous order. The moment he announced his credentials Hall was often in harm's way. Another Irishwoman, a Mrs. O'Brien, an ugly hag, large and powerful, responded to Jimmy's investigation by brandishing a huge butcher-knife. She chased Jimmy round and round the table in her kitchen. He was saved only because she was drunk at the time and not as dexterous as she would have otherwise been. He made his life-saving escape when O'Brien tripped, but Hall was not free from peril until he had dodged the missiles that she threw forcefully at his head as he made his hasty retreat out the entryway below.

There were other, more subtle threats, the handsome young society agent faced. Of these Jimmy wrote:

> Not all mothers of neglected children were hideous, middle-aged creatures. Some were extremely attractive, not spiritually or intellectually of course, but physically. Now and then I was assigned to cases that should have gone to Miss O'Rourke or Miss Marsters . . . Delinquent mothers may be far more dangerous and aggressive than delinquent girls; at least, that was my guess, having confronted a fair number of them. They were never bothered by moral scruples. Their attempts to contribute to the moral delinquency of an agent of the M.S.P.C.C. sent out to investigate them for the same offense were, sometimes, of so bold a nature that the only possible course of action was to *flee.* At least, that is what I would do. Fortunately, I survived four years' experience as an agent of the M.S.P.C.C. without becoming a 'case' to be investigated rather than the investigator of the case; but when I recall the manner in which some of the temptations were offered, I wonder that I had the strength of character to resist them. Perhaps I flatter myself in calling it that. It may have been fear, and a consciousness of the everlasting shame that would be mine, if I were to fall.[112]

Jimmy did not claim youthful perfection. On the contrary, Hall often in his autobiographical writing emphasized his failings over his virtues. But in dealings of this nature he found it expedient to follow the example of Joseph, son of Israel, who when tempted by Potiphar's wife said to her, "How then can I do this great wickedness?" Nevertheless, she persisted until finally the seductress corned him alone. So bold was the wife of Potiphar in this sexual advance that there was nothing that young Joseph could say to dissuade her. The record simply states that Joseph, "fled, and got him out." Hesitation is always fatal in such circumstances. A man cannot hope to prevail if he attempts to arbitrate with his seducer or his conscience. A man, who desires to be free of shame, must flee or fall.

Hall writes that another Grinnell Vesper Choir hymn came into his mind on such occasions. It was *Dear Lord and Father of Mankind,* by John Greenleaf Whittier.

Dear Lord and Father of mankind,
Forgive our foolish ways;
Reclothe us in our rightful mind,
In purer lives Thy service find,
In deeper reverence, praise.

In simple trust like theirs who heard,
Beside the Syrian sea,
The gracious calling of the Lord,
Let us, like them, without a word,
Rise up and follow Thee.

O Sabbath rest by Galilee,
O calm of hills above,
Where Jesus knelt to share with Thee
The silence of eternity,
Interpreted by love!

With that deep hush subduing all
Our words and works that drown
The tender whisper of Thy call,
As noiseless let Thy blessing fall
As fell Thy manna down.

Drop Thy still dews of quietness,
Till all our strivings cease;
Take from our souls the strain and stress,
And let our ordered lives confess
The beauty of Thy peace.

Breathe through the heats of our desire
Thy coolness and Thy balm;
Let sense be dumb, let flesh retire;
Speak through the earthquake, wind, and fire,
O still, small voice of calm.

Jimmy worked for the M.S.P.C.C. until 1914. He realized how intently he had become involved in this work and how completely it had consumed the lives of the dedicated social workers with whom he associated. If he stayed this would soon be his life, as it was theirs. Hall knew that the time he had given to the society was extremely worthwhile but he also believed there something else in his future. This something was still as intangible as ever. His salary had been raised to one hundred dollars a month—a very good income for the time. However, Jimmy had already demonstrated by refusing the generous offer from the clothier, Mr. Gould, that he was not money-motivated. What should he do? First he would return home to Colfax for a short season. Then—then he decided, he would herd sheep in Montana.

CHAPTER 13

THE END OF AN INDIAN SUMMER

How am I to give a really vivid picture of trench life as I saw it for the first time? I watched the rockets rising from the German lines, watched them burst into points of light, over the devastated strip of country called "No-Man's-Land" and drift slowly down. The desolate landscape emerged from the gloom and receded again, like a series of pictures thrown upon a screen. All of this was so new, so terrible, I doubted its reality. Indeed, I doubted my own identity, as one does at times when brought face to face with some experiences which cannot be compared with past experiences or even measured by them. [113]

—JAMES NORMAN HALL

BACK IN COLFAX LITTLE HAD CHANGED in four years except the outhouse was gone from behind the Hall home and an upstairs room had been converted into a bathroom. Jimmy's dad apologized "for having gone so thoroughly 'modern.' "

Jimmy had corresponded with an old classmate who had become the editor of the *Daily Star* in Miles City, Montana. His friend, appropriately named Chester, had written back telling Hall there were indeed openings for shepherds. In fact, Chester explained, "At this moment a partner in one of the big sheep outfits is lying in the hospital here, hovering between life and death as the result of a punctured chest from a Luger 38 in a fight with a homesteader over a water hole." Chester went on to say that a shepherd could expect to earn $50.00 per month and had absolutely no chance of spending a thin dime of that money. Furthermore it was a solitary life (with the exception of meeting an occasional homesteader at the water hole), perfect for endless reading and entertaining one's self. What an opportunity! Jimmy thought. He imagined himself in the cozy shepherd's wagon on long blustery winter nights, by the warm stove with his books and writing materials. He reasoned that such an adventure would provide ample material to compose *The Memoirs of a Sheepherder* and net him six hundred dollars in a year.

When Jimmy met with Professor Payne and told him of his plans to herd sheep in Montana, the professor was simply incredulous—how could Hall even consider such a proposition? He told Jimmy that he admired his romantic tendencies. At the same time he should guard himself against the totally unrealistic, for this absurd plan would lead nowhere. Rather, his old teacher counseled, he should himself become a teacher. Payne told Jimmy that he had the ability to inspire young people and would make an outstanding shepherd of students.

Hall knew there was wisdom in his former professor's advice. However, the idea of being a teacher terrified him. He knew what would happen, just as it did when he gave the commencement address at his high school graduation—his mind would go blank. Well if sheep herding out west was ridiculous, what was he to do? He feared that by staying in Iowa he "might yield to Professor Payne's plea to enter the teaching profession." And so in May of 1914 he left, or rather fled to England.

Jimmy's object in going to Great Britain was to jump start a literary career—to give himself three months and prove to himself that he had commercial ability. He felt that if he could visit the places where the great English poets had composed their masterpieces it would aid in his own writing. Write he did; sell his manuscripts he did not.

Jimmy also wanted to visit personally the greatest living author of his time—Joseph Conrad. One day Hall bicycled south of London to Capel House in Kent. He found Conrad's house and stood for some time staring at the home of the illustrious writer. On a sudden he straddled his bike and rode away as fast as he could. He wondered, what would have been the result of an actual visit had he only mustered the courage to ring the door bell? In his mind's eye he could see Conrad patiently waiting to hear Jimmy's faltering attempt to speak, thinking, "I believe this young man has something to tell me, if only he can get it out."

As Jimmy peddled north he was struck by the incredible beauty of the countryside and the British way of living. He wrote:

> I caught glimpses of family groups having afternoon tea in their gardens, of others looking on at cricket matches, or fishing from the grassy banks of streams, or strolling through the fields, or floating dreamily along in punts on gently winding rivers. It seemed to me that I was passing through an earthly paradise. Here were people who had long since learned the art of living; who kept broad margins of leisure around their lives. Business in England seemed to be an avocation rather than the be-all and end-all of existence . . . I had not the faintest premonition that I was enjoying with all England the last days of the Indian summer of an age that was all but gone.[114]

It was a season full of wonder for Jimmy Hall. From May through the first week in August, 1914, he read, cycled from village to village, and wrote. Traveling he kept to himself and did not disturb his tranquility of mind with newspapers or discussions of current events.

One perfect evening, after pedaling all the day, he found a haven of tremendous comfort and peace in the hamlet of Beddgelert in northwest Wales. He stayed at Llewellyn's Cottage, an inn of tremendous antiquity. Hunger can be a great feeling when it has been earned through strenuous physical activity and one knows that he is soon to dine sumptuously. As Llewellyn's only guest he was afforded noble hospitality and was provided a generous supper of roast spring lamb with fresh greens and vegetables. As the fading light of day shimmered through the leaded windowpanes of his ancient room, he read *Wild Wales: Its People,*

Language and Scenery. Jimmy was still in pursuit of the bird in the bush, at his leisure, and he found the journey immensely satisfying. He was young and free, with no obligations or demands on his time; with meager financial demands and therefore few financial constraints, living a life he had dreamed of living. The season, the day, and now the evening had been idyllic. For Jimmy Hall, that night ended his quiescent world—for *years* to come. Peace had already been taken from the earth, but in Jimmy's isolation he knew it not. Hall would be awakened in the dawning day to a higher quest, still in search of the unseen, but a far more glorious intangible than his student mind had been capable of imagining.

At first light Hall began an ascent up Mt. Snowdon to view the new day from its summit. However, clouds had set in and before he had gone far, a hard rain fell. The clarity of the preceding day, and this morning's obscurity were for Jimmy a harbinger. His plans frustrated, Hall returned to the inn where he observed a group of uniformed men at the post office. He struck up a casual conversation with one soldier, asking if he was stationed nearby. No, was the reply. The soldier was a reservist, called into action, he said, because of the war. Jimmy's reaction was one of shock. He said:

> War? What war?

The soldier replied in disbelief.

> Where have you been? Don't you know that England, France and Russia are at war with Germany and Austria?[115]

Jimmy's immediate response to this incredible news would have astonished Professor Payne. Who, when discouraging Hall from his Montana scheme, had frankly told him: "You think too much about yourself." The day after Jimmy had learned of the Great War he sold his bicycle and caught the next train to London. Hall never considered that he was heroic by nature. At this critical moment in his life, upon which everything else would depend, possibly including life itself, he was not resolute. Jimmy's feelings were mixed. He yearned for the safety and comfort of home. At the same time he felt something akin to the spirit of adventure—that nebulous heart swelling when a man feels the promptings to join a crusade which may demand of him the ultimate sacrifice. Early one morning Jimmy found himself in a long recruiting line at Scotland Yard. He was in no hurry for the line to advance. At length he approached the line's front and could see the desk of the recruiting sergeant. He left the line.

Great acts of courage may often be divided into many small, hesitant steps. Self-doubt and diverse emotions are not pusillanimous. A coward is one who looks for an escape when he is compelled to advance in the threatening storm. A hero *in the making* is a man who searches his soul and finds the will to press forward into great danger, particularly in the absence of edictal command.

The following morning Hall again joined the seemingly endless line of volunteers. All of these men had the look of vagrants, for they wore their worst clothes, knowing that these would soon be discarded for rags and exchanged for army uniforms. There was symbolism in this act—replacing the base with the noble. The appearance of these masses of men in tatters gave birth to their popular name—*Kitchener's Mob*—so named after Horatio Herbert Kitchener. Lord Kitchener was England's Secretary of State for War at the outbreak of WWI. He quickly increased the army from twenty to seventy divisions establishing the greatest volunteer army in history consisting of some three million soldiers. Under his direction this *mob* of men was molded into a magnificent fighting machine.

Jimmy again eyed the decreasing numbers in front of him. In his pocket was his steamship ticket for America. When only a few recruits separated him from the Rubicon just ahead, he again withdrew. A third time he joined the line and when he came face to face with the recruiting sergeant his fears vanished and he unhesitatingly moved forward when the officer barked, "Now, then, you! Step along! Jimmy wrote:

> Was it an act of weakness, a want of character, evidenced by my inability to say no? Or was it the blood of military forebears asserting itself after many years of inanition? . . . I was the grandson of my Civil War grandfather, and the worthy descendant of stalwart warriors of a yet earlier period.[116]

James Norman Hall was probably the first American to join the British Army. That this is so is evident by the reaction of the recruiting officers to his frank admission that he was a citizen of the United States. The British administrators did not know how to handle such a situation. After consulting one another, they informed Jimmy he would be permitted to enlist—if he would just *say* that he was an Englishman. He knew at that moment that here was an honorable way to refuse enlistment. Already he had envisioned nightmares of blood-soaked battlefields, of fatigue and fevers, of pain-filled years as a cripple. No sooner had this temptation to abandon his resolve entered his mind than he rejected it. Hall vowed to the officers that although he was an American he was placing himself in subjection to the British Crown and with an oath would "bear true allegiance to the Union Jack." Jimmy left the parade grounds as Private J. N. Hall, 9th Battalion, Royal Fusiliers.

Initially, as Hall considered his new comrades he concluded that he had little in common with these Brits. Although his fellow soldiers-in-training welcomed Hall into their ranks, fondly calling him "Jamie the Yank," Jimmy had difficulty accepting the English class system that went beyond military subservience. He wrote:

> I had to accept, for convenience sake, the fact of my social inferiority. Centuries of army tradition demanded it; and I discovered that it is absolutely futile for one inconsequential American to rebel against the unshakable fortress of English tradition . . . my comrades were used to clear-cut class distinctions in civilian life. It

> made little difference to them that some of our officers were recruits as raw as were we ourselves.[117]

When Hall attempted to even discuss such a system his comrades promptly rebuked him with statements like:

> Look 'ere! Ain't a gentleman a gentleman? I'm arskin' you, ain't 'e?

When Jimmy confided to his peers that he would enjoy chatting or sharing a joke with the officers they responded incredulously:

> Don't be a bloomin' ijut! They could jolly well 'ang you fer that!

For seven months, from the crack of dawn until the setting of the sun, the new recruits of the Royal Fusiliers were conditioned and trained for trench combat. The physical and emotional demands placed on these men, who were about to fight the first "modern" war, were truly exhaustive. Jimmy's leisure hours and days were lost luxuries. The hour between Reveille and breakfast was given to Swedish drill—"a system of gymnastics which brought every lazy and disused muscle into play." The rest of the day was given to "musketry practice," followed by company and battalion drills, marches, parades, boxing and wrestling. Taps sounded at exactly at 9:00 p.m. The daily routine was often altered, the men engaging in lengthy marches, field maneuvers, and bayonet charges. War games were truly exciting and consisted of twenty thousand men on each side employing all aspects of a real battle including infantry, air support, artillery and cavalry. After the strenuous activities of the day were finished, the men marched back to their barracks in cadence to:

> Left! Right! Left! Right!
> Why did I join the army?
> Oh! Why did I ever join Kitchener's Mob?
> Lor Lummy! I must 'ave been balmy![118]

However, despite the complaining tones of drill songs, the men grew *happier* as their training progressed. They all knew they were soon to face the enemy and their success in this life and death struggle for victory would depend entirely on one another. Bonds of brotherhood were being forged and in the heat of vigorous preparation, individual prejudices fell as dross from each unifying weld. Jimmy wrote:

> The friendships I formed . . . and the memories of them still are beyond price to me . . .[119]
>
> Plenty of hard work in the open air brought great and welcome changes. The men talked of their food, anticipated it with a zest which came from realizing, for the first time, the joy of being genuinely hungry. They watched their muscles harden with the satisfaction known to every normal man when he is becoming physically efficient. Food, exercise, and rest, taken in wholesome quantities and at regular intervals, were having the usual excellent results. For my own part, I had never before been in such splendid health . . . my fellow [soldiers] were living, really living, for the first time. They had never before known what it means to be radiantly, buoyantly healthy.[120]

As their bodies hardened so did standards of discipline. At first allowances were made for "civilian frailties." Soon the men adhered to a code of conduct that brought the order of a precise parade into their individual lives. After two more months of specialty training (Hall's was given to machine gunnery) Lord Kitchener ordered Hall and his comrades to battle. Accompanying their orders each man was given the following letter:

> You are ordered abroad as a soldier of the King to help our French comrades against the invasion of a common enemy. You have to perform a task which will need your courage, your energy, your patience. Remember that the honor of the British Army depends upon your individual conduct. It will be your duty not only to set an example of discipline and perfect steadiness under fire, but

> also to maintain the most friendly relations with those whom you are helping in this struggle . . . you can do your own country no better service than in showing yourself, in France and Belgium, in the true character of a British soldier.
>
> Be invariably courteous, considerate, and kind. Never do anything likely to injure or destroy property, and always look upon looting as a disgraceful act . . . Your duty cannot be done unless your health is sound. So keep constantly on your guard against any excesses. In this new experience you may find temptations both in wine and women. You must entirely resist both temptations, and while treating all women with perfect courtesy, you should avoid any intimacy.
>
> Do your duty bravely.
> Fear God.
> Honor the King.
>
> Kitchener,
> Field-Marshal.[121]

It is most interesting that the last exhortation which Lord Kitchener gave his troops was not regarding valor on the battlefield, but rather to be valorous in virtue! The result of Kitchener's leadership was recorded by Hall when he wrote:

> In France, [the conduct of British troops] has been splendid throughout. During six months in the trenches I saw but two instances of drunkenness. Although I witnessed nearly everything which took place in my own battalion, and heard the general gossip of many others, never did I see or hear of a woman treated otherwise than courteously. Neither did I see or hear of any instances of looting or petty pilfering from the civilian inhabitants . . . Active service as we found it was by no means free from temptations. The admirable restraint of most of the men in the face of them was a fine thing to see.[122]

In our day, when scandals are loudly touted by a prurient and sensationalistic media, who with a broad brush attempt to color the character of our military men and women, many Americans may be led to erroneously believe that our soldiers are trained to be blindly and barbarically obedient to their superior officers. True there have been perverse individuals who, when given the opportunity, exercise dominion unjustly and sometimes wickedly —more often than not such are recompensed by court-marshal. However, the shining examples set by hundreds of thousands of our military professionals reflect standards of high moral training.[iv]

[iv] In the summer of 2004, as an honorary commander of the 388th Fighter Wing, the author was invited to tour the U.S. Air Force Academy in Colorado Springs. Along with civic leader Mel Kemp and other officials, I met with Brigadier General Johnny A. Weida, Commander of the Academy. Reminiscent of Lord Kitchener, General Weida, in his briefing to us, stressed personal conduct above all else in the Air Force training of cadets. Moral development is foundational to manhood and will never be outdated. He provided us with a pamphlet entitled *Officer Development System—Building Leaders of Character.* In this document, directly after the airman's Oath of Office, the Air Force Core Values are defined, in part, as follows:

> ***Integrity*** is the willingness to do what is right even when no one is looking. It provides our 'moral compass'—the inner voice of self-control; the basis for trust. *Integrity* is the single most important part of your character and forms the very foundation of the military profession. Elements of this first core value are:
> ***Courage.*** A person of integrity possesses moral courage and does what is right regardless of personal cost.
> ***Honesty.*** . . . one's word is binding.
> ***Responsibility.*** Airmen acknowledge their duties and take responsibility for their own successes or failures.
> ***Accountability.*** No person of integrity tries to shift the blame to others or take credit for another's work.
> ***Justice.*** A person of integrity treats all people fairly and with respect, regardless of gender, race, ethnicity, or religion.
> ***Openness.*** Airmen . . . value candor as a mark of loyalty, even when offering dissenting opinions or bearing bad news.
> ***Self Respect.*** Airmen respect themselves as professionals and as human beings . . . [they] behave in a manner that brings credit upon themselves, their organization, and the profession of arms.
> ***Humility.*** Airmen comprehend the awesome task of defending the Constitution of the United States of America and realize they cannot do it alone. While airmen should be proud, they should be neither arrogant nor boastful.

Kitchener admonished his men to "fear God." Today's Air Force instructs its airmen to foster, through integrity, their "'moral compass'—the inner voice of self-control." And in the "Oath of Office" each airman vows: ". . . I will well and faithfully discharge the duties of the office upon which I am about to enter. So help me God." It is impossible, under the extreme circumstances of war, for a soldier who relies solely upon his own intelligence to make choices, with life and death consequences, to always act appropriately—*unless,* he combines his military training with a God fearing conscience. Within each human being there is placed from infancy an "inner voice" that whispers promptings to

---

Honor. A person of integrity upholds the traditions of sacrifice, courage, and success that mark Air Force heritage. Airmen strive to adhere to what is right, noble, and fair.

Service before Self . . . to obey *lawful* orders and to accomplish the mission despite personal sacrifice. This Service core value includes:

Duty. . . . Airmen have a duty to fulfill the unit's mission . . . They follow rules unless there is a clear operational, legal, or moral reason to refuse or deviate.

Respect for Others. Airmen always act with the knowledge that all persons possess a fundamental worth as human beings.

Self-Discipline. Air Force leaders must act with confidence and cannot indulge themselves in self-pity, discouragement, anger, frustration, or defeatism.

Self-Control. Airmen *must* refrain from exhibiting behavior and/or expressing attitudes that would bring discredit upon themselves, the Air Force or the United States. *This especially includes exercising control over anger, sexual conduct, use of alcohol, and other discrediting or criminal behavior.* (Italics added)

Tolerance. Military professionals must remember that religion and other personal choices are a matter of individual conscience.

Loyalty. Airmen should be loyal to their leaders, fellow airmen, the Air Force and their country. American military professionals must demonstrate allegiance to the Constitution and loyalty to the chain of command, especially to the President and the Secretary of Defense, regardless of political affiliation.

Excellence in All We Do challenges you to do your best at all times with all tasks . . . by elevating excellence to a core value, we, as an institution are saying that our mission is so vital to our nation's security that achieving excellence is imperative. As warriors, we know this to be true. Excellence is not a luxury, but rather a fundament element of our daily performance that allows us to accomplish our mission safely and effectively. Without a true commitment to excellence we put lives in jeopardy.

Warrior Spirit. . . . all officers must embody the warrior spirit; tough-mindedness, tireless motivation, an unceasing vigilance, and a willingness to sacrifice their own lives for the country if necessary. While always preferring peace to war, officers hone their skills to ensure the Air Force is every ready to 'fly, fight and win.

do right and warns against error. Like the mechanical compass, it is a delicate instrument and may be easily damaged by neglect. Disobedience to this still, small voice within mutes the whisperings—silences the oracle. We can be taught correct principles, such as those in the *Officer Development System*, that when put into practice by the individual, frees the "moral compass" to provide direction in every aspect of life, especially in the critical moment when life itself hangs in the balance. John, the Apostle, testified of the universality of the inner compass. He wrote:

> There was a man sent from God, whose name [was] John. The same came for a witness, to bear witness of the Light, that all [men] through him might believe . . . [That] was the true Light, which lighteth every man that cometh into the world.[123]

Every man and woman born into this world is given *Light*—a portion of divine intelligence from the Creator, the Light Giver, the Law Giver. Another ancient prophet entitled our conscience *"the light of Christ."* He told us that if we do not judge by that Light, our judgment will be erroneous; furthermore the faulty scale of our own making will be the very scale upon which our deeds shall be weighed in the final balance of eternal judgment. Therefore, he stated, for our sake and for the sake of our fellowman, we must probe deeply this internal light, for there is right and wrong, there is in reality good and evil. It is also of extreme interest to know that this ancient prophet was the last survivor of his race—all of his kindred were exterminated by war.

> . . . ye know the light by which ye may judge, which light is the light of Christ, see that ye do not judge wrongfully; for with that same judgment which ye judge ye shall also be judged . . . search diligently in the light of Christ that ye may know good from evil.[124]

In the 1990s, as part of a relief team of five hundred volunteers, the author assisted victims of devastating tornados in northern Georgia. There had been a tremendous loss of life and property. On the beautiful morning that followed the night of terror, we drove inside the disaster perimeter. The contrast was startling between profound normality and utter destruction. On one side of a street stood elegant homes with manicured lawns; yet on the other side of the same street homes had been reduced to skeletal ruins, imploded by bomb force winds.

Such was the condition of France in 1915 when James Norman Hall arrived on her shores as a soldier in Kitchener's Mob. Jimmy and his fellows traveled on a troop transport through the quiescent and quaint villages of Normandy. It was springtime and the train windows were opened to the "country fragrant with the scent of apple blossoms." Children played in the fields and towns, waving heartily to the soldiers as they swiftly passed. The only suggestion of the awful storm was farm workers, who pausing to rest upon their hoes, silently watched the army train pass. These were not as exuberant as the children, for they were all women and girls—and the sight of soldiers was a melancholy reminder of their own war-lost men.

Kitchener's soldiers disembarked from the railway twenty-five miles from the firing line of the front. They marched from the depot through a small village of charming well-kept homes with spring flowers blooming from window boxes, down a poplar-lined road and past magnificent fields painted with verdure of new crops. Again, it was the absence of an essential element that was the precursor to the desolation they were soon to see. Jimmy wrote:

> It was a land swept bare of all its fine young manhood . . . Those who were left went about their work silently and joylessly. When we asked of the men, we received, always, the same quiet, courteous reply: "À la guerre[v], monsieur."[125]

[v] Translation: "Gone to war, sir."

Marching forward they began to hear the first low groans of thunder that signaled the approaching vortex of war. It took one day to march across the street from normalcy to a land obliterated. Gone were the forests and fields, green replaced by brown and gray, shattered remnants of villages, profiled ruins. This was a surreal world of ammunition and artillery depots, endless columns of khaki-clad men, horse drawn Red Cross carts, countless supply wagons, and field-kitchens that bounced along the cobbles filling the air with the scent of boiling caldrons.

After nightfall this fledgling army, "the meekest of undergraduates," marched in platoons, at intervals of one hundred paces, into the "fire zone." Hall wrote:

> As we came within the range of rifle fire, we again changed our formation, and marched in single file . . . The sharp *crack! crack!* of small arms now sounded with vicious and ominous distinctness. We heard the melancholy song of the ricochets and spent bullets as they whirled in a wide arc, high over our heads, and occasionally the less pleasing *phtt! phtt!* of those speeding straight from the muzzle of a German rifle . . . We wound in and out of what appeared in the darkness to be a hopeless labyrinth of earthworks. Cross-streets and alleys led off in every direction. All along the way we had glimpses of dugouts lighted by candles, the doorways carefully concealed with blankets or pieces of old sacking. Groups of [soldiers] were boiling tea or frying bacon over little stoves made of iron buckets or biscuit tins.
>
> I marveled at the skill of our trench guide who went confidently on in the darkness, with scarcely a pause. At length, after a winding zigzag journey, we arrived at our trench.[126]

When day dawned Jimmy was awed by the world he had entered. The trench works formed a virtual city of thousands. The thoroughfares, like a giant mosaic, ran fifteen feet, then turned perpendicular about a centerpiece of six square feet of solid ground, then continued onward for another fifteen feet where the pattern was repeated for scores of miles. The firing trench lay forty-five feet beyond this traveling trench. There were underground passages, also miles long, linking lateral trenches. Off from these and from the thoroughfare lay incredible dugouts serving variously as sleeping quarters, lavatories, field clinics for preliminary treatment of the wounded, and kitchens. The quarters for enlisted men and N.C.O.s were all of equal dimensions and were built with wooden walls and floors. Ceilings of corrugated iron were covered with four feet of earth. Accommodations for officers were more spacious. The officer's mess was "a café de luxe" with glass panels in the door, a fine stove and wooden dining tables. Outside the dugouts, trench walls were held in place by fine-mesh wire. Boardwalks, equipped with drains, were laid out over the trench floors. It was a spectacle of engineering, amazingly clean and orderly. Jimmy was yet to experience trench living when the rain fell so hard that the drains overflowed and turned the trenches into canals of mud.

Hall marveled how orders were quietly passed from "sentry to sentry, with the speed of a man running." From the signaling corps ran mazes of telephone wire, connecting outposts with headquarters. The protocol of traversing the trenches was explained to Hall in this manner: "Outgoin' troops 'as the right o' way. They ain't 'ad no rest, an' dead beat fer sleep. Incomin' troops is fresh, an' they stands to one side to let the others pass." Beyond the firing trench lay the "entanglements"—barbed wire twisted between firmly set posts fifty feet in width. This jumbled maze was impossible for a man under fire to get through, even with cutters. There were sections of this fencing that could be opened to one side from which attacks could be launched. The German fortifications were patterned after a similar manner. Deadlock continued month after month with little movement along the front lines of the war. However, every day was an adventure in sulfur and shrapnel. Each morning sky hailed tons of bullets and bombs. Soon Hall and his comrades forgot that they had "ever known the security of civilian life." Each new day was a wonder to the soldiers that they were still alive. Hall wrote:

> We lived without comforts which formerly we had regarded as absolutely essential. We lived a life so crude and rough that our army experiences in England seemed Utopian by comparison. But we throve splendidly. A government, paternalistic in its solicitude for our welfare, had schooled our bodies to withstand hardships and to endure privations . . . the indescribable horrors of modern warfare at its worst . . . [127]

Hall's duty was one of the most dangerous in trench warfare. Under the cover of darkness he and other machine gunners crawled out of their trenches and stealthy maneuvered through the openings in the British entanglements onto "No-Mans-Land." At predetermined positions they then rendezvoused with men from "listening patrols," who had previously discovered the location of German working parties. The enemy, as a whole, never slept and always worked to advance their position or repair damages of the previous day's battle. The machine gunners then set their sights upon the coordinates given and delivered heavy fire at five hundred rounds per minute. The moment they ceased fire, Jimmy said, "the exciting part of our work began." Hall and his comrades changed positions as quickly as terrain and cover

James N. Hall, 9th Battalion, Royal Fusiliers, Machine Gunner

allowed. A moment's hesitation meant certain death. For what always followed was an immediate deluge of return rifle fire from hundreds of angry Germans. Two or three minutes later German artillery commenced firing upon the allied machine gunners, seeking their absolute destruction. On their bellies and knees Jimmy and the other fusiliers made their way homeward over open ground. When the rain of explosions split the dirt near their position, they lay flat on their faces "listening to the deafening explosions and the vicious whistling of flying shrapnel."

To be wounded on such a patrol in "No-Man's-Land," or upon the same desolate soil during an infantry attack was an ordeal from hell. Jimmy wrote of one such sufferer:

> One plucky Englishman was discovered about fifty yards in front of our trench. He was waving a bit of rag tied to the handle of his trenching tool. Stretcher-bearers ran out under fire and brought him in. He had been badly wounded in the foot when his company was advancing up the slope fifteen hundred yards away. He had not been seen by his comrades when they were forced to retire and had been left with many other dead and wounded, far from the possibility of help by friends. He had bandaged his foot with his first-aid dressing and had started crawling back, a few yards at a time. He secured food and water from the haversacks and water bottles of dead comrades and after a week of painful creeping, reached our lines.[128]

It was not only in "No-Man's-Land" that life was lost. The trenches were no protection from heavy bombardment. Even the dugouts, except those few that were twelve to fifteen feet below the surface, were easily penetrated from a direct hit. A seemingly insignificant event oft times made a fatal difference. Jimmy and six of his C Company gun team were in a surface dugout making tea. Their sector was quiet and only two of their company stood as sentries on the firing line by their silent gun. One sentry, Richard McHard, asked Jimmy to trade positions while he searched for his misplaced water bottle. Hall had no sooner reached the firing trench, when German artillery made a direct hit on the dugout where Jimmy had been relaxing only a moment before. The repercussion of the explosion blasted earth and timber. This first shell was only the beginning of a massive barrage of bombs that fell up and down their sector. Hall and the other sentry, Freddy Azlett, were instantly half buried but received no major wounds. Their gun team, in the dugout, was not so fortunate. Hall and Azlett scurried back to their comrades. Three of the seven were dead, including McHard who had just exchanged positions with Hall. His head was split in two. Another's head was completely blown off his torso. Three others died within the hour. The seventh man survived as an amputee. The entire line suffered casualties while the sector trench works had been destroyed. Immediately those who were physically able began to dig with all their strength, rebuilding their fortifications. Hall wrote:

> The worst of it was that we could not get away from the sight of the mangled bodies of our comrades. Arms and legs stuck out of the wreckage, and on every side we saw the distorted faces of men we had known, with whom we had lived and shared hardships and danger for months past. One thinks of the human body as a beautiful thing. The sight of it dismembered, disemboweled, smeared with blood and filth and trampled in the bottom of a trench, is so revolting as to be hardly endurable. Nevertheless, we had to endure what there was no escaping, and worse, even, than the sight of the dead were the groans of desperately wounded men waiting to be carried back to the field-dressing stations.[129]

Jimmy Hall's description of how the men he served with kept their reason in the heat of battle, agrees completely with Rickenbacker and Saint-Exupéry. Hall said "the real danger comes when the strain is relaxed, "for then they were free to survey their surroundings instead of fixating on the firing positions of the enemy. What Hall and his fellow soldiers saw, during these times, was their friends mutilated horribly as if by "fiends." Hall recorded some actual pleas for help:

> I'm shot through the stomach, matey! Can't you get me back to the ambulance?
>
> Stick it, old lad! You won't 'ave long to wite. They'll be some of the Red Cross along 'ere in a jiffy now.
>
> Give me a lift, boys, can't you? Look at my leg! Do you think it'll 'ave to come off? Maybe they could save it if I could get to 'ospital in time! Won't you give me a lift?
>
> Don't you fret, sonny! You're a-gon'n' to ride back in a stretcher presently. Keep yer courage up a little w'ile longer.[130]

Hall said there were those who, in anguish, forgot everyone but themselves. He wrote of one man, who having looked about at the carnage, sat down and wept, suffering a complete breakdown. However, Jimmy knew only of few such cases. For the most part, although the men were "shaken and trembled from head to foot," they did not falter in their duty. Drawing upon reserves of strength they did not know they possessed, men—who before battle had seemed very ordinary demonstrated during the fight "heroic qualities . . . endured fearful agony in silence," and readied themselves with nerves of steel for the next onslaught.

It was not only the soldiers who exhibited extreme valor under fire. There were French women in the war zone who refused to leave their homes—though their houses had been blown to ruins with scarcely a wall standing. It was one of these, a mother, who, Hall said, summed up in five words all the heartrending misfortune of war's innocent victims. Only a few thousand feet from the front lines, this mother had a small store in the bombed out village of Armentières. The British soldiers would stop there to buy candles, chocolate, and her savory French bread. She kept her little shop stocked by daily pushing a handcart from the far side of Armentières where the market had not been laid waste, as in her district. Jimmy said there "was a spiritual fineness about her." On one occasion, while purchasing candles, he caught her staring towards the battlefield and beyond to the skeletal war-ruined towns behind German lines. Why, thought Hall, did she tolerate such a miserable and risky existence, living within the range of the big German guns? With the little French that he knew, he asked her. After a period of silence she pointed to occupied France, on the far side of the front and simply said, "Monsieur! Mes enfants! Là-bas!"—meaning: "Sir, my children! Over there!" So few words told the story of the tragedy she suffered when the war erupted. During the invasion this mother had been separated from her little ones and for the better part of a year she had been watching and waiting without knowledge of whether or not they even survived. Jimmy wrote:

> To many of the soldiers she was just a plain, thrifty little Frenchwoman who knew not the meaning of fear, willing to risk her life daily, that she might put by something for the long hard years which would follow the war. To me she is the Spirit of France, splendid, superb France. But more than this she is the Spirit of Motherlove which wars can never alter.[131]

Another time Jimmy and his comrades were enroute to the Armentières's baths. The Germans knew the town to be a place of retreat for British troops in reserve and frequently hurled bombs to the near-reaches of the village in hopes of killing a few enemies. The explosive shells fell near Hall's company who marched undisturbed, indifferent, so familiar had they become to extreme peril. Suddenly a bomb exploded into a nearby house sending the shattered brickwork in all directions. Hall wrote:

> A moment later, a fleshy peasant woman, wearing wooden shoes, turned out of an adjoining street and ran awkwardly toward the scene of the explosion. Her movements were so clumsy and slow, in proportion to the great exertion she was making, that at any other time the sight would have been ludicrous. Now it was in-

evitable that such a sight should first appeal to [the English soldier's] sense of humor, and thoughtlessly the boys started laughing and shouting at her.

"Go it, old dear! Yer makin' a grand race!"

"Two to one on Liza!"

"The other w'y, ma! That's the wrong direction! Yer runnin' right into 'em!"

She gave no heed, and a moment later we saw her gather up a little girl from a doorstep, hugging and comforting her, and shielding her with her body, instinctively, at the sound of another exploding shell. The laughter in the ranks stopped as though every man had been suddenly struck dumb.[132]

Most good Samaritans would run to the aid of those in danger after the shelling had ceased. However, true maternal love far exceeds the love of self and the bounds of charity. Every new creation of life is born of the travail of near death. Wondrous then that this matriarch flew to cuddle and console the child who could not comprehend the horrific sound and destruction, and defend the frail frame of the *petite enfant* with her only shield—her weathered and worn body. It mattered not to this mother if the comfort she could lend lasted but a moment, for another shell might send the two far from the firing line to a place of peace removed from this world. She knew the instant the child was nestled to her bosom, the panic and awful fear of an innocent would ameliorate, if only by a degree—and for that she was willingly to sacrifice her life. The succeeding shell, missing its mark, carried thunder only. The old was left cradling the young; and the hardened soldiers who thought *themselves* brave were left speechless at this sight which emulated the condescension of God.

Of all of Jimmy's war experiences, the failed offensive of the Battle of Loos undoubtedly ranked supreme on the appalling scale of death and suffering. In three days the British suffered fifty-thousand casualties. From the perspective of Hall's company they were convinced that they had captured "at least one trench"—but were mistaken. So many dead—nothing gained. On the fateful day of the first attack Hall arrived, with his company, to see the support trenches "filled to overflowing with troops in fighting order." They had no sooner obtained their assigned position when English artillery began to rain down upon enemy trenches only a few hundred yards to their front. It was an incredible bombardment. Jimmy wrote:

> The earth was like a muddy sea dashed high in spray against hidden rocks.[133]

The first wave of men anxiously awaited the order to mount the parapet and attack. Their ranks were composed of "bayonet-men" and "bombers," the latter loaded down with numerous grenades. Hall surveyed his friends. When he first enlisted Jimmy thought to himself, how would he endure living with these strangers? Now he thought of the hardship it would be to live without them, without the inspiration of their "splendid courage" and the "visible example of unselfish devotion." Everything about him seemed surreal, especially the soldiers—some nonchalantly inspecting their gear and adjusting their equipment; others were *singing*. There was in the ranks a cheerful spirit, despite the *sure knowledge* that most would die or be wounded savagely! The security and freedom of their families, their country, their posterity was at stake—and these placed on the balance carried a far greater weight than did their own lives. They chatted with each other in good humor:

> Are we downhearted? Not likely, old son!
>
> I'm a-go'n' to arsk fer a nice Blightey one! (A blightey wound was serious enough to be hospitalized in England, but not an injury that required amputation.) Four months in Brentford 'ospital an' me Christmas puddin' at 'ome!
>
> Good luck to you, Sammy boy! If you sees my missus, tell 'er I'm as right as rain!

Suddenly there was silence. The artillery attack had ceased. Then came the order, "Now, men! Follow me!" Not a man shirked and in a matter of seconds the front line trench was emptied and the second wave of troops poured into the vacuum. The German guns had been "reserving fire"—but now answered in full force. Jimmy wrote:

> Then came the "boiler-factory chorus," the sharp rattle of dozens of machine guns. The bullets were flying over our heads like swarms of angry wasps. A ration box board which I held above the parapet was struck almost immediately.[134]

The first wave ran with all their might, heads down, against this fearsome storm of suffocating lead. Men fell like grass before a mower. *Yet each succeeding wave faithfully charged forth when the order was given.* All were not infantry. There were Royal Engineers who carried picks and shovels instead of rifles. There were men from the Signaling Corps who ran while unwinding spools of telephone wire. And there were medics who ran carrying stretchers to retrieve, while under fire, as many of the wounded as they were able. At four the next morning Hall was positioned just outside of the trenches, lying prone with his machine gun, but otherwise exposed. He gazed down upon the "endless procession of casualties." Some, he said, groaned pitifully, while others were "laughing despite their wounds." These men, all very young, bore their injuries with a spirit of elation. Hall wrote:

> Their courage had been put to the most severe test and had not given way.[135]

For Jimmy, the worst of it was that a battle was really never over. There were no truces. Within his narrow field of vision he could see hundreds of bodies, and no opportunity for burial, except what could be done at night. Even then there was constant sniping. Certainly many of those who lay inanimate were not dead, but unconscious. Imagine the difficulty of the Red Cross Corps in trying to find the living in such conditions. To use a light to search a victim for life would be to draw the fire of instant death. If a man had not the strength to call for help, when help was near, he would unavoidably perish.

There were miracles in this madness. One English soldier was found by a listening patrol *six days* after he had been so badly wounded that he could not crawl. Although his discovery was providential, his survival for so long was even more so. How was it that he was still alive without the ability to secure water? Hall recorded that two German sentries had seen the plight of the sufferer. Although forbidden to take injured prisoners, each night they left their stations long enough to give him hot coffee, to warm his body and replenish it with liquid. Certainly, if they could see the poor soldier, they would have spotted the listening patrol who rescued him. However, no alarm sounded, no guns fired—as the injured man was borne homeward by his comrades.

Chapter 14

Where Is Home?

Saw pure Aspiration seeking
Heavenly light through human darkness,
Gain of power by world experience,
Wisdom's apple, sweet and bitter.

Saw the truest and the worthiest—
Winnowed grain, the wind-blown refuse
Lost in Lucifer's down-whirling—
Spirit's loyal, Michael's legion . . .

War was done, and Peace sat brooding
O'er a realm redeemed from darkness,
Darkness of oppression's scepter,
Shadow of ingrate rebellion,
When my comrade, homeward sailing,
Scarred with battle's badge of honor—
Wounds that won him swift promotion—
On his native shore descended. [136]

— Orson F. Whitney

After fighting six months in France, C Company was given leave and James Hall requested that he be allowed to spend this time with his family in America. He very much wanted to see his father who was suffering from Parkinson's disease. Initially he was told by battalion headquarters that unless he could persuade President Wilson to allow him to return with "a million or two"

American soldiers, the answer was no. At this time the United States had not yet entered the war. Hall mentioned his desire to be given a short leave home in his correspondence with his Bostonian friends. Several weeks later, and to Jimmy's surprise, he was summoned to regimental headquarters in London. There, at Hounslow, an officer explained to Hall that "someone has been pulling wires for you." Although leave could not be extended all the way to America, Jimmy was given the option of an honorable discharge, retaining the privilege of reenlisting; or taking leave with C Company and returning to France when their leave was over. Hall accepted the former offer. Lance Corporal James Norman Hall's discharge papers read that he was being released from military service "on the ground of being an American citizen" after serving 1 year, 99 days with the colours" and "172 days with the British Expeditionary Force in France—character: very good." Jimmy wrote:

> I doubt whether in the whole of London there could have been found that day a happier, more miserable man than former Lance Corporal 690, J. N. Hall. It may seem incredible that one could experience these conflicting states of feeling at the same time, but so it was in my case. I was going home, leaving that band of brothers whose friendship was one of the finest things that had ever come to me, and many of whom I would never see again.[137]

On his way to Iowa, Jimmy stopped in Boston to see his old friends at the Society. The Boston *Globe* reported that a former agent of the M.S.P.C.C., James Hall, had "just returned from the battlefields of France." The editor of the *Atlantic Monthly*, Ellery Sedgwick, heard of this and sent Hall word that he would like to see him. Sedgwick had no idea that Hall had, without success, repeatedly submitted articles to his magazine. In fact in this first meeting the editor asked Jimmy if he had ever done any writing. Tactfully Jimmy answered, "Yes, a little." Sedgwick explained that most Americans did not have much knowledge of the "actual battle experience" in France. He told him that the magazine wanted Hall to "write some articles for the *Atlantic* about the experiences of a private in the British Army." Sedgwick continued:

> The fact that you are an American will make them all the more interesting to readers over here. And you will be doing a real service to the Allied cause; I can assure you of that. Except for a few towns and cities on the Atlantic seaboard America is not awake to the significance of this war. Most people still believe that it is merely another of Europe's perpetual squabbles to be settled by Europe alone . . . [However, there should be], no preaching, or exhorting, or reproving the American people for their neutrality . . . I want you to write a simple, straight-forward narrative of your experiences: your day-to-day life in the trenches; the kind of men you served with; the hardships and dangers you shared together . . . and don't leave out any touches of humor.[138]

Jimmy left the office of the *Atlantic Monthly* with mixed emotions. Two years earlier he would have been elated to have been given the opportunity he had dreamed of. However, now he wanted to simply see his father, his family, a few friends and *return to war.* How could he take the time to write what Mr. Sedgwick had requested?

Jimmy enjoyed the Christmas holidays in Iowa. Not once did he mention his plans to his parents. Everything at home was *so* normal. At times this evoked a deep emotional response from Hall, "How can they be so happy when the young men of Europe are dying in their tens of thousands." He feared that if America remained neutral, Germany would win the war. He wrote:

> The enlightened, live-and-let-live Pax Britannica would be destroyed, and I could well imagine the Pax Germanica that would takes its place: one of complete domination . . . [139]

Soon thereafter Jimmy paid a visit to Professor Payne at

Grinnell. To his old mentor Hall was completely honest. He told Payne of his resolve to return to the war, of the offer from the *Atlantic*, of his feelings since arriving at home. At first the professor told Jimmy that this was a decision no one could make but himself. Also, if he supported Jimmy in his thinking, Hall might be dead before spring came. They continued their conversation for some time and Jimmy read to Payne some of the initial draft material he had started for the magazine. Professor Payne stopped Jimmy when he arose to leave, saying:

> Wait a bit, Norman. Let's come back to your problem. I've been considering it in the back of my mind while we've been talking here. I see that you are still an incurable romanticist, which prevents you from taking a common-sense view of things. You believe that because you resolved to return to service after a month of leave, you are bound to do so . . . How long do you think the war will last?

Hall responded that the fighting would last for several more years. The Professor went on:

> That is my opinion. Furthermore, I believe it cannot be won without the help of the U.S.A. and that we are bound to come in. Well, then, the articles the *Atlantic Monthly* wishes you to write may be of real service in making America more conscious of what English soldiers are enduring in a cause that is ours as well. I think you should stay here and finish them. What will it matter if you miss two or three months of service with your battalion . . . You will have plenty of time to be killed before the war ends.[140]

Jimmy was asked to speak to the townspeople of Colfax. He found the predominate attitude to be typical of the Midwest—namely that the Great War was no cause for American concern. Rather, let the Europeans follow the peaceful example of the United States, and if they could not, "let them stew in their own juice." His address failed to arouse the sympathy and support of his old friends. He returned to his home in "deep anguish of spirit." That night he penned these words:

RETURN TO FLANDERS

Hearing the voice, as in a dream
He rose and followed. Nothing stirred
Save that the air was ringing still
With the call he'd heard.

Before him stretched a level land
Where it was neither night nor day;
How forlorn, how desolate
No words could say.

Along a road, what had been trees,
Though dead, seemed begging still to die.
That evil place seemed very heaven.
He knew not why.

Musing, he stood, as still as stone;
Then, in a flash, his body knew
And cried in anguish, 'What is this
You make me do?'

Little could his body guess
Why spirit found that stricken plain
So beautiful, or what it said,
"Home! Home again!"[141]

Jimmy kept in constant touch with his comrades on the front by letter. He knew his duty lie with them. Yet there was a duty to fulfill before he could return to that *home,* that evil place made heaven by the consecration of heroic blood. He followed the advice of Payne and stayed in America to write the articles requested by the *Atlantic Monthly.* They were all published as he wrote them, and when finished as a whole, published again as Hall's first book, *Kitchener's Mob.* According to scholar Robert Roulston *Kitchener's Mob* was "well received" by the American audience, for it was an "honest account of life in the trenches"—with "power to engross and affect the reader." One need only read the book in its entirety to know that both Professor Payne and Editor Sedgwick were right on the mark. The pen of James Norman Hall wrought a tremendous "service to the Allied cause"—for it awakened America to "a cause that is ours as well."

Eleven months after the book *Kitchener's Mob* rolled off the presses, the United States declared war on Germany. By then Hall had long since returned to the war. At the time of his return Jimmy did not bring with him the host of American soldiers that British Regimental Headquarters sarcastically suggested would qualify him for leave in the states. However, thousands upon thousands of Hall's fellow citizens followed him to the front only months after his departure to Europe. Jimmy was in part responsible for their enlistment, for he had inspired our nation with a simple, straight-forward narrative of his experiences, of day-to-day life in the trenches, of the heroism of the men he served with and the hardships and dangers endured.

Hall inspired his countryman with a vision of home as a place, not of peaceful isolation, but of needful *belonging,* united with "a band of brothers" whose bond of friendship was the "finest thing" to which a true man can aspire. When a man answers the call to this home he assuredly sanctifies and preserves the home, and loved ones, he leaves behind. Beside these two homes there is yet a *third home;* the Apostle Paul called it *a third heaven.* Such men as James Hall *feel deeply* a longing for a home they seem to have known and aspire to regain—an intangible that few are able to put into words. Hall called it the "pursuit of the bird in the bush"—always beyond our vision and our grasp in this life, yet nonetheless *real.* Some day all men will know that the leaving of father and mother, the leaving of family and friends, of comforts and familiarity, to voluntarily enlist in a great cause in a far away land, is but a *type*. For this noble action is actually a continuation of the heroism of leaving our eternal home, to strive on the deadly battlefields of mortality, consecrating not only the life of the warrior, but also his loved ones, preserving their abode in the Home of God.

CHAPTER 15

ESCADRILLE LAFAYETTE

The pilot on top was doing beautiful renversements . . . I was so certain it was our patrol that I started over at once . . . it was getting dusk and I lost sight of the machine lowest down for a few seconds . . . You know how difficult it is to see a machine in that position. Suddenly he loomed up in front of me like an express train . . . I realized my awful mistake, of course. His tracer bullets were going by on the left side, but he corrected his aim, and my motor seemed to be eating them up. I banked to the right, and was about to cut my motor and dive, when I felt a smashing blow in the left shoulder. A sickening sensation and a very peculiar one, not at all what I thought it might feel like to be hit with a bullet . . . After that I knew that I was falling . . . my brain refused to act. I could do nothing. Finally, I did have one clear thought, "Am I on fire?"

—THE ACCOUNT OF "DREW" FROM HIGH ADVENTURE,
BY JAMES NORMAN HALL

AFTER HAVING SERVED FIFTEEN MONTHS with the Royal Fusiliers and six months in the death trenches in France—after receiving an honorable discharge and spending a brief period in the states writing *Kitchener's Mob*, Hall returned to France. Upon leaving the states Sedgwick of the *Atlantic Monthly* had commissioned Jimmy to write several additional articles on the Escadrille Lafayette, a newly formed flight squadron of the French Foreign Legion composed entirely of American fighter pilots. As the United States had still not officially joined the war effort, France had organized this Franco-American Corps to accommodate U.S. citizens who

Allied Airfield

aspired to aerial combat. Hall was thrilled with his editor's assignment. Ever since he had seen on display in London, in 1909, Blériot's famous aircraft, the first to cross the English Channel, Jimmy had been fascinated by manned-flight. He planned to write the commissioned articles, which, he thought, would not take long, then enlist in the Royal Army Medical Corps. Incidentally, one of the principal men involved in the expansion of the Lafayette Escadrille was Dr. Edmund L. Gros. Gros also had responsibilities with the American Ambulance Service. It was natural then, for Hall to approach Dr. Gros and explain his dual purpose in meeting with him. After listening silently to Jimmy's introduction, Gros said:

> Do you feel obliged to re-enlist as an infantryman in the British Army? Why not join up as an airman with your compatriots over here?
>
> Hall was stunned! He had never considered such a prospect. He wrote:

I stared blankly at him. I heard his words, but their significance did not come home to me for a moment or two.

"As an airman! You mean, it would be possible to do this?"

"Why not?" Dr. Gros replied. "Would you like to fill [out this form]? My name is the only reference you will need."

"Dr. Gros, I know nothing whatever about flying."

"Neither did the other men who are now *pilotes de chasse* with the Escadrille Lafayette."

"And I know nothing about internal-combustion engines."

"That isn't necessary . . . there are expert mechanics to take care of the planes and engines. Your only duty would be to learn to fly and to fight in the air."[142]

In three days time ex-Lance Corporal J. N. Hall, number 690 of the Royal Fusiliers, became "*Engagé Volontair* [number] 11921 in the Aviation Section of the French Foreign Legion . . . *pour la durée de la guerre*"—enlisted for the duration of the war. After receiving the initial Penguin Class training in 1916 at the École Militaire d'Aviation and the last phase of training at the "School of Acrobacy" in November of 1917, Jimmy awaited his orders to the front. During this respite there was a period of time where he and his fellow American pilots where free to fly whenever they liked, without the restrictions of the schools. They were now considered aerial combat ready. However, Hall and his friends did not feel as confident as their credentials. He wrote:

We were not all good acrobats. One must have a knack for it . . . The French have it in larger proportion than do we Americans. I can think of no sight more pleasing than that of a Spad in the air, under the control of a skillful French pilot. Swallows perch in envious silence on the chimney pots, and the crows caw in sullen despair from the hedgerows.[143]

The American pilots used this free time to increase their skill, flying numerous sorties of their own design—practicing formations, dogfights, and charade air strikes on poor villages, whose inhabitants must have been greatly relieved when they perceived that the roaring, low flying aircraft were French Spads! Hall wrote:

> It was forbidden to fly over Paris, and for this reason we took all the more delight in doing it. . . . We were as happy during those days as any one has the right to be. Our whole Duty was to fly, and never was the voice of Duty heard more gladly. It was hard to keep in mind the stern purpose behind this seeming indulgence . . . War on earth may be reasonable and natural, but in the air it seems the most senseless folly. How is an airman, who has just learned a new meaning for the joy of life, to reconcile himself to the insane business of killing a fellow aviator who may have just learned it too?[144]

The aerodromes at the front, by no means could be compared to the front line trenches of the war, with which Hall was so familiar. At the base, airmen rode about in automobiles, slept in comfortable beds, and (except when flying) were sheltered from the harsh weather. Upon Jimmy's arrival at the aerodrome he was met by two aviators that he had known in military aviation school. Miller and Dunham had been assigned to the front two months earlier. Sixty days experience may not be much of an advantage in many occupations. However, two months time flying combat is quite another matter. After a hearty handshake Dunham gave Jimmy some sound advice. He told his friend that he had flown over the front for two weeks before he saw his first enemy plane—not because they weren't there—he just couldn't *see* them. The French combat pilots, on the same patrols, would engage the enemy, while he spent most of his time just trying to keep track of his squadron. Dunham knew that he was fortunate to survive those early flights. He told Hall not to "be too anxious to mix it up with the first German you see, because very likely he will be a Frenchman, and if he isn't, if he is a good Hun pilot, you'll simply be meat for him—at first," that is. For a while, Dunham told Hall, he would be practically helpless.

Escadrille Lafayette Combat Pilot — James Norman Hall

The pilots of the Escadrille Lafayette were given four objectives, namely to protect photographic reconnaissance planes, to escort bombers, to patrol the front, and to harass the enemy. Any of these objectives could result in dogfights with the enemy. This Franco-American squadron shared their airfield with three other pursuit squadrons—all French. Together they formed *groupe de combat 13* and were assigned a particular sector in the war zone. In the flight operations bureau hung a detailed map of their sector, along with a series of aerial photographs of the same territory. Hall and his comrades spent hours studying "every trench, every shell hole, every splintered tree or fragment of farmhouse [that] stood out clearly." Still, Jimmy found that Dunham was right—on his very first patrol Hall made serious mistakes.

Jimmy was already awake and alert before his fellow flyers began to stir. When he walked onto the airfield the earth was still in night's shadow, the sky broken with clouds that were gradually dissipating. Stars could still be seen through the breaks in the overcast. A deep throated rumbling permeated the air, like the muffled roar of distant thunder. However, the storm was man-made and the reverberation was the bellowing of big guns along the front. The dutiful mechanics had risen before the aviators, for in front of the hangers were two rows of perfectly aligned Spads, machine guns armed and engines running, growling like angry dogs. Ace pilot, Eddie Rickenbacker, said the Spad had the appearance of a shark, streamlined towards the tail, but possessing mighty jaws up front. On each aircraft was painted the insignia of the Escadrille Lafayette, the head of an Indian, and the individual mark of the particular airship's pilot. The air was supercharged with excitement. The Squadron leader's mark was a big "T," for "Talbott" fixed on the fuselage. Above the din Talbott shouted to Hall to join formation, following his lead, over the aerodrome at two thousand meters. He was ordered to "stick close" and if he lost sight of the patrol, he was to head home, straight to the southwest. Soon the planes were taxing to the far end of the field. One by one they turned into the wind and departed. Hall's aircraft had seen plenty of action, but it was fitted with an overhauled engine. It was his "*avion*," and would carry him aloft to potentially his first air combat. His life depended in large measure upon the strength of this Spad. Jimmy loved it as if it were imbued with life.

Imagine the feeling of, for the first time, strapping one's self into the cockpit of the Spad war bird, the most powerful and agile combat plane of WWI. When Jimmy turned this magical machine into the wind, he opened the throttle and, he later said, the "veteran Spad lifted its tail and gathered flying speed with all the vigor of its youth, and *we* were soon high above the hangers, climbing to the rendezvous."

The first airplanes to depart did not just patiently circle while waiting on the others. They looped and rolled, performed *renversements* and *retournements.* One Spad, much higher than Jimmy, dove down upon him slipping gracefully beneath him; then converting his tremendous speed back into altitude, zoomed high overhead. Moments later the aerobatics ceased, every man took his position in formation, flying northeast. The sky was still dark enough, when they crossed over "No-Man's-Land" to see "thousands of winking lights, the flashes of guns and bursting shells." It must have seemed odd for Jimmy to look down upon the death trenches, so personally familiar to him. Hall wrote:

> I knew that shells of enormous caliber were wrecking trenches, blasting out huge craters; and yet not a sound, not the faintest reverberation of a gun. Here was a sight almost to make one laugh at man's idea of the importance of his pygmy wars. But the Olympian mood is a fleeting one . . . To look down from a height of more than two miles, on an endless panorama of suffering and horror, is to have the sense of one's littleness even more painfully quickened.[145]

As Hall surveyed the incredible sights below, his eyes constantly scanned the skies with a twofold purpose: be vigilant to enemy assault and keep a watch upon his own patrol. Suddenly, after only few seconds, Jimmy lost sight of every aircraft in his patrol, but one. Obviously the others had spotted an opportunity to attack the enemy, while Hall had not even seen the enemy. The aircraft to his front was already on its side, plummeting headlong. Hall closed his throttle and nosed his bird over, but he had not yet "learned to fall vertically." Then he spotted evidence of his patrol—narrow, crisscrossing ribbons of white, trails of tracer bullets pouring forth from unseen German fighter planes! The enemy aircraft were equally invisible to Jimmy as the aircraft of his comrades. The thought occurred to Hall that if he followed these streamers of gunfire he would be led to his patrol! This is precisely what Jimmy did, spiraling seven thousand feet earthward until he leveled his Spad at around six thousand feet. At that moment he saw a rare sight indeed. A large caliber anti-aircraft shell was peaking only a few feet away, having reached the apex of its arc and was just beginning its fall to earth. Jimmy thought it beyond incredible that he had seen a live shell—and yet could not see his own patrol!

This unlikely curiosity was soon replaced with obvious comprehension—Jimmy realized the enemy had accurately fixed their guns on his precise position! Anti-aircraft shells began to explode all around his Spad, buffeting his aircraft so violently that he momentarily lost control. One shell ripped the air so close to his tail that the "terrific rending sound" made Hall fear that he had been hit. Until that instant Jimmy had not given thought to his position, relative to the batteries of German gunners—whose sole responsibility was to shoot down allied aircraft. Had the shell he had seen exploded at the top of its trajectory, Hall would have surely have been shot down. Talbott's words came into Jimmy's mind that he should "never fly in a straight line for more than fifteen seconds." At his altitude a predictable flight pattern would make him an easy mark. And so in the air, blown wild with the repercussions of anti-aircraft fire, Hall maneuvered his Spad in a highly irregular manner. Again Talbott's orders came to him that if lost he should immediately set a southwestern course to home. Just how, he thought, was he to accomplish that miracle, when his compass bobbed, in its liquid case, in utter confusion? A pilot can only trust his compass when he holds the plane straight and level for approximately a minute, with no acceleration or deceleration. That Hall could not do and stay alive. All the while he was attempting to escape from the expert gunners below, Jimmy was actually flying deeper into German held territory. Before long, with his fuel supply dwindling, he would be forced to land. Unless Hall reversed his course soon, his first flight might well be the last. However, unknown to Jimmy, his old classmate Miller had been within five hundred meters of him all the time, keeping an eye on his fledgling friend. Literally out of the blue Miller overtook Hall.

Jimmy wrote:

> My love for concentric circles of red, white, and blue dates from the moment when I saw the French *cocarde* on his Spad.
>
> "And if I had been a Hun!" Miller said, when we landed at the aerodrome, "Oh, man! You were fruit salad! Fruit salad, I tell you! I could have speared you with my eyes shut."[146]

Oft times in dangerous straits, a loyal friend is the only thing that saves one from utter ruin. In air combat that doesn't mean the hero is necessarily modest, as with Miller. Nor does it save the near-victim from the wisecracks of his other veteran comrades. Back at the squadron, Hall was greeted with the following banter:

> You should have seen [Hall] following us down! Like [an] old rheumatic going into the subway.
>
> You want to dive vertically. Needn't worry about your old 'bus. She'll stand it.
>
> Well, the Lord has certainly protected the innocent today!
>
> One of them was wandering off into Germany. Bill had to waggle Miller to page him.[147]

In his book *Kitchener's Mob* Hall refers frequently to "Tommy" who is actually a composite character representing the unified spirit, humor, courage and determination of the British soldier. In his book *High Adventure* Hall uses a similar literary tool in the character of "Drew." Sometimes "Drew" is a fellow aviator who rises with him through the ranks of training and shares his initial adventures in the Franco-American Corps. At other times, as we learn from Hall's autobiography, "Drew" is actually himself. Also, it is important to keep in mind that both *Kitchener's Mob* and *High Adventure* were published during war time; Hall was careful in revealing names and places for obvious reasons. Additionally, Hall was forever modest in writing of his own exploits and the dangers he faced. When he does refer to himself, Jimmy revealed how human he was—*in his own mind*, and how, like the rest of us, he often made dreadful mistakes. Most autobiographers prefer to dwell on exemplary events in their own history. While Hall, in his extreme modesty, does the opposite—even to the point of sharing moments of foolishness and laughter, at his own expense. Part of Hall's greatness lies in the fact that he does not consider himself great (despite the remarkable accomplishments of his life). Jimmy admired the lack of ego in others as well. Consider Hall's observation of his commander, sending out a patrol on a vital mission to shoot down enemy observation balloons. Balloon hunting was a dangerous enterprise as anti-aircraft batteries surrounded each site. Knowing the balloons altitude the gunners could accurately fix their sights on attacking aircraft.

> As a squadron leader Talbott has many virtues, *but the most important of them all is his casualness*. And he is so sincere and natural in it. He has no conception of the dramatic possibilities of a situation—something to be profoundly thankful for in the commander of an *escadrille de chasse.* Situations are dramatic enough, tense enough, without one's taking thought of the fact. He might have stood there, watch in hand, counting off the seconds. He might have said, "Remember, we're all counting on you. Don't let us down. You've got to get that balloon!" Instead of that, he glanced at his watch as if he had just remembered us. "All right; run along, you sausage-spearers. We're having lunch at twelve. That will give you time to wash up after you get back."[148]

A final point on Jimmy Hall's humility—nowhere do we learn from *High Adventure* that Hall attained the coveted designation of *ACE PILOT*, or that he rose from the rank of corporal to major. Humility is a *hall*mark of true manhood. An editor's note in the book *My Island Home* states:

In all, Hall was accredited with five[vi] German planes, and for his service in the air he was decorated with the *Croix de Guerre,* with five palms, the *Médaille Militaire,* the *Legion d'Honneur*, and the Distinguished Service Cross.

After being lost on his first patrol and the commensurate feelings of vulnerability that accompany such a circumstance, Hall penned a few lines in the manner of Alan Seeger's poem, *I have a Rendezvous with Death.* The poem of Hall's, entitled *The Airman's Rendezvous,* had a direct impact on financing the war effort. Jimmy's poem was utilized by the "Liberty Bond Campaign." A leader in this effort, Curtis Coe, wrote to Hall explaining that he had "sold tens of thousands of dollars worth of bonds merely by displaying this "exhibit from the front." *The Airman's Rendezvous* was taken from Jimmy's uniform pocket and was stained with his own blood.

THE AIRMAN'S RENDEZVOUS

And I, in the wide fields of air
Must keep with him my rendezvous.
It may be I shall meet him there
When clouds, like sheep, drift slowly through
The pathless meadows of the sky
And their cool shadows move beneath . . .
I have a rendezvous with Death
Some summer noon of white and blue.

Oh, he must seek me far and wide
And track me at his fleetest pace,
For there are lonely depths in space—
Solitudes where I may hide,

---

vi Captain Eddie Rickenbacker reported that Hall scored six official victories. See Rickenbacker's summary "Hall of Fame of the Air" in the color section.

Laughing at him when he has gone
On a false scent, with laboring breath . . .
But I've a rendezvous with Death
Over Verdun, as night comes on.

Perhaps some autumn afternoon
Of cloudless skies, far in the blue
Beneath a ghostly waning moon,
I shall be flying without care
Or thought of war, or thought of death;
Unwarned that he is coming, too,
Swiftly through the upper air
Straight to his well-planned rendezvous,
Until I hear, with darkening brain:
'Well met! We shall not meet again.'[149]

Approximately two months before Jimmy wrote this poem America had officially entered the war. The ink was hardly dry on his poem when a number of American Air Service officers came to inspect the Escadrille Lafayette, for they were now in the process of organizing American air combat units. Although it was late and the patrols for the day had already returned, it was decided that an "exhibition patrol" be dispatched to show the Americans how it was done. Among the flyers chosen for this late patrol was Jimmy Hall, who felt "keenly the honor" of demonstrating his skill. Unfortunately, Jimmy's mechanic had difficulty in getting his Spad's engine to run. The others waited as long as they could for Hall, engines idling, but finally left without him. All the while the French mechanic worked furiously on Hall's Spad. With a sudden slap to his head, the Frenchman exclaimed, "Voilà! Ça Gaz!" and the engine roared to life. By then the spectators, along with Captain Thénault, had walked back to squadron headquarters. Hall felt that had the Captain been there he would have excused Hall from the patrol, as it would now be difficult for him to join the formation. However, Hall was excited and anxious to fly. He strapped himself in the cockpit of his Spad and a moment later was airborne.

In the fifteen kilometers from the airfield to the front, Hall climbed his Spad four thousand meters—to over twelve thousand feet. The sun had set in the trenches and anti-aircraft fire began to blossom around his flight path. At his altitude there was not much reason for alarm, as the odds were definitely in Jimmy's favor. For fifteen minutes he flew up and down the front, trying to spot his patrol, but to no avail. Finally he spotted a formation of aircraft, five kilometers behind enemy lines. Five planes were grouped tightly, with one plane well above the others "doing beautiful renversements"—that, Jimmy decided, would most likely be Raoul Lufbery. As Hall was certain this was the Escadrille Lafayette, he turned his Spad to join them at once. Another plane was approximately two hundred meters below the formation, at the same altitude as Hall's Spad. It is very difficult for a pilot to see a plane converging head-on at the same altitude he is flying, particularly at dusk. Hall lost sight of this lowest aircraft, just for a few seconds. When he again caught sight of this plane, he knew *it was not a Spad* and, that again, he had made a terrible mistake. Jimmy wrote:

> Suddenly he loomed up in front of me like an express train. . . only ten times faster; and he was firing as he came. I realized my awful mistake, of course. His tracer bullets were going by on the left side, but he corrected his aim, and my motor seemed to be eating them up. I banked to the right, and was about to cut my motor and dive, when I felt a smashing blow in the left shoulder. A sickening sensation and a very peculiar one, not at all what I thought it might feel like to be hit with a bullet. I believed that it came from the German in front of me. But it couldn't have, for he was still approaching when I was hit, and I have learned that the bullet entered from behind . . . I tried to shut down the motor, but couldn't manage it because my left arm was gone. I really believed that it had been blown off into space until I glanced down and saw that it was

> still there . . . although there was no more feeling in it. Blood was trickling into my eyes so that I could scarcely see and my flying-goggles were hanging down over my ears in two parts; they had been cut through at the nosepiece . . . after the bullet that creased my forehead I couldn't see anything . . .
>
> After that I knew that I was falling . . . my brain refused to act. I could do nothing. Finally, I did have one clear thought, "Am I on fire?" This cut right through the fog, brought me broad awake. I was falling almost vertically, in a sort of a half *vrille.* No machine but a Spad could have stood the strain.[150]

One more bullet grazed his body, and then the Germans, who had attacked Hall from the front and the rear, ceased firing. They had riddled his plane which fell obviously out of control. At full power Hall's Spad was plummeting to the ground faster than the Huns could safely descend. The Germans, no doubt, continued to observe Jimmy's fall, then saw his Spad partially recovery (which planes will sometimes do even when the pilot is dead at the controls) and then crash into the trenches. Hall wrote that "some proud Boche airman is [probably] wearing an iron cross on my account."

In reality it was Jimmy who pulled his plane out of the half spin when he momentarily came out of trauma induced stupor. Holding the control stick between his knees, he reached over with his good arm and closed the throttle to ease the awful acceleration. Instead of the engine slowing to idle, it simply quit and the propeller "stopped dead." There was no way for Hall to start the engine again. In his mental lethargy, induced by blood loss, he wondered if he should even *care.* He was extremely drowsy and struggled to catch his breath, for he felt as if he had been struck hard in the stomach. Again Hall lost control of the Spad and it fell earthward; and again he recovered, this time only a few hundred feet above earth. Below him he saw trenches and thought: are they friend or foe?

> It was a wicked-looking place for landing: trenches and shell holes everywhere, dimly seen in the gathering dusk. I was still wondering in a vague way whether they were French or German *when I fell into a most restful sleep.*[151]

As he was to later learn, his Spad slowed considerably just before impact, then "fell squarely into a trench, the wings breaking the force of the fall." Jimmy had lost consciousness before he hit the earth. Never did he recover memory of the crash. When Hall awoke he was at once alert and perceived that he was being carried on a stretcher. Though breathing was still difficult, he felt little pain. He attempted to move his limbs and to his great relief found they responded, except for his left arm. Jimmy later wrote that he "accepted the miracle without attempting to explain it." His thoughts turned to the men who carried his stretcher. Were they allies or enemies? He tried to focus but could only see a red blur, as his forehead was still bleeding. Wiping his eyes, he looked again. The uniform of the stretcher-bearer was indistinct to his bleary eyes and covered with mud. Hall looked higher and to his delight saw the helmet was of French design! He wrote:

> If ever I live long enough in one place, so that I may gather a few possessions and make a home for myself, on one wall of my living-room I will have a bust-length portrait, rear view, of a French *brancardier,* mud-covered and battered tin hat.[152]

Jimmy relaxed on the stretcher as his benefactors bore him along the zigzag corridors of earthworks. He experienced "perfect happiness" with no thought of past or future. Hall simply enjoyed the present miracle. He was alive, back-*home* in the trenches, and with friends. Jimmy said nothing for five minutes. Then, as he could not contain himself any longer he chirped from his bloody throat, "Bonjour, messieurs!" The lead bearer turned his head in amazement. The Frenchmen spoke to Jimmy in their native tongue, which he easily understood, with exclamations of astonishment. They had seen his fall from the sky. Fortuitously his Spad had over-flown the German trenches, entanglements, and no-man's-land, and had come down on the French first-line trench. The Spad had hit the earth behind a little hill, where the Germans could not fire upon the wreckage. To hit at this precise spot his plane made a turn and was actually flying back towards German territory! The Frenchmen pointed out that had the Spad been just a few feet higher Hall would have crashed in the heart of no-man's-land. When Jimmy was pulled from his ruined plane he was unconscious. The miraculous manner of the crash and now Hall's alertness, led the Frenchmen to marvel, "This is something wonderful!"

Even as they spoke, enemy artillery was pounding the French trenches. When the shells posed immediate danger, the stretcher-bearers carried Hall down a long staircase into a deep dugout. Here they waited while listening to muffled explosions and the whine of casings and shrapnel. After a time they continued their journey and at length, came to the underground field hospital, lit only by candles. Jimmy had lost a tremendous amount of blood from a bullet that entered his left shoulder and exited in a larger wound under his arm. This was the cause of the copious blood loss that had caused him to slip into unconsciousness. The bullet had fortunately missed his shoulder blade. French doctors dressed his wounds and transferred him to an evacuation hospital near the front. Dr. Gros arranged for another transfer to the American Ambulance Hospital outside of Paris where Jimmy made a complete recovery.

Upon his release from the hospital Hall was not reassigned to the Escadrille Lafayette, but by mistake to an all-French squadron, Spad 112. Nonetheless Jimmy thoroughly enjoyed the comradeship of flying with these veteran airmen of France. There he was given an assignment to provide air escort to the King of Italy, who was traveling near the French Alps. During this mission he seldom saw enemy aircraft. Hall loved every minute of this flying adventure—aerial sight-seeing over glorious mountain country, looking down upon picturesque alpine villages, untouched by war. When this mission was complete, Hall departed Belfort, intending to return to the Verdun Sector. Without warning the Spad's engine began to sputter, and suddenly the beautifully rugged landscape below took on a dreadful aspect. The fuel pump failed and fuel pressure was falling rapidly. Immediately Jimmy began to operate the auxiliary hand pump, when it failed as well. His last backup was a small gravity fed fuel tank which provided approximately ten minutes of flight—just enough time to land under power—provided he could find a suitable meadow or field in which to land the Spad in the mountainous terrain.

All Jimmy needed was a solitary flat spot of five or six hundred feet to safely land his Spad. As he quickly surveyed his options, the best landing site he could see was the summit of a sugarloaf hill with a small area of pastureland at its crest. Everywhere else, within his limited range, was forest or orchard covered slopes. His fuel was rapidly reaching the point of exhaustion—he could make one approach and one only. As Hall descended he found the landing hill to be of a much steeper grade than it had previously appeared. He found he had to *climb* as he flared to land to avoid smashing into the ground. This was the first of Hall's difficulties—for out of nowhere dozens of *cows* came into view. Jimmy explained, "Their natural camouflage of browns and whites and red prevented my seeing them earlier." The next few seconds would have been a sight to see as Jimmy, nearly at stalling speed with no options remaining, deftly dodged the animals, missing "collisions by the length of a match-stick." He reached the apex of the mountain still slightly airborne. Hall touched down just as he was clearing the pasture's edge marked prominently, from the ground-level perspective only, by a wire fence. His Spad drove through the fence with no deceleration whatever, and began rolling and bouncing *down hill* into an apple orchard. Two large trees sheared the Spad's wings, but the velocity of the aircraft was such that it continued undeterred on its flightless journey. Ahead was a stone wall that would certainly capture the rolling fuselage

Hall's First Victory by Herb Kawainui Kane

for good. Fortunately for Jimmy the interim slope was covered with brush, which slowed his impact considerably. Jimmy wrote:

> There was nothing left of my machine but the seat. Unscathed, I looked back along the wreckage-strewn path, like a man who has been riding a whirlwind in a wicker chair.[153]

True to Hall's belief that all French Mayors must constantly scan the skies with binoculars "searching for wayward aviators," the kind-hearted Mayor of the village was soon on the crash site. Despite the fact that Jimmy had panicked his cows, laid waste a good section of his fence, and lopped off huge limbs from his apple trees, the Mayor gave Hall a hero's welcome. Soon he was on his way to Verdun, by ground transport, with funds loaned Jimmy by this good benefactor.

Later that fall Jimmy was reassigned to the Escadrille Lafayette. Although delighted to see his old friends, Hall was disappointed—for although he had shed his blood in the war effort, he had not yet gained a single victory in aerial combat. On New Year's Day, on patrol with Bill Thaw, Jimmy was so elated with the thrill of flying that even the extreme cold of his open cockpit biplane seemed scarcely an annoyance. However, the emotion of the day once again took its toll. In the lead, Thaw had been only one hundred meters ahead of Hall. In Jimmy's spirit of exhilaration his attention was diverted to the glorious vistas and away from the bleak realities of war. When Jimmy again focused on the business at hand, Thaw was simply gone from sight. Hall scanned the skies trying to visually reestablish contact. His eyes fell upon a "speck" of a biplane, profiled a half-mile distant against a billowy cloud. Jimmy thought of the time his friend Miller had spied him out, and descended on him from nowhere. So Hall planned to maneuver high above Thaw's rear and repeat the same stunt, then later gloat as Miller had done.

Bill Thaw was obviously enjoying himself with New Year's Day flying as much as Jimmy, for below Thaw rolled and looped to his heart's content. Careful not to give away his approach, Jimmy skillfully positioned his Spad in an ideal posture for attack. So stealthy was Hall that the other pilot truly had no idea that an *enemy* aircraft was about to dive upon him—for as Jimmy plummeted, as an Eagle with talons extended, he saw in his gun sights, not tri-colored *concardes*, but black crosses fixed on the wings of a German single seat fighter plane. Soberly Hall continued the attack full throttle. Joy gave way to grim duty. At one hundred yards Hall's bullets riddled the black crosses and with deadly accuracy pounded into the German's engine. Without hesitation, the enemy plane fell off on one wing completely out of control. A wing sheared free, either weakened by Jimmy's spray of lead, or from the extreme forces of a violent descent, and the combat plane of his adversary crashed in no man's land.

When Hall returned to his squadron he was first met with a censorious look by Lieutenant Verdier at headquarters. Bill Thaw had been on the ground for twenty minutes and the officer demanded an explanation as to why Hall had lost his lead patrol pilot. Jimmy responded by simply relating his encounter with the enemy. Verdier immediately telephoned Group Headquarters. After a brief conversation he hung up the receiver, looked at Jimmy with a new respect and said:

> *Bon! Merci,* you got him. Congratulations on your first victory . . . That's the way to begin the New Year.[154]

Jimmy wrote that he "felt no elation whatever." A noble soldier never delights in bloodshed; Hall did not—neither did Rickenbacker or Saint-Exupéry. An ancient warrior accurately expressed the true sentiments of all strong men of liberty. This man was a general and a prophet. Empowered with righteous indignation, he wrote an epistle to the commander of his enemies, saying:

> . . . we do not desire to be men of blood . . . we have not come out to battle against you that we might shed your blood for power; neither do we desire to bring any one to the yoke of bondage. But this is the very cause for which ye have come against us; yea, and ye are angry with us . . . [we fight for] that liberty which binds us to our lands and our country . . . we will seek not your blood, but we will spare your lives, if ye will go your way and come not again to war against us . . . if ye do not this, behold, ye are in our hands, and I will command my men that they shall fall upon you, and inflict the wounds of death in your bodies . . . and then we will see who shall have power over this people; yea, we will see who shall be brought into bondage.[155]

Of personal subsequent victories Jimmy's pen is silent. However, during the ensuing months Hall became "one of the most spectacular American airmen." With the advent of the first squadrons of the United States Army Air Force, Hall was promoted to captain and made a flight commander in the 94th Aero Squadron. On April 29, 1918, Captain Jimmy Hall accompanied a new airman, Eddie Rickenbacker, into enemy skies. The account of this sortie, which ended successfully with Rickenbacker's first victory, is recorded in *Part One* of this book. Regarding the event, Eddie Rickenbacker wrote a remarkable tribute to James Hall, stating:

> Hall was immediately beside me. He was evidently as pleased as I was over our success, for he danced his machine about in incredible maneuvers. And then I realized that old Archy (anti-aircraft fire) was back on the job. We were not two miles away from the German anti-aircraft batteries and they put a furious bombardment of shrapnel all about us. I was quite ready to call it a day and go home, but Captain Hall deliberately returned to the barrage . . . Machine-guns and rifle fire from the trenches greeted us and I do not mind admitting that I got out quickly the way I came in without any unnecessary delay, but Hall continued to do stunts over their heads for ten minutes, surpassing all the acrobatics that the enraged Boches had ever seen even over their own peaceful aerodromes. Jimmy exhausted his spirits at about the time the Huns had exhausted all their available ammunition and we started blithely for home. Swooping down to our field side by side, we made a quick landing and taxied our victorious machines up to the hangars. Then jumping out we ran to each other, extending glad hands . . .[156]

Captain Hall awarded the Croix de Guerre on the Champs Elysés

CHAPTER 16

CAPTURED

My mind to me a kingdom is;
Such present joys therein I find,
That it excels all other bliss
That earth affords or grows by kind:
Though much I lack that most would have,
Yet still my mind forbids to crave.

I laugh not at another's loss,
I grudge not at another's gain;
No worldly waves my mind can toss;
My state at one doth still remain:
I fear no foe, I fawn no friend;
I loathe not life, nor dread my end.

Some weigh their pleasure by their lust,
Their wisdom by their rage of will;
Their treasure is their only trust,
A cloaked craft their store of skill;
But all the pleasure that I find
Is to maintain a quiet mind. [157]

—SIR EDWARD DYER

ON THE MORNING OF MAY 7, 1918 Captain Jimmy Hall, piloting a Nieuport Type 28, crashed for the third time. As late comers in the war the American Air Services acquired old Nieuports from the French, a plane far inferior to the Spads Hall had been flying in the Escadrille Lafayette. Had Jimmy flown the Spad on this fateful day, instead of the weaker Nieuport, he would have been the victor rather than becoming the vanquished. The Nieuport had the infamous habit of shedding wing fabric at high speed!

Responding to a call from the front lines to intercept five German fighters near Pont-à-Mousson, Captain Hall, Eddie Rickenbacker, and Eddie Green took to the skies. They spied their antagonists south of Metz. Skillfully Hall maneuvered his team to an advantageous position to the rear and above the enemy. When nearly on top of their foes Jimmy nosed his plane over and dove vertically.

The acceleration is incredible when a plane, already at high speed, leaves a level attitude and plummets straight for the earth. A predator screaming down upon his prey in this manner must fly with absolute precision for his target is anything but stationary. The line of fire of his guns corresponds exactly to the pitch and longitudinal axes of the airplane—this he must align in a split second and bring his enemy within gun sights. Any error in perception will cause him to miss his target, forfeit the element of surprise, plunge past his opponent, and surrender the advantage of altitude.

This technique was not difficult for Jimmy Hall, now an ace pilot with five aerial victories to his credit. He plunged straight down, he said, standing on his rudder bar. In an instant he had the German combat plane dead centered in the gun sights. Hall narrowed the distance to where his bullets could not possibly miss the mark, and was about to unleash his machine guns, when suddenly he heard a horrific sound just above his head. At that critical moment fabric began tearing away from Hall's upper right wing! Jimmy was forced to immediately abandon the attack and quickly decelerate by pulling up hard, lest he suffer a catastrophic wing failure. As it was, enough damage had been done that it was impossible to hold altitude. Leaving the battle to Green and Rickenbacker, Jimmy attempted to fly his crippled Nieuport homeward. However, by the time Hall approached the front lines,

Captain Jimmy Hall — 94th Aero Squadron

he was within range of the big German anti-aircraft guns. With altitude constantly decreasing, he became even more vulnerable. The defense of flying erratically, giving the enemy little opportunity to fix the aircraft's position, was not an option. Jimmy was barely able to keep his Nieuport level by displacing his control stick to one side. Any evasive maneuver would have caused him to lose directional control completely. Hall was the proverbial sitting duck—the dream target of German gunners. A large 37-millimeter shell found its mark in the Nieuport's engine. Miraculously the round did not explode, but impact was sufficient to cause the already disabled biplane to literally fall from the sky. Hall tumbled one thousand meters while he saw the earth rushing to meet him at diverse angles. His controls did not respond until the instant before impact. At that moment Hall was able to stop the Nieuport's gyrations and flared just enough to crash in a horizontal attitude. When he hit the landing gear was demolished and the badly broken fuselage skidded abruptly to a stop. Except for the life-saving flare the Nieuport had plummeted entirely out of control. Hall could not have directed his biplane to the open field in which he'd gone down. Looking around, he saw that this little clearing was wholly encircled by forest. As bad as things were, a slightly different course to the ground and Jimmy would have fatally crashed in the woodlands.

German troops had earthen bunkers in the wood that surrounded this open field. Scarcely had Hall's plane come to rest when he saw a number of enemy soldiers rush to towards him from every direction. Jimmy was not greeted with hostility—rather several Germans kindly assisted him out of the wreckage. Jimmy could not bear weight upon his injured feet. Therefore, his captors carried him to a field dressing station. A corpsman who attended Jimmy found he had severely fractured his right ankle, his nose and perhaps his left ankle as well. His injuries were bound and he was given refreshments. Hall was somewhat surprised with the humane treatment he received, leading him to think, "This is not as bad as it might have been." In his pocket he carried orders for the 94th Squadron and when left for a moment alone, he quickly wadded the document into his mouth and, with a little difficulty, swallowed. Later, when asked for his papers, Hall presented his identification card and his wallet, which contained a fair amount of money. Jimmy's billfold, including his money, was promptly returned.

Remarkably, an hour later, Jimmy was visited by the very combat pilots he had attacked earlier in the day. Through an interpreter he spoke with the German airman whose plane had filled Hall's gun sight. What a strange feeling it was to meet personally his antagonist, a man who would have been dead had not the Nieuport's wing fabric failed. Calmly these officers explained to Hall that his patrol's attack had proven successful for one of their comrades had been "shot down in flames." As it turned out, this triumph was Eddie Rickenbacker's second aerial victory. Still the Germans bore Hall no ill will. In fact, Hall was taken to their squadron at Mars-le-Tour, only a short drive from the field dressing dugout, before making the longer journey to the hospital.

Their headquarters was situated in a French town home—much nicer by far than any accommodations of the French or American Air Services. Jimmy was made comfortable on a sofa while a fine meal was prepared for the airmen—Hall included.

Awaiting dinner, one of the Germans played popular French songs on a piano. The others engaged Jimmy in friendly conversation. It was extremely rare to meet an American pilot. They knew he flew for the hat-in-the-ring squadron from the insignia on his Nieuport. From the emblem on his helmet, they discerned that Jimmy had also flown with the Escadrille Lafayette. At first Hall was cautious, thinking perhaps they were attempting to retrieve vital information through a relaxed interrogation. But the questions they asked had nothing to do with intelligence gathering. Rather, these airmen considered him truly a fellow aviator, one who had fought against them illustriously. Now they paid him considerable homage. Perhaps they knew who Jimmy was—the author of *Kitchener's Mob.* This book had drawn considerable publicity, as it was first published as a series of articles in the renowned *Atlantic Monthly.* In *Kitchener's Mob* Jimmy had given an honest account of war in the trenches—*including* depicting his opponents as human beings with the capacity for compassion. This is not the norm of propaganda. Fairness is always esteemed by just men, even though circumstances dictate an unfortunate adversarial state of affairs. However, Hall's modesty would never allow disclosure in his writings of personal recognition, and so on this point we can only speculate.

Nonetheless Hall's *manner* and *mindset* certainly affected his captors. There was no bitterness in his heart for this third misfortune. Rather he was grateful for miraculously surviving his literal fall into enemy territory. It was clear to the Germans that Jimmy appreciated the assistance and care given to him. Thankfulness is a cardinal virtue and ennobles the sufferer as well as the caregiver. Consider the ten lepers whom Jesus cleansed. Only one, a Samaritan, fell at the feet of the Son of God and gave thanks. This man was a stranger to the Lord's race. Nonetheless, Christ praised him and acknowledged his faith. Regarding the others Jesus asked in disappointment: "Were there not ten cleansed? but where are the nine?" Jimmy's sincerity quickly captured the hearts of his former adversaries. True, it was fortunate that Hall crashed in the midst of men, *men who were men*, and not fallen *former*-men. In the next world war there would exist some *no-longer-men;* creatures that, having lost their humanity, evolved inversely into Gestapo-created carnivores. However, the German captors who cared for Jimmy possessed inherent goodness and were soon drawn to a kind man in bonds of friendship.

Later an intelligence officer did question Hall. Still he was treated respectfully and not coerced in any way. When Jimmy was finally taken to a hospital, he was placed in a large ward of enlisted men. However, his escort, a German officer, strenuously objected. Emphatically he stated that it made no difference that Hall was a prisoner, he was an airman officer, and ordered that he be treated as such. Accordingly they placed Jimmy in a semi-private room reserved for men of rank.

Jimmy was given a photograph of his wrecked Nieuport by the German he "failed to kill." It plainly showed the wing shorn of fabric and the engine knocked from its mount by the un-exploded shell. Explaining his conflicting emotions Hall later wrote:

> I regretted, as a pursuit pilot that I had not shot him down, and was deeply grateful, as a human being, that the event fell out as it did.[158]

Additionally, his German friends extended Hall the courtesy of dropping a message on the French side of the lines to inform the 94th Squadron that Hall had survived the awful crash of his Nieuport. Jimmy learned afterward that the "German pilot who dropped it was himself shot down . . . and made prisoner."

Jimmy was transferred to a hospital prison where his broken ankle and injured feet kept him flat in bed for six weeks. He was confined in the lovely village of Landshut, Bavaria and was treated "generously" by the warden and prison staff. In this isolated world he was surrounded with "an ocean of silence and slow time . . . abundant leisure," although deprived of "personal liberty," as a P.O.W. His fellow captives were mostly officer aviators, like himself, and were likewise recovering from wounds. Some had been terribly disfigured and maimed, or savagely burned. Of this period Jimmy wrote:

> We talked of old combats which seemed to have taken place centuries ago, in the course of a previous existence . . . We bore on our persons and uniforms evidence of the mischances that had brought us tumbling out of the air and had swept us to that quiet old town in Lower Bavaria, far beyond the tumult and clamor or war . . . We had youth in common, memorable adventures in common; whatever our nationality, we spoke a common language, the vivid picturesque slang of the Air Service . . . and we had met a common fate, or, more accurately, perhaps, an uncommon one, for we were still living.[159]

Best of all Jimmy was provided with volumes of British and American literature published at Leipzig. In his writing he revealed the extreme austerity of prison life regarding physical comforts—while at the same time he glorified in *mental* opportunities:

> A fifteen cent lunch at a Child's restaurant would seem a feast to me, and a piece of milk chocolate—are there such luxuries as chocolate in the world? But for prisoners, I for one, have no complaint to make . . . we have a splendid little library here . . . I didn't realize, until I saw it, how book-hungry I was. Now I'm cramming history, biography, essays, novels . . . A prisoner of war has his compensations. Here I've come out of the turmoil of a life of the most intense nervous excitement . . .
>
> We are like monks in a convent. We're almost entirely out of touch with the outside world . . . Until now this cloistered life has been very pleasant. I've had time to think and to make plans for a

future which, comparatively speaking, seems assured. One has periods of restlessness, of course. When these come I console myself as best I may. Even for prisoners of war there are possibilities of adventure, adventure in companionship . . . By Jove! this is an interesting place![160]

Just as James Hall had been plane-wrecked three times, there was another man who was shipwrecked "thrice." This man endured incredible hardships, including being stoned and whipped. Like Hall and Dyer he learned to *maintain a quiet mind*, the core virtue of that state which always presages true joy—the state of contentment. This man was the Apostle Paul who wrote:

> I have learned, in whatsoever state I am, therewith to be content. I know both how to be abased, and I know how to abound: every where and in all things I am instructed both to be full and to be hungry, both to abound and to suffer need. I can do all things through Christ which strengtheneth me.

In mid November, 1918, the prisoners kept in Landshut at the Schloss Trausnitz numbered four airmen, namely Hall, Browning, Codman, and Lewis. Although isolated from world events Jimmy and his comrades felt that something of great importance was shaking the foundations of the old German regime. For the first time the camp guards displayed almost an indifferent manner. They saw one soldier actually throw his uniform cap on the ground and stamp on it, while another ripped off his insignia—unthinkable acts for disciplined soldiers of the Fatherland.

The prison inspector approached the four inmates with a friendly greeting asking them how they were enjoying the fair autumn days and the quietude of their lives at Landshut. One of the airman was bold enough to ask the inspector what had happened on the "outside." The inspector was hesitant but at length answered:

> Yes you are right. Something has happened. I'm sure that you'll all be sorry to learn of it, but the fact is the war is over. An armistice was signed at eleven o'clock this morning.[161]

The allied airmen were simply stunned. When after a profound silence they responded to this news, it was in an almost humorous manner. Codman replied that it was nice of Herr Inspector to come and say goodbye and that in the future they would often think of him. Then Codman asked if he and his friends should leave the prison at the main or the side gate. The inspector was not taken back by Codman's impudence, but simply replied that no provision had yet been made for the release of prisoners. It would be quite some time, he explained, before such a possibility could be realized. Then all four spoke at once, trying to reason with Herr Inspector. They asked what purpose was served keeping them locked up with the war at its end. Why occupy the guards' time watching over four unimportant airmen? Couldn't the Germans simply look the other way while they escaped through an inadvertently unlocked gate? All the while Jimmy and his comrades pleaded their arguments, the inspector paced back and forth, obviously perplexed. Finally, he brought the discussion to an abrupt end, telling the airman that it was "quite impossible"—they were still prisoners of war and until such time as orders were received, authorizing an exchange or release, they must remain incarcerated.

Germany had been defeated—the old dynasty was rapidly losing power. The country was, in fact, on the verge of civil war. Rioting had broken out in Munich, not forty miles from Landshut. The four prisoners of war in Schloss Trausnitz knew nothing of this. Nonetheless, that evening they found it impossible to sleep. After all that Jimmy had been through—from trench warfare to aerial combat, surviving three crashes and spending months as a prisoner, it seemed totally unreal that the Great War was over—especially as they were still confined in Trausnitz. This too, was about to end. Their remonstrance to the prison camp inspector had been far more effective than the four airmen could possibly have believed. Late the next morning the good man visited the captives, and said in a casual manner:

> You may go. I think it will be best for you to make for the Swiss border, by way of Munich, Lindau and Lake Constance. I have wired to a friend, an artillery officer, at Lindau. He will meet you at the station there, so be on the lookout for a well set-up man of thirty-five, with ruddy cheeks, blue eyes, and a small blonde mustache. He wears a captain's uniform.

Jimmy could scarcely believe it and responded saying: "And we may go now?" A fellow airman incredulously asked, "And do you mean that we are to go by train?" The German inspector answered:

> You don't want to walk to Switzerland, do you? There is a train for Munich at twelve-thirty. You will have to stop there for the night and leave for Lindau the following morning. If you succeed in getting through you will be at Romanshorn, in Switzerland, before dark tomorrow evening. Remember, this is an escape . . . I have no right to let you go and am doing so on my own authority. The commandant is strongly opposed to the idea, and I have promised to take the blame in the event that you are re-captured. Don't let that happen. You might make it very awkward for me. But with the revolution on in Bavaria, if you have your wits about you, you should be able to get through.[162]

In a matter of minutes Jimmy Hall and his three friends gathered their few possessions and bade a hasty goodbye to their benefactor. The inspector had already purchased train tickets to prevent unnecessary scrutiny at the station ticket office. He accepted reimbursement from the *escapees* in prison-camp currency, which of course was useless. Amazingly this officer not only permitted their escape, risking personal reprisal, but also paid for their transportation and arranged with an accomplice in Lindau to assist with their passage into Switzerland. He did not, however, provide the men with a change of clothes or papers. When they left the prison castle, the four wore their American Army uniforms with the Air Service insignias on their jackets! There are many accounts of P.O.W. escapees with stolen or cleverly forged papers, dressed to blend in with the population. Not so with these fugitives—they were anything but inconspicuous. With elated emotions Jimmy and his friends hurried down to the Landshut station. After waiting only a few minutes they boarded the train for Munich, sitting in a compartment occupied by an older gentlemen and a nun. The old man looked the airmen over from top to bottom. The escapees avoided eye contact with him and thankfully no words were spoken by anyone in the compartment for the length of the journey.

When the train pulled into the crowded Munich depot the four made for a station exit as expeditiously as possible, without attracting attention. The train to Lindau was scheduled to depart the following morning. There were soldiers and policemen everywhere. To their advantage the city was in obvious confusion, and despite their eye-catching allied uniforms, no one questioned them. Jimmy wrote:

> If we loitered about the streets the chances were that we should be taken up, for men in the uniform of any of the Allied nations were not then to be seen in Germany except in prison camps . . . Not far from the station we saw a hotel, and, as it was necessary to take a chance somewhere, we agreed to take one there . . . [Codman] asked for a room large enough to accommodate the four of us. The man at the desk looked at us in a bewildered manner and said, "*Bitte schön*?" Codman repeated the request and added that we should like lunch served in our room. He did this with admirable casualness, as though it were a customary thing for American army officers to be touring Germany.[163]

The hotel clerk simply checked them in and soon room service provided a wonderful meal—the first bounteous dinner the airman had enjoyed in a great while. Fearful that at any moment their room might be raided by military police they anxiously passed the afternoon and evening. However, they were undisturbed and the following morning boarded the train for Lindau without the least difficulty. Leaving the station in Lindau an artillery officer with a blonde mustache approached and in English asked if they wished to go to Switzerland. In was difficult for Jimmy to fathom after long captivity as a P.O.W., and after all of the failed schemes he and his associates had devised to escape, that they were actually being "escorted" out of Germany by a captain wearing the enemy uniform! The artillery officer led them to the shore of Lake Constance. Off in the distance the magnificent Swiss Alps could be seen. Near the loading platform the German captain directed their attention to a particular boat, which he said would take them to Switzerland. He expressed the hope that they would be able to board without being arrested. However, he advised that if they were, he could do nothing more for them.

Boarding the vessel two customs officers scrutinized the four American airmen "suspiciously," but again, said nothing. Soon they sequestered themselves in an obscure corner of the ship. At length the boat cast off and through a small porthole the aviators could see the shores of Germany growing more distant. Nervous tension broke as liberty seemed "assured." It had scarcely been more than a day since Herr Inspector announced his plans to help them gain their freedom. Having avoided seizure from Landshut to Lindau the ex-captives stepped confidently on the neutral soil of Romanshorn, Switzerland—when, ironically, they were promptly *arrested by* Swiss authorities. The Swiss officials explained that their arrival *by steamer* was most unorthodox. Escapees traditionally arrived by row boat or swam to safety. Furthermore, the Swiss government had not received communications "either from the Central or Allied Powers, with respect to the release of prisoners." There was nothing in their policy manuals to cover so extraordinary an arrival as four uniformed American aviators stepping offhandedly down the gangway from a German ferryboat. Codman quickly answered that theirs was "an escape de luxe!"

In response to Codman's quick wit the Swiss administrator sent off a wire to the United States authorities in Berne. A short time later the American officials answered, requesting that the prematurely released prisoners be re-released. Within forty-eight hours the four airmen were in Paris, France, enjoying the sweet air of true liberty. Although the armistice commenced on November 11, 1918, it should be remembered that the definition of armistice is a *truce* in a war to discuss terms for peace. The Treaty of Versailles was not signed until June 28, 1919. Article 214 of the Versailles Treaty stated:

> The repatriation of prisoners of war and interned civilians shall take place as soon as possible after the coming into force of the present Treaty and shall be carried out with the greatest rapidity.

Thus the war was *not* over for the vast majority of P.O.W.s for seven long months *after* Hall's astonishing "escape de lux."

One may say that Jimmy was just incredibly lucky; lucky to have fallen from the sky into the hands of humane enemies; lucky to have been befriended by officers in the German air corps and treated as one of their own in a German hospital by kind and skillful attendants; lucky to have a castle prison inspector who was so benignant as to act as both architect and financier of his escape to freedom; lucky to have escaped successfully; lucky to enjoy freedom from captivity many months before other prisoners of war. However, the odds of such luck exceed those of a state lottery. Rather, there is a law of the harvest. Fair consequences follow a field cleared of stones and noxious weeds, where growing life is encouraged, appreciated, nourished, and cultivated. For the good fruit man labors, but God miraculously provides the increase. Jimmy developed a quiet and contented mind, cleared of stones of bitterness and weedy depression. Hall's sincerity, his appreciation, his contagious love of friendship, his willingness to be useful and to be of service—affected everyone whose life touched his. Jimmy followed the maxim found in Ecclesiastes to "cast thy bread upon the waters." Simply stated, the good Jimmy lived returned to him *increased* by God.

CHAPTER 17

INCREASE

Lord and the Life-giver,
Thine is the quickening power that gives increase;
From Thee have flowed, as from a pleasant river,
Our plenty, wealth, prosperity, and peace. [164]

—WILLIAM CROSWELL DOANE

AT THE LATTER END OF NOVEMBER, 1918, Paris again became the City of Lights. In the evening hours every lamp once more brightened the homes and hearts of men. Each light reveled in the glow of thousands of other lights. The universal glimmering of Paris sparkled like stars of Andromeda Galaxy—each beam a luminous pinpoint woven in a blanket of radiance. The ebony shade of the surrounding French countryside contrasted sharply with the resplendent city, enhancing the illusion of a Parisian constellation set in the depths of space. Gone were the horrid blackouts that had for so long stained the night with dark shadows of war. The sinister blemish was lifted and night seemed as bright as day. Sunrise no longer brought war's escalation, although the Champs Élysées was still fringed with German cannonade. Rather, young Parisians played on the big barrels of steel, the cannon roar now transformed and softened by children's laughter. Jimmy wrote:

> Those who were in France shortly after the Armistice of 1918 will never forget the universal feeling of blessedness—there is no other word for it—prevailing then. Bitterness, sorrow, even

> mourning for the millions dead, seemed to have been put aside, for the moment at least. I doubt whether, in all European history, there had ever been a time when the hearts of men were so filled with serene hope for the future . . . The war that was to end war had run its appalling length.[165]

Jimmy searched the old airman haunts of Chatham and Maurice's. There he met again several comrades whom he thought dead. Ironically, these men thought Hall had perished as well. Reunions of this sort were not uncommon as order replaced chaos—as it always does in times of peace.

Although prospects were high for an officer in the Air Service, Hall decided to resign his commission—after one more flight. He personally requested from General Patrick the opportunity to fly a final mission over the front, "Solely," he said, for his "own pleasure." Surprisingly the General acquiesced with the admonishment: "Don't get yourself killed now that the war is over." When Jimmy went out to the Spad hangers he was told: "Take your pick. We've got 'em to burn, now." There were literally hundreds of factory new Spads lined in formation. Sadly, nearly all were deliberately destroyed by the military later that winter—by fire. Jimmy chose a beautiful new machine that had never seen combat. In a matter of moments he was high above the airfield of Orly. Jimmy wrote:

> What a glorious sensation it was, after six months in a prison camp, to be traveling by route of the air again! I am grateful for the fact that I never became used to flying in the sense of being wearied by it. Every time I left the earth I felt exhilarated, lifted up in spirit as well as in body. It was, rather, as though I had left my body behind, and all the slowness and heaviness of corporeal existence . . . And there was nothing, now, to mar the fullest enjoyment of that upper world: no danger of ambush; no need to scrutinize the sunlit peaks of curling shifting vapor for the presence of enemies. My only companions seemed to be bands of seraphim and cherubim hidden somewhere in the depths of blue sky.[166]

Nancy Hall Rutgers and the Author
(Painting of the Bounty in Background by Herb Kawainui Kane)

Nicholas Rutgers, Jr. – a Valiant Aviation Veteran of WWII

Jimmy Hall Guides Eddie Rickenbacker to His First Victory by Herb Kawainui Kane

Final Victory by Rich Thistle

The 13th Aero Squadron by Jim Laurier

Balloon Buster Extraordinaire by Stan Stokes (Hanriot flown by Willy Coppens de Houthhulst)

Balloon Buster by Robert Taylor (Sopwith Camel flown by Henry Botterell)

Dawn Patrol by Robert Taylor (SE5A Fighters of the 85th Squadron)

Between Heaven and Hell by James Dietz (RAF squadrons tangle with two Jastas literally filling the sky with airplanes)

Circus Rolls at dawn by James Dietz (Albatross D.V. Scout)

Encounter with a Legend by Rich Thistle

Gotcha by Stan Stokes (Fokker D VII downed by Eddie Rickenbacker)

Jimmy Hall's First Victory by Herb Kawaninui Kane

The Fokker Scourge by Stan Stokes (Max Immelmann flies an Eindecker equipped with prop synchronized machine gun)

Mud in Your Eye by James Dietz

The Kaiser's Battle by Stan Stokes (CL IIIa strafes British Mk IV tanks during the Spring offensive of 1918)

Coming In Over the Estuary by Robert Taylor (The P38 was the last plane flown by Saint-Exupéry)

In large measure, Jimmy flew this flight *in memorial.* He thought of all the young men who had taken to these skies in temerarious adventure, from war's beginning to the Armistice—so many gifted, high spirited, men of valor had fallen. Hall thought of Lufbery, Chapman, McConnell and scores of other friends. He thought of others fliers of great courage, of many nationalities, like Richthofen, who braved enemies and elements. All these were gone "in their excellence." Jimmy flew over Dontrier, where he had witnessed a French reconnaissance plane pounded into flames by the bullets of a German fighter. It fell a thousand feet when its wings collapsed. There were three crewmen in the photographic aircraft. Jimmy saw the trio leap into mid-air, their "flying-suits afire." Below his Spad the battlefields lay silent but the air through which he flew seemed to carry still the death-cries of the slain.

Oh men who dwell safely in lands of liberty, *think* of the cost of our ease. We who mature to manhood and grow old with cares only of *living,* who each day face life and not death—remember, remember our young brothers who fell in the trenches or from the skies; who left a sweetheart's embrace, never again in mortality to feel her warmth, who never held sons or daughters, and who died before parents. To these valiant young men we owe a debt that can never be repaid and may only be partially settled by devotion to the ideals for which they gave their life's blood.

Jimmy's last assignment in France was to write a history of the Escadrille Lafayette, assisted by another aviator, Charles Nordhoff. The two writers had never met, since Nordhoff had trained at the *Ecole d' Aviation* after Hall. Initially, Jimmy thought Charles rather bombastic but soon came to regard him as "a delightful companion." Ultimately their partnership would sire their personal fortunes as they co-authored the timeless book, *Mutiny on the Bounty.* During the period these two new friends were engaged in writing the Lafayette Corps History, they discussed future plans. Ever since boyhood Hall had dreamed of the South Pacific world of Melville's *Typee*. Interestingly, Nordhoff's grandfather had sailed the tropics and instilled in his grandson a vicarious love of the islands. Jimmy and Charles decided that together they would visit the South Seas when released from active duty.

In late 1919 two former combat pilots called on Mr. Sedgwick of the *Atlantic Monthly* magazine. Hall and Nordhoff approached Sedgwick with the idea of composing a series of articles from first hand experience in the South Pacific. They explained that financially neither had sufficient funds to commence the journey. Sedgwick liked the idea but felt *Harper's* magazine would provide a better fit. He gave the writers a letter of introduction to Thomas Wells, editor of Harper's. Wells embraced the project with enthusiasm and advanced a sufficient sum to begin the adventure. In no time the duo set sail from San Francisco, bound for Tahiti, for an "indefinite sojourn in the South Seas."

Upon arrival, it was delightfully necessary to wander about the islands and learn of the natives "before setting pens to paper." Nordhoff preferred the more settled regions, while Hall spent most of his time in the lagoon islands of the Low Archipelago, more suited to his love of solitude. When at length they found each other again, the two collaborated on their second literary work, *Faery Lands of the South Seas,* which Harper's serialized and then published in book form. *Faery Lands* stayed in print for a decade. Years passed before Nordhoff and Hall again co-authored a manuscript. In the intervening period they separated and enjoyed vastly different experiences. For Jimmy this was a time of immense happiness coupled with absolute poverty.

In the Tahitian Islands, thirty-five miles from the capital town of Papeete of French Polynesia, Hall found the perfect residence. It was a single-room house remotely situated on one acre of ground, totally suited to his taste and pocketbook. Rent was a meager three dollars a month. From his veranda Jimmy viewed the infinite blue of the Pacific. A pure mountain stream flowed past his home, providing drinking water and added beauty. Palm trees graced the land. Truly this was a paradise where he could live and compose literature undisturbed.

Life undulates like waves of the ocean. Jimmy's writing hit low tide. Despite his extremely modest life style, he found his fortunes reduced to five American dollars. With seemingly no literary prospects and pressed with the immediate need of replenishing his nearly exhausted food supply, Hall turned optimistically to farming a little plot of land next to his home. The ground was fertile, but a multitude of ants devoured most of the seed before it could sprout. What did germinate was sheared away by an army of land crabs the moment green shoots appeared. His total harvest consisted of several ears of corn, a couple of tomatoes and a single squash. Disheartened after months of labor, Jimmy put away his gardening tools and oiled his neglected typewriter.

As Jimmy was preparing to resume writing, he saw a Chinese neighbor whom he had never met, driving an old wagon down the road. This man, named Hop Sing, lived with his family a quarter mile from Jimmy in a shack built from packing cases. Although Sing's carpentry skills were doubtful, his gardening prowess was not. Hall had before observed that Sing's plot of sweet potatoes heartily survived the ants and crabs. Jimmy never thought to ask Hop Sing how he succeeded raising produce in spite of these pests.

Hall still possessed a few packages of American seed which he had purchased for one dollar. On seeing Hop Sing approach, Jimmy called out to him to stop his wagon, then ran out to meet him in the roadway, offering the packets of seed as a small present. The seed was of the highest quality—beans, lettuce, sweet corn, pumpkin and squash. It was a simple gift, but Sing did not understand and thought that Jimmy was trying to sell him the seed. Most likely the Americans Sing had met were strictly profit motivated. Certainly Hop Sing could not have supposed that a virtual stranger would *give* away something which Sing considered to be of great value.

To a true husbandman there is no such thing as seed that is *worth* only a dollar. I learned this from my father who cherished earth and sky. Aviation was Dad's *second* love and he acquired the skills to build aircraft of his own design and fly them. His first love, however, was *growing*. Not that he preferred farming to flying. Rather Dad preferred growing sons and daughters to any other vocation. In humble circumstances, Father found that he could not pursue his career in aviation without sacrificing vital responsibilities to his beloved wife and emerging family. So he set aside his aspirations of flight and sunk his shovel into deep rich soil. Dad established Gibby Floral and Greenhouses and raised flowers, while he raised his family. One day he said to me:

> Bryce, look at this seed. It is a brown seed that we put in brown earth. Yet it grows a plant that springs green from the ground and blossoms into every color of the rainbow.

Another time my father asked how much commission I made on an aircraft sale. I answered and he replied that to receive a percentage of the whole was not much of an increase. This puzzled me and I asked him what he meant. Dad said:

> I plant a seed and it grows into something worth far more than the seed.

Then I understood that increase was not a percentage of the whole. Rather, increase is multiplication of the original into something far greater than itself. The financial cost of a tiny seed is very little compared to the price of a luxurious, blooming plant. A seed without scent can become a flower of immense fragrance. Blossoms from a single seed will yield a thousand thousand seeds. The increase of life from seed is a miracle. You cannot put a price on a miracle. Edgar Guest wrote:

I paid a dime for a package of seeds
And the clerk tossed them out with a flip.
"We've got 'em assorted for every man's needs,"
He said with a smile on his lip,
"Pansies and poppies and asters and peas!
Ten cents a package! And pick as you please!"
Now seeds are just dimes to the man in the store,
And dimes are the things that he needs;
And I've been to buy them in seasons before,
But have thought of them merely as seeds.
But it flashed through my mind as I took them this time,
"You have purchased a miracle here for a dime!
You've a dime's worth of power no man can create,
You've a dime's worth of life in your hand!
You've a dime's worth of mystery, destiny, fate,
Which the wisest cannot understand.
In this bright little package, now isn't it odd?
You've a dime's worth of something known only to God!"[167]

When Jimmy placed the packets of seed into Hop Sings hands, Sing was of course interested, but he wondered if he could afford the price? He queried Hall saying, "How much?" Jimmy answered that he wanted nothing in payment; this was just a little present. Sing had to grab hold of the seatback to prevent his falling out of the wagon. Such was the shock of the gift from Jimmy, who now was a stranger no longer.

The incident soon passed from Jimmy's mind as he had other things to consider, such as where his next meal would come from. Fortunately he had prepaid several months rent in advance. There were bananas and coconuts on the property but the owner had excluded rights to these edibles from the lease. Jimmy could not even glean leftovers, as this fruit was picked green and sold to Papeete markets. He was, however, working on a new idea for a manuscript called *Settling Down in Polynesia*. Yet even if finished soon, Hall would have to send it to America and wait three months for a check—*if* the publishers liked it. With his few remaining francs Jimmy purchased a little food. He kept just enough money to post the manuscript.. What would he do when his rations were gone? Hall decided to "worry about that when the time came."

After several days of intense mental labor, try as he might, Jimmy could not get the typewriter to put ink on page three of his story. He said, "The mere fact of *having* to work seemed to make the accomplishment impossible." His food stock was down to several tins of beef, and he was no doubt hungry as well as frustrated with his writing progress. Jimmy recorded:

> I was aroused from a mood of profound dejection by a knock at the door. It was Hop Sing, and with him were his wife, their three small children and [Sing's] 'fadda-law.' I felt embarrassed and could think of nothing to say.
>
> "What name, you?" he then asked.
>
> I told him. Another interval of silence. I gave my forefinger to the child on Mrs. Sing's lap. It clasped it gravely and held on. Mrs. Sing smiled. Her father, too, smiled; at least, his face wrinkled suddenly . . . Sing took from his pocket one of the packets of seeds I had given him.
>
> "What name, this?" he asked . . . I brought out a seed catalogue and showed him the illustrations in color of various kinds of vegetables. He was much interested and exchanged remarks in Chinese with his father-in-law.[168]

Jimmy and the Sing family enjoyed a wonderful visit. Obviously the Sing farmers were completely delighted with the prospects of higher quality vegetables than the tough Tahitian varieties. A thunderstorm had kept the new friends indoors for a short time. When the storm broke, Hop Sing went out to his wagon and returned with three large watermelons, a live chicken, a basket of eggs and a bottle of Dubonnet. Jimmy was "astonished and genuinely moved." Hop Sing said simply, "Littly plesent, you." They all shook hands warmly and bid each other good bye. Hall wrote of this occasion:

> It would be difficult to exaggerate the value, to me, of their generous gift. Tinned beef is a nourishing food, but I had lost all relish for it during the First Great War . . . How welcome, then, was this more palatable food! I thought of having a chicken dinner at once, but on second thought decided to preserve my fowl. Perhaps she would lay . . . I might from this small beginning raise enough chickens to provide for all my needs. So I staked the hen out in the dooryard with a string tied to her leg.[169]

After Jimmy had finished a sumptuous six egg omelet and a large slice of watermelon he settled down to work with zest and renewed inspiration. All day his typewriter clanged through line after line. By early evening he had completely finished his manuscript! In several days the steamer from New Zealand to San Francisco would stop at Papeete. As the ship ran only once a month, Hall had just enough time to post his manuscript in the northbound mail. Not trusting a courier and possessing insufficient money to pay for postage and round trip bus fare, Jimmy set out on foot the thirty-five miles to Papeete.

Walking along the road that wound its way from the village of Taravao, the beautiful day was transformed into a magnificent evening. Jimmy was truly contented. He had a new friend in Hop Sing, whose generosity had relieved his hunger. More importantly the hours spent with the Sing Family had helped to remove a mental block which seriously frustrated his efforts to write while lifting him from a rare state of depression. Now with a genuine sense of accomplishment and a sincere feeling of gratitude toward the kind islanders, Jimmy walked briskly in the wondrous night. Miles fell behind him as he crossed valleys, edged his way past lagoons of calm waters mirroring the lights of the firmament. At times the roadway hugged the mountains—huge black shadows where slits of silver marked the descent of high, tumbling waterfalls. Now and then he drew near Tahitian homes, filled with evening's life—lamps glowing, strains of soft guitar, Polynesian voices flavored with harmonies of France. Jimmy wrote:

> If it were true that a man's wealth may be estimated in terms of things he can do without, then in that sense I might hope soon to achieve affluence. Material possessions added little to the sum of one's happiness, and I could always earn enough at writing to provide for the simple necessities of life. Whenever the mild-eyed, melancholy tropical wolves came sniffing apologetically at my door, I could write a story of one sort or another, and live on the proceeds of the sale of it.[170]

A thirty-five mile trek expends a great deal of energy. Near midnight Jimmy began thinking of the delicious omelet that had provided his day's strength. Hall knelt at fresh water stream and drank heartily, then tightened his belt. He knew he needed nourishment but what, he thought, could he do about it now? He walked on, growing weaker as he went.

Soon he came to a solitary beach whose sole inhabitants were profiled in the light of their small hut. It was an old Polynesian couple, enjoying a midnight meal over a wood fire. Jimmy paused to admire the beautiful domestic scene framed by palms, waving gently from the breath of a cool, salt scented, ocean breeze. The old woman saw the traveler and called out, "Haere mai ta maa!" which means "come and eat." This is a customary greeting and should not always be taken literally. Jimmy responded with the polite and typical, "Paia vau," meaning, "I'm not hungry." However the old native would not take no for an answer and begged him to share their supper. Shell fish and a nutlike vegetable roasted over the coals. The aroma from their meal kindled Jimmy's already keen appetite and he did not need to be asked again. The old man and woman were pleased with Jimmy's fondness for their cooking and insisted: "We have plenty, enough for a dozen."

When at length Jimmy had eaten his fill, he asked his hosts what type of shell fish and vegetables they had served him. They answered: land crabs and *mapé*, or Pacific chestnuts. Jimmy was amazed, as land crabs literally overran his home. There was also a grove of *mapé* on the property that littered the ground with nuts, which his landlord never harvested. For this reason Jimmy had supposed that neither was edible. Hall thought of all the time he had wasted in trying to grow a garden when a steady supply of food was right under his nose. Then he thought how difficult it was trying to rid the leased land of crabs. They would dart in their holes the moment he appeared and infested his garden the minute he turned his back. Jimmy asked the old man how he had caught so many crabs. The native demonstrated the simple procedure. He took from his hut a long staff from which a cord was tied, much like a fishing pole. To the end of the line he attached hibiscus blossoms and leaves. Next he cast the line onto the beach where crab holes were visible and quietly waited. In no time a number of crabs had fixed their nippers on the bait. Then he jerked the line to his feet and quickly emptied the crabs into a bucket. He gave the pole to Jimmy who performed the same task with ease. Now Hall could not wait to return home and "begin fishing [his] garden." He said goodbye to his new friends and, with renewed strength, set out again for Papeete.

The following day Jimmy arrived in the capital town in time to see the northbound steamer dock in the harbor. As he posted the parcel he said, "I breathed over it a silent prayer." After postage was paid, Hall still possessed enough francs for a one way return ticket plus change. Killing time until the bus left, Jimmy strolled through the market district and down to the waterfront. He was enjoying the day immensely. While he was walking along the Quai de Commerce, a squatty little Chinese man came running after him, out of breath, speaking in a Tahitian-Chinese mix that was completely incomprehensible to Hall. The only words Jimmy understood in the gibberish were "Hop Sing." He asked the man to slow his speech down and take a breath. The man's name was Lee Fat, a local merchant and Hop Sing's brother-in-law. Hop Sing had written Lee, telling him of a new friend who had given him wonderful new seeds for his garden, *without charge.* Lee finished his narrative telling Jimmy, "Maitai! Maitai! Hop Sing glad. Me glad." Then the enthusiastic man abruptly said goodbye and ran into his nearby store. Jimmy was amazed at the gratitude of Hop Sing and his family for the "trifling" gift of seed.

A short time later Jimmy boarded the bus for Papéari, the village closest to his home. As Hall was getting off at his stop the boy who unloaded parcels and baggage handed Jimmy a box. Jimmy protested that it was not his. However, the boy insisted it certainly was, for the parcel had been presented to him by a Chinese man who directed that it be given to Hall at his destination. Jimmy could scarcely believe the boy's story until he opened the box and found it was a gift from Lee Fat, with a hand written note stating simply, "Mr. Hall, for you." Jimmy wrote:

> The parcel contained the following articles: a two-pound box of New Zealand chocolates, a pager bag of litchi nuts, one quart of champagne, and a Chinese lacquered box with a gold dragon on the lid. In the box were two silk handkerchiefs and a silk pajama suit.[171]

Returning home, Jimmy discovered a newly laid egg beneath his contented hen. Hall immediately thought of the remaining eggs Hop Sing had given him. He made a nest of Lee Fat's gift box and within placed the eggs. He then set the mother fowl atop who seemed delighted to have a larger family to hatch. Next Jimmy began "fishing for crabs" in his garden. His skill, acquired from the previous night's adventure with the old man, proved extraordinary. Within a short time Hall caught more land crabs than he could eat. One morning, three weeks later, Jimmy observed his hen leaving her nest. Behind the proud mother four baby chicks followed in trail.

When the landlord and his children came to harvest bananas

and coconuts on the property, Jimmy invited them in for a meal. This was apparently something new for the landlord, whose tenants typically could scarcely afford rent, let alone host a dinner. Jimmy served his guests tasty shellfish and roasted Pacific chestnuts. For desert Hall shared with his guests some of the chocolates he had received from Lee Fat. Of course goodwill followed this kindness. Jimmy wrote:

> The next morning I found on my back veranda a bunch of bananas and a copra sack half filled with mangoes and oranges, gifts from my landlord and his family. Not infrequently, thereafter, Mata, his wife, would send me baked fish, breadfruit, and mountain plantain, fresh from her native oven, and I remembered with deep gratitude that I really owed these benefits to Hop Sing.[172]

Jimmy found it easy to maintain these new friendships. For example, often he stopped to visit the Sings whose industry was simply amazing. Mrs. Sing could be found sorting vegetables with her hands while she rocked the baby's cradle with her foot. Near her head was a cord which, answering a frequent pull from Mrs. Sing, animated a scarecrow that disbursed birds and land crabs alike from the flourishing garden. The old father-in-law continued his life-long trade as a baker. Nearly every week Jimmy found a delicious loaf of bread left at his gate. When Hall first met the Sings he was thin and waning; in a matter of weeks Jimmy put on a healthy fourteen pounds.

Three months passed and although Hall's typewriter chattered away continually, he failed to submit this new work. Jimmy's modest nature was indelibly linked to his self-confidence, and currently was as low as his bank balance. Despite the fact that he had written several successful books, Hall had serious doubts as to the long term commercial viability of his compositions. This may seem unreasonable until it is remembered that Hall's published works primarily were written at the request of publishers. The *Atlantic* had asked Jimmy to write of his experiences in the trenches and thus *Kitchener's Mob* came into print. Sedgwick also commissioned Hall to write *High Adventure,* Jimmy's experiences in the Escadrille Lafayette. Dr. Gros assigned Hall and Nordhoff to write the history of the Escadrille Lafayette while both were still on active duty. Although it was Hall's idea to coauthor *Faery Lands of the South Seas* with Nordhoff, the work did not commence until after they were commissioned by *Harper's.* Aside from these efforts Jimmy had written newspaper and magazine articles paying him from ten to fifteen dollars. Hall knew that selling an *unsolicited* manuscript for substantial profit was quite a different matter from his previous exploits.

The southbound steamer carrying the U.S. mail had docked in Papeete. It was time for Jimmy to visit the post office and determine what fruit, if any, the manuscript *Settling Down in Polynesia* had borne. Again Jimmy walked thirty-five miles to Papeete. This time there was no buoyancy in his step for he visualized another rejection notice. Pathetically, he took a seat on a bench outside the post office and watched as mail clerks disseminated letters and packages to delighted recipients. Even as the sun was setting behind the Tahitian mountains Jimmy sat dejectedly, feeling certain that if a response had reached the Papeete post office it probably would be nothing more than a letter declining the manuscript.

Courage has many faces. A man may confidently meet a battle-hardened enemy in fierce aerial combat and yet lack the self-assurance to approach a postal clerk—particularly if that man has repeatedly met with successive disappointments. Hall could have wall-papered his study with past literary rejection letters.

The fear of failure is one of the most difficult fears to overcome. It takes a man of extraordinary mettle to repeatedly exert himself toward a goal when past experiences seem to prove the improbability of success. Although with renewed vigor he may instigate the enterprise, when the pivotal moment is near and the outcome is about to be unveiled, the returning fear of failure is often magnified horribly.

A classic and sad example of this truth is the story of Charles Yelverton O'Connor, an Irish engineer who immigrated to Australia in the late 1800s. In 1896 a loan of 2.5 million pounds was authorized by the Australian Parliament to fund the Goldfields Pipeline project, a scheme designed to pump five million gallons of water per day, uphill, across three hundred and thirty miles from Perth to Kalgoorlie. Charles O'Connor was appointed chief engineer of this history-making venture. Many thought the plan impossible, subjecting O'Connor to constant cynicism. Undoubtedly O'Connor's greatest critic was himself. As the project grew close to completion, the monster fear of failure loomed unconquerable before the brilliant engineer. On March 10, 1902 O'Connor took his own life. Incredibly his suicide note included detailed final instructions to finish the pipeline. A short time after O'Connor's death the pumps were engaged and life-giving water flowed as per his calculations from Perth, elevation 67 feet, to Kalgoorlie, elevation 1,203 feet! To this day O'Connor's thirty inch diameter pipeline still supplies millions of gallons of water a day to vast desert reaches and to the cities of Kalgoorlie and Boulder. Had O'Connor not succumbed to illusionary horrors, who can say what other magnificent feats of engineering his genius might have created?

Under the stress of this same fear, Jimmy Hall sat quietly on the postal bench. He wrote:

> I waited until the sun was sinking and the post office was about to close. Then, summoning all my resolution, I mounted the steps and walked to the delivery window, saying inwardly: 'It's useless to ask. I'm quite certain to be disappointed.' The girl who presided there went hastily through a small number of letters from the 'H' box.

"No, there's nothing for you," she said with a smile . . .

I made a ghastly attempt to smile in return and was going toward the door when she called after me:

"Oh! Just a moment! Yes, there is one letter," she said. "Fifty centimes postage due."

Having paid this I had left only a twenty-five-centime piece, the smallest coin used in French Oceania. But little that mattered. The letter contained a gracious note accepting my manuscript, and a check for five hundred dollars.

To those living luxurious lives in the high altitudes, five hundred dollars may seem a trifling sum, but it was a fortune to me. I had never before received even a half of that amount for anything I had written.[173]

The old adage "It is darkest before dawn" is true. There never was a night eternal. Day always follows, and in its light shapeless dread evaporates as dew.

Looking back on this experience Hall wrote that the "upward trend" in his career began around the time he met Hop Sing. With newly acquired financial independence Jimmy decided to leave the islands for a time and return home to America. Hop Sing and Lee Fat came to see Jimmy off and wish him bon voyage. Sing gave Jimmy baskets of tomatoes and golden sweet corn, freshly harvested from the crops grown from Jimmy's gift of seed. Lee gave his friend, reluctant to receive such lavish presents, slippers and an exquisite silk fan.

On board the America-bound steamer, Jimmy gave Sing's produce to the steward and asked that it be served at his table. At mealtime Hall was seated with only one man. This dining companion was a passenger who boarded in Wellington—a tall, dour man who, according to the steward, constantly complained of the ship's food. The two were first served canned salmon, which brought immediate disapproval from the "bilious" diner who nonetheless picked at the unappetizing fish. Then the steward brought in a steaming plate of eight ears of sweet corn. The man was astounded! Pushing the canned salmon away he feasted with extreme delight on the fresh corn, asking, "Steward, where does this corn come from? It's not on the card." The attendant explained that it was a gift from the young mean seated across from him. After the tall man finished his wonderful meal he apologized to Hall for his abrupt and rude manner. He further explained that he suffered from the miserable stomach illness of dyspepsia. Fresh corn, he said, was one of the few foods he could eat without suffering afterwards from indigestion.

As they chatted, the now cheerful companion asked Jimmy what line of work he was in, besides providing others with delicious corn. When Hall responded that he was a writer, the man's interest was peaked and asked if Jimmy had any manuscripts with him. Hall answered that he did—six compositions of two thousand words each, on various island topics. He then queried further if Jimmy would be so kind as to allow him to see the texts. Jimmy retrieved his writing and his new friend said in a rather commanding tone, "Come back an hour from now and I'll tell you what I think of them." At the appointed time Jimmy returned and the man frankly said he thought two of them "worthless," while he liked the other four. Hall's new friend then introduced himself for the first time, a director of a publishing syndicate in the states. He wanted to purchase the four manuscripts and asked Jimmy his price. Hall asked if one hundred dollars would be too much for all four compositions. The publisher responded *no*—he would give Hall one hundred and fifty dollars each, or six hundred dollars!

Later that night, Jimmy wrote down "a list of benefits, direct and indirect, accruing to me from my trifling gift to Hop Sing." We may imagine his list to be something like the following:

Increase of seed—originally purchased for one dollar:

1. Sing family-of-friends;
2. Three large watermelons, a live chicken, a basket of eggs and a bottle of Dubonnet;

3. The physical and spiritual nourishment necessary to finish the manuscript *Settling down in Polynesia*;
4. Inner joy;
5. A midnight meal of crab and chestnuts;
6. More friendships with the old man and woman;
7. The newly acquired skill of fishing for crab in my garden;
8. A new friend in the person of Lee Fat;
9. A two-pound box of New Zealand chocolates, a pager bag of litchi nuts, one quart of champagne, and a Chinese lacquered box with a gold dragon on the lid, two silk handkerchiefs and a silk pajama suit.
10. A brood of chicks;
11. New friends in the landlord and family;
12. Bananas, mangoes, oranges, baked fish, breadfruit, and mountain plantain;
13. Weekly fresh bread;
14. Increased health and fourteen pounds in body weight;
15. $500 for the sale of manuscript *Settling down in Polynesia*;
16. Baskets of tomatoes and golden sweet corn;
17. Slippers and silk fan;
18. Another new publishing friend;
19. A new source for future publications;
20. Six hundred dollars for four brief island sketches.

CHAPTER 18

ROOTS AND BRANCHES

If I had my life to live over again, I wouldn't have the strength.

—BOB HOPE[174]

All aspects of life are in perpetual flight before us. Darkness and light alternate: after a flash, an eclipse; we look, we hurry, we stretch out our hands to seize what is passing; every event is a turn in the road; and suddenly we are old.

—VICTOR HUGO

AGING INHERENTLY MAGNIFIES THE VIRTUES of the man who *prefers* goodness as it also amplifies the deformity of one who desires evil. Years wear away the muscle of pretext revealing in character the essence of what *is*. There is always beauty in youth while a person is still *becoming*. However old age possesses either splendor or ugliness. A youth has the flex of a sapling. The young may choose to sink deep roots, able to withstand wind and drought, and send straight growth skyward with sun-seeking branches. For these, suppleness becomes stately strength. Or the immature may choose to encumber the ground of early years, leaving roots, trunk, and branches stifled, withered and knarred. The promise, once held, is lost—leaving what *is* a fruitless, decrepit thing.

Jimmy Hall's kindness was evident in each stage of his life, but the power of this virtue grew in him as he grew older. One evening, Jimmy sat reading on his veranda. Although he was surrounded by the sights, smells and sounds of the tropics, his psyche was transported to wintry northern Russia—so much so that a native visitor approached unnoticed, just beyond the corona of lamplight. The man remained so quiet that when Jimmy chanced to see the dim figure, he momentarily thought it was an apparition. Only after Hall had put down his book did the native greet him respectfully. His name was Maitua and was both a courier and a captain. Maitua carried a written message from a Ronald Crichton. Crichton was scarcely an acquaintance, having met Hall only twice before. On both occasions Crichton had avoided conversing with Jimmy. More remarkable was the fact the Maitua had sailed seven hundred miles for the sole purpose of delivering Crichton's letter. It read:

> Dear Sir:
>
> The service I am about to ask of you is one that I would hesitate to ask even of an old friend, but you are the only white man I know in this part of the Pacific and I must appeal to you however reluctantly.
>
> I am ill, and as I have grave doubts as to my recovery I must try to put my affairs in order. I have no one with me but an old Chinese servant, Ling Foo, whom you may remember. Could you come to see me? I have chartered a Paumotu cutter for the purpose of carrying this letter, and if you find it possible to come this same cutter will bring you to the island. I realize that you may not be able to leave at once and I have, therefore, instructed the man who brings you this letter—he is the owner of the vessel—to await your orders.
>
> Yours very truly
>
> Ronald Crichton[175]

His handwriting was little more than a scrawl suggesting weakness of the author. This Maitua confirmed, stating that unless they departed soon, it was doubtful Crichton would be found living.

Years earlier in 1920, Hall, recently discharged from the army air services, was traveling in the South Seas on a trading schooner. In his desire for English-speaking comradeship Jimmy attempted to befriend another traveler, Ronald Crichton. However, Hall found Crichton preferred solitude to camaraderie. Their association over several weeks of ocean travel was less than one might experience in a short ferry crossing. The little Jimmy learned of Crichton was that he had purchased a tiny island called Tanao from an old Polynesian lady as a place of permanent retreat from civilization. When the schooner reached Tanao, Jimmy went ashore and was amazed at the bleakness of the isle. Furthermore, he was astounded that the only inhabitants of Tanao, aside from the former aging owner, was to be Ronald Crichton and his servant. Hall soon left, feeling that Crichton "would be heartily glad" to have him leave. Crichton was not abrupt in speech, but rather tacit in manner.

Time passed and Jimmy had many adventures. His voyages took him, not only throughout the tropics of the Pacific, but as far away as the northern climes of Iceland. When he returned to Tahiti, four years later, he wondered what had become of the reclusive Crichton. Could any man actually live a life so solitary and isolated? Upon inquiry, Jimmy learned the odd Englishman still lived on Tanao. The natives had a name for him, "the Forgotten One." In his empathy Hall decided to again travel the Low Archipelago and visit Tanao. He learned that once a year the schooner *Toafa* diverted from its normal course and set anchor off Tanao, leaving Crichton supplies for twelve months and picking up the little copra that Crichton harvested. When the *Toafa* set sail for the annual visit, Jimmy was aboard.

Due to the other stops of the *Toafa,* it was a long journey of thirty-eight days. As Jimmy walked up the beach to Crichton's home he was impressed with the improvements the Englishman had made to his island. The small eight by five mile isle had been transformed into a garden paradise. Hall met Crichton near his impressive house, which was much larger than Jimmy had imagined. The inside of the residence was immaculate, furnished with upholstered settees and chairs, reflected in the luster of carefully polished tables. The heart of the home was a vast library of fifteen hundred volumes. Noticeably absent were the voices of family—of a wife and children that, wrote Jimmy, "should have been there."

Strangely Crichton said little to Jimmy, vaguely mentioning trouble with his eyes. He excused himself shortly thereafter, leaving Hall in the care of his servant Ling Foo. Crichton and Hall were not to speak again before Jimmy's departure the next day. Hall wrote:

> I was as forlorn as it is possible for a man to be: a guest in a house where I knew that I was not wanted . . . I felt that he was lacking in consideration to abandon me as he had . . . Almost any excuse would have been better than no excuse.[176]

Jimmy spent a portion of that evening in Crichton's library. There he picked up a book; in the preface was underlined the following:

> Those who love not their fellow beings live unfruitful lives and prepare for their old age a miserable grave.[177]

Now years later, Jimmy sat on his veranda, the letter from the dying Englishman in his hand. Maitua, captain of the cutter, stood patiently awaiting Hall's instructions. What man among thousands would take six weeks out of his life to aid another who had been as discourteous as Crichton had been to Hall?—but these were not the thoughts in Jimmy's mind. Rather, he considered how terribly sad it was, that of all the thousands of souls in the South Pacific, that he—a mere acquaintance—was the only man Crichton could turn to in a time of desperation! The very next morning Jimmy left with Maitua for Papeete. By noon Maitua's cutter left the Tahitian harbor on the seven hundred mile voyage to Tanao. The fourteen day journey itself was eventful and dangerous, beleaguered by heavy squalls, and great glassy-sea calms.

Hall found Crichton emaciated but alive. Jimmy allowed Maitua to leave the island with instructions to return for him in two weeks—for Hall felt that Crichton could last no longer. Surprisingly, when his strength allowed, Crichton was talkative. He was a man of tremendous wealth, as Hall had surmised. Jimmy wrote:

> All of his property in England was to be divided equally between a nephew and a niece, his only surviving relatives. What he particularly wished me to do was to send to his attorney—with a personal letter which I wrote at his dictation—the official papers to be secured from the French authorities at Tahiti, establishing the fact of his death. He had something over five hundred pounds on deposit in a Papeete bank, and this money was to go to Ling Foo who had served him so faithfully all these years.[178]

Over the next several days Jimmy administered kindness to the dying man, who had never reciprocated in the past and whose death would prevent his doing so in the future. Crichton had become blind and for some time had been unable to enjoy his beloved books. Hour after hour, at Crichton's request, Jimmy read those passages most dear to the poor man. Near the end, Crichton made an attempt to apologize for his "strange behavior." Jimmy interrupted, saying there was no need. Nonetheless, the failing man unburdened his soul to Hall, the only confessor able to hear Crichton's voice before death would silence it. Three days later the two *friends* chatted away about "common things"—of the beauty of the island and the infinite leagues of the sea. Then Crichton fell asleep. Later Jimmy and Ling Foo laid Ronald Crichton in his chosen burial place.

> It was near the lagoon beach at the head of the small cove that could be seen from his house. In accordance with his own wishes,

no stone, not even a border of sea shells, was placed to mark his grave. It is marked, adequately and beautifully, by the shadows of palm fronds moving to and fro over the coral sand.[179]

Hall possessed in a remarkable manner the promise spoken of by Malachi the prophet—Jimmy's heart was turned to his fathers, and to his children, and to his children's children. This love of ancestry and progeny filled Hall's bosom long before he realized fatherhood. Years before, while a prisoner of war in Landshut Germany, Jimmy wrote a letter to his unborn posterity. It read:

My Dear Grandchildren,

Many years from now, when this narrative is placed in your hands, you may wonder why I should have written it, with you in mind, long before any of you were born, when in fact, I had no idea who your grandmother was to be. Let me tell you, then, that I have a sense of family that none of the Halls, up to my time, seem to have had, or the Youngs, my mother's people. Like many of the families of Middle-western America, who, toward the fifties of the last century, peopled the prairies of the Mississippi Valley, we know almost nothing beyond our grandparents, and little enough concerning them. A few have a vague existence in that their names and the dates of their birth and death can still be deciphered on moldering tombstones in country cemeteries, but the earlier ones no longer exist, even in this shadowy sense. They have vanished without leaving a trace behind them, with no word of farewell, of counsel, of friendly greeting, to those who should come after them, and we shall never know what manner of men and women they were.

This seems to me a great pity, and I have resolved to do what I can to remedy matters, for even in families of no particular distinction, such as ours seems to have been, if intimate and truthful records should be prepared and handed down from generation to generation, we should have, at last, the means for judging of the worth of our blood. We might then see what our family virtues are—

> or be assured, at least, that we have none—and what shortcomings have been carried over from one generation to the next.
>
> But my real purpose in preparing this narrative is a selfish one at the bottom. The thought that I shall live for you in these pages and that I shall perhaps be something more than a name to your children and your children's children, gives me the keenest pleasure. And I cannot urge you too strongly to follow my example in this matter, otherwise, your own grandchildren may know of you, if at all, only through hearsay. With such a precedent once established and followed faithfully by our descendents, we should eventually accumulate a library of family history more interesting than the most fascinating of fiction could be; for those who come after us could say, as they read: "This is my great-great-grandfather (or grandmother) who is speaking. These things really happened to members of my kindred."
>
> In the mind's eye, I see the pleasant book-lined room of the house, where, five centuries hence, these records would be kept—an old house, high-walled and secret from the outside world. Here, young men and women of our own line would come, now and then, to spend some time with the family ghosts, to read of joys and sorrows, once as keen as theirs, of hopes as bright, of disappointment that seemed catastrophic and were yet survived. And so again and again, our shades would assume the shapes of men and women of flesh and blood, and none of them, I am sure, would frisk about more gaily than mine, knowing that I was the Nestor of you all.[180]

As young men, Hall and Crichton were both green and pliable. Hall, in his modesty, would never tolerate a comparison in their lives. However, from our distant perspective the choices each man made in life and the commensurate results are readily apparent. One man died as stubble without root or branch. The other lived a fruitful life filled with adventure, but centered in family.

In 1925 Jimmy Hall married Sarah Winchester. The couple happily settled in Tahiti. A year later Sarah gave birth to their son Conrad, and in 1930 their daughter Nancy was born. Seventy-four years later, the author of this work met with Nancy and her loving husband Nick. They provided wonderful insights into the family life of James Norman Hall. Interviewing this amazing couple it became readily apparent that Jimmy and Sarah had instilled in them a love of roots. Nancy spoke from the heart, without referring to pedigree charts:

> My great great grandmother married an American whaling captain by the name of Richmond. They had twelve children, among them my great grandmother, whom I knew. She married a Scottish sea captain, by the name of Rose from Inverness, Scotland. They also had many children, among them my grandmother, Marguerite Rose. She married Joseph Winchester a sea captain from Liverpool—they were all sea captains. (Nick further explained that "Joe" was a war hero in the Great War and had also fought professionally as a boxer in Australia.) My Grandfather, Joe Winchester, had come to Tahiti around fourteen years of age. He became a seaman, trading between the islands in schooners. One time, his captain and crew with passengers and a big hull full of pearls went to Chile and the captain took off with the money and left the boat and the crew. Grandpa Joe brought the ship back to Tahiti and that was when he was made Captain. He also was able to get French Citizenship, which had been denied him up to that point.

Nancy described the first time her father met her mother. Jimmy had known Joe Winchester previously, having accompanied him as he sailed the South Seas. These two adventurers became fast friends. One day Joe invited Jimmy to his home for lunch and there for the first time Jimmy met Joe's daughter, young Sarah Winchester. However, Jimmy could not possibly have known that Sarah would someday be his wife. He was engaged at the time to another girl from Tahiti and Sarah Winchester was still very young. Shortly thereafter Hall left the tropics for Iceland and then traveled to America to visit his family. When he finally returned to Tahiti he found that his fiancée had jilted him in preference to a French Sailor. Nick said he felt she broke her relationship with Hall because Jimmy was so poor. Although Jimmy was disappointed by the broken engagement, he nonetheless honored an invitation extended by his former fiancée's family to attend the wedding reception. As it turned out, this proved to be the best thing that could have happened to Jimmy Hall. At the wedding party he met again Sarah Winchester, now a beautiful young lady with exquisite European features accented by flowing hair that fell to her knees. Sarah's rich abundant hair was the only outward trait of her one-eighth Polynesian heritage. She had been waiting for someone just like Jimmy. As for Jimmy, he had found at last the perfect compliment to his quiet personality. Nancy said:

> This was meant to be. Mom and Dad had a wonderful love affair and had such a wonderful life together. She was the keeper of the flame, because my Dad was up in the air all the time, dreaming about books. Sarah was totally practical. She fed him, made his rum punch, and loved him to death.

Nick added that Sarah literally kept Jimmy alive. Nancy continued:

> They did everything together. They loved to go out dancing and to parties. They loved planning their lives. My grandmother bought their house for them—they didn't have a penny. But Dad paid her back.
>
> When Father brought Mother to Boston to introduce her to his friends, they simply loved her, she was so genuine. My mom was always so dignified and lovely.

Their first child, Conrad, was born in Tahiti. Later they suffered the loss of a stillborn child. This prompted Doctor Casio,

Jimmy Hall with his beloved daughter, Nancy.

the only doctor on the island, to recommend that in the future Sarah travel to America to deliver. In 1930 the Hall family stayed with Jimmy's brother, Fred, in Southern California until Nancy was born in the Sisters of Mercy Hospital, San Diego. Near midnight, the evening of Nancy's birth, Jimmy wrote what he called a "Commemorative Ballad." Every birthday thereafter Hall again authored a poem in honor of his daughter. Two months later the Halls returned to their home in the islands.

When asked what it was like to grow up with her mother and father in Tahiti Nancy responded:

> It was heaven! It was paradise! You can't imagine how simple life was—how beautiful. Everybody cared for everybody. We met interesting people who would get off from the monthly boat that would arrive. Our only contact [with the outside world] was that monthly steamer. During the Second World War we finally got a radio. We listened to Chet Huntley for the news.

I made my own toys. I would find a half of a coconut that was cut to make copra, and send it out to sea. We would make cars with old butter cans.

Mom taught me how to deal with any situation—whether I was in the company of rich or poor, common or with royalty—she taught me to be comfortable and sincere.

My Dad gave me a few great tips. He said, "Never underestimate the common man."

Ah—and he asked me when I was ten or eleven, *"What do you want to be when you grow up?" and I answered, "A mother!" He said, "That's the most wonderful occupation a woman can have!"* Instead of saying, "Oh don't you want to be a doctor or a lawyer or an Indian chief?" He never put me down. He always gave me such a wonderful sense of self-worth. You know, I have never done anything great. But you know what, *I am happy in my skin.* I always have been. I have tried to teach that to my children.

Year after year Jimmy continued writing his annual birthday poem for Nancy, until she became the wife of Nicholas G. Rutgers. Jimmy held this handsome and accomplished young man in the highest regard. In 1949 Nancy and Jimmy compiled the birthday verses into a unique treasure, published as *Her Daddy's Best Ice Cream.* Set to rhyme, these words of a father to his daughter are sometimes humorous and always poignant. They speak a universal language of love and provide insight into a noble relationship. Three examples of this poetry follow. The first work is remarkable, as we consider the former ace combat pilot could not be intimidated by enemies or elements, yet was completely taken aback by the steady gaze of his precious infant daughter.

THE STARE

There is nothing much to fear
From a child the first half-year,
But the second half, beware

Of that more than searching stare!
Mothers never seem to mind;
Father always do, I find.

I would rather have nine owls
Sitting by me, cheeks by jowls,
Than Miss Nancy when imbued
With her 'watch-my-father' mood.

She outstares the wide-eyed lynx
And could disconcert a sphinx.

Then her mood will change. A smile
That was lurking all the while
Buds and blooms and quickly chases
Soberness from both our faces.

And the fussed and frightened dad
Then relaxes, more than glad.[181]

My wife, Jean, was my companion as I met with Nick and Nancy Rutgers. After a delightful lunch we retired to the lower room in their home. Nancy picked up the small book of poems and held it to her heart, exclaiming, "Of all my treasures . . ." Then turning to page 18 she began to read, or rather I should say *recite*, for the words are a part of her heart like a melody often sung:

PAEAN OF GRATITUDE TO NANCY ELLA WHO, UPON BEING ASKED BY DENNY HOLMES WHAT KIND OF ICE CREAM SHE LIKED BEST, REPLIED: "MY DADDY IS MY BEST ICE CREAM."

I who have sometimes wished to spank her,
How can I ever truly thank her
For such a tribute high?

The wreath upon her father's head
I know, is quite unmerited.
What matters that? say I.

My little Nancy placed it there
For all to see, for me to wear,
And what I can, I will
To swell the head that bears the crown
So that it can't go slipping down.
But what a crown to fill!

"My daddy is my best ice cream" . . .
Did she say that? She did. No dream
It was, for others heard.
"Nancy, which kind do you like best?"
Was asked. The choice was then expressed
As stated, word for word.

Proclaim it south! Thunder it north!
Ye heralds, trumpets! Send ye forth
The news both east and west!
Of all the sherbets, ices, creams
Of childhood's rich and sumptuous dreams
Her father is the best![182]

Nick and Nancy's home is extraordinary. Books by Hall and other great authors line many of the walls. Tropical plants, reminiscent of Tahiti, thrive in the atrium that serves as an open staircase. Polynesian paintings adorn the walls, the most notable on the main floor being a magnificent oil painting of *The Bounty.* On the lower floor are two spectacular paintings by Herb Kane depicting the aerial exploits of Jimmy Hall and Eddie Rickenbacker. Everywhere are portraits of family.

The bonds of family are meant by our Creator to be eternal. There is no question that undying love permeates the Rutgers' home, as it did the Hall home of Nancy's youth. A true father's affection extends beyond his corporeal life—it reaches forward and backward and cannot envision separation without anguish. The poetry found in this small book of verse is intensely profound. On August 10, 1937 Hall wrote:

THE DREAM

We had been walking hand in hand.
Paradise itself the land;
I had no thought or care.
Nancy was singing 'Papio;'
Suddenly I seemed to know
She was no longer there.

I felt the chill of coming night;
Nowhere was the landscape bright.
The wind began to moan.
The road sloped steeply down before;
Nancy's song I heard no more.
I was there alone.

I could not halt. I tried, but no,
Faster yet I had to go
Down that forbidding hill;
And all the while I knew that she
Was trying to catch up with me,
Crying as children will

When left behind, alone and lost.
Countless stony fields I crossed.
I could not check my gait.
And then I heard, a world away,
It seemed, from where I could not stay:
"Daddy! Wait! Please wait!"

If ever heart was wrung to hear
The voice of one it loved most dear,
Helpless to reply,
My heart was wrung. If ever man
Tried all that strength and willing can
To halt, that man was I.

I could not even turn my head;
And then I knew that I was dead
Or just about to be.
Oh, I have tasted bitterness.
I heard the voice grow less and less
Of Nancy, calling me.[183]

True fatherhood is the highest manifestation of manhood. Fatherhood is more than begetting. Rather, fatherhood is a kingly protectorate. A man receives his coronation when his firstborn breathes the breath of life. For Sovereignty in this kingdom to be long-lasting it must be merited by unconditional love, never tainted with hypocrisy or guile. A father's position of power is not one of privilege only, for he bears the burdens of defender and teacher, sacred and secular. He can increase dominion only by expanding his children's horizons. The regal symbol of his authority is a scepter of integrity, for he cannot reign in any sphere where he first does not rule himself. Although he possesses the power to command, the Sovereign of the family *prefers* instead to *persuade* and disciplines only with abundance of affection.

Jimmy tenderly acknowledged that his daughter, at an early age, placed both wreath and crown upon his head. To Nancy he was champion and king. Always modest, Hall felt such honor was undeserved. However, never did he abdicate by unworthy behavior. Jimmy and Sarah created in their home a realm of happiness for their children. They so linked heart to heart that Paradise itself would be a bitter land if any *one* were left behind. With such parents it was a natural thing for Nancy to aspire to become a mother herself. For the Halls and Rutgers, *family* is the primary occupation of life.

Civilizations rise in proportion to adherence of codes of true family values and fall proportionally as family responsibilities are abandoned. Many scholars have speculated as to the cause of the rapid rise to power of the ancient Republic of Rome. Roman military structure and tactics are touted by most authorities as the basis for their progressive empowerment. The truth is that Rome grew from the strength of strong families whose religious faith exceeded all their neighboring states, with the exception of Israel. In fact, in the time of the Maccabees, Israel and Rome were allies, bound by a mutual appreciation of liberty and family values. (Later, under a degenerating Rome, Israel became a vassal state.) Writing on the Republic of Rome the noted historian Will Durant stated:

> Every part of [the family] and every aspect of its existence were bound up in a solemn intimacy with the spiritual world. The child was taught, by the eloquent silence of example, that the undying fire in the *hearth* was the sign and substance of the goddess Vesta, the sacred flame that symbolized the life and continuity of the family; which must never be extinguished, but must be tended with 'religious care' . . . Hovering invisible but potent over the threshold was the god Janus, two-faced not as deceitful but as *watching all* entry and exit at every door. The child's father, he learned, was the ward and embodiment of an inner *genius*, or *gen*erative power, which would not die with the body, but must be nourished forever at the paternal grave. His mother was also the carrier of a deity and likewise had to be treated as divine; she had a *Juno* in her as the spirit of her capacity to bear, as the father enclosed a *genius* as the spirit of his power to beget. The child too had his *genius* or *Juno* . . . a godly kernel in the mortal husk. Everywhere about him, he heard with awe, were the watchful *Di Manes,* or Kindly Shades, of those male forebears . . . warning him not to stray . . . and reminding him

that the family was composed not merely of those few individuals that lived in his moment but also of those that had once been, or would someday be, members of it in the flesh, and therefore formed part of it in its spiritual multitude and timeless unity.[184]

Although the gradual decline of Rome is said by some scholars to have begun with the death of the republic and its transformation into a dictatorship, Durant indicates the declination began when "houses became larger as families became smaller." Evils grew in the Roman society, licentiousness protected under the banner of a free society. Divorce became common place, many women "doubted the wisdom of bearing children in an age of urban congestion," prostitution flourished and "homosexualism was stimulated by contact with Greece." Furthermore, Durant wrote,

> Men became brave by proxy, they crowded the amphitheater to see bloody games . . . In the upper classes manners became more refined as morals were relaxed . . . In the widening middle classes commercialism ruled unhindered . . . everyone longed for money, everyone judged or was judged in terms of money.[185]

Jimmy Hall never considered himself an islander, although Tahiti had become a sanctuary for himself and his family. His roots would always be in Midwest America. The machine age had overtaken his Arcadian homeland, and commercialism was gradually replacing the core values that Hall cherished so deeply. Jimmy wrote:

> Life in the U.S.A. is so vastly different now from what it was during my boyhood and youth.

Nevertheless, homesickness for Iowa, particularly at Christmas time, would lead Jimmy to exclaim, "What am I doing in this part of the world? I don't belong here." Jimmy beautifully expressed his sentiments in his poem entitled *December in the Tropics:*

The palm trees slope against the sky
As still as they were painted so . . .
Very strange it is that I
Stand under them, knee-deep in snow.

In other lands as green as this
Are other men, perhaps, like me,
Listening to the seething hiss
Of snowflakes falling endlessly.
Oh, kindly hills of home! That keep
For us who left them years ago
A wintry silence, muffled deep
In newly fallen, immortal snow.[186]

In 1950 Jimmy received a letter from Samuel Stevens, president of Grinnell College informing him that his alma mater desired to confer the "honorary degree of Doctor of Literature" at his "40th Commencement Anniversary." The letter went on to request his height, weight and hat size for the purpose of fitting his cap and gown. Jimmy wrote:

> The size of my hat is, customarily, #7, but one of 8$\frac{1}{4}$ would have perched precariously on the top of my head at the moment when I read President Steven's letter.[187]

Across the seas and continents Jimmy journeyed home. Back in Colfax, Iowa, Jimmy visited his brother Fred, who with his wife and family still lived in their boyhood home. Jimmy was taken back by his home's beauty, made sacred by loving memories that came flooding into his heart. He wrote:

> It was comforting to feel so strongly the presence of my father and mother in the old house. I could hear my father singing one of his favorite songs, "I Dreamt That I Dwelt in Marble Halls," as he climbed the steps carrying a bucket of water from the one hydrant in the cellar; and I could see my mother sitting at the dining-room

> table, and hear the faint scratching of her pen as she wrote the wonderful letters to her grown-up and far-scattered children.[188]

Jimmy's last literary work was his autobiography, which he was unable to finish before his death. Hall said that if he were not to leave a gap in his narrative he must:

> [Of necessity find a] different manner of writing [that would demonstrate] the spiritual effect of brute incident upon [his] character . . . and how it moulded his later life. But would this be interesting enough to the general reader who usually wants to know of the adventures themselves rather that the effect of them upon character?[189]

This work seeks to answer Hall's question in the affirmative. Again we quote Edwin Markham who said, "Nothing is worth the making if it does not make the man." There are too many protagonists in today's media who nihilistically exhibit bravado in thrill seeking audacity, whose escapades are exploitive, without merit—counterfeits of true adventure. Adventures in manhood should appeal to man's duality—he is body and spirit. Neither can be neglected or abused. Jimmy Hall lived a courageous life in times of global brutality. Never did Hall allow the effects of horrific war to mold deformity in his character. Rather his experiences, although physically hardening, softened his heart towards humanity. Never did Jimmy lose faith in the basic goodness of people—always did he grow in compassion toward his fellowman.

Hall left America for Tahiti with a premonition that he had not long to live. One day, not long after Jimmy's return, he asked his beloved wife Sarah to sit by him so that he might explain what he wished done in the event of his death. Of this poignant meeting, a close friend of the family, Walter Smith, in a letter to Edward Weeks, wrote:

> He wanted no mourning or weeping or wailing. On the contrary

> he desired that the natives of the district should assemble and sing their songs, songs that he so loved, and not alone their songs of sadness, but also their joyous hymns, and especially those of a humorous character. He wished that wine and food be furnished to them, and that they be regaled to their hearts' content. Mrs. Hall, as any wife would, at first refused even to listen to him, but he was so insistent that she heard him out and finally succeeded in diverting his thoughts into other channels. But the significance of this was not lost on the wife, and thereafter she kept him under watchful and loving attention practically from hour to hour. She had doctors visit him under the guise of friendship—everybody in Tahiti was a friend of James Norman Hall—and advise her what course to follow in case of unfavorable eventualities. He himself never repined or complained.[190]

On July 6, 1951, in the middle of the night, Sarah Hall cried aloud for help. Smith lived nearby and quickly answered her summons. Soon they were joined by Hall's physician, Dr. Andrea de Balmann. Recently Hall's blood pressure had been high, but now Dr. de Balmann "failed to register any pressure at all." Jimmy, suffering with pain, found it very difficult to breath. However, there was nothing that could be done for him, except to ease the pain; his coronary arterial system had collapsed. For two hours Jimmy Hall held on to life; then finally, after a few gasps, he slipped quietly into death.

Even before dawn, the home of Jimmy and Sarah Hall was surrounded with friends from all over the island. Polynesian flowers were given in such quantity that soon the floor of their great room was carpeted in exquisite beauty. All day long neighbors came, and as they did not leave, the numbers grew into a vast throng. The following day Jimmy's body was placed in a coffin and the pall bearers, the young men of the Arué Football Club, lovingly bore him on his final journey in mortality. Hundreds of islanders, dressed in white, colonial government officials, British and Chinese consuls—all were among the mourners of this remarkable man. The church choir sang Jimmy's favorite melodies. The procession, led by the young men bearing the casket, walked to the temple of Out-aiai where his pastor presided over the services. The funeral assembly then continued on to the graveside where Chief Teriieroo, leader of Papenoo, eulogized Jimmy's life. Smith wrote:

> Teriieroo . . . recalled his services in the war of 1914-1918, spoke of his fame as an author, but particularly emphasized his constant readiness to aid the distressed and contribute generously to whatever might be for the benefit of the local inhabitants.[191]

After the services concluded eighty Tahitians returned with Sarah Hall to the beach house and asked if they could offer testimonials and bid farewell to Jimmy Hall in their accustomed native manner. Sarah gratefully consented. Walter Smith wrote:

> For the ensuing three and one-half hours there poured forth, as from a brook that goes on forever, address after address . . . Women as well as men arose . . . and each in the smoothly-flowing Tahitian tongue, expressed his or her feelings. These addresses were interspersed with songs, not all songs of mourning—far from it, but it was all just as Hall would have had it . . . An address by a young workman of Arué . . . expressed these words: "We all knew and loved Papa Hall. He was one of us in his interest in our sports and our other activities. We knew him especially as a *kind* man, a simple man, to whom the interests of the poorest were more important than those of the rich and comfortable. No one ever in vain approached him with a request for aid. These things I knew and we all knew. But today my eyes are opened. When I look upon the cushion upon which are pinned his medals and decorations from the leading governments of the world, I for the first time realize that we have had living amongst us a great man. I know now, but never knew before, that in our midst dwelt a hero."[192]

Jimmy Hall possessed a "splendid courage" which had never given way. He lived his life a "visible example of unselfish devotion." With the great campaign of life complete, we almost hear him echo the words of his comrade from the Battle of Loos:

> Good luck to you! If you see my missus, tell her I'm as right as rain!

Dawn, Sunday, the first day, vernal equinox, summer solstice—nightfall, Saturday, month's end, autumnal equinox, winter solstice,— beginnings, endings; days into months into seasons into years into centuries into millennia. This seemingly endless cycle is essential for man's earthly sojourn. Every day, week, month, season, century, is a new creation. Each creation a powerful symbol, quantitatively unique, yet in type similar to other creations. New beginnings are requisite for our progression. In all of history there was only One Life that built successive successes, never failing—perfect. For every other person who has lived, now lives and will live, success comes only after rebuilding, re-creating, refining—falling, failing, climbing, healing. Symbols are wonderfully directive to the wise, but the fool dreadfully misinterprets symbols. Nature's constant renewal often leads to the false perception of never ending opportunities. Youth is especially vulnerable to this grievous error. The power of God-given emblems is discovered in the many layers of truth found within the representation. Although it is *day*, it is a different day than yesterday. Nothing is stagnant in a cycle. Transformation is the only constant, the only "never ending." How soon the flexible becomes fixed, the young become old. *Each man possesses only finite time and limited opportunities.* Man has but one birth, one childhood, one season of virility, and one era of age—then all revolutions of mortality cease and death seals the record of endeavors. Life offers no guarantee even these limits will be granted, for life may end in the morning as well as at night.

Young men do not misconstrue the miracle of your being. God gives you only one earthly possession—*time.* It is the only thing you can truly label *mine.* How much of this wonderful substance is granted you, heaven alone knows. This commodity may seem prolific in the springtime of life. Hence, you will be tempted to trade your precious allotment of it foolishly. However, do not be deceived and do not waste that which you cannot replace. With the time given you, adhere deeply to noble roots. If misfortune has given you an unfit heritage, remember that early life is capable of being grafted. Bind yourself to a legacy with taproots that will ever feed your growth and enable you to send forth mighty branches. It is a matter of choice and the choices must be made while change is possible. The aptitude for change is greatest in youth. Procrastination is the choice of self-deceivers. Only *now* is in your control. The past is already engraved, the future beyond reach. *Now* may never be held—"we stretch out our hands to seize," but we cannot grasp "what is passing."

Certainly the present impacts the future. The course we are flying makes possible our destination. Think of Jimmy Hall in captivity in Landshut. What an appropriate name for a prison—shut off from the land of home. Yet Hall did not languish without hope. It takes faith to grow branches. Incarcerated, Jimmy used his *time* to develop his faith. He wrote: "I've had time to think and to make plans for a future which, comparatively speaking, seems assured." The future Hall envisioned stretched beyond his own years. He envisioned life that would come *from* him—life that was yet unborn! Jimmy wrote to his posterity, "*I shall live for you . . . I shall be something more than a name to your children and your children's children.*" Oh men of youth, live for life which you will yet create. Do not be as Crichton, leaving material wealth only to kinsmen who are strangers to you, to whom *you are only a name.* The sad Crichton cut himself from roots and sent forth no branches. He moved to a winterless land, yet winter overtook him and buried his stubble beneath coral sands. Rather be as young Jimmy Hall and establish a legacy. "Papa Hall" was a *kind* man of such generative power that he nourished many branches—some natural and hundreds grafted. Become as he, the "embodiment of an inner *genius,* or *gen*erative power, which [will] not die with [your] body" but will become a "Kindly Shade," watching over and warning those who will "someday be."

To Jimmy's children, born of his wife Sarah or self-adopted to

Inset — Jimmy Hall, 94th Aero Squadron Wing Commander, WWI
Far Right – Nicholas Rutgers Jr., Hall's son-in-law, WWII
Far Left – Nicholas Rutgers III, Hall's grandson, Vietnam War
Center – Nicholas Rutgers IV, Hall's great-grandson, War Against Terror

him because of his love given without prejudice to the "poorest," he fulfills that which he promised as a young captive of war:

> I see the pleasant book-lined room of an old house, high-walled and secret from the outside world. Here, young men and women of our own line come, now and then, to spend some time with the family ghosts, to read of joys and sorrows, once as keen as theirs, of hopes as bright, of disappointment that seemed catastrophic and were yet survived. And so again and again, our shades assume the shapes of men and women of flesh and blood, and none of them, I am sure, frisk about more gaily than mine, knowing that I was the Nestor of you all.

The author considers it very appropriate to include as a footnote to this chapter a letter he received from Nicholas Rutgers III, to accompany the photograph below. This brief account of a remarkable family is unprecedented, not only as a testament to the sire of their legacy, but as a singular record of four generations of their family history that encompasses the history of military aviation.[vii]

[vii] I cannot forget two other valiant men, old and young that have greatly inspired me throughout my life, my father Nick senior and our son Nicholas. As a young volunteer Marine during all of World War II, my father proudly and heroically served as a very young 16 year-old Marine radio-gunner aboard the amazing Grumman TBM Avenger, flying throughout the China-Burma-India Theater, recalling night bombing missions over Okinawa, where sixty years later our son Nicholas would serve a three year tour of duty as an F-15C fighter pilot. Throughout my entire life, my father has always been my mentor, a man of tremendous integrity, generosity and with a sense of humor second to none. Our son Nicholas has been a sense of pride in our family that I only wish more families in this country could be fortunate enough to experience in their lives. As a 2000 graduate of the U.S. Air Force Academy where young Nicholas was the distinguished graduate in the Department of Aeronautical Engineering and Mathematics, the recipient of the Air Force Academy's top research and development award, saving the Air Force millions of dollars in the operation of the AC-130 gunship. After attending the Euro-Nato fighter pilot training facility at Sheppard Air Force Base in Texas, where Lieutenant Nicholas Rutgers was once again the distinguished pilot graduate, top formation pilot, and recipient of the Daedalian award for the state of Texas (His Great-Grandfather was one of the first Daedalians in history), our son Nicholas was selected for the extremely demanding six month F-15C air superiority combat aircraft transition course, where he graduated as the Topgun in his class. While assigned to the 67th Fighter Squadron on Okinawa, Japan, now Captain Nicholas Rutgers, better know as stitch to his fellow fighter pilots excelled as usual, receiving the Wingman of the Year and Flight Lead of the Year awards, and also participated in two Red Flag fighter pilot exercises at Nellis AFB in Las Vegas; where this year CPT Nicholas commanded a 70 aircraft exercise and is featured in a recent Imax Boeing movie Fighter Pilot, which was filmed during his first Red Flag operation. Recently transferred back to Sheppard AFB in Texas, CPT Rutgers is completing a four month instructor pilot course in the T-38 Fighter trainer, at the same Euro-Nato fighter school he attended three years ago. Guarantee F-22 Raptor Stealth Fighter in three years, our son Nicholas has a bright future to fly into and the sky is the only limit.

As the very proud father of an Air Force fighter pilot, the son of a WW II veteran Marine radio-gunner, and the grandson of a remarkable valiant man for all seasons, I am approaching the mandatory retirement age of 60, a time when I will have to relinquish the flight controls of the incomparable Boeing 747-400 transport that I fly for United Airlines as a Captain rated First Officer, and three years ago retired from the Army National Guard as a Sikorsky UH-60 Blackhawk aircraft commander. I proudly served our country during six years of active duty in the U.S. Army, to include a one year combat tour in the Republic of South Vietnam, and deployments worldwide during 17 years of flying in the Army National Guard.

As I fly off into the sunset, I am incredibly proud to be a part of a unique aviation legacy, proud of the support my wife and I and our extended family have given our son as he becomes one of many of this generation's valiant young men. To Bryce Gibby, thank you for the opportunity to be a small part of this invaluable literary work, and for undertaking a vision to insure that the fine young men of this country will continue to be inspired by careers in aviation and follow the path of those valiant young men of the past, our heroes of flight.

Nicholas G. Rutgers III — Grandson of James Norman Hall, B-747-400 First Officer, United Airlines, CW4 (Ret) U.S. Army, Former Aircraft Commander, UH-60 Blackhawk

Bibliography – Book 2

Primary Sources

Hall, James Norman: *High Adventure* (Arno Press, A New York Times Company, New York)

Hall, James Norman: *Kitchener's Mob* (Grosset & Dunlap Publishers, New York)

Roulston, Robert: *James Norman Hall* (Twayne Publishers, A division of G. K. Hall & Co., Boston)

Hall, James Norman: *My Island Home, an Autobiography* (Mutual Publishing, Australia)

Hall, James Norman: *The Forgotten One* (Little, Brown and Company in association with The Atlantic Monthly Press, U.S.A.)

Hall, James Norman: *Her Daddy's Best Ice Cream*

Durant, Will: *Caesar and Christ* (Simon and Schuster, New York)

The Scriptures

Antoine de Saint-Exupéry

CHAPTER 19

CYCLONE

For him alone have I compassion who wakes in the great ancestral night, thinking himself sheltered under God's canopy of stars, and suddenly feels himself a wayfarer—whither bound he knows not.

—ANTOINE DE SAINT-EXUPÉRY

LONG BEFORE THERE WAS AIR FRANCE, there was its predecessor, Aéropostale, and before Aéropostale there was the Latécoère Company, the grand sire of the proud French Airline. Tonio was among Latécoère's first pilots. Passengers were rare in the pioneering days of the airlines—their primary purpose was to carry the mail. The aircraft, by today's standards, were extremely primitive, unreliable, and equipped only with rudimentary instruments. Cockpits were open to the elements so that the pilot could feel the relative wind in his face—could sense whether he was slipping or skidding and therefore could properly coordinate aileron and rudder.

Tonio departed from the field at Trelew, Argentina, bound for Comodoro-Rivadavia. His route would take him across an incredible wasteland, a wind-ripped region devoid of vegetation. Here the Pacific and the Atlantic Oceans are scarcely 300 miles apart. When high pressure dominates the Pacific, a breach in the Andes forms a venturi, a corridor 50 miles in breadth, through which the winds rush towards the Atlantic at velocities that could match the maximum cruise speed of Tonio's airplane. Surface winds alone in this strip commonly reach 100 miles per hour!

This route was a familiar one to Tonio. This day, as before, his eyes scanned the horizon for the "gray-blue tint in the atmosphere," the unmistakable signature of the super-charged winds. When sighted he would instinctively tighten his seat belt and shoulder harness. A pilot does not *fear* the approach of foul weather, but has an intense *respect* for its power. When immersed in doubtful elements he must take their measurement, calculate their probable impact—then either traverse or reverse, circumnavigate or set down, as his judgment dictates. Again, a pilot does not feel fear when his hands are on the controls and he is busily engaged in his profession. It is said that fear leaves the battlefield once the battle commences and the soldier is focused on the task at hand. It is hard to be analytical and emotional at the same moment. There is time for emotion when the fight is over.

Today there was no tint to the sky. It was cloudless, crystal clear and beautifully blue. Too blue. Tonio felt a growing uneasiness—the harbinger of an approaching storm, but one he could not measure because it was invisible. He drew nearer to the "razor-edged mountains" and could see from their peaks dingy streamers of earth scraped off by the wind. He cinched his belt and harness as tightly as he possibly could, griped the controls with one hand while the other tightened around the longéron near his seat. Yet the air was perfectly calm.

There was a slight warning. The wings minutely quivered. The controls sent light vibrations to Tonio's hand. Then suddenly he entered the unseen vortex of the "blue storm" and it seemed that everything around him simply exploded. He had flown, not just into the west-east high-wind corridor, but into a cyclone—"the whole sky blown down" upon him from the Andean chain! So convulsive was the paroxysm of his stout, but small craft, it appeared, not that the plane was being violently buffeted, *but that the earth itself, around him,* was in spasms, epileptic, buckling then trembling, fiercely contorting, writhing painfully. Later Tonio wrote:

> Horizon? There was no longer a horizon . . . A hundred transversal valleys were muddled in a jumble of perspectives. Whenever I seemed about to take my bearings a new eruption would swing me *round in a circle or send me tumbling wing over wing . . .* All those peaks, those crests, those teeth that were cutting into the wind and unleashing its gusts in my direction, seemed to me so many guns pointed straight at my defenseless person.[193]

We now have a term for this unseen monster, we call it CAT—*clear air turbulence.* It can occur at any altitude, near the boundaries of the jet stream or near the earth's surface. But when 150 miles per hour winds assault disruptive mountainous terrain, and when flying low, it is a condition equivalent to white-water rapids that is simply off the scale. For the first time this pioneer aviator understood the reason for certain accidents. Planes had crashed in the mountains, under blue skies—no storm, no fog. They had been seized by CAT and tumbled out of control into granite arms.

The maelstrom held Tonio tightly in its clutches. To fight this phenomenon required every ounce of strength his muscles could deliver and every stratagem his mind could conceive. The landscape, although pitching and rolling, was not changing. Under normal conditions the scenery always transforms itself into new and infinite vistas. At full throttle, Tonio could make no headway—like a boat fighting a current that it cannot overcome. Then there were downdrafts that plummeted earthward at rates exceeding the aircraft's ability to climb. A downdraft cannot pierce the earth for when it nearly reaches ground it flattens out into horizontal winds or rebounds back aloft. Certainly severe eddy currents, such as Tonio experienced, can cause structural failure, or blast control away from the pilot's exhausted hands. Or these downdrafts, can in a moment, plunge the pilot into valleys, box canyons, and cap his ability to *climb.* Thus the pilot is trapped with no feasible escape route. If he continues successful in his attempts just to stay airborne with no release otherwise from the element's grip, he will ultimately exhaust his only ally—his fuel. Such was Tonio's predicament. Thrust earthward he could not climb higher than two hundred feet above the surface. Nearly an hour went by mercilessly, gobbling his precious gasoline. There was no respite from the onslaught—his *resources*, seen and unseen, pitched in battle against the powers of the cyclone. It was a physical fight; it was hand to hand combat.

Off to his right he recognized the massive peak of Salamanca, which he knew towered above the sea. The sea! Flat—where air currents flow without the disheveling interference of rock and ridge. Whatever preternatural foes the sea might set against him, it could not be worse than the fatal certainty of his present course. He banked his aircraft and skidded crosswise with the cyclonic winds. There came a two second reprieve. The air-pressure built powerfully beneath his wings. A pilot learns to recognize the *feel* of a forthcoming volley—updrafts can equal the might of downdrafts. With no gain in forward direction he was yet virtually stationary. He wrote:

> Before I knew it [I was lifted] fifteen hundred feet straight into the air . . . the plane quivered as if in boiling water. I could see the wide waters of the ocean. The valley opened out into this ocean, this salvation.—And at that very moment, without any warning whatever, half a mile from Salamanca, I was suddenly struck straight in the midriff by the gale off that peak and sent hurtling out to sea . . . I had not flown out to sea. I had been spat out to sea by a monstrous cough, vomited out of my valley as from the mouth of a howitzer.[194]

As quickly as he had accelerated above and beyond the mountains, he as rapidly decelerated and dropped seaward. He found himself five miles from shore at only sixty feet above the ocean's vast expanse. Once again he was stationary—cutting through the air, maximum power, at 150 miles per hour, but the headwinds he fought were near the same velocity. Over the ocean he would appear to hover, like a seagull whose forward speed matches that of the wind into which it flies and to our eyes appears suspended mid-air. The battle ground had changed from land to sea, but the relentless war raged on. He now faced the shoreline, if it could be called a *line*—for his eyes were jostled so rigorously that the coast was a blur. The landing strip at Comodoro-Rivadavia was the only safe harbor in this remote area—it lay still to the south of his position. However, should Tonio angle the aircraft towards this destination in the least degree he would be blown downstream—further out to sea. As long as he kept his heading straight into the wind, he could hold his own. Any deviation from that course gave the enemy gale the advantage and it would drive him further from the continent. Five miles from shore might as well have been five hundred! Although not as violent, the turbulence was still *extreme* and so close to the water there was the dread possibility that if the buffeting dropped a wing, momentarily dumping his lift, there would be no space to recover. His tanks were now half-empty and the gas sloshed in every direction causing transitory fuel starvation. At times his engines sputtered, critical thrust fell to practically nothing, then fuel pumps, catching the vital fluid, revived their prime and the engines roared back to life.

The drama created a fantastic seascape. Windspouts clashed against the sea in a "succession of horizontal explosions." Pools of deep emerald adjacent to vast stretches of pure white sea—sea whipped to a frothing crème. Now and then he could peer down to the very bottom of the ocean. After twenty minutes and making no headway Tonio had to face the possibility that he might run out of fuel before he could find a breach in the still clear cyclone. The idea of the engines sputtering dead and then the necessity of ditching the plane in the ocean frenzy below was a terrible mental image. Was escape impossible? His hands were numb. They still gripped the controls and fought the enemy, but he could feel nothing. What if they were to simply let go, relax into useless stumps? The steel control cables had been brutalized—as had the ribs and spars. Any moment Tonio expected a cable to snap, or the plane's very structure to fail. There would be no reprieve from any of these catastrophes. In any of these events he would tumble to the water where his heavy flight gear would weigh him down like concrete and in the tempestuous swirl forfeit his life.

Then came very brief periods, what he called "green zones" of relative calm. He seized these moments and *climbed*. First three hundred feet, then six hundred feet, then finally nine hundred feet above sea level. Now he could maneuver. He looked at the thermometer on his wing. It read twenty degrees below zero yet he was dripping wet in sweat from head to toes. Every muscle, every joint in his body ached painfully. How had he endured so long?

He spied a "sort of blue stream" on the ocean that trailed towards the mainland. The idea came into his mind that this faint *lane* of color could possibly indicate that the air above it was somewhat sheltered from the horrific winds. How that could be possible, he could not theorize, only that something was causing this phenomenon, and that it indicated a slight change of conditions—good or bad. If he could only reach that stream perhaps he would be able to reach the coast where he might at least survive a land-crash. He allowed himself to drift left, losing precious distance in the hope of gaining a slight advantage over the horrendous headwind. As his plane intercepted this pathway of hope Tonio felt, at least he thought he felt, a slight decrease in the force of the wind.

It took an hour to reach the shore, indicating that the winds had decreased from a velocity of 150 miles per hour to 145 miles per hour—a mere 5 miles per hour improvement! It is interesting that when Tonio had truly exhausted every potential solution through extreme personal effort, an idea, an *impression,* entered his consciousness. Acting upon this inspiration did not result in a quick solution. As he gazed at the blurred coast, without the aid of modern instruments, it would for a time, have been agonizingly difficult to ascertain if he were actually advancing. When he finally made it, he miraculously found shelter close to a ridge that traversed the shoreline a great distance. The ridge created a sort of a buffer providing Tonio with his escape route south. Incredibly he landed safely at his destination. When he inspected his plane he discovered that his wing ribs had come unglued and that a number of his control cables had "been sawed down to the last thread" How much longer could his airplane have held together? Minutes—maybe only a moment more. Had that happened Tonio still would have been victorious. His plane would have failed before he did.

Pilots, like all pilgrims, often have great cause to faint—to become numb in the clench of adversity. But their mission is to endure to the end of their travels; regardless of the cyclones they encounter enroute.

CHAPTER 20

TRAVELER

Our birth is but a sleep and a forgetting;
The soul that rises with us, our life's star,
Hath had elsewhere its setting,
And cometh from afar:
Not in entire forgetfulness,
And not in utter nakedness,
But trailing clouds of glory do we come
From God, who is our home. [195]

—WILLIAM WORDSWORTH

[We are] strangers and pilgrims on the earth.

— PAUL THE APOSTLE[196]

MAN IS A TWO PART BEING—PHYSICAL AND SPIRITUAL. Our mortal bodies are sired by our earthly fathers. Our intelligence—our *spirits* are sired by, as Paul said, the Father of Spirits, God, our Heavenly Father. Birth is the union of body and spirit; death is the separation of the living spirit from the lifeless body. The spirit body is immortal.

Man is a traveler, an adventurer, a pilgrim on earth. A pilgrim does not come from the country of his sojourn. Therefore the soil of earth is not our native soil. If this sphere on which we temporarily reside is not home, then where is home? How far have we come? What is the purpose of our pilgrimage and where lies our final destination?

Literally, our spirits have flown from the home of heaven, from a distant Star, across the immensity of space we traveled at incomprehensible speed, landing safely upon the earth, within our mother's womb, within our miraculously forming physical body, awaiting the advent of our birth into mortality. Birth!—a continuation of the life of the spirit, an expatriation of ourselves from the pre-mortal world, a separation of our new body from the body of our mother, an awakening to a new life and a forgetting of a former, preparatory one, a debut into a world of limited sight where we can best learn faith, agency, individual responsibility, service and sacrifice. To each mortal life is given a purpose, a God-given mission, and an all-important *test.* How we fulfill this life's mission, how we measure up to this test, will determine when this life is over, where next we will *fly!*

Have you ever dreamed you were *flying*—flying without wings, independent of artifice, without machinery, without bounds, hovering at will or traveling at the speed of *thought?* Deep in sleep, the conscious mind subdued, the subconscious mind freed from the effects of somatic amnesia, we vaguely recollect our autonomous *spirit,* and act out in our dreams our former mobility. We fly down arcadian valleys, soar over snow-capped mountains, glide effortlessly above crystal seas, ascend higher than the atmosphere and gaze down upon a paradisiacal world, perhaps faintly remembering our former home—nostalgically joyful.

There are those among us who are restless with earth-bound confines, whose subconscious mind remembers the freedom of flight and cannot be cowed by the conscious mind—men whose very nature despises the practical, the safe, the sedentary, the known, whose inward spirit envies the *eagle.* The eagle, endowed by the Creator with incredible strength, vision and with the kinetic power to move freely in all dimensions. Fearless of storms, their great wings capture the power of the wind. At will the eagle ascends to dreadful heights or swoops down, wings tucked in perfect control, diving within inches of the ground. Men who felt this kinship with the lord of the sky, must have been tormented to live their lives earthbound—that is until the Giver of truth inspired such men with the knowledge to deliver themselves, even while mortal, from flightless existence. This gift was given a short one hundred years ago, on December 17, 1903, at Kitty Hawk, North Carolina. Tonio, already full of adventure, was just three years of age when the Wright Brothers made the first powered flight in history.

CHAPTER 21

THE SUN KING

We live in deeds, not years; in thoughts, not breaths;
In feelings, not in figures on a dial.
We should count time by heart-throbs. He most lives
Who thinks most, feels the noblest, acts the best.
And he whose heart beats quickest lives the longest:
Lives in one hour more than in years do some
Whose fat blood sleeps as it slips along their veins. [197]

—PHILIP JAMES BAILEY

ANTOINE JEAN-BAPTISTE MARIE ROGER DE SAINT-EXUPÉRY was born on June 29, 1900 in Lyons, France. As a child he was known by the sobriquets "Tonio," short for Antoine and "the Sun King," due to his golden locks and his childish sovereignty. He playfully sought to exert dominion over his mother, Madame Marie de Saint-Exupéry, and his siblings. Tonio had one brother and three sisters, namely Marie-Madeleine—three years his senior, Simone—two years older than Antoine, François—his younger brother by two years and Gabrielle—his favorite sister, born in May 1903. Their father, Jean de Saint-Exupéry died a young man of forty-one years of age, by stroke, less than a year after Gabrielle's birth, leaving Madame de Saint-Exupéry a widow at the age of twenty-eight.

Antoine's nickname, the Sun King, was indeed appropriate for another reason—he was born a noble. The family name, *Saint-Exupéry*, is one of the oldest in France and dates back to the time

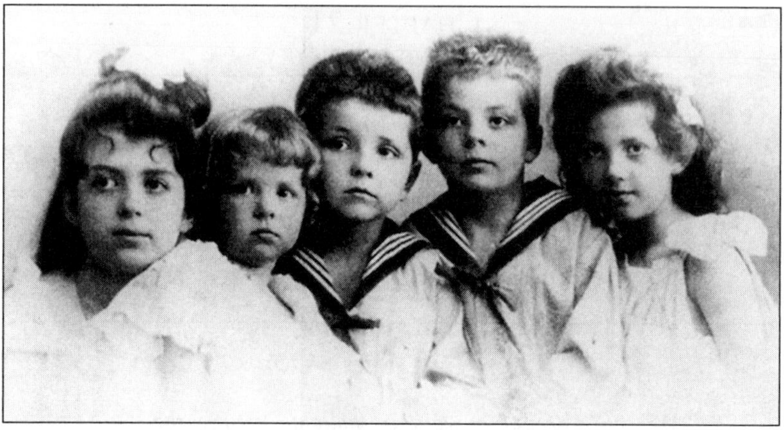

Antoine with his sisters and brother—
Marie-Madeleine, Gabrielle, François, Antoine, Simone

of the Crusades. His ancestral aristocracy, on both sides of the family, were extremely distinguished and included a host of knights, military officers, counts, barons, an archbishop, and a court chamberlain (a high-ranking steward who manages the household of the Sovereign). Although his widowed mother was a countess, she personally possessed no fortune. Her husband, Jean, had been an insurance professional, an unlikely occupation for a count—but these were the 1900s and royalty no longer necessarily meant riches.

Madame Saint-Exupéry was a wonderful and resourceful mother to her five little children. She was a trained nurse, yet she retained the dignity and grace of her high birth. A very tender woman, she was talented, perpetually compassionate and devoutly religious. Her great aunt and godmother, the Countess de Tricaud, lovingly came to her aid when Jean died. Madame Saint-Exupéry's small apartment on the rue du Peyrat in Lyons was vacated and her family moved to the Countess de Tricaud's château in Saint-Maurice-de-Rémens. Six months of each year was spent at this château while they spent the rest of year in the countess's apartment in Lyons or with Madame Saint-Exupéry's parents. They lived in a converted medieval monastery known as the

Antoine de Saint-Exupéry

château de La Mole, close to the town of Saint-Tropez. This old home had been in the family since 1770 and was truly enchanting, with its two ancient towers, its own tropical forest and its close proximity to the warm waters of the Mediterranean Sea. Tonio loved this area and much later in life commented that it was "the only corner of the world, apart from Greece, where even the dust has a fragrance."

Tonio was an exuberant child, to say the least. At the château at Saint-Maurice, bars were placed over the third story windows so that Tonio could not venture out onto the roof for his nighttime adventures. When it was time for his bath he could nearly always outmaneuver Paula, a girl who helped with the children. Tonio would run naked down the hallway with Paula in hot pursuit, the sponge dripping water in her hand. Yet Tonio possessed a creative and introspective side to his personality. He loved stories and shadowed his mother constantly until she took the time to sit at his side and tell him a tale from Hans Christian Andersen or Jules Verne. As soon as he could write he began to compose little poems, stories and plays, often late in the evening. For ideas he perused his uncle's library, assisted by his sister Simone. The hours of the day that are traditionally appropriated meant very little to him. He often stalked the house at night, waking his brother, sisters and cousins to join him in some enterprise, which normally included his theatrical readings. To the great amusement of the adults in the château, Tonio's troupe performed his plays or adaptations at family gatherings.

From his mother, Tonio inherited tenderness. There was one way that the rowdy son could be calmed—it was to simply place an infant cousin in his arms. Tonio would bottle-feed the baby with paternal gentleness and with loving attention. For an hour neither the baby, nor the boy, uttered a sound. He, along with his siblings, shared a tremendous love for animals and small creatures. They tended wounded birds or field mice, tamed crickets and built earthen homes for snails, whom they trained as *racers*.

His mother also imbued Antoine with a profound sense of spirituality. She taught him "the real riches of Christianity." Yet, as he grew older he did not fully embrace the orthodox views of the organized religion to which he was born. He seemed to relay his personal feelings in his first novel when he lamented that in the cathedral of Notre-Dame-de-Paris one left dissatisfied and saddened. But his faith in God was well founded by his mother and his spirituality matured as he did. His insight into *truth* can be found throughout his writings—which ultimately became his greatest earthly accomplishment.

As a child and later as a man, it was to his mother that his thoughts turned whenever he was lonely or sad. Later, when he was far from home, his letters to her were unceasing and brimmed with expressions of appreciation for her love, support, encouragement, for the rich treasure she had given him in his childhood—the memories that were more real to him than the often hard world around him. She was ever his source of peace and the genesis of his knowledge. In 1930 he wrote her saying:

> What taught me the meaning of infinity was not the Milky Way, or aviation, or the sea, but the second bed in your room.[198]

There was still another facet to his character that surfaced early in Antoine's life. Once he pestered his piano and voice teacher if she knew how a piston worked, for which she, the daughter of the conductor of the Lyons Opera, had no reply. Father Monessuy, the local curé, pronounced that Antoine was "extraordinarily talented in the sciences." One of his first engineering projects was a design for a flying bicycle. After a diligent search in the village, he procured a small hot-oil engine. However, it was never fitted to his bike, having blown-up while his young brother was playing with it. Nonetheless he pursued his objective. It had only been nine years since the Wright Brothers first flight and Tonio was determined to follow their lead. A carpenter, endeavoring to help the now twelve year old boy achieve his dream, helped him fix wicker supports to his bicycle to which he rigged old sheets for wings. He made a good run, pedaling for all his young legs were worth, aided by a steep ramp, but fortunately he could not get his bike airborne. Had he been successful it would have no doubt ended in a spectacular crash! One wonders if his lovely mother Marie could have ever dreamed that her adventurous boy, with his unusual whims and daring imagination, would one day *fly* from Toulouse to Casablanca, then across the great Sahara to Dakar!

Although Tonio was extremely attentive when the subject caught his interest, he was *easily* distracted when schooled in other areas that did not appeal to his intellect. He is often described, by classmates and teachers alike, as having a short attention span, fidgety in his seat, and given to daydreaming. Later he would be recognized as a great mathematician, but in the Jesuit school at Le Mans he was detained after class repeatedly for failing a series of math tests. He grew quickly in size and it seemed that his coordination was always a step behind his growth—particularly, when the activity was not to his liking—as in learning to *dance*. Odette de Sinéty, who was often relegated with the unpleasant task of being his partner, commenting years later said that Antoine danced with the grace of a "bear" and made no effort whatever to disguise his annoyance with this "duty."

The one element—the one common denominator in his educational years was his writing—so much so that it irritated his professors. When thirteen years of age Tonio published his first *magazine*; he recruited a friend as a sportswriter, another as a cartoonist, and several others as columnists. He wrote a poetry column that must have been controversial to say the least—for as a result, he and all of his fellow editors were given detention. The magazine met its demise after only one edition. Classmates often leaned over Tonio's shoulder to read his clever verse. This caught the attention of the instructors who chastened him for distracting the class. This, in turn, led to gibes by the other students. Tonio's solution to this problem was a masterful one—he taught himself to skillfully write entire sentences in *reverse,* which confounded his comrades and teachers alike.

The luckless magazine revealed Tonio's two budding passions, composing literature and flying, where rapidly maturing in unique harmony. He was *becoming* gifted as a poet as he would later become gifted as a pilot. In this juvenile work these loves where conjoined. Later their union would bring him nothing less than world fame! He designed the magazine's cover featuring an airplane and on the pages within he penned a poem, only three lines of which remain in existence:

> The wings tremble under the evening breeze,
> The engine, with its song, rocks the sleeping heart,
> The sun's pale warmth shines down upon us . . .[199]

Although America was the birth-place of modern aviation, the science of flight was weaned, not in the United States, but in France. The Wright Brothers had three times failed in their attempts to sell their invention to the War Department in Washington. The British Government also rejected their curious, but seemingly impractical wizardry. But France, already infatuated with flight, embraced the young inventors and the French were the first to profit from the Wright's wealth of new found knowledge.

Long before the Wright brothers, France was steeped in aeronautical history. In 1783, the French brothers Joseph Michel and Jacques Etienne Montgolfier, built the first practical hot-air balloon. The first living aeronauts to ascend in the balloon were an unlikely French trio—a duck, a sheep and a rooster. Later the same year the Montgolfier's recruited a French physicist, Pilatre de Rozier to pilot the first manned flight. Although a Roman will tell you that the word *pilot* comes from the old Italian *pilota*, a French aviator will defend to his death the doctrine that *pilot* is derived from the name of the very first man to fly—*Pilatre.* Established in 1898, the Aéro-Club de France was the first of its kind in history. The French-born Engineer, Octave Chanute, gave considerable support and encouragement to the Wright Brothers. After their historic first flight, Chanute reported the success in a landmark speech to this preeminent aeronautical association. Even the word *aviator* comes from the French *aviateur.* The first powered flight in Europe was on September 13, 1906—flown, of course, in Paris. On November 13, 1907, Paul Cornu was first to fly in a helicopter, near Lisieux, France. Henri Farman was the first airplane passenger, flying with Leon Delagrange at Issy, France on March 28, 1908. The first hydroplane was flown at Martiques, France by Henri Fabre; the Frenchman Louis Bleriot was the first person to fly across the English Channel on July 25, 1909.

The latter of these French successes was made possible by the knowledge gained from an agreement which licensed the Wright Flyer to a French syndicate. Wilbur Wright came to Le Mans in March of 1908 and, before the year was over, had flown scores of demonstration flights, culminating in an astounding 2½ hour flight in bitter winter weather. The great American inventor, slighted by his own government, returned home bearing the highest accolades the French could bestow upon him—he was inducted into the Légion d'Honneur and awarded the Michelin Cup.

And so it was that Tonio was nurtured not on the fantasy adventures of Jules Vern alone, but was reared in the very atmosphere of the adventurous early days of aviation. While on vacation in July of 1912, home at Saint-Maurice, he and Gabrielle often rode their bikes to the aerodrome at Ambérieu. There he would hound the mechanics with questions, eye enviously the all-metal

Berthaud-Wroblewski airplanes, and worry his mother to death that he might actually try to go up in one of those bat-like contraptions (which she absolutely forbade). Late in the month Tonio fibbed to Gabriel Wroblewski, telling him that Madame de Saint-Exupéry had given her son permission to fly. He proudly announced that he was ready to receive his *baptême de l'air*, or his aerial baptism. He received his first flying lesson that very afternoon. The following year when he wrote, "the wings tremble under the evening breeze," he did so from personal observation.

Tonio had just turned 14 years of age when all adult French males were drafted at the outbreak of the Great War. Overnight he witnessed more than a million men leave their homes and families to defend France. Although too young to serve, nevertheless, his noble blood was stirred by the dangerous crusade and he longed to be part of a cause far greater than himself. A boyhood friend said that more than the other young men, Antoine longed to prove his manhood, to face peril calmly and withstand the rigors of action. He believed that Tonio felt that "he had missed forever some vital test." Already he possessed the body of a man and was described by another friend as "monolithic, massive and gauche" yet possessing an "intensely radiant personality." Later in the original French version of *Wind, Sand and Stars,* which in France was titled *Terre des Hommes,* literally the *Land of Men*, he wrote:

> The world teaches us more about ourselves than any number of books, because it resists us; a man discovers himself only when he faces up to its challenge.

Certainly his ardor must have been further roused by his mother. Marie no doubt told her son the somber stories of the brave soldiers, wounded and maimed, who came under her gentle touch as she nursed them in the hospital trains that passed through Ambérieu station.

During the early days of the war Madame de Saint-Exupéry removed her two sons from the school in Le Mans and enrolled them in the College of Saint Jean in Fribourg, Switzerland. Also known as the Villa Saint-Jean, the school was far better suited to Tonio's disposition than the harsh Jesuit environment at Le Mans. Situated above and overlooking Fribourg, the campus was indeed picturesque, equipped with extensive playing fields and bordered by a charming forest. No walls surrounded the Villa Saint-Jean, providing a mien of trust and freedom to its 1,000 students. The general milieu was more relaxed than most boarding schools, yet dignified and certainly academic. Tonio wrote his mother that he liked Saint-Jean. He found it a bit harsh but appreciated the "great sense of justice" which seemed to permeate everyone and everything in the institution. To his professors, he was anything but extraordinary. Although he excelled in Latin and French composition, they chided him for failing to speak the required German at the dinner table. His grades in geography were at the bottom of the class and his math scores were average at best. His teachers mostly regarded him as cumbrous, apt to knock over the milk pitcher, but his large size suited him well for the soccer field. It was hard indeed to get a shot past Tonio the goalie.

Tragedy struck when his younger brother, François was stricken with "cardiac rheumatism" known now as rheumatic fever. After months of convalescing at Saint-Maurice, his condition failing, Antoine was summoned home from Fribourg. On July 10, 1917 at 4:00 a.m. François asked his nurse to get Tonio. His pain was unbearable but he reassured his older brother that he was all right. Then this fifteen year-old boy bestowed his possessions on his best friend.

> Had he been a builder of towers he would have bequeathed to me the finishing of his tower. Had he been a father, I should have inherited the education of his children. A reconnaissance pilot, he would have passed on to me the intelligence he had gleaned. But he was a child, and what he confided to my care was a toy steam engine, a bicycle, and a rifle.[200]

Then he whispered:

> Antoine, go and fetch Mamma, because I am going to die soon.

In a moment his widowed mother was at his side.

> Mother, you must not worry about me. I have already sensed certain things about life which are very ugly, and I don't think, if I had grown up, I should have been able to face them. I shall be better off in the place where I am going to now.[201]

He did not cry out, but gently slipped from life to death. Gabrielle, so close in age to François, wrapped herself in Tonio's arms and sobbed. He assured his little sister that as her only brother he would do his very best for her, more than all the brothers in all the world.

Failure is one of the most difficult forms of adversity. Dis*courage*ment, simply put, is a lack of courage. The two needn't go together. Life is a test. If something is fair then it cannot be a test. So by divine design, life cannot be fair. Is failure then a factor in all lives? Yes—*especially* in lives of merit. Only through opposition can a man grow in strength. Without opposition our muscles and our minds become weak. When hopes are reduced to ashes one can either lose courage, and truly fail—or courageously plow the ashes into the soil of enterprise and nourish future success. George William Russell wrote:

> THOUGH now thou hast failed and art fallen, despair not because of defeat,
> Though lost for a while be thy heaven and weary of earth be thy feet,
> For all will be beauty about thee hereafter through sorrowful years,

And lovely the dews for thy chilling and ruby thy heart-drip of
tears.
The eyes that had gazed from afar on a beauty that blinded the
eyes
Shall call forth its image for ever, its shadow in alien skies.
For thou hast but fallen to gather the last of the secrets of power;
The beauty that breathes in thy spirit shall shape of thy sorrow a
flower. [202]

In France, the key to higher education was turned when a student successfully completed his *baccalauréat* exam. Tonio passed the baccalauréat, and the future looked bright for the young aristocrat. As aviation was still in its military infancy, the adventurous youth sought to be admitted to Ecole Navale, comparable to the US Naval Academy. World War I was raging—there was certainly a demand for new officers to replace those killed at sea. War creates opportunities as well as destroying them. As Tonio could point to a history of naval officers in his family, he could envision an illustrious career in the navy. He enrolled in Lycée Saint-Louis in Paris in the fall of 1917 to prepare for the extremely difficult entrance exam.

Life in Paris, as a prep student, was unlike anything else he had ever experienced. His new friends were lively and unrestrained. However, Antoine was bound to a higher code. Stacy Schiff wrote:

> As for any fears Madame de Saint-Exupéry might have had about her adolescent son in the City of Light at a time when its morals were more than usually lax, he assured her that "I believe I will always remain your same Tonio who loves you so."[203]

It was a time of great excitement. Paris was host to thousands of soldiers from all branches of the military, coming or going, on leave or in transit, freely mixing with the students at the cafés near

Lycée Saint-Louis. Windows were papered over to prevent shattering from the concussion of explosions, an everyday occurrence. In the evening the city was transfigured, but not as you might imagine it in times of peace. Paris was blue. From the blue train lights to the blue cable car lamps—even the hall lights at school were blue. Most street lights were put out. Saint-Exu, as he was now nick-named, delighted in the atmosphere. He wrote that when looking down at night from a high building the city looked like a "giant ink stain," without halos or reflections. He also commented that a clear and beautiful sky would surely precede a horrific rain from Big Bertha. That great German gun hurled 265 pound shells, carrying 15 pounds of explosive, to the very edge of space, 24 miles high, then continued on a trajectory that would carry it to a maximum range of 80 miles! Tonio wrote his mother:

> I wish you were here to experience the artillery barrage just once. You would think yourself in the middle of a terrible storm, of a hurricane. It's magnificent.[204]

On June 28, 1919, one day before Tonio reached the age of conscription, the Treaty of Versailles was signed. Formally, World War I was over. Gone were the terrible dangers, but also gone were the commensurate opportunities. However, Tonio continued his studies and nearly a year later he felt ready for the Naval Academy exams. His euphoria in passing his written tests was shattered when afterwards he *failed* the oral portion of the examination. This failure was a direct hit to his career. Could he retake the exam? No. Recovery was impossible as his age prevented subsequent attempts. Even worse, Lycée Saint-Louis was a preparatory school only—he had earned no diploma. He was an aristocrat, without fortune, a well educated young man, without academic credentials, and he was also without a father to sure up his failing confidence or to assist him in charting a new course.

Although he expended a great deal of effort during this fruitless era to his writing, most of his manuscripts ended up crumpled and discarded. Even though hostilities had ceased, two years conscription was still mandatory for all young men. When Tonio was called up he put in his request to serve in aviation. This request was granted and he was assigned to the Second Fighter Group, but not as a student pilot. He had hoped to be a military officer, however he was inducted as a private-second class, known derisively among the French military elite as a *rampant*, the lowest of the low. It is one thing to lead a servile existence when experience has offered nothing better. It is quite another thing when a boy is raised a blue-blood, immersed in a family history of nobility, raised on stories of knights—not from fairy tales, but from true accounts of worthy ancestors. The German "von" and the French "de," when signed preceding the last name, are equivalent designations of aristocracy. Antoine *de* Saint-Exupéry owned the title "Count." Imagine the degradation of the young Count, when he was addressed by his so-called superiors as "rampant," taken from the Franch *ramper* meaning literally to crawl.

Antoine's perspective in this regard may best be understood from a discourse he wrote much later in life in his book, *The Wisdom of the Sands*, wherein through the voice of the King he stated:

> Whoever has played a lofty part and been honored may not be laid low. He who has reigned may not be divested of his kingship, nor must you reduce to beggary him who has given alms to beggars. Acting thus, you would be shattering the very design and fabric of [nobility]. Therefore, I have my punishments befit the standing of those whom I punish. I execute those whom I have thought fit to ennoble, if they have proved unworthy, but I do not degrade them to the estate of slaves.[205]

In other words, it is better to *kill* a nobleman, if he betrays his nobility, than to enslave him. For to enslave such a man dishonors, not him alone, but nobility itself. A groveling subservient aristocrat is but fodder for the envious masses, who, with no vision of *exalted man*, desires to pull down all who would excel to kingly character. Such minds, wallowing in the contemptuous mire, can conceive of nothing that is grand, gracious, lordly, majestic, royal. They delight in what is common and base and would seek to reduce all to their democratic misery. Saint-Exupéry's thinking is not autocratic—it does not uphold the treason of infidelity but demands the severest penalty of one who has dishonored his high trust—an immediate death both dignifies the office he held and banishes forever the person who failed that office. The divine law upholds this philosophy, as the rebel Lucifer was not enslaved by God, but was eternally cast out of His presence.

There is, however a great advantage to unjust humiliation as it can aggravate a man to tremendous exertion. A good man so ridiculed and humbled is roused from his sleepy descent. With a start he sees clearly the rising of the ground before him and its near term deadly convergence with his flight path. Every control he has is brought to bear to check this fall—to reverse this course. Every power within himself and within his reach is employed to lift him skyward, away from his *almost* ruin. This change of direction, this ascent, is seldom spectacular and nearly always perilous. Life is never static. While struggling to gain altitude and perspective he must move forward. To stall is to crash. Initially there is little maneuvering room. He is hedged about with deadly terrain. It will be sometime before he rises above the obstructions that now appear on every hand. Also, it is nearly always true that as he climbs the ground elevation increases. You cannot fly far without encountering mountains—that is the way this earth is built and that is also how mortal life is designed.

Tonio was determined that he would *merit* a higher station in life than that of a *rampant*. For himself he knew that such a life of mediocrity was synonymous with ruin. His first move was a bold one for a private-second class—he appealed to a Major de Féligonde for the opportunity to become a student pilot. The major seemed to respond sympathetically to Tonio and promised to look into the possibility.

In the meantime Tonio would increase his qualifications civilly for he knew that if he could acquire a civil license he would be immediately eligible to become a military student pilot. There was a commercial aviation firm that shared the Neuhof field with the Second Fighter Group. Its only staff pilot was a man named Robert Aéby. The cost of a ten minute lesson was fifty francs—expensive, especially for Tonio, whose military pay was meager to say the least. He had not flown since he was twelve. Aéby took him aloft in a Farman F-40. They had no sooner landed and taxied back to the hangar when Tonio requested another lesson—straight away. Aéby was surprised and delighted as he put another fifty francs into his billfold.

His funds exhausted, Tonio supplicated the pilots of his fighter group to take him along whenever there was a vacant seat. This was not an unusual request, as experienced flyers often enjoy taking up a fledgling. Normally, one flight was sufficient to quell such appeals, for these sessions were typically aerobatic in nature, frightful, and to the novice, simply nauseating. However, Tonio was not typical—the more a young ace would roll, spin, loop, and swoop, the more Tonio loved it. He was especially thrilled when he rode in a SPAD. He wrote his mother that "It holds the air like a shark holds the water, and even looks like a shark!" Of course, riding as a passenger, though beneficial, does not impart the skill of structured lessons. Once again Tonio spoke with Robert Aéby. Aéby was reluctant to assist him, and for good reason. The firm he flew for, Compagnie Transpaérienne de l'Est, was not a flight school. They chartered aircraft, took passengers on pleasure rides, and flew aerial photo missions. In fact there was no flight school on the field. Aéby was also concerned that Saint-Exupéry was full time military—did he really have time he could call his own? Additionally Aéby acknowledged that he had not actually given formal instruction—he had never taught anyone to fly. In any case it would be very expensive, at least 2,000 francs! Did Tonio have such resources? He did not, but Tonio promised he would get the funds. Aéby insisted that he would need authorization from his company, as well as permission from Saint-Exupéry's commanding officer.

His mother was naturally fearful for her son—aircraft accidents were common in those days and often fatal. Still she agreed to help him and borrowed the requisite 2,000 francs. Not long afterwards Tonio's commanding officer met with him, Aéby and Aéby's supervisor. Technically, Commandar Garde explained, Saint-Exupéry did not have control of his time and it was against the regulations to release a rampant to the custody of a civilian firm for training, even if he paid for the lessons himself. Certainly if a young man obtained his civil license *before* he was drafted, he could qualify as a military student pilot, but it was highly unorthodox for a private-second class to begin flight training, and never with a civilian flight facility. There was no precedent for exception. At that point it seemed certain that Tonio's plan would never see the light of day. He was shocked, therefore, when Commandar Garde conditionally approved of his flight instruction. Each man in the room was placed on his "honor to keep the enterprise a secret [and] no photographs were to be taken of the student with a CTE plane or in Aéby's company!"

On June 18, 1921, only 2 1/2 months after Saint-Exupéry had been inducted into the military, he began his career as an aviator with his fourth flight lesson. He was allowed to fly early in the morning, at the noon break, and after 6:00 p.m. He also began gunner flights, his official duty as a rampant. His lessons with CTE were initially in the Farman F-40, then later in a British Sopwith. As is often the case when a student loves his learning, Tonio progressed quickly and demonstrated the potential for excellence. On July 8, twenty-one days after he began formal training, and after two warm-up flights around the traffic pattern, Aéby yielded to his students repeated requests to solo. Tonio had flown approximately twenty three "circuits" or twenty three flights around the traffic pattern, presumably taking off and landing with each circuit. He had amassed a mere 2½ hours of flight time when he flew his first solo flight! Tonio had never been so happy. He had proven his worth to his superiors and later that very month he was transferred to the 37th Fighter Group, stationed near Casablanca, not as a rampant, *but as a pilot!* Here Tonio learned to love the desert for it seemed like home to him. By November he was ready for his reserve officer exams in Rabat. This time there would be no failed tests.

When a man is really motivated and prepared, an examination is simply an affirmation—there is no doubt in his mind that he will pass. A professional pilot does not wonder if he can safely land his airplane; he just does it. He does not doubt his capabilities to perform any aspect of flight. If he did he could not be a captain of an aircraft.

CHAPTER 22

EROS

You cannot think that the buckling on of the knight's armor by his lady's hand was a mere caprice of romantic fashion. It is the type of an eternal truth—that the soul's armor is never well set to the heart unless a woman's hand has braced it; and it is only when she braces it loosely that the honor of manhood fails. Know you not those lovely lines: [206]

Ah, wasteful woman!—she who may
On her sweet self set her own price,
Knowing he cannot choose but pay—
How has she cheapen'd Paradise!
How given for naught her priceless gift,
How spoiled the bread and spill'd the wine,
Which, spent with due, respective thrift,
Had made brutes men, and men divine!

—JOHN RUSKIN (POEM BY COVENTRY PATMORE)

IN 1922 TONIO WAS COMMISSIONED a second lieutenant with a salary of 1,000 francs a month—more money than he had ever earned in his life. Unfortunately he was transferred to the 34th Air Regiment in Paris. The desert had proven, and would prove again, to be Tonio's fertile soil, while the seductive and sophisticated "City of Light," appearing lush and green, would prove barren and treacherous. In the soft Parisian summer he met a young woman of incredible beauty, intelligence, daring, mystery and charm, Louise de Vilmorin. Like Antoine, she was an aristocrat.

Unlike Tonio, her family still possessed wealth. Nothing in his experience had prepared him for such a mesmerizing assault on his character. Had his father been alive he might have helped his son see clearly the misalliance. Not in name, for his noble name, de Saint-Exupéry, exceeded that of de Vilmorin. Not in wealth, for Antoine, surrounded by relations who possessed fortunes, yet possessing none himself, had already learned the value of merit. However, his father might have helped his son recognize a misalliance of mind, which is nearly impossible to overcome. Tonio and Louise appeared to have similar acumen. They were both poetic, both enjoyed composing verse and prose. They seemed to both be idealists, with imagination and whimsy. However, where he was fervent, she was frivolous. Where he had been raised to think deeply and seriously, she had been indulged and her thinking reflected a pampered life. Nonetheless, he quickly fell under the spell of this shallow minded princess and thought himself deeply in love.

Tonio courted Louise with fervor. He listened intently to her compositions and complemented her eagerly. Sometime in 1923 they became engaged. As far as we know he said little to his mother about his fiancée. Louise's mother thought Tonio a poor match for her exquisite daughter. Although his nobility was taken for granted, his poverty and his profession were appalling to Madame de Vilmorin. For a time Louise turned a deaf ear to her mother.

On May Day, 1923, Tonio took a friend flying, most probably to celebrate the arrival of Spring. He was scarcely airborne when, for an unknown reason, he lost control of his plane and plunged 270 feet to the earth. Both he and his passenger survived, although severely injured. He had not been checked out in the plane he had taken up, a Hanriot HD14. The official report reprimanded the young lieutenant for "his too-lively interest in trying all types of planes." At the same time the report praised his natural abilities and his flying skill. In that era particularly, bravado and daring were essential elements in an aviator's character. Today aviation accidents are rare, but in 1923 every flight had the potential of misadventure. However, this crash ended his military flying career. How? His superiors did not end it, rather they quickly forgave Tonio. He was nearing the end of his two year obligation and was now a trained pilot, who could provide valuable service to the French Air Force. But Louise, recognizing her mother's viewpoint, saw the real possibilities of widowhood if her betrothed continued his flying. Through her sister Louise issued Tonio an ultimatum, while still in the hospital—give up aviation or their relationship would end. He was kin to the eagle, had dreamed of flying since a small boy, had first flown when only twelve, soloed scarcely two years before this time, remarkably, after less than three hours of training, had risen from rampant to officer; this aeronautical prodigy cowed under the auspices of love and acquiesced to Louise's demands. On June 5, 1923, Tonio left military aviation behind along with his lifelong aspirations.

Although this sacrifice appeased Louise for a short time, it did little to satisfy Madame de Vilmorin. She thought Tonio intellectually deficient—she could not follow his conversation. One wonders when, years later, he became famous for his exceptional intelligence, insight, and eloquent skill in writing if Madame then realized her own inanity. Probably not—the ignorant are most ignorant of themselves. In any case, her daughter was of the same fabric and not long afterwards Louise terminated their engagement.

Tonio *thought* he had lost the treasure of his life. The effect of this estrangement cannot be understated—for a time he lost his health, his direction and purpose. It would be several years before he became again the man he was in the deserts of Africa. Later it would be those same deserts that would resurrect his greatness. However, he learned from this tragic relationship and increased in wisdom. Considering the power this petite coquette held over Tonio, had they married, she could well have *diminished* him, *turned* him from his life's purpose and obstructed his mortal mission. Had they continued together we may never have heard of Antoine de Saint-Exupéry. We may never have been enriched by his life and the truths he discovered and disclosed in his writings.

Louise *did* lose a treasure, more substantive than she could ever have imagined. Her thinking was bent and as such her course in life was set on ever changing delusional destinations—mirages. She became famous for a line, lived more than spoken: "I shall love you, forever, tonight." She led a life of vanity, turning heads and breaking hearts. Her first marriage was to Henry Hunt, a Las Vegas Developer and globe trotting entrepreneur. Henry settled his bride in Las Vegas of the 1920s, population 5,000. Wind swept, dirty, coarse—where Louise was left alone while he continued his travels. Their marriage lasted four years.

Love is not a god—it is a gift from God. However love, or rather one of its counterfeits, is often *believed* a deity and therefore worshipped with sacrificial offerings. When one gives their all to the true God, blessings unmeasured are returned. When a lover sacrifices all that is of value to Eros, he sacrifices to a false god, who returns nothing because he is nothing. This was a hard lesson for Tonio to learn, but he did learn it. True-love is a triangle, a three way relationship between God, a man, and a woman. Such *companions* have learned to put God first, each other second, and all else *after.* Therefore their all-powerful Benefactor continually renews His gift to them of true love. His ultimate reward is not Eternal Life only, but Eternal Love. Victor Hugo wrote:

> To love is the only thing that can occupy and fill up eternity. The infinite requires the inexhaustible . . .
>
> God can add nothing to the happiness of those who love one another, but to give them un-ending duration. After a life of love, an eternity of love . . .
>
> What love begins can only be finished by God . . . Love is a celestial breathing of the air of paradise.
>
> What a great thing, to be loved! What a greater thing still, to love! The heart becomes heroic through passion. It is no longer composed of anything but what is pure; it no longer rests on anything but what is elevated and great. [207]

CHAPTER 23

WINGS AS EAGLES

And he shall be led in paths where the poisonous serpent cannot lay hold upon his heel, and he shall mount up in the imagination of his thoughts as upon eagles' wings.

—THE LORD[208]

IN NEED OF WORK, SAINT-EXUPÉRY naturally sought positions in aviation or as a writer, the two areas of his expertise. He was unable to land a job as a journalist. He received news that China was in need of flight instructors but nothing developed for him in that regard. Facing his situation realistically he recognized that he had to work at whatever he could find. He felt the impact of his failed entrance exam now more than ever before. His friends were completing their advanced degrees with a multitude of opportunities on their horizons. By comparison his future looked bleak and he felt himself "the most discouraged man in the world."

Nonetheless and unknown to himself he was still gaining altitude. Pride keeps many young men from taking positions which they consider beneath themselves. Tonio humbly took an entry position with the firm of Tuileries Boiron, filing and bookkeeping. To a flyer a bureaucratic position is odious. It is not lofty, destination oriented; but it was honest work and he reported dutifully to his little cubical every workday. Eventually he landed a sales position with the Saurer Truck Company. He was not cut out for sales either and only sold one truck during the year in lieu of the expected three or four trucks per month. One highlight for Tonio during his tenure with Saurer was a three month training program where he was taught the mechanics of their engines. He reveled in grease and the feelings of accomplishment when he successfully disassembled and reassembled a complicated truck engine. This skill would prove literally life-saving to Tonio in the not distant future. Most of all he enjoyed the camaraderie with his fellow workers in overalls—surely to their surprise, as he was the only "Count" among them. Of these friends he wrote:

> I like people who have been tied more closely to life by the need to eat, to feed their children, and to survive until the end of the month. They are wiser.[209]

The fulfillment he found in brotherhood would lead Antoine to amazing spiritual conclusions, when later he would daily put his life on the line, defending his homeland against the atheistic Nazis.

1926 marked the end of his slow climb above the treacherous landscape into which he had nearly crashed. He had planned, prepared, worked and waited, never giving up on the dream he nourished deep within. Isaiah wrote:

> They that wait upon the LORD shall renew their strength; they shall mount up with wings as eagles.[210]

Antoine de Saint-Exupéry published his first commercially successful story in the April edition of *Le Navire*, entitled *"L'Aviateur."* He was also hired by Compagnie Aérienne Française Airlines, receiving his Airline Transport Rating on June 23, 1926. (The ATR license, now known as an ATP, Airline Transport Pilot, is the highest level of certification to which a pilot can aspire. It bestows the official title of captain and authorizes the carriage of passengers for commercial purposes on scheduled lines.) Most of his flights were scenic flights or very short "aerial baptisms."

Tonio seldom logged more than one hour a day.

The best airline opportunities were those lines that carried the mail. Passenger travel had yet to come into its own due to the expense, danger, and deafening attributes of the passenger lines. An old mentor of Tonios, Abbé Sudour, was a long time friend of Beppo de Massimi who managed Compagnie Latécoère, the premier mail service. Tonio aspired to leave the short-hop pleasure flights behind and become a Latécoère pilot. After much coaxing he prevailed upon Sudour to arrange for him an interview with Massimi. In October of 1926 he met first with Massimi and later in the month with Latécoère's Director of Operations, Monsieur Didier Daurat. Men like Daurat were (and still are) demi-gods to inexperienced pilots, like Antoine. Daurat was a highly decorated World War I ace, a hero of Verdun and the sole surviving pilot of the second battle of Marne. As a young student Tonio had witnessed first hand the bombardment of Paris by Big Bertha. Now he met with the aviator who had obtained the vital reconnaissance information of Big Bertha's location. Since 1919 Daurat had been engaged by Latécoère to fight a different type of war, one that required military precision and unrelenting endurance to accomplish a mission, regardless of seemingly insurmountable obstacles. On the average ten pilots lost their lives each year! Mail line pilots were fighters who were willing to sacrifice their all, even their lives, for something greater than themselves.

Neither Massimi or Daurat was impressed with Saint-Exupéry's piloting experience—he had logged only 300 hours in the air. However, both were strongly affected by the intensity of Tonio's desire to fly for Latécoère. They easily discerned that he was not the typical swaggering, assertive aviator. Rather he spoke softly saying that he wanted to fly, only to fly. Daurat observed that Tonio "possessed a clear moral and intellectual distinction." Saint-Exupéry was hired with the stipulation that he would begin his work with Latécoère, not on the flight line, but as an aircraft mechanic. Soon he would take to the skies, but he would first learn to enter knowingly the bowels of the planes he would fly.

Daurat was pleasantly surprised by Tonio's enthusiasm in donning mechanic's blues and his aptitude for wielding a wrench. Unlike the veteran flyers who often felt maintenance responsibilities below their lofty skills, Tonio loved this work almost as much as he loved piloting. And for the first time in his life, he began to love discipline. He quickly learned that he was entering a life that was as exacting as that found in a monastery and nearly as fraternal. In his first interview with Daurat he was tardy by an hour. Later he would write:

> I learned that any delay is a dishonor, regardless of why it occurs.[211]

Several weeks after his arrival he passed his flying tests with Latécoère and he was officially assigned to fly the Breguet 14 A2. His first flights were between Toulouse and Perpignan, a distance of only 100 miles. Then Daurat assigned Tonio to ride with his best pilot, Henri Guillaumet, from Toulouse to Alicante, via Barcelona—a flight of 420 miles that crossed the treacherous ten thousand foot Pyrenees mountains. This route carried passengers as well as mail. Twice Antoine accompanied Guillaumet on this run, not as a pilot but strictly as an observer. Late one evening, in the early winter of 1926, Daurat summoned Tonio in to see him. He said simply, "You leave tomorrow." Early the next morning he was to fly mail and passengers on the same route he had flown with Guillaumet. His mental reaction to this assignment was made evident by the fact that he stood before Daurat speechless and motionless. It was one thing to accompany the experienced Guillaumet and quite another to fly it as pilot-in-command, solo. He thought of the engine that often would "drop out, without warning and with a great rattle like the crash of crockery" send the pilot gliding earthward, with no other option than a rapid descent. He knew, by limited experience and by reputation, the formidable dangers of the Pyrenees. More perilous than the higher Alps, they are given to greater convective currents, extreme turbulence and

Breguet 14

cloud obscuration in any season. However, the winter storms of the Pyrenees caused the greatest concern and Saint-Exupéry was struck by a memory—a comment made by one of the veteran flyers said with great sympathy:

> I feel sorry for the man who doesn't know the whole line pebble by pebble, if he runs into a snowstorm. Oh, yes, I pity the fellow.[212]

Flying above an ocean of clouds is a celestial experience. The early morning sun reflects from the cloud's summit a soft radiating whiteness, whiter than snow. A pilot sees the beauty, but is not deluded by the fair white Sirens that lay beneath his gaze—for the ethereal mists mask towers of granite, millennial mountains that seek to beguile mariners of the air and destroy them in an instant.

Another image and warning entered Tonio's mind:

> Navigating by the compass in a sea of clouds over Spain is all very well, it is very dashing, but—but you want to remember that below the sea of clouds lies eternity.[213]

When Tonio left Daurat he was nearly overcome with conflicting emotions. He felt pride that he was given the responsibility to fly travelers who trusted implicitly in his skill and the charge to safely delivery the mails destined for Africa. Tonio also felt "ill-prepared." The merciless terrain of Spain does not lend itself to emergency landings should the engine quit or the pilot get himself boxed in with bad weather in the Pyrenees. Tonio's plane was not equipped with a radio—there would be no way to access help should he find it necessary "to hunt a landing-place." Saint-Exupéry wrote:

> I fled to spend this night of vigil with my friend Guillaumet . . . When I walked in he looked up and smiled. "I know all about it. How do you feel? . . . Don't worry. It's easier than you think."
>
> On this night, sitting in his shirtsleeves, his arms folded in the lamplight, smiling the most heartening of smiles he said to me simply: "You'll be bothered from time to time by storms, fog, snow. When you are, think of those who went through it before you, and say to yourself, 'What they can do, I can do.' "
>
> I spread out my maps and asked him hesitantly if he would mind going over the hop with me. And there, bent over in the lamplight, shoulder to shoulder with the veteran, I felt a sort of school boy peace.
>
> But what a strange lesson in geography I was given. Guillaumet did not teach Spain to me, he made the country my friend . . . He did not talk about Lorca, but about a humble farm near Lorca, a living farm with its farmer and the farmer's wife. And this tiny, this remote couple, living [far] from where we sat, took on a universal importance. Settled on the slope of a mountain, they watched like lighthouse-keepers beneath the stars, ever on the lookout to succor men.
>
> The details that we drew up . . . no geographer had been concerned to explore. Because it washed the banks of great cities, the Ebro River was of interest to map-makers. But what had they to do with that brook running secretly through the water-weeds to the

west of Motril, that brook nourishing a mere score or two of flowers?

"Careful of that brook: it breaks up the whole field. Mark it on your map." Ah, I was to remember that serpent in the grass near Motril! It looked like nothing at all, and its faint murmur sang to no more than a few frogs; but it slept with one eye open. Stretching its length along the grasses in the paradise of that emergency landing-field, it lay in wait . . . Given the chance, it would transform me into a flaming candelabra.[214]

Far into the night Tonio was instructed by his friend, Guillaumet. In lamplight his map of Spain was transformed into virtual reality. He marked the haven of the farm of Lorca, the emergency strip of Motril with its hidden snake-like trough that could catch his landing gear and send him cart wheeling. He marked areas of refuge as well as the traps that could snag the unwary. When at last they finished he walked confidently into the freezing night air. In his heart he carried a feeling akin to the first infatuation of love. He possessed a skill and knowledge unimaginable to those he passed on the streets of Toulouse. He looked at those whom he passed on that frigid evening. They knew nothing of him, yet he would be entrusted with their intimate thoughts, cares and life-sustaining business in their letters that he would carry—and a few would trust him with their very lives when they boarded his plane bound for Alicante. He felt for these unknown passer-bys the emotion that a Protector feels for his lover. Tonio also knew that among all these, he alone received certain messages given to him by the dark wind—and the stars, that one by one, ceased to shine in the firmament. A snowstorm was approaching. In this era, planes had no de-icing capabilities, yet the flyers of Latécoère were expected to launch just the same. To fly a primitive aircraft into such a storm is to enter a battle field. He wrote:

These messages of such grave concern were reaching me as I walked between rows of lighted shop-windows, and those

> windows on that night seemed a display of all that was good on earth, of a paradise of sweet things. In the sight of all this happiness, I tasted the proud intoxication of renunciation. I was a warrior in danger.[215]

At three-thirty a.m. Tonio was dressed in leather and harness, sitting on his flight case on glittering pavement, wet from the first attack of the storm. A while later an old bus picked up the expectant aviator, whose heart beat within his breast with the delicious heightened regularity of one ready to meet and conquer his adversary. Of all those who slowly filled the bus he was the only one of his profession. Most were clerks or inspectors, bureaucrats. For a short time he had, of necessity, been one of them. Now it seemed to him that such a life causes a man to sink "as into quicksand." He surmised that those with whom he rode led lives of monotony clogged with red tape. What joy had they in a life devoid of creativity, of challenge, *of significance!* Could their minds, anesthetized by the numbing tedium of sameness, even imagine the universe to which he now belonged? He felt sorry for these comrades—blameless in their sedentary security—they knew not that they were travelers, on a quest to discover *exalted man.* At day break he would penetrate the gray overcast of Toulouse as a sovereign of far horizons. Flowing in his veins was the blood of knights. Now Antoine would measure up to his ancestry as a knight of the skies. As a pilot combatant he would engage the tempestuous elements of winter, above the palisades of the Pyrenees—a feat his royal progenitors could never have dreamed possible. In the space of five hours, if he were victorious, he would have defeated the snowstorms, the perils of towering mountains, and would descend in the sweet summer scented air of Alicante.

Tonio departed Toulouse, on schedule in the midst of the storm. His navigation was flawless. He vaulted his aircraft over the Pyrenees and landed safely in Barcelona. Next he flew down the Spanish mainland, past Villanueva, Castellon De La Plana and Valencia and touched down, as planned, in Alicante. His return flight was also successful, although he was forced, due to heavy fog, to land southeast of Toulouse, near the fortress of Carcassonne, in a field. It was a perfect emergency landing with no damage to the aircraft. He was found waiting patiently beneath the shelter of the plane's wing, seated on wet grass.

From that day on Tonio routinely crossed the Pyrenees on the Toulouse-Alicante line. In early 1927 he was occasionally dispatched as far south as Casablanca and Tangier. He proved himself capable of the exhausting long hauls and by February was flying the route between Casablanca and Dakar. From then till early summer Saint-Exupéry flew the African line which ran along the coast from Casablanca to Cape Juby, to Villa Cisneros, to Port-Étienne, to Dakar—a fifteen hundred mile run. In a Breguet 14 aircraft, at an average groundspeed of around 80 miles per hour, with three stops, it would take 20 hours one way, plus layover time at each stop. Tonio's thin logbook quickly became fat with experience. Later in 1927 Latécoère was purchased by Marcel Bouiloux Lafont and henceforth became known as Compangie Générale Aéropostale.

On one flight Saint-Exupéry's engine overheated and began to misfire and sputter. Accompanied by a mechanic named Lefèbvre, they had departed Villa Cisneros bound for Port-Étienne. Tonio turned his aircraft toward the cooler air above the ocean and flew extremely low, just skimming the waves. When a plane flies less than one wing span above the surface induced drag is greatly decreased, allowing the plane to stay in the air at a speed below normal stalling speed. The misfiring engine continued to run but produced far less power than usual. Lefèbvre prepared for what he thought was the inevitable ditching and removed his shoes and clothing to facilitate floatation should they survive the ocean crash. Water does not compress, and struck at right angles is as hard as cement. Meanwhile Tonio seemed busily engaged in the cockpit. It soon became apparent what had been occupying his attention—he passed sketches back to Lefèbvre that he had just made. Lefèbvre couldn't believe it. In the first sketch Tonio portrayed himself and Lefèbvre as deep sea swimmers. In the second he had drawn the two as "Robinson Crusoe look-alikes on a tiny island—prisoners of the desert." The engine gradually cooled and ran a little smoother. Ultimately he was able to turn landward and put down at Port-Étienne without mishap. Clear thinking, coupled with humor, prevailed.

Engine failures were common in the Breguet 14 resulting in frequent forced landings or ditchings. For this reason, on the African line, Daurat assigned an escort plane to fly along side the mail plane. When one plane was forced to make an emergency landing the downed pilot, if uninjured, would direct the other aircraft to the safest place of landing as close to his plane as possible. The two planes were equipped with field tools, a mechanic and a Muslim interpreter. Often a field repair rendered the disabled aircraft airworthy and both aircraft could depart the sands. Mechanics were therefore obvious members of the flight crews, but why did Daurat employee native interpreters? For the same reason he armed his pilots. Only a year prior to Tonio's arrival in the desert, two of his fellow Aéropostale pilots, Bourp and Erable, had been murdered by the Moors and a third Frenchman later succumbed from injuries he received as a captive awaiting ransom. Not only did the Moors know the value of a French aviator, they had discovered the mail often contained franc notes, worth far more than their weight in gold. As the airfields were always guarded by a detachment of soldiers, the pilots were safe, provided they did not venture into the desert. However, this was a small refuge indeed. Saint-Exupéry wrote:

> . . . more than sixty feet beyond the fort one was shot at. At 150 feet one was killed or sold into slavery.

Therefore a pilot and mechanic might well survive a forced landing but awful was their plight if captured by the Moors. The Muslims that rode on these flights amid sacks of mail, swords at their sides, were not only official interpreters, they were negotia-

Cape Juby

tors of ransoms! What Daurat needed was an emissary, an envoy of Aéropostale. He turned to the young aristocrat, with the soft voice and granite nerve—who possessed the intelligence of an ambassador and the noble name of Saint-Exupéry.

Tonio had been on a short leave of absence in Toulouse due to a bout of Dengue Fever. On October 19, 1927 he returned to Africa and was appointed Chief of Cape Juby. His field responsibilities included making ready a small fleet of standby aircraft, receiving and dispatching line flights, and repairing and maintaining line aircraft. Uniquely he was also commissioned to rescue any downed aviator anywhere in the Sahara—with a specific charge to somehow influence the Spanish Moors to a more hospitable attitude toward French flyers.

Shortly after his arrival at Cape Juby, Tonio tamed a

chameleon, a gazelle and a sand fox. He wrote his mother and explained that he had discovered his role in life—it was to "tame." Saint-Exupéry then moved on to the more difficult species—the desert nomad. He studied Arabic, and more importantly, Antoine carefully observed the Arabian mores. The children of the Sahara loved him! He was funny, clever with tricks, a wonderful mime, gave them chocolate, and he was pleasant and kind. When not flying he discarded his European style of dress and donned a long cloak, very similar to the burnous worn by the Moors. He grew a beard, his skin tanned to a deep brown, and with his dark brown eyes he became "almost indistinguishable from the Moors." Tonio spent so much of his time in the desert, walking in the deep sands, that he soon emulated the slow-paced, rhythmic step of the Arab. Chieftains became his frequent guests for tea. But even more amazing was that he accepted their invitations to dine with them in their desert strongholds. Without reservation, he would walk miles into the Sahara alone. No one—absolutely no one, whether an armed soldier or a government inspector, would hazard such an effort. The Moors respected this man with the gentle voice, beloved of children, fearless as fire!

Saint-Exupéry also befriended the Spanish officers of the fort. His barrack was always open to them for a meal or a game of chess. Evening discussions often extended for hours into the night as Tonio held his friends spellbound with his marvelous stories. The soldier's quarters, although guarded and fortified, had the marks of many a rifle shot drilled in their panels—symbols of defiance from the surrounding Moors. Tonio's barrack was unprotected, lock-free and unmolested. Daurat said:

> Locks and bolts did not interest Saint-Exupéry much, as the magic of his own personality was enough to protect him.

He told his brother-in-law that he was "one part aviator, one part ambassador, one part explorer."

The Arab chieftains lived in the exclusive world of their own dominion. Scarcely one lifetime has passed from that era to the present day—so short a time. Yet when Antoine and his fellow aviators first flew over the sands of the Sahara they traversed a continent and a civilization that had remained unchanged for thousands of years. A sultan of a citadel or a chief of a wandering tribe of Bedouins possessed the same fierce arrogance. Their word was law. At their command the infidel was *allowed* to live or was condemned to die. Very few of these Arabian masters had ventured outside the boundaries of their own sovereignty. Saint-Exupéry wrote:

> Their pride was born of the illusion of their power. Many a time a chief has said to me, pointing to his army of three hundred rifles, "Lucky it is for France that she lies more than a hundred days' march from here."[216]

When the Frenchmen walked by them in the safe zones of Cape Juby or Cisneros, the Moors would

> . . . turn away and spit; and this not by way of personal insult but out of sincere disgust at having crossed the path of a Christian.[217]

Tonio sought to *tame* these Muslim leaders in a truly diplomatic manner. First, he demonstrated a sincere respect for their authority and way of living. There was no impious condescension in his diplomacy. He possessed no airs of superiority. He showed deference not only to chieftains, but he was courteous and kind to all he met—including children and even slaves. Secondly, he sought to build relationships of trust. Antoine had the gift of molding friendships. By dressing as they dressed, walking as they walked, learning their language and not forcing them to speak in his tongue—by taking interest in their interests, showing no revulsion to their idiosyncrasies and by delighting in the beauty and solitude of their desert home, Antoine soon forged ties of brotherhood. Thirdly, he and his French comrades assuaged the pomposity of the chiefs by expanding their universe. They did this by opportunely taking the Bedouins with them on their flights. It was marvelous for these provincial minded men to be conveyed by air, in a matter of hours, to worlds beyond their imagination.

Unless a person has lived in the arid region between Cape Juby and Port Etienne it is difficult to imagine such scarcity of water and greenery. Saint-Exupéry described how in Port Etienne the children begged, with tin cups in their small hands, not for money but for water. On one flight Tonio flew several Arabs, whose entire lives had been spent in the Sahara near Cape Juby, to Senegal. Although still on the African coast Dakar is a world apart from Juby. When these men saw large and leafy trees, growing prodigiously, they "burst into tears." Later three others were flown to France. Upon their return Saint Exupéry was amazed at their indifference to the accomplishments of *civilized* man. The Eiffel Tower meant nothing to them; nor did the great steamships and locomotives. What did impress them? It was the bounty of nature. Antoine wrote:

> Here were men who had never seen a tree, a rose; who knew only through the Koran of the existence of gardens where streams run, which is their name for Paradise . . . the chiefs mused . . .
>
> "You know the God of the French, He is more generous to the French that the God of the Moors is to the Moors."
>
> They had seen pastures in France in which all the camels of Er-Reguibat could have grazed! There were forests in France! The French had cows, cows filled with milk![218]

Several of their chieftains were led up a trail to a thunderous waterfall high in the French Alps. The plaited tresses of water fell from the escarpment in prolific abundance, hitting the rocks at the base of the waterfall with tremendous force, the spray rising like steam and settling like morning dew on the Arabs who gazed in disbelief! When they cupped their hands and drew the water to their lips, again they were filled with wonder.

It was sweet water. Water! How many days were they wont to march in the desert to reach the nearest well; and when they had arrived, how long they had to dig before there bubbled a muddy liquid mixed with camel's urine! When rain has fallen anywhere, a great exodus animates the Sahara. The tribes ride towards that grass that will have sprung up two hundred miles away. And this water, of which not a drop had fallen in Port Etienne in ten years, roared in the Savoie with the power of a cataclysm as if, from some burst cistern, the reserves of the world were pouring forth.

"Come, let us leave," their guide had said.

But they would not stir.

They had stood in silence . . . That which came roaring out of the belly of the mountain was life itself, was the life-blood of man. The flow of a single second would have resuscitated whole caravans that, mad with thirst had pressed on into the eternity of salt lakes and mirages. Here God was manifesting Himself: It would not do to turn one's back on Him. The three Moors had stood motionless.

"That is all there is to see," their guide had said. "Come. We must wait."

"Wait for what?"

"The end."

"But that water has been running for a thousand years!"[219]

Saint-Exupéry was more successful in his efforts to effect détente in the Sahara than even Daurat had expected, especially among the Izarguin clan. Still he was but one man among so many Arabian tribes. He wrote:

One does not pacify the nomads any more than one pacifies the international underworld . . . Above all the Moors admire force, and a conversation will influence them only insofar as it is an expression of power, even if that power is not put to use.

This he knew first hand. On June 30, 1928, two of his friends

Reine and Serre were scud running when their low flying plane, midway between Cape Juby and Villa Cisneros, struck a sand dune. Although they survived, they were captured by the R'Guibat. The chief demanded a ransom of one million rifles and a million camels (the negotiations always began at the ridiculous). Through his Moorish friends Antoine had sent Reine and Serre clothing and rations. Additionally, he attempted numerous times to save his friends. Said Antoine:

> For Reine and Serre I landed more than ten times, without a radio, without an escort, in the most remote corners of dissident territory.[220]

But each time the intelligence Tonio garnered was in error. Hostages were constantly moved by the R'Guibat, frustrating rescue efforts.

Another Friend, Jean Mermoz, was captured by the Arabs and torturously caged like a wild animal. In this manner he was moved about for days, from place to place, with little food and drink, baking beneath the desert sun by day and nearly freezing unprotected at night. Not once did he see the face of the Chieftain, whose countenance was always masked by a black veil. Eventually he was ransomed for one thousand pesetas. Antoine, while flying low over the dunes, had himself been shot at "like a rabbit by razzias of 300 men."

On July 18, two Aéropostale Breguet 14s, one carrying the mail, and the other aircraft acting as a safety escort, departed Villa Cisneros bound for Cape Juby. Only twenty miles south of Cape Juby the escort plane's engine failed and the pilot was forced to make an emergency landing in the soft desert sand. The mail plane flew on to Juby and notified Saint-Exupéry of the mishap. Unfortunately the escort plane had set down in a very dangerous area frequented by the murderous Ait-Toussa clan, an Arabian tribe Tonio had not in the least been able to restrain. The downed pilot, a Frenchman named Riguelle, was safely rescued. Now could the disabled Breguet 14 be salvaged? Anyone else, but Tonio, would have said no. The surface in the Sahara varies greatly. At some places the surface is hard packed and smooth—suitable for landing and taking off. There are other areas where the sand is firm enough to allow a skilled aviator to attempt marginal operations. However, Riguelle had no choice but to land his Breguet in very soft sand surrounded by dunes. It would be impossible to cut a trail through those dunes to retrieve the plane by truck. Even if the aircraft was repaired how could one take off with landing gear buried past the hubs? Worst of all there was the Ait-Toussa to deal with. The company had regulations that covered this extremity—policy required that this would simply be a loss for Aéropostale. However, Saint-Exupéry was not one to be governed by the book.

Tonio flew to the site of the downed Breguet and found a suitable place to land his plane within a reasonable hike from Riguelle's aircraft. To his dismay not only was the engine beyond field repair, but the airframe had been damaged in the emergency landing. He had brought two Moors with him, whom he left on the site to act as guards. He then returned to Cape Juby to plan his salvage operation. First he donned his burnous-like garb. It was actually a bathrobe but it served the purpose well. He walked to the camps of the Moors and met with their chiefs. Initially he said nothing regarding his objective but spoke to them poetically of wind and sky. Occidental cultures are matter of fact. There is little symbolism in western speech. But the oriental mind thinks in terms rich in second meanings, in imagery, in layers (the oriental way of thinking is superior, as evidenced by the manner of thought and expression employed by the greatest Communicator and Teacher of all time). Antoine had long cultivated his mind to think deeply; his powers of expression were sincere and eloquent. When the chieftains scorned his heathenish culture with questions such as: "You eat greens like the goat and pork like the pigs. . . . What good are your airplanes and wireless . . . if you do not possess the Truth?"—Tonio would answer intelligently, lyrically, and without taking personal offense. In any case on this day, although his needs were urgent, yet he followed the protocol of the desert. After polite conversation and supping tea, he requested an armed escort to retrieve the Breguet. His request was granted.

Within two days he organized a caravan consisting of eight horses, three camels, two mules and eighteen men. Six of the men were Moorish guards, nine were laborers; the last two were Saint-Exupéry and an Aéropostale mechanic named Marchal. Tonio rigged a cart, cleverly using two aircraft tires that would easily glide over the dunes; to which he secured a Breguet engine, a saw-horse and a block and tackle lift. He had never seen camel act as oxen, nevertheless he fashioned two harnesses for the camels to pull his makeshift cart. The Moors laughed at his contraption. Yet when they set out in the evening it worked perfectly. The following morning the caravan arrived on site. The two guards Tonio had left there previously had evidently been frightened off and the Breguet 14 had been vandalized. Still, Tonio thought it could be saved.

Tonio stationed guards as sentinels while Marchal removed the failed engine. Two of the engine mounts had been severed by a piston rod and Tonio sent a courier by camel back to Juby for replacements. Antoine now became a civil engineer designing an improvised runway. He and his men set to work leveling a strip, removing rock obstructions with pickax and employing novel techniques to firm the surface. Toward the end of the runway he put considerable effort into packing the sand as hard as possible to hopefully allow the Breguet to accelerate to flying speed. In the event the airplane began to stall and sink earthward after the initial lift-off, Tonio constructed another section of hard-packed surface in line with the runway to allow the aircraft one final attempt to be airborne. Failing that, the additional strip would allow him to settle down and roll out to a stop without endangering himself needlessly. This was a tremendous endeavor, considering that only manual laborers were constructing the runway. Additionally, the dangers of the region required completion within three short days.

As the sun disappeared below the horizon they were alarmed by the sound of distant gunfire—then silence. Soon thereafter the courier safely returned from Juby with the engine mounts. Several hours later an Izarguin tribesman raced into their camp warning that the Ait-Toussa were about to descend upon them. He predicted they would all be killed if they did not leave at once. He said he was sent by Colonel de la Peña, commander of the fort at Cape Juby, with orders to immediately return. Within minutes Antoine and his men were off. However, when the caravan was nearly half way to the fort, the Izarguin admitted that he carried no orders from the Colonel. He alone had sounded the alarm and had used the Colonel's name to add urgency to the cause. He believed the Ait-Toussa was planning a razzia and felt compelled to warn his friends. Antoine was livid! Of course the Ait-Toussa would raid their camp if they could. He knew that and was racing against time. It was most likely the gunshots of Ait-Toussa they had heard earlier in the evening. Now the Izarguin had wasted time Antoine could ill afford to lose. Saint-Exupéry ordered the caravan to turn around. The Moors refused. He accused them of cowardice. They all had known this was to be a dangerous undertaking. The only thing that had changed was a warning from an overzealous ally. Warily the Moors turned their horses and camels and obeyed the "Captain of the Birds," as he was now known by the Bedouins. The sun had risen well into the sky before they were back at the Breguet.

The drone of aircraft engines broke the morning silence. Two Spanish aircraft flew low over head dropping a package that contained, now curiously, an actual order from Colonel de la Peña to retreat to the safety of the fort. Obviously the Ait-Toussa were near. Saint-Exupéry did not share the order with his men. They were back at work; Marchal was busy installing the new engine—a half a day more and they could attempt the takeoff. Antoine wrote:

> I folded this paper carefully, as a souvenir, and decided to head back, but by plane, that evening.[221]

When the sun was directly overhead the desert silence was again broken with gunfire, now much closer. Antoine commanded the men to continue working. Did the Ait-Toussa know of their exact location? Certainly, even with his armed guards Saint-Exupéry's group would stand little chance of survival against the assault of the most barbarous tribe of the Rio de Oro. It was six o'clock when Marchal finally had the plane marginally readied for flight. Saint-Exupéry held the Breguet stationary while he advanced the engine to full throttle. When the engine was at full power he released the brakes. The makeshift airstrip was short and anything but ideal. The Breguet 14 would have accelerated slowly at first; for the sands, although smoother and firmer than they had been when Riguelle was obliged to put down, still would have but reluctantly released hold of the landing gear. However, when Tonio reached the hard packed sector at the end of the strip, the Breguet rapidly accelerated to flying speed, almost as if it were bounding into the air from a "spring-board." Twenty minutes later Antoine and Marchal landed safely at Cape Juby having successfully recovered a valuable airplane. The caravan also escaped back to the fort before the Ait-Toussa discovered their whereabouts. Antoine was becoming legendary among the pilots of *la Ligne* and among the Arabians of the Sahara.

In October of 1928 the Moors shot down a Spanish aircraft. In response, two reconnaissance aircraft, also bearing the flag of Spain, left Cape Juby with a Moorish interpreter on board. Their purpose was to gather intelligence, as it would be unlikely that the Moors would release the crew, if alive, without ransom. Misfortune followed misfortune. Well before they reached the riddled aircraft one of the reconnaissance planes suffered an engine failure and the pilot desperately crash-landed. The pilot and interpreter were both badly injured. The second reconnaissance pilot, observing the discordant terrain, was fearful, lest in attempting to land in such precarious conditions he would also crash. He returned to Cape Juby.

At that time the Spanish airlines were in fierce competition with Aéropostale and the Spanish had shown a great deal of animosity against French flyers. They had taken this to the extreme by obstructing the release of Reine and Serre, who were now nearing their fourth month of incarceration by R'Guibat. Saint-Exupéry had, since his appointment as Chief of Cape Juby Airfield, been doing all that he could to lessen hostile feelings. As he had entertained the Moors, dining with them in his quarters, showing them card tricks, telling them stories—so had he with the Spanish flyers, soldiers and officers. Now he saw an opportunity to do much more than card tricks. He immediately set off to rescue the wounded reconnaissance crew. Tonio departed in a flight of two, the other aircraft was, once again, a Spanish plane. This Spanish pilot had the courage to attempt a landing, but not the skill. He crashed as soon as he touched down. The two wrecked airplanes on the ground attested to the impossibility of a pilot negotiating the harsh topography. No one could have blamed Antoine, had he returned to Cape Juby alone. In such a situation, Colonel de la Peña would of course order a ground rescue attempt. Most likely, however, ground rescuers could not reach the two crews before the Moors—who would either kill or take them hostage.

Saint-Exupéry was fearless. He saw in the tragedy unfolding before him a rare opportunity to serve his fellowman. Antoine truly believed in brotherhood—race, politics, religion—these were not weighty considerations when fragile life was on the other end of the scale. Without hesitation he expertly and successfully landed his plane. Quickly he placed the two wounded men in his Breguet and executed a takeoff some would call miraculous. No sooner had he delivered the Spanish casualties to Juby than he returned to retrieve the second crew. This rescue was likewise triumphant. By no means was this daring deliverance a singular feat! By "the more modest accounts, [Antoine] rescued fourteen aviators" while acting as Chief of Juby. Under his watch Reine and Serre were finally ransomed from the R'Guibat after one hundred and seventeen days of captivity.

Toward the end of 1929 Tonio was transferred by Aéropostale to South America, promoted to Argentine Operations Manager. Along with the new job title came a new pay scale—225,000 francs annually (only a few years earlier he had felt fortunate to receive a second lieutenant salary of 12,000 francs annually). After so many years of receiving financial help from his mother, he was finally able to send home the significant sum of 3,000 francs each month.

While in South America Saint-Exupéry was inducted into the Légion d'Honneur for his previous service in Africa. Antoine was cited for his equanimity and "rare sense of self-sacrifice" and for "his devotion, combined with his readiness to face all the hardships of the desert and to expose his life every day to danger" in the cause of humanity; and the development of commercial aviation, to further the "cause of French aeronautics," particularly in the establishment of the routes from "Toulouse, to Casablanca, to Dakar." Added to this accolade was yet another—along the North African coast a bay was given his name, "the Baie of Saint-Exupéry!"

In 1931 when Tonio returned to once again fly the African Line, a journalist named Jean-Gérard Fleury accompanied him as a passenger. When they landed at Cape Juby, enroute to Port-Étienne, Fleury was amazed at the reception Saint-Exupéry received. They had no sooner taxied to the operations area and deplaned, when Antoine was greeted by a "troop of blue-veiled Moors" who "threw themselves upon Saint-Exupéry, kissing his hand." Tonio, still a young man, was greeted with the honor of a tribal chief. And as a chieftain, they encircled him, seeking his counsel on some troublesome matter. He responded in Arabic and settled the issue put before him. But not without embarrassment, in light of the fuss they made of him in front of Fleury and other nearby Frenchmen. It had been over two years since Tonio's departure from Cape Juby. Yet he was not only remembered by the Bedouins but had become even more renowned and esteemed by them with the passage of time. News of this event soon reached Paris, enhancing his reputation as a diplomat with the unique ability to *tame*.

Aéropostale schedule and fares

CHAPTER 24

PUNTA ARENAS TO MOSCOW

Remember that in life thou shouldst order thy conduct as at a banquet. Has any dish that is being served reached thee? Stretch forth thy hand and help thyself modestly. Doth it pass thee by? Seek not to detain it. Has it not yet come? Send not forth thy desire to meet it, but wait until it reaches thee. Deal thus with wife; thus with office, thus with wealth—and one day thou wilt be meet to share the Banquets of the Gods. [222]

—EPICTETUS

ON OCTOBER 12, 1931 TONIO'S ship docked in Buenos Aires. He was warmly greeted by Marcel Reine, Jean Mermoz, and his closest friend, Henri Guillaumet. Antoine soon began his new responsibilities directing operations, opening new routes and airfields. Bureaucrats had always annoyed Antoine. At Cape Juby he had proven that an administrator need never be simply a dull functionary. Now in Argentina, with greatly expanded duties, he proved himself an extraordinary manager. Guillaumet wrote to Mermoz saying:

> The Argentines are crazy about him. . . . The mail goes through despite the winds, and—despite his absentminded demeanor—our friend manages the Aeroposta Argentina with a firm hand. He flies all day, delivers the mails, lands suddenly 600 miles from Buenos Aires on an airfield whose chief—thinking himself far outside anyone's purview—is tending to his bridge game and not to his field. Saint-Exupéry rights the situation, takes off again, returns to

> Pacheco as night falls, picks up his car, races home at full speed, and spends the rest of the night writing. I wonder when he sleeps, this phenomenon![223]

These were aviation's pioneering days in South America. A windsock might be a handheld handkerchief. Airports were primitive roughed out fields, often overrun with snakes and scorpions. Antoine thrived in the face of challenge and improvised ingeniously. He said that to land at Comodoro Rivadavia required the pilot to combine "elements of harpoon-fishing and rappelling." This east coast port city is notorious for its extremely high winds. Even today the port authority cautions: "Waiting time for mooring between two to five days must be considered due to strong winds."

Fourteen soldiers comprised the Comodoro Rivadavia aerodrome ground crew. When the surface winds exceeded the landing speed of the airplane, the pilot could not land safely without the ground crew capturing it, as it were, in mid flight! They formed two lines on the field, straight into the wind, one line of seven men on each side of the landing aircraft. On the underside of the wings Aéropostale had installed metal rings. The pilot brought his plane down near the ground, flanked by the two rows of ground crew; all the while keeping a level attitude. He then reduced power, slowing the plane's airspeed to match the wind speed. When this was achieved the aircraft's groundspeed would be close to zero, its movement in relation to the earth nil. The linemen then inserted the hooked ends of long poles into the rings on the wings, snagging the plane mid-air. At the same time they rolled a cart beneath the plane's tail skid. This maintained the level attitude as the main gear touched down. Captured "Lilliputain" style and with the strength of a number of men holding the aircraft securely to prevent capsizing, the pilot powered the aircraft towards the hangar's open door. Of course, high winds are turbulent and dynamic. They roll, twist and gust.

One can only imagine the sight that was presented when Saint-Exupéry or one of his fellow aviators landed in this manner—the pilot, fighting gale force winds, trying to maneuver his craft to within several feet of the ground, keeping a level attitude, carefully avoiding being blown into the fourteen ground crewmen; while these men attempted to insert their long poles into eyelets, dodging the deadly propeller, fighting the same wind that is bucking the aircraft. There was at least one incident where this procedure failed terribly. After the men had hooked the plane, a strong gust of wind whipped the aircraft skyward. One row of men was shaken loose, falling six feet. With their weight suddenly gone the aircraft careened violently towards the other side where the men still held fast. The plane plunged to the ground on its side; the falling wing crushing two men to death in an instant.

Aéropostale Advertisement

The South American era was a period in Tonio's life of great adventure and romance. He flew over jungles and rain forest, over coastal wind swept badlands and through high Andean passes. He brought air service to the most southern town in the world, Punta Arenas. Above the Straits of Magellan, south of the Gallegos River, he marveled at the ancient lava flows, the numerous low rising craters. He wrote:

> No Vesuvius rises up to reign in the clouds; merely, a flat on the plain, a succession of gaping howitzer mouths. . . . There is something surprising in the tranquility of this deserted landscape where once a thousand volcanoes boomed to each other in their great subterranean organs and spat forth their fire. I fly over a world mute and abandoned, strewn with black glaciers.[224]

The very town of Punta Arenas was to Antoine so isolated that it was a world unto itself, the climate so harsh that life was a fragile luxury. It was to him an allegory of humanity. After one flight he walked alone in the town square. Near the fountain he saw a girl whose eyes lowered as she passed by. Tonio wondered about this graceful beauty, of her beliefs, life patterns, secrets and confidences so isolated from *civilized* dominions. He wrote:

> Born yesterday of the volcanoes, of greenswards, of brine of the sea, she walks here already half divine. . . . Out of the thoughts, the voice, the silences of a lover, she can form an empire, and thereafter she sees in all the world but him a people of barbarians.
>
> A child, his head against a wall, weeps in silence: there will remain of him in my memory only a beautiful child forever inconsolable. I am a stranger. I know nothing. I do not enter into their empires.
>
> How shallow is the stage on which this vast drama of human hates and joys and friendships is played! Whence do men draw this passion for eternity, flung . . . as they are upon a scarcely cooled bed of lava, threatened from the beginning by the deserts that are to be, and under the constant menace of the snows.
>
> By the grace of the airplane I have known a more extraordinary experience than this, and have been made to ponder with even more bewilderment the fact that this earth that is our home is yet in truth a wandering star.[225]

The extreme geography of lower South America presented Saint-Exupéry with limitless opportunities for adventure. Antoine marveled as he flew low over Tierra del Fuego, whose sheep slept unseen, buried in a blanket of winter snow, but whose frozen breath rose in the air like “hundreds of tiny chimneys.” He flew in awe, carefully, when downwind of the Cordilleras Mountains; which land, according to journalist J. G. Fleury, was known as the “country of the flying stones.” Here hurricane velocity winds blasted through stony gaps, catapulting rocks through the air “annihilating flocks." At times Tonio was forced to land in dry lagoons, or on slender beaches hemmed by primeval forests through which no man could emerge alive. On one forced landing, due to the rough terrain and his heavy load, four longerons split in the fuselage. The only mechanic that Tonio could enlist was the town blacksmith. Of course he carried no inventory for repairing aircraft. With the materials at hand he helped Antoine with a temporary fix. The blacksmith attached fence wire to the ends of the longerons; then he twisted the wire into knots to draw the ends tightly together. On the ground, without a flight load, it looked operational. Airborne the wire stretched; the gap grew ever wider—so much so that the radio operator was able to admire the landscape through this new and expanding portal. When Tonio reached his intended destination the chief mechanic, Raoul Roubes, could see the massive crack even before the plane touched down. Safely on the ground Tonio proudly displayed the ingenious field repair to which Raoul replied, "But you're sick. The fuselage was on the verge of breaking in half!"

It was during this era of bravado that the young aviator chose his life long companion. He met and fell in love with an exotic El Salvadorian beauty. When he returned to France in 1931, he returned a happy man. His writings had been widely published. He was known to all of France as an aviator adventurer extraordinaire and he was engaged to Consuelo Carrillo. Soon thereafter Consuelo became the Countess de Saint-Exupéry. She was unfortunately extremely "capricious" and as unpredictable and volatile as the Andean winds. Yet he loved her and *hoped* for her the remainder of his life.

In the esoteric Moroccan city of Casablanca Tonio and Consuelo made their first home. He was once again a line pilot for Aéropostale flying mail and passengers to the outposts of the Sahara. Technology had advanced in the intervening years since his departure from Africa and now it was possible to extend outboard of the fuselage a three hundred and fifty foot long UHF antenna. A VHF radio allows only line-of-sight transmissions, such as from cockpit to tower. But a UHF transceiver accommodates long distance communications. Furthermore, a bearing could be obtained on the signal and with the bearings from two or more stations a navigator could triangulate the aircraft's position.

On one night flight between Villa Cisernos and Agadir Saint-Exupéry's radio operator found the hole through which the antenna would be trailed was completely blocked. After repeated attempts to open the hole the man creatively made a new one by hammering a screwdriver through the plane's metal skin. After he had extended the antenna through this new aperture he attempted to insulate it with his socks. But the moment the radio operator applied power, sparks bloomed everywhere. Tonio passed back a note asking him what the heck he was doing. The operator past his written answer forward saying: "It's not as bad as that. We have parachutes, don't we?"

There was an obvious grin on Tonio's face as he turned around. The radio operator increased the insulation by adding his

Saint Exupéry's Night Flight

scarf. This time it worked and he industriously began his duties, communicating with Agadir and Villa Cisernos. However the antenna did not trail the plane as it normally would if extended through its usual port and it repeatedly bounced against the left side of the plane sending out into the sky a nearly continuous shower of sparks. As the operator was thus busily engaged in his work, he was startled and frightened by the sudden appearance of a brilliant flame, also on the left side of the aircraft. There was no question in his mind that he had set their plane on fire. Nothing is as devastating as a rapidly advancing in-flight fire. Besides the horrific thought of being burned to death if caught in the spread of the flames, all crewmembers understand the effects of fire when it penetrates the fuel tanks—explosion! Immediately he radioed the SOS distress call. Saint-Exupéry had as swiftly begun to leave his seat exclaiming: "Parachute, buckle up quickly, we're going to jump!" So frustrated and anxious was the poor operator that he strained uselessly with his straps and buckles. Each micro-second must have seemed an eternity; aggravation and fear increased as he remained stuck in his seat. At that moment he looked portside to assess the progress of the emergency. What he saw stopped him cold. The light of the fire was moving away from the plane at the speed of a bullet. Suddenly it dawned on him that Tonio had intentionally and harmlessly fired off a flare, knowing that the burst of light in the peripheral vision of the navigator would be mistakenly interpreted as if the plane had caught fire. When he looked forward he saw that both Tonio and the interpreter had erupted in uncontrollable laughter.

Tonio's career as a novelist continued to blossom when in the same year he published *Night Flight*, a captivating tale that has been compared to such classics as *The Old Man and the Sea.* Although told as fiction, it is largely an autobiographical work enumerating poetically the adventures of his Aéropostale days in South America. Many literary works have skillfully and beautifully told of ships and sails. *Night Flight* was the first composition of the same genre set on the stage of aviation. It was a huge success.

For it Antoine was awarded one of the most esteemed and celebrated literary awards of France, the Prix Fémina. Two years later *Night Flight* reigned larger than life on the silver screen. The film, released by MGM in 1933, starred John Barrymore as Riviere, Helen Hayes as Madame Fabian, Clark Gable as Jules, Lionel Barrymore as Robineau, Robert Montgomery as Auguste Pellerin, and Myrna Loy as the wife of a Brazilian pilot.

Night Flight was not written to merely entertain; no work of value is. Saint-Exupéry opened to his readers a window on the world he so intimately knew. Through his writing we experience the wonder and awe, the daring and danger of the pioneer flights over the great Andean Mountains and the vast reaches of South America. But more importantly, he illustrates masterfully the requisites of manhood. In his pilgrimage man is thrust far from the security of the home he had to leave behind. He is ordered to achieve an objective greater than himself at heroic peril. When appointed a leader, a captain's actions are life or death to those entrusted in his care. He cannot succumb, no matter the personal cost, for others depend upon him. He must reach his destination or be brought down fighting. Wetherald wrote:

> My orders are to fight;
> Then if I bleed, or fail,
> Or strongly win, what matters it?
> God only doth prevail.
>
> The servant craveth naught
> Except to serve with might.
> I was not told to win or lose,—
> My orders are to fight.[226]

Antoine wrote in *Night Flight* of a pilot named Fabien who, in black obscurity, encounters a horrific storm. It is a battle of physical and mental dimensions, perhaps beyond endurance. His endless exertion upon the controls has numbed the muscles in his arms, hands and legs. The constant demands of navigation, his primitive instruments dancing wildly in reaction to the severe turbulence of flight, are on the point of numbing his brain.

> Somewhere, even now, there still were lands of calm, at peace beneath the wide moon-shadows. His comrades down there knew all about them, poring upon the maps beneath their hanging lamps, pretty as flower-bells. But he, what could he know save squalls and night, this night that buffeted him with its swirling spate of darkness.
>
> It was as if dead matter were infected by his exasperation; at every plunge the engine set up such furious vibrations that all the fuselage seemed convulsed with rage. Fabien strained all his efforts to control it; crouching in the cockpit, he kept his eyes fixed on the artificial horizon only. For the masses of sky and land outside were not to be distinguished, lost both alike in the welter as of worlds in the making. But the hands of the flying instruments oscillated more and more abruptly, grew almost impossible to follow. Already the pilot, misled by their vagaries, was losing altitude, fighting against the odds, while deadly quicksands sucked him down into the darkness.
>
> He made up his mind. He would land no matter where, even if it meant cracking up! To avoid the hills anyhow, he launched his only landing flare. It sputtered and spun, illumining a vast plain, then died away; beneath him lay the sea!
>
> His thoughts came quickly. Lost—forty degrees' drift—yes, I've drifted, sure enough—it's a cyclone—where's land? Without another flare, he thought, I'm a goner. Well, it was bound to happen one day.
>
> But now the pilot's anger had ebbed away. He had only to unclasp his hands and their lives would slither through his fingers like a trivial mote of dust. He held the beating heart of each—his own, his comrade's—in his hands. And suddenly his hands appalled him.[227]

No destiny attacks us from outside. But, within him, man bears his fate.[228]

On August 30, 1933 Aéropostale, plagued by the effects of the Great Depression and internal scandal, dissolved in bankruptcy. One fourth of the airline was owned by the State and from these publicly owned roots grew its successor, *Air France*. In the new company's re-organization Saint-Exupéry lost his job. Why? It was also in 1933 that Hitler attained power in Germany. Indirectly this affected Antoine on a very personal level. In his writings Antoine had taught the truths of manly greatness. There always have been and will always be dark forces opposing those who teach *truth*. Enemies are the birthright of greatness. Clandestine groups fight truth with deception—they are masters of misinformation. When the public at large perceives a growing evil, the allies of evil seek to discredit the teachers of truth by associating them with the malevolent threat feared by the masses. *Night Flight* espoused manhood, by putting forth the call for men to espouse gallant enterprises. It called for men to be selfless and willing to sacrifice their all. It was a hit in Germany. The virtues Saint-Exupéry proclaimed were prostituted by the spin artists as being pro-Nazis. Nazism was not a high cause, but a low crime—the basest the world had yet seen. To compare what Antoine taught and what Hitler brutally enforced would be to compare the rallying cry of God to the bullying actions of the Devil. After the propagandists promoted their "spin" on *Night Flight*, Saint-Exupéry found himself unemployed.

His old boss and good friend, Didier Daurat, was also discarded by *Air France* but had hired on with Latécoère, now exclusively an airplane manufacturer. Daurat helped Tonio get work with Latécoère as a test pilot. This position came to an abrupt end, nearly a mortal one, when on December 21, 1933 Saint-Exupéry crashed a Latécoère floatplane. On landing the Latécoère he inadvertently caught the tips of his pontoons in the water, flipping the plane on its back. There were three others on board with Tonio who managed to escape the doomed plane; but Antoine became disoriented in the murky water and was unable to get free of the submerged aircraft. His lungs began to fill with water and he realized that he was in fact drowning. It was a gentle feeling, he said, without hysterics. Dying, he thought, was not so hard a thing to do. However, he would not give up and calmly worked his way back through the fuselage towards the tail. "There, as though by an act of grace, he found an open hatch, through which he floated up to the surface." A patrol boat saw the aircraft go under and speedily came to the rescue. Antoine was the last to be hauled into the boat, barely conscious. Later he said that his return to life was ironically brutal; he convulsively, violently, painfully, coughed up sea water for several hours.

In March of 1935 Antoine was offered a position with Air France; oddly enough, not to fly, but to write. This was a time of great unrest in the world and particularly in France. Revolution was in the air. The Air Ministry realized that Saint-Exupéry was an icon whose writings had popularized and romanticized the very airline that had "blackballed" him from commercial aviation. The power of his pen could either do tremendous damage to Air France, or it could provide a great service. Although Antoine was not flattered by the offer, he accepted out of financial necessity. His salary was only a fraction of what he made when acting as director of operations in Argentina—a mere 3,000 francs a month, plus bonuses. Shortly thereafter he produced two documentaries—the first was *Week-end à Alger,* and the second was *Atlantique Sud.* The later film was very successful and played in theaters for the next twelve years. Air France made a single engine airplane available to Saint-Exupéry—a Simoun. The Caudron-Renault Simoun was an incredible plane for its time, fast and economical. With only a one hundred and eighty horse power engine, the three thousand pound plane could cruise at one hundred and seventy miles per hour, with a range of over nine hundred miles. A skillful mechanic, Andre Prévot, was assigned to accompany

Antoine on his flights. Together they flew thousands of miles in the Simoun. On a public relations fact finding mission Tonio flew a month long trip to Indochina. Characteristically, it turned out to be adventurous; his engine failed while flying a floatplane in Viet Nam. Tonio made a perfect emergency landing on the Mekong River. The engine ran again after a little attention from their mechanic, but after being airborne for just a few minutes, it died again. Saint-Exupéry had no choice but to land in a marshy area between the Soirap and Vaico Rivers. Far from being discouraged, Tonio was delighted with the prospect of spending an evening in a "snake and spider-infested tropical swamp" with his plane moored to a mangrove tree. The following day the problem was resolved and he departed the swamp without further difficulties.

Also in 1935 the editors of the *Paris-Soir* newspaper asked Antoine if he would travel to Moscow and report on the Russian celebration of May Day, which would include an imposing demonstration of Soviet air power over Red Square. The Soviets must have considered his presence potentially harmful for when he arose early on the morning of May 1, he discovered that he had been locked in his hotel room. Not one to be easily discouraged, Tonio escaped this unofficial incarceration by climbing out of a window.

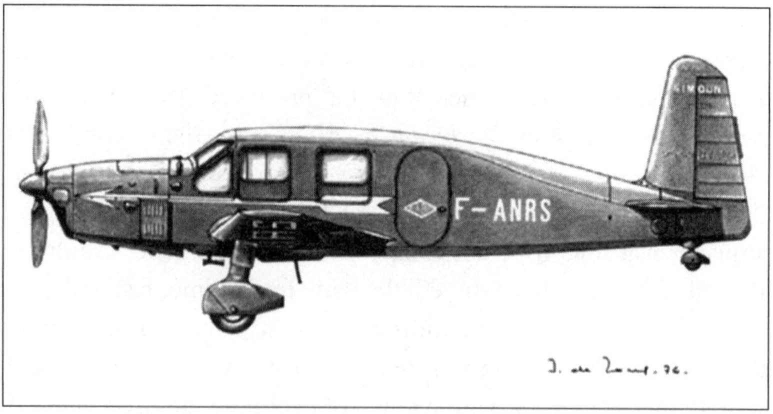

Caudron-Renault Simoun, Drawing by Joseph de Joux

8 Engine ANT-20 Maxim Gorki in which Saint-Exupéry flew

Saint-Exupéry's reports evidently must not have been perceived by government officials as detrimental; for on May 19, 1935 he was honored as the first foreigner allowed to fly in the *Maxim Gorki ANT-20.* This aircraft, an incredible feat of Russian technology, weighed forty-two tons, had eight engines that developed seven thousand horsepower and was designed as a powerful propaganda weapon. Saint-Exupéry found onboard a cinema, a photo lab, a radio broadcasting station and a loudspeaker system that could be heard above the din of the engines from the ground. It was also equipped with its own printing press, which could be operated in flight, allowing for the airborne distribution of thousands of leaflets. The secretarial staff and telephone operators could pass paperwork between their stations using a pneumatic tube system. On May 20, the day after Antoine's flight in the Maxim Gorki, a young fighter pilot named Blagin, broke formation with the other escort planes. The cocky youth pulled his plane up with the idea of performing an eye-popping loop above the Maxim Gorki and rejoining his fighter group at the conclusion of his unauthorized maneuver. His imagination exceeded his skill and he flew right into the wing of the massive aircraft—sending both planes tumbling to the earth.

Chapter 25

Risk

Passage—immediate passage! the blood burns in my veins!
Away, O soul! hoist instantly the anchor
Cut the hawsers—haul out—shake out every sail!
Have we not stood here like trees in the ground long enough?

Sail forth! steer for the deep waters only!
O soul, exploring, I with thee, and thou with me;
For we are bound where mariner has not yet dared to go,
And we will risk the ship, ourselves and all.

O my brave soul!
O farther, farther sail!
O daring joy, but safe! Are they not all the seas of God?
O farther, farther, farther sail! [229]

—Walt Whitman

Risk. One cannot be a traveler without exposure to risk; it is inherent in every notable adventure. However risk is not the same as temerity. The latter is a reckless, foolhardy disregard of danger. A thrill-seeker is temerarious when he puts himself in harms way, not to accomplish some great good, or to advance a worthy cause, but to gratify his senses senselessly. One may scale a cliff to build strength, skill and fortitude, but if he is wise he will belay himself as securely as possible. It is not courage, but stupidity to place one's health or life on the line to experience "a rush" or to win a base-metal trophy. In fact, to needlessly imperil ourselves is an insult to our Creator, who gave us irreplaceable, marvelous bodies. Death, or the loss of faculty or function, can preempt a life otherwise destined for great purpose. Hence, the Adversary tempts men to foolishness as well as to wickedness.

Conversely, a man may gravely err by seeking the pretense of security. Mortality is designed for motion. Running involves risk, and a man may think himself secure who only sits. But the law of entropy dictates deterioration of a sedentary system. This truth supercedes the adage, "Ships are safe in harbor, but that's not what ships are for." Ships are *not* safe left idly in port. As a charter pilot back in the 1970s I flew from Albuquerque to Santa Monica. There on the Santa Monica ramp was a Convair 440—a fifty passenger airliner built in 1959. The paint had peeled off, the metal skin had badly oxidized and corroded. I thought it was a worn out relic, more deserving of space at a scrap yard than on a corporate jet ramp. I learned from one of the operators on the field that it was owned by Howard Hughes who had personally flown the airplane to Santa Monica when it was a shining new airliner. The eccentric Hughes gave then orders that it be left where he parked it; it had not flown again from that day to the day I saw the derelict airliner. In its day the 440 was the most efficient piston-powered, pressurized, all weather aircraft in its class, capable of flying over two thousand miles non-stop. At the time I saw it hundreds of Convair sister ships were still proudly flying all over the world, each having logged tens of thousands of hours. These grand ships of adventure were still airworthy while this particular aircraft simply rotted—no longer capable of flight.

When a man sets out to traverse vast distances and worthily prepares himself for the journey, he will prevail if he endures to the *end*—even if the end may not be what he envisioned. The very immensity of the expanse that lies before him normally prevents him from seeing the end from the beginning. What he learns during the odyssey is often of far greater value than what he thought he might have gained upon arrival at the intended port.

One of the colonial jewels of the French Empire was Indochina. Over seven thousand five hundred miles separated Paris from Saigon. Today records are set for the sake of setting records. Not so in the early days of aviation. Prizes were offered to induce men to finance and advance technology. Pilots of the era were typically underpaid. A record setting purse offered much more than headlines—it made possible a better livelihood. To set a *record* also gave a grand purpose to the aviator. For humanity to eventually fly great distances safely, tremendous progress was necessary—it would be won at the *risk* of the pioneer pilot. Such a man knew that he might well lose his life. However, most flyers possessed a common vision of the importance of their profession. It was to them a higher calling—an objective greater than themselves. Mermoz had said that it was worth it—"worth the final smash-up."

The purse offered by the French Air Ministry for the fastest flight from Paris to Saigon, commenced before the end of 1935, was 150,000 francs! This was well over a years salary for a prosperous pilot and it could be won in under four days of strenuous effort. Tonio was determined that he had the resources and skill that would enable him to fly his 180 h.p. Simoun the vast distance from France to Indochina. He came to this conclusion when the contest year was near its end. Mermoz, Daurat, Lucas and other friends came to his aid, preparing the Simoun so that it would be in peak condition for the enterprise, assisting in the calculations of navigation logs and gathering the necessary aeronautical charts and equipment. Andre Prévot, his able mechanic, requested the privilege of accompanying Tonio to Saigon. This was not an audacious lark, but a well planned quest. Antoine made one crucial decision that could have life saving consequences—he would fly without a radio. A wireless in that day was heavy. No radio on board would allow him to carry a greater load of fuel.

For such a flight one would normally wait for propitious weather. Tonio's route would take him from Le Bourget Field, in

Paris, to Marseille, Tunis, Benghazi, Cairo—then five thousand miles more to Saigon. A challenging route, especially since storms in North Africa are unlike any other in the world. Antoine wrote:

> Desert storms turn the sky into a yellow furnace and wipe out hills, towns, and river-banks, drowning earth and sky in one great conflagration.[230]

In his last visit to the weather bureau, conditions were anything but ideal. The briefer was especially concerned about a "coiled demon" forming in Basra but he assured Tonio that it was not a sand-storm. For this effort Tonio would not have the luxury of waiting for fair skies. It was the morning of December 29, 1935—the record would have to be set now or the purse would go to André Japy, who had flown the trip in ninety-eight hours, fifty-two minutes. Saint-Exupéry knew that he was capable of flying the journey in seventy hours, including refueling stops. The winds aloft forecasts were favorable. He was expected to have a tailwind all the way to Cairo.

Tonio and Andre Prévot took off in a light drizzle before the break of day. The Simoun responded with grace to his every touch, although heavy with fuel. He had confidently flown this little plane eight thousand miles. The engine sang its smooth resplendent song. The instrument panel glistened "like a constellation in the dark of the night." Saint Exupéry loved this finely crafted machine as his knight forebearers had, no doubt, loved the steeds they rode in battle. Due to rain showers he flew low, beneath the overcast.

There is much more to see, especially when visibility is limited, when you hug the earth. You fly over sparsely settled country lying black and foreboding beneath you. Then over villages illumined, not with light only, but with the vision of hearth and happiness you imagine in each dwelling. Next a city bursts in view, gleaming like a carpet of diamonds set against ebony velvet.

Antoine was flying far, far away and said the morning passed magically away as if "in a dream."

Antoine de Saint-Exupéry and André Prévot

He had just passed Marignane, barely out to sea, when he noticed a smoke like vapor emanating from the left wing fuel guage. Prévot checked their fuel load—they had leaked almost twenty gallons of gas. Tonio quickly reversed his course and set down at Marignane, just to the northwest of Marseille. Although it didn't take much time to repair the faulty tank, the lost time "hurt like an open wound." Airborne, once again, Antoine encountered intense rain over the Mediterranean Sea and was forced to scud-run. He flew so low that he feared encountering the masts of ships. Less than sixty feet below him the ocean seethed, driven mad by the downpour of rain. Finally, Tonio penetrated the last squall line, greeted by affable rays of sunshine. This meant that the island of Sardinia would warmly and openly welcome the two adventurers instead of rising like a deadly behemoth in their flight path. He climbed the Simoun to four thousand, five hundred feet. Soon the pleasant isle came into view, tops of mountains scantly shrouded in clouds—then hamlets encompassed by farms and forests. All too soon, the genial landscape passed from sight and the ocean spread before him as if to infinity. Tunis lay 160 miles ahead. An hour later he touched down safely at the African aerodrome.

A short time after landing, as he was leaving the airport office he heard the sickening muffled grunt of two automobiles as they collided head-on. He was drawn by the sound to the roadway adjacent to the airport. There two cars were impaled, statue like, into each other. He heard a voice shout for a doctor. Someone's skull had been crushed. Antoine wrote:

> My heart sank. In the peace of the evening light . . . A beauty, a mind, a life—something had been destroyed. It was as sudden as a raid in the desert. Marauding tribesmen creep on silent feet in the night. The camp resounds briefly with clashing tumult of a razzia. A moment later everything has sunk back into the golden silence. The same peace, the same stillness, followed this crash. . . I had no mind to be told about that crushed and bloody cranium. Turning my back to the road, I went across to my ship, in my heart a foreboding of danger. I was to recognize that sound when I heard it again very soon.[231]

Daylight was nearly spent when Tonio and Andre departed Tunis for Benghazi. The subdued twilight rays of the sun cast a luminous carpet of gold over the ceaseless sands. Tonio was struck, as he had been so many times before, with the vast emptiness of our earthly home.

The diminutive habitations of man are seen, even today, by aviators in true perspective. In contrast the city dweller perceives that the entire world is densely populated. But the pilot leaves behind the city of millions within minutes of takeoff and from his swift and lofty throne observes what *is*—a sparsely settled expanse that varies but minutely, regardless of where over earth or sea he flies. Upon the deserts or oceans may reside a scattering of nomads, whether Bedouin or sailors. As surprising as this may seem to grounded man, Europe and America are only marginally more populated. Man is microscopic. The interior space of a sole Alp is sufficient to act as the sarcophagus of all humankind. Even when multiplied by billions man is a small organism compared to the earth, the living host of his pilgrimage.

Miles upon hundred of miles were left in Tonio's wake. Below him a wild land, uncultivated, void of life signs. The cloak of night descended. Saint-Exupéry wrote:

> A novice taking orders could appreciate this ascension towards the essence of things, since his profession too is one of renunciation: he renounces the world; he renounces riches; he renounces the love of woman. And by renunciation he discovers his hidden god.
>
> I, too, in this flight, am renouncing things. I am giving up the broad golden surfaces that would befriend me if my engines were to fail. I am giving up the landmarks by which I might be taking my bearings. I am giving up the profiles of mountains against the sky that would warn me of pitfalls. I am plunging into the night. I am navigating. I have only on my side the stars.
>
> The diurnal death of the world is a slow death. It is only little by little that the divine beacon of daylight recedes from me. Earth and sky begin to merge into each other. The earth rises and seems to spread like a mist. The first stars tremble as if shimmering in green water. Hours must pass before their glimmer hardens into the frozen glitter of diamonds.[232]

When at last they reached Benghazi the moon had set and the sky was stygian black. Field lighting consisted only of red lights marking the triangle shaped perimeter of the airport and a pivoting search light that rose like a radiant wand, sometimes blinding Tonio as he dropped from the sky, landing without difficulty. Only twenty minutes were required to refuel and they were off in the jet-dark night bound for Cairo six hundred and fifty miles away.

The magnetic course from Benghazi to Cairo is 97 degrees,

nearly directly east. Antoine had set his bearings to avoid "danger zones along the coast" and approach his destination on a line midway between Alexandria and Cairo. In this manner he would pick up the lights of Alexandria portside or would see the lights of Cairo starboard. He determined that with the tailwind he should make 190 miles per hour groundspeed, and considering his climb to six thousand feet would make this leg in three hours and forty-five minutes. Prévot succumbed at last and fell into a deep sleep. Tonio felt anything but somnolent. With the progress they had made the trip seemed to him almost a short one. In fact he intended to push himself for at least another day without rest. He was tranquil and happy. The lights of his panel were an extension of the stars in the heavens. The first indicated that his plane purred with perfection—the second that his course was true. His poetic mind had time to reflect and compose simile and metaphor, relating this journey of wonder to life and its meaning.

Three hours had passed when the first irritant troubled what had been a faultless flight. A glow began to halo his wing-tip lights, indicating that he had flown into a cloud, the moisture of the mists reflecting light from the lenses. Obscured by clouds he could neither take his bearings from the stars, nor see the lights of the Nile Valley. However, all he would need would be an adequate break in the clouds to determine his position. That failing, he would descend below the overcast once sufficient time had elapsed to ensure that he crossed the Nile and was flying over elevations near sea level and then reverse his course back to Cairo. Turbulence began to increase and Tonio knew that he was in a cumulus cloud. How far did it extend? How high were the tops? He climbed to seven thousand five hundred feet and found himself still in its bowels. He descended to three thousand feet, his vision still completely obscured. He knew that his altitude as displayed on his altimeter only approximated his actual altitude as he could not adjust for changes in barometric pressure—he had no radio to obtain the setting for Cairo. His last setting in Benghazi would certainly be in error.

Occasionally he would pop out of the clouds for a few seconds. But the respite was too short to take his bearings from the stars, while below, left and right, he saw only the blackness of night. This was not a new phenomenon for the experienced pilot. Surely a small window to the heavens or to the world beneath would open, allowing him to determine his position from whence he could accurately plot his course to the airfield. He had flown "blind" so many times, and he had always found safe harbor. Thirty minutes later, conditions still unchanged, he began to be a little annoyed but felt no real concern—just that he was "wasting time." At this point he could descend no further as he was, without doubt, over higher terrain. Perhaps as he crossed the Nile he would be able to obtain a glimpse of the river below him through the narrow breaks in the clouds. Although, from the information given him in the weather briefing, he knew it unlikely that the tailwind would have died down to nothing. His true airspeed had been steady at 170 m.p.h.—with no winds pushing him he should be over Cairo four hours after departing Benghazi.

Prévot awoke precisely at four hours and five minutes into the flight commenting that they must be close to Cairo. Then both saw a light—was it a phantom light, a reflection from the sky mirrored from a cloud, or an all important sign welcoming the travelers to their destination? Saint-Exupéry began a slow descent confident that the ground below his aircraft lay near sea level. In reality the winds aloft had turned traitor—he had been bucking a headwind for hours. He was still one hundred and twenty five miles west of Cairo. And what was far worse, the terrain directly below the Simoun was a least 800 feet higher than Cairo. Tonio maneuvered north, then north-north east, descending slowly. Knowing that his altimeter was substantially off, he leveled at twelve hundred feet, indicated altitude. He was actually much lower, but had the ground been at sea level, as he believed, he would have had nearly a thousand feet of precautionary space. *In truth he was only a few feet above the ground*, veiled completely beneath the opaque overcast.

Again Tonio and Prévot saw the phantom light—just for a glittering moment. They drew their eyes close to the windshield, seeking intently that illusive signal. Still flying at one hundred and seventy miles per hour and in a level attitude they hit. Neither felt the least emotion. There was the same sickening grunt of impact they had heard only nine hours earlier at Tunis. The fuel remaining was ample to power an explosion, which according to all odds, would be forthcoming in an instant. Tonio more than expected a blinding light, the precursor to being burned to death or blown to bits. But instead the airplane continued on and on while the craft around them was being ripped apart, the sound of the crash increasing to a loud and awful crescendo. Suddenly the starboard wing struck something that clutched it tightly and the Simoun spun violently—then abruptly ceased its motion. Both Tonio and Prévot leaped through a fractured window and ran as fast as they could from the explosion they both thought was still to come. It did not. All was still. It was the silence that followed the razzia.

Why the Simoun did not explode cannot be explained, save through divine intervention. The fuel and oil tanks had not escaped unscathed. Like the rest of the wreckage the tanks had been torn asunder, spilling the incendiary agent freely against grinding metal into the sands. The aircraft had struck the ground nearly horizontal, plowing angrily up a gradual incline at the top of an arid plateau. For over eight hundred feet the plane had ripped the surface of the earth, snake-like on its belly until the right wing was caught by higher ground. In such a horrific impact a plane would normally disembowel its fragile carcass and with a force equal to the one hundred and seventy mile per hour velocity of the crash, hurl its metallic members helter-skelter. But the Simoun was still largely whole, although twisted and contorted grotesquely, gaping with holes where sheet metal had been rent from fuselage, wings, and tail. Wrote Saint-Exupéry:

> We owed our lives to the fact that this desert was surfaced with round black pebbles which had rolled over and over like ball-bear-

The crashed Simoun in the Libyan Desert

> ings beneath us. They must have rained upward to the heaven as we shot through them.[233]

When daylight broke the two castaways were better able to assess their dire predicament. They had crashed in a hellish region, where the sand glistened like "coats of mail"—caused by the strange layer of ebony stones. There were no life signs, not a living twig or blade. Tonio knew only that the forecast winds were horribly in error. He could only guess how strong the actual winds aloft were and from what direction. A stronger tailwind would have blown them east of Cairo—the most likely scenario considering the weather briefing they had received. A headwind would mean they were well short of their destination. A crosswind from the north could have blown them far south of their course, deeper into the continent. Sadly he faced the reality that they might be anywhere "two hundred and fifty miles more or less in the desert." Worst of all the supply of drinking water had also been lost, all but a solitary flask they filtered from coffee and wine. Of their food all that was left was an orange, some cake and a few grapes—an emergency reserve of less than a half day supply. They sat next to the wreckage. Prévot turned to Tonio and said:

> You know it's a shame.
> What's a shame?
> That we didn't crash properly and have it over with.[234]

The first day after their crash Tonio and Prévot decided to search for an oasis, returning to the plane at nightfall. Although extremely unlikely, it was possible that the wreckage might be spotted by another plane, especially if they were not too far off the airway from Benghazi to Cairo. It would be much more difficult to catch sight of two men walking—seen as mere specks from the air. At the end of the day they had covered nearly 40 miles and had drunk their meager supply of water. From wing fragments they kindled a bonfire and threw sheets of magnesium coated sheet metal on the blaze. The magnesium produced a "hard white flame" that penetrated miles into the dark night. Their signal fire was seen by no eyes but theirs. When their last drop of water had been drunk Prévot began to weep, his tear filled eyes reflecting the grim light of their fire. He did not cry for himself. He sobbed for his wife and loved ones at home. They would be suffering! With their plane overdue and no news as to their whereabouts or condition, their families would know they had crashed and would believe them badly injured or dead. Prévot knew that sorrow is greatest for the love bearer who waits—whether by the bedside of their beloved or powerlessly biding time for the *lost.* When there is no response, when the condition is unknown, when life and death hang in the balance, when there is the probability of great need and painful, torturous consequences, the ones left waiting in silence must bear the unbearable. Prévot and Antoine could withstand the challenge that lay before them. It was likely they would die. Their own suffering they could take, but the thought of those whom they left behind pierced their hearts. Antoine wrote:

> Nothing is unbearable. Tomorrow, and the day after, I should learn that nothing was really unbearable . . . despite the bonfire I had decidedly given up hope that our cries would be heard by the world . . . Prévot was a level-headed fellow. He loved life. And yet Prévot no more than I was wringing his hands at the sight of death the way we are told men do . . . I was perfectly ready to fall asleep, whether for a night or for eternity . . . But that cry that would be sent up at home, that great wail of desolation—that was what I could not bear. I could not stand idly by and look on at *that* disaster. Each second of silence drove the knife deeper into someone I loved. At the thought, a blind rage surged up in me . . . Why does our conflagration not carry our cry to the ends of the world? Hear me, you out here! We are coming to save you.[235]

When a man cares for the hurt he causes those who love him more than he cares for his own suffering, that man *is a man*. Had these two truly been alone in the world, if their loss would effect only a casual concern among associates, had there been only a selfish will to survive, death would have been the only possible outcome. Self-centered motivation is always insufficient when conditions are dire. It was not themselves Tonio and Prévot would save. Their lives were not their own to abandon, to succumb. *"We are coming to save you,"* our wives, our mothers, our families, our friends!

The second day Antoine left Prévot with the wreck of the aircraft and he searched alone, hoping he would have the strength to return. He knew that the humidity in the Libyan desert in which he trekked was half that of the Sahara. The Bedouins had told him that in Libya, after nineteen hours without water, your eyes begin to fill with light. When you see the light you know that the end is near, that death will come with awful celerity. The night before they had set snares at the mouths of burrows; even a snake, rich in blood, would be life to them. The snares were empty. As the sun rose in the heavens Tonio began to see mirages. At first he knew them for what they were—illusions. When a man sees an illusion he knows something is playing a trick on him. There is a difference between illusion and delusion. When you believe the illusion is real, that is delusion. As Saint-Exupéry's stamina ebbed with time and heat so did his cognitive powers. He saw a man. He shouted and waved to him. The black rock did not wave back. As he trudged in the sand he came across a Bedouin, sleeping peacefully. He tried to waken him but the Arabian transmogrified himself into a black tree trunk. He looked around and laughed to himself. He had found a forest. Unfortunately he was too late to enjoy the shade. The living boughs that cradled birds and cooled the green grass in its shadow had petrified into Cimmerian marble. He held in his hands a limb whose veins once flowed with sap and counted the rings, the years of its life. The rings, symbol of fleeting mortality. The stone, a type of eternity.

On a far distant dune he saw the profile of a caravan. It was plain to see. He focused intently on the train of camels and men. It vanished. "Fool!" he cried to himself. On the top of a hill ten miles away he saw a cross and his mind flashed back to the previous evening. He had been scrutinizing his map and had observed such a cross, annotated with the words: "Permanent well." Could it be? His delirious mind convinced him that it must be, and with the conviction came a history of that cross—a vision as clear as if he now supped its cool waters. The well provided life for a Coptic monastery. The cross had been placed there on the hill as an atoning sign for men agonized by thirst. The cross was salvation. The monks were Dominicans who possessed a red tile kitchen with sweet meats. Water flowed from the rusted pump in the garden courtyard. What joy his deliverers would feel when he laid hold of the rope at their gate, ringing their bell. There is ecstasy when you redeem one near death. We are all Prodigal Sons. The feast awaits our return to our Father's home! Suddenly the vision evaporated beneath the blazing sun. He realized that he was describing to himself a house he knew in Provence. Yet the imagery was true.

He had been plodding to the west. Tonio now turned north towards the Mediterranean Sea. He saw an illusionary city, the most beautiful he had ever seen but this time he knew that it was a mirage. Still he enjoyed its splendor. He felt drunk, drunk with thirst. As the day cooled at sunset his senses returned. Did he have the strength to return to his solitary friend? Hours later he saw the light of a fire, a homing beacon lit by Prévot. The last few yards seemed like miles to Tonio. His legs were so heavy. His feet moved so slowly. If he didn't make it, he thought, it would make no difference to him now. Although he was only one hundred and fifty feet from the fire he did not cry out for help. He was ready to rest, rest forever. Then he saw an incredible sight. In the light of the fire he plainly saw *three* men. Prévot and two Arabs. His approach had been so silent and slow that he had not caught their attention. He was suddenly filled with joy and with new energy he called out of the darkness into the circle of light in which they stood. Instantly the two men saw him and gazed at him intently. Prévot only came forward and caught Antoine by the arm, helping him the short distance to the warmth of his fire. Tonio exuberantly said:

> At last, eh?
> What do you mean?
> The Arabs!
> What Arabs?
> Those Arabs there, with you.
> There are no Arabs here.[236]

Another delusion? Perhaps—but perhaps not. To a dying man without hope, fifty yards might just as well be fifty miles. Paul wrote:

> Some have entertained angels unawares. Remember them which suffer . . .[237]

Stories abound of men who died when almost *there*. Through no fault of his own, Antoine was ready to yield, but for what he saw and for what he *felt.* There is divine grace when we have fought and done all that we could possibly do. Angels are not myths. They are true messengers sent to strengthen and aid travelers in mortality when weighed down with fatigue that is nearly beyond corporeal endurance. Sometimes they are seen. Most often we only feel their eyes upon us. It is not their mission to remove the trial, but to make it endurable.

> God [is] faithful, who will not suffer you to be [tried] above that ye are able; but will with the [trial] also make a way to escape, that ye may be able to bear [it].[238]

Preternatural aid is grace, not only given to us when we have done all that we can do for ourselves, but also meted to us in connection with the help that is available through mortal means. We are exhausted and God sends a fellow traveler—a Prévot, a true friend, who takes us by the arm and leads us to the warmth of his fire.

Prévot, while going through the wreckage had found another orange. He, of course, could have eaten it while he was alone, but had saved the sweet nectar to share with Tonio. Antoine held his half in his hands and said to himself that a man had no concept of what an orange was. He felt condemned to die—a strange emotion—to believe that this night, of all the nights in his life, would be his last. Yet he was happy and lay supine facing the star lit sky, sucking the delicious juice slowly. He thought:

> The joy I take from this half of an orange which I am holding in my hand is one of the greatest joys I have ever known.[239]

A north wind had been blowing from the far off sea increasing the humidity. Tonio and Prévot thought to take advantage of this by spreading sections of their parachutes to collect the morning dew. At daybreak they could not believe their good fortune. Wringing the cloth in a salvaged fuel tank they had produced nearly two quarts of water! Although the water was yellow green from either the parachute sizing or the magnesium lining of the tank, Tonio and Prévot drank eagerly. The aftertaste was one of "poisonous metal." Prévot was the first to swoon and vomit. Tonio was soon seized likewise with heaving convulsions—expelling the deadly bile. Nothing else came up, for there was nothing that could.

This was the third day. When they had recovered somewhat from the nausea the two determined to leave the "cursed plateau" and seek relief elsewhere or die trying. On the side of the Simoun's fuselage Saint-Exupéry wrote what he knew might be his final words. However what he wrote is unknown. On the other side Prévot wrote:

> I ask my wife's forgiveness for whatever hurt I have caused her.

Together they tramped a thirty-foot high message in the sands:

> We have headed northeast. SOS.[240]

Tonio still believed that Cairo was west, that the tail wind had pushed him beyond the Nile. He started westerly but "felt a vague foreboding" that he "could not explain." Instead he settled on a course that would take them east-northeast. For most of the day the wind bearing moisture from the sea continued, helping to slow the dehydration process. Tonio's hand held compass was another ally, preventing the legendary circular pattern of the lost. They walked and rested, walked and rested. Mirages and delusions tormented them constantly. As the sun was setting they again spread a few sections of parachute to catch the dew, but the wind direction had changed. The dry breeze felt to Tonio like the foul breath of a predator closing on his face for the kill. In the three days he had tramped one hundred miles with only a little water. Prévot looked at his comrade. He was parched and so dreadfully pale. Prévot believed Tonio was close to dying and felt it was his turn to search. It prompted him to lie. He told Tonio enthusiastically that he could see a lake, not too far distant. He explained that it could not be a mirage, for the sun was down. Antoine argued with him that there was no lake, or if there was, it was a lake of salt. But Prévot was stubborn and leaving Tonio to rest, struck out to reconnoiter.

Alone, Saint-Exupéry pictured Prévot's death and his own, separate—"He somewhere, and I somewhere else. Not that it was important." Again, he was near the point of surrender. He felt himself swaying as if he were on board a ship, rising and falling with the waves that bore him to a port that he would reach effortlessly. This port was close and in a strange way, pleasing. He thought fleetingly of Prévot—how he had not murmured, how he had proven himself a man.

A moment later he saw Prévot's electric torch, his lamp! Saint-Exupéry did not have a flashlight and could not signal him—so he rose to his feet and yelled. What he saw next amazed and thrilled him. He wrote:

> A second lamp, and then a third! God in Heaven! It was a search party and it was me they were hunting!
>
> "Hi! Hi!" I shouted.
>
> But they had not heard me. The three lamps were still signaling me.
>
> "Tonight I am sane," I said to myself. "I am not out of my head. Those are certainly three lamps and they are about five hundred yards off."[241]

The three lights began to turn a different direction. Saint-Exupéry found new strength. He ran toward them faltering and stumbling, calling and beckoning. At length a voice responded to his pleadings. He ran reeling toward the voice. When he reached Prévot he dropped to the ground. Catching his breath he realized, once again, that Prévot was alone. There was now only one light, Prévot's lamp. Prévot was in the process of returning, having found no oasis, and was attempting to find Tonio in the darkness.

The night was cold, so very cold. Tonio was without a coat and buried himself in the earth. He felt peace in the embrace of the sand. His mind was clear. His thoughts paralleled those of the ancient king Mosiah who said that God preserves us from day to day, lending us breath, and literally supporting us from one moment to another. Saint-Exupéry thought how the common man thinks he is so independent, so self-sufficient. He does not comprehend that he is bound to the River of Life, like an

> . . . umbilical cord tied to the womb of the world. Let man take but one step too many . . . and the cord snaps.[242]

Or as John wrote of the Creator:

> If a man abide not in me, he is cast forth . . . withered.[243]

Antoine thought of his life, of the opportunities and gifts he had been given and he was filled with appreciation. He thought how a man cannot live a creative life in the cities; how he had been blessed with wings to carry him away from congestion and pettiness. He wrote:

> The airplane is a means, not an end. One doesn't risk one's life for a plane any more than a farmer ploughs for the sake of the plough . . . Flying is a man's job and its worries are a man's worries. A pilot's business is with the wind, with the stars, with night, with sand, with the sea. He strives to outwit the forces of nature. He stares in expectancy for the coming of dawn the way a gardener awaits the coming of spring. He looks forward to port as to a promised land.[244]

When the sky was only dimly lit by the daystar, Tonio, rested, quickly stood on his feet and commanded Prévot to do the same. This was the fourth day and they must move now. This push would be their last. His tongue was thick, as was his indolent blood. Worst of all, light was beginning to fill his eyes. Of this day he does not write of mirages or illusions. He makes no comparisons, thinks no metaphors. Tonio's mind had no energy left to think, but only to tramp. The days previous he had taken pleasure in the thought of gardens, wells and orchards. On this day he could no longer believe that such things ever existed. He felt no grief, no distress. Later he wrote that sorrow is proof that you still live. He did not know what it meant to live, only to stagger on for the sake of those few feet just ahead. Tonio and Prévot had covered one hundred and twenty four miles. They had left in them only the ability to travel a few more feet.

Before they *saw* anything that could make a difference, before their scorched skulls were capable of thinking again, something "awakened" in their hearts. Tonio looked at Prévot and knew that he *felt* this something, so intangible, yet so real. The desert retained its vast emptiness. The sun still struck its steady blows on the smooth anvil where they reeled. Yet incomprehensibly both men knew they were near salvation. It was a matter of faith, for their sun burnt eyes apprehended only the eternal sands; that is until they saw footprints, of two men—and the imprint of a kneeling camel. They strained to hear a *sound*. For the last four days they had only heard the wind's breath. Again it came. It was a cock crowing. Happiness began to swell in their breasts. Over a sand dune rode a Bedouin. Tonio and Prévot were outside his field of view. They shouted for all they were worth, but their shouts were only whispers. The Arab did not see them and slowly traveled out of sight, like a vanishing mirage. But it was not a mirage for they had seen the same thing. No sooner had he gone from view when a second Bedouin came in sight. Again he moved in a direction that would pass them by and again they waved and tried to shout, but their lips produced only faint and muffled words. Saint-Exupéry described:

> At last, slowly, slowly he began a turn in our direction . . . Let this man but make a quarter-turn left and the world is changed. Let

> him but bring his torso round, but sweep the scene with a glance, and like a god he can create life.
>
> The miracle had come to pass. He was walking towards us over the sand like a god over the waves.
>
> The Arab looked at us without a word. He placed his hands upon our shoulders and we obeyed him: we stretched out upon the sand. Race, language, religion were forgotten. There was only this humble nomad with the hands of an archangel on our shoulders.
>
> Face to the sand, we waited. And when the water came, we drank like calves with our faces in the basin . . .
>
> Water, thou hast no taste, no color, no odor; canst not be defined . . . Not necessary to life, but rather life itself . . . By thy grace, there are released in us all the dried-up runnels of our heart.[245]

A short time after Tonio and Prévot drank their life saving draught the Arabs helped them mount a camel. After three hours, in their weakened condition, they could go no further. They rested at a small oasis while the Bedouins went twelve miles ahead to the home of Monsieur Raccaud, the director of a salt and soda company. Monsieur was not home but Madame Raccaud immediately sent a company truck to fetch the two men. When her husband returned in the early evening he had in his hands a newspaper whose headlines announced that Antoine de Saint-Exupéry, and his mechanic, Andre Prévot, had disappeared while attempting to break the speed record from Paris to Saigon. Raccaud was shocked to find his wife caring for these very men in his own living room! Although night had fallen Antoine asked Raccaud if he would drive them to Cairo to enable them to send word of their safety. Monsieur Raccaud promptly responded and, due to the late hour, arranged for an armed Bedouin guard to accompany them. The first telephone they came to was fifteen miles from Cairo at a Giza hotel. Antoine phoned Pierre de Witasse, the French minister in Cairo. The minister's secretary doubted the authenticity of the caller and told Monsieur de Witasse, as he brought him the phone, that it was a dubious call from a hotel bar.

When Saint-Exupéry and Prévot finally arrived at the Hotel Continental in Cairo, Monsieur Raccaud left them at the front steps while he went to park his car. The Frenchmen were accosted by the porter who proclaimed with indignity that his hotel would not provide accommodations to beggars. Ironically, true beggars would have been better attired and certainly would have been cleaner. While the porter was thus engaged in deriding the famous French aviator, who attempted to explain that he was Antoine de Saint-Exupéry, he was immediately recognized by several doctors who were returning from a banquet. Later Raccaud found Saint-Exupéry in a private room, being examined by several of the most notable surgeons in the world.

On New Year' Day, the day before their rescue, newspaper hawkers in the streets of Paris loudly announced that Antoine de Saint-Exupéry was long overdue. He had simply vanished and had presumably crashed. His mother, Madame Marie de Saint-Exupéry, his wife Consuelo, along with Daurat and many other close friends, awaited the outcome at the Hotel Pont-Royal. For two days they anxiously kept vigil. The veteran flyer Daurat was asked what he thought had happened to the lost Saint-Exupéry. Daurat replied:

> Have no fear, he is a man of great battles. Of course he'll make it. I've seen him disarmed only by the little things.[246]

On January 2, very late at night, Saint-Exupéry called his wife from Cairo. When the hotel told Madame Consuelo that Monsieur de Saint-Exupéry was on the line she let out a shriek that Antoine said "would ring forever in his ears." His friends were ecstatic. On January 3, *Paris-Soir* released a special edition of its newspaper announcing Saint-Exupéry's dramatic emergence from the Libyan Desert. Although he was under contract with a competitive newspaper, *L'Intransigeant,* to write the story of his flight from Paris to Saigon, Antoine had spoken with reporters briefly at breakfast. The scoop by *Paris-Soir* upset *L'Intransigeant,* whose representative called on Antoine reminding him of his obligation. Tonio smiled at the man and replied:

> Tell them for me that the accident was not included in our agreement.[247]

Saint-Exupéry returned to Paris more of a celebrity than ever. His photograph was on the cover of every newspaper. He was in the minds of the French more of a hero than if he had won the race to Saigon. Of course he had hoped to return home 150,000 francs richer. Instead, the failed expedition had extracted a severe toll on his finances. He wrote a series of six articles for *L'Intransigeant* on his desert ordeal. Edited and reduced this material is the basic content for chapter eight of his later book *Wind, Sand, and Stars.* Although his country and much of the world knew, from a myriad of reports, the facts of Tonio and Prévot's incredible journey, nothing could have prepared them for the mesmerizing, poetical accounts published in *L'Intransigeant.* Many were brought to tears; all were astounded—not only with the miracle of their survival but were amazed in the manner Antoine told his story. This was especially true when on rare occasions Tonio spoke of the odyssey. Princess Marthe Bibesco, wife of the President of the International Aeronautical Federation, after hearing Saint-Exupéry speak of his Libyan crash, said:

> He described it so graphically that we felt our mouths getting drier and drier, and when the lecture ended there was a stampede to the buffet for drinks. We clamored for wine, for lemonade, even for water—for anything which would quench our thirsts![248]

CHAPTER 26

SONS, BROTHERS AND ANIMALS

If souls were visible to the eye we would clearly see the strange fact that each individual of the human species corresponds to some species of the animal kingdom; and we would easily recognize the truth, scarcely perceived by thinkers, that from the oyster to the eagle, from the pig to the tiger, all animals are in man . . . Animals are merely the forms of our virtues and vices, wandering before our eyes, the visible phantoms of our souls. God shows them to us to make us reflect.

—VICTOR HUGO[249]

SEVERAL MONTHS INTO THE YEAR another of Saint-Exupéry's works was slated for the cinema. Writing the screenplay for *Courrier Sud,* produced for the French audience, (the English version of this book is known as *Southern Mail)* occupied a great deal of his time. In July of 1936 the Spanish Civil War erupted and *L'Intransigeant* retained Antoine as their foreign war correspondent. His articles read, not in the staccato fashion of the stereotypical journalist, but as fine literature. Again, part of this work ended up also in *Wind, Sand and Stars.* He speaks of the men on the front who volunteered to enter the fray—who left behind the comforts of home for a cause, again, greater than self. These men could not answer him when questioned why they left security and ease.

> You never really wondered about the imperious call that compelled you to join up. You accepted a truth which you could never

translate into words, but whose self-evidence overpowered you. And while I sat listening to your story, an image came into my mind, and I understood.

When the wild ducks or the wild geese migrate in their season, a strange tide rises in the territories over which they sweep. As if magnetized by the great triangular flight, the barnyard fowl leap a foot or two into the air and try to fly. The call of the wild strikes them with the force of a harpoon and a vestige of savagery quickens their blood. All the ducks on the farm are transformed for an instant into migrant birds, and into those hard little heads, till now filled with humble images of pools and worms and barnyards, there swims a sense of continental expanse, of the breadth of seas and the salt taste of the ocean wind. The duck totters to right and left in its wire enclosure, gripped by a sudden passion to perform the impossible and a sudden love whose object is a mystery.

Even so is man overwhelmed by a mysterious presentiment of truth . . . he discovers the vanity of his bookkeeping and the emptiness of domestic felicities. But he can never put a name to this sovereign truth.[250]

Job was asked by God where he was when the earth was being created and the "sons of God shouted for joy."[251] If the spirit of Job, his mind, his intelligence did not exist when the earth was formed, God would not have asked him where he was at the time of Genesis. Job could not answer—he, like all of us, could not remember. God told Jeremiah that before he was formed in the belly of his mother, before he came forth out of the womb, that He knew him—knew the spirit intelligence that came to occupy his physical body. The Creator also told Jeremiah that he had been foreordained, fore appointed, to a vital mortal mission. How did God know us before our birth? Who were the "sons of God" who shouted for joy when our mortal home was constructed? Are we barn yard foul whose entire existence, beginning through end, is to be lived and lost within the confines of a cage? Or rather is there a sovereign truth known to the subconscious mind, yet lost to the conscious memory? Are we overwhelmed by this "presentiment of truth?" (A mystery veiled in the forgetfulness of our life before we began our "pilgrimage" on earth?) Who are we? Are we animals, kin only to subspecies of mammals? Or are we placed on this earth, not only by a Creator, but by a literal *Father in Heaven*, to travel through mortality to fulfill a vital mission, to prove ourselves worthy of a divine heritage! Within our hearts we hear a wild, mysterious call, it descends upon us from far away, a call of greatness, striking within us "with the force of a harpoon." Our blood is quickened, true nature, true manhood, stirs our souls and we aspire to that which now seems unattainable. The hold of a superficial and egocentric world loosens and is replaced by visions of celestial flight! The image of soaring to impossible heights beckons, but our pilgrimage is not complete and we are bound to the earth by a vital mortal mission (and never should we succumb to the temptation to attempt flight before the *time* of our departure). However, the immortality within us awakens a forgotten understanding and we perceive our divine destination. Who are we? We speak of the brotherhood of man. This is not figurative. Psalms declares "all of you [are] children of the most High." Paul wrote

> God that made the world and all things therein . . . And hath made of one blood all nations of men . . .For in him we live, and move, and have our being. . . For we are also His offspring.[252]

We are the "sons of God!" He created us, but not as the other creatures of His creation. We alone are His children, created in His image, in His likeness—all the nations of men are of His race. If we are His children then we, in truth, are all brothers.

The world known to Saint-Exupéry was forgetting the Fatherhood of God and the Brotherhood of Man. His world was beginning to be believe that all of humanity were as worthless as barnyard foul, nothing more than evolved animals. Darwin's doctrine was, and is, being institutionalized in governments and kingdoms. To Darwin, Man is *not* a traveler, *not* sired by an Eternal Father, *not* placed as a pilgrim on the earth, *not* destined to travel beyond mortality to immortal Manhood. To Darwin, Man *is* a lower life-form who may rightly devour one another. It is the doctrine of the superior animal—the survival of the fittest! It is the world of Hitler. Weak men on a global scale are to be annihilated or made slave by the delusional Arians. In the third century the scholar Arius denied that Jesus was the Son of God, denied that Christ was of the race of God—denied that He was of the same *substance* as God. Instead Arius dictated that Jesus was only the highest of all earth beings. Arianism of the Third Reich proclaimed that they, the true Arians, were the highest animals, not only of earth's creatures, but were superior to all humans. With this conviction came the justification, not of war only, but of extermination.

In March of 1939 Saint-Exupéry decided to see, first hand, Nazi ruled Germany. However, he found it impossible to assess conditions independently. Said Tonio, "Curious how totalitarian countries always prefer guided tours!" Otto Abetz escorted Antoine throughout Berlin and Pomerania. He visited three *Führerschulen* where he observed the product of National Socialism personified in Hitler's youth. As he rode in the car with Abetz, Antoine spoke frankly; he had no use for a society that prohibits the free agency of ideas. Later he wrote:

> Human respect! Human respect! There is the touchstone. When the Nazi respects only what resembles him, he respects nothing but himself. He denies the creative . . . [and] ruins any hope of man's ascent, and in place of man, creates an ant-hill robot. Order for order's sake deprives man of his essential power which is to transform the world and himself. *Life creates order, but order does not create life.*[253]

On the first day of September, 1939, the Nazi *blitzkrieg* devastated Poland. Two days later the French Minister of Foreign Affairs issued the following declaration:

> M. Georges Bonnet, Minister for Foreign Affairs, to all the Heads of Diplomatic Missions accredited to Paris. Paris, September 3, 1939.
>
> YOUR EXCELLENCY,
>
> In conformity with Article 2 of Convention III of The Hague, dated October 18, 1907, I have the honour to send you herewith the notification relative to the State of War existing between France and Germany.
>
> The aggression which the German Government, scorning the methods of peaceful settlement of differences to which it had bound itself to have recourse, and the appeals to free discussion or to mediation addressed to it by the most authoritative voices, committed against Poland on September 1, in violation of engagements most freely accepted both towards Poland herself as well as towards all the signatory States of the Pact of renunciation of war of August 27, 1928, has confronted the French Republic with its obligations to assist Poland, obligations resulting from public treaties and known to the Government of the Reich.
>
> The supreme effort, attempted by the Government of the French Republic and by the British Government with a view to maintain peace by the cessation of aggression, was frustrated by the refusal of the German Government.
>
> *In consequence, as a result of the aggression aimed by Germany against Poland, a state of war exists between France and Germany as from September 3, 1939, at 5 p.m.*
>
> The present notification is made in conformity with Article 2 of Convention III of The Hague, dated October 18, 1907, relating to the outbreak of hostilities.[254]

France was ill prepared for war. As Antoine put it, "Forty million farmers must lose an armament race run against eighty million industrial workers." But France could not stand as an idle witness to the homicidal crimes waged against her Polish neighbors and the weak declared war against the mighty.

Saint-Exupéry was, at this time, a Captain in the Air Force Reserve. Was he obliged to enter the fray as a combatant? The previous year he had nearly been killed in Guatemala when his Simoun crashed on takeoff, caused, most likely, by a weight/density altitude miscalculation by Prévot. Antoine had been critically injured, his entire body mangled. Worst of all were the wounds to his head and left arm. The Guatemalan doctors believed his arm was beyond repair and was so badly infected that they recommended amputation; if the infection spread it would mean his death. Antoine would hear nothing of it—determined to remain whole, and he did! The better part of 1938 was spent recovering. However, when he presented himself for active service and for a physical examination in September 1939, he was still so affected by this latest crash, and the combined effects of all the previous accidents he had survived, that the French doctors stated that he was medically incompetent to pilot an aircraft. His body had been subjected to all of the rigors of an aviation pioneer and now was stiff and arthritic from his many fractures. His left shoulder was nearly immobile. The authorities wondered why in the world this man of letters wanted, so uncompromisingly, to engage the enemy, in the most dangerous of all places, *behind* their lines?—which is exactly where a French pilot would be required to operate.

After his Guatemalan accident, for the first time Tonio met his wealthy father-in-law. When the older gentleman saw the pitiful condition of his daughter's husband, a direct result of Antoine's profession, he proposed to Saint-Exupéry a generous new life style. He wanted Tonio and Consuelo to live a secure and peaceful life in El Salvador. If they would settle near his home, he would *give* Antoine "more plantations than you can cross in an entire day in a powerful car." Naturally, the injured pilot was deeply affected and appreciative, but he replied that he could not accept this offer. He was not meant to grow coffee beans. Said Antoine: "My job is to till the clouds."

During the first World War, Tonio had been considered too young to enlist. He was determined that this time he would not be excluded from the fight regardless of the orthodox limitations others sought to impose on him. He knew what he was capable of doing. He would demand supernatural strength from his worn and tired body and he knew that it would deliver, regardless of pain. He appealed his case all the way to the *Ministre de l'Air*, who finally waived the regulations in favor of the courageous, experienced aviator.

On November 26, 1939 Saint-Exupéry was assigned to the 2-33 Reconnaissance Group based in Orconte. It was no ordinary pilot who joined his fellow flyers that day. Saint-Exupéry was more revered by the French than the Wright Brothers! Most of the young aviators carried a sort of an aviation bible in their bags—*Terre des homes—Wind, Sand and Stars.* To this day there is not a more profoundly moving book on the *spirit* of aviation than this work of Saint-Exupéry's. Also, nearly all had read his other books, seen his films and documentaries, had read the newspaper accounts of his victories and his tragedies—now this demigod of flight stepped into the barracks of the 2-33 Squadron, surrounded by idealistic pilots, ten to fifteen years his junior. He was greeted by Lieutenant François Laux, announcing that he was the Commander of the 2-33rd. Antoine, a Captain did not pull rank. Instead he simply replied, "Saint-Exupéry, pilot." A junior pilot of the squadron named Gelée, later became a General in the French Air Ministry. Regarding Saint-Exupéry he said:

> We were proud yet a little apprehensive when we heard he was coming to us, for by then he was quite an illustrious figure. But our fears proved groundless. What impressed us most about him was his humility. There had been a conspiracy amongst his friends to get him a safe job, and he was almost pathetically grateful to be

> accepted in a fighting unit. He had a horror of being cut off from the fighting man. Far from expecting any special privileges, he seemed actually to enjoy discipline. . . . He loathed affectation and shallowness, and even mere worldly polish. . . . Our reconnaissance work was arduous . . . But Saint-Exupéry thought nothing of the discomfort and risks. He only made a fuss if he felt he was being cheated of his fair share of flights.[255]

Jean Israël, another fellow pilot, said simply of Antoine, "He tamed us."

Tonio loved brotherhood and he could be a highly entertaining companion. Besides his story telling abilities, he was an incredible magician and he had an infinite store of astounding card tricks. He loved to "ennoble another human being,"[256] to help a friend gain confidence in his own worth and manhood. When Antoine came to someone's aid, it mattered not if *he* suffered consequences, whether such consequences were physical, social, monetary or political. Antoine loved to "raise [a] drowned face above the current."[257] He could not tolerate gossip and although he often absorbed personal insult, he would not allow insult or injury to the innocent. Stacy Shiff tells of one incident in a restaurant near Laon where Saint-Exupéry may have given the "only order of his military career." Antoine had just returned from a reconnaissance flight and was probably very tired, looking forward to a peaceful dinner. Also in the restaurant was a woman, obviously distraught, with her two young daughters. They appeared to be mourning the loss of a loved one and were waiting for someone to come for them. A group of soldiers, noncommissioned officers, were there as well, drinking copiously. They were drunk and their conversation evolved into lewd boisterous singing. Antoine caught their attention and motioned towards the mother and her daughters. They not only ignored Captain Saint-Exupéry but their conduct became increasingly more offensive, vulgar and salacious. Antoine, who, for a Frenchman, was extremely tall and large, suddenly stood to his full height and quickly crossed the room, confronting the insolent and loathsome soldiers. His command was direct and coolly spoken: "I order you to be quiet." As he returned to his table, the only sounds in the restaurant came from "rattling dishes" in the kitchen. He had been obeyed, not only on the basis of his rank but by virtue of his moral authority. The mother appreciatively turned to him and said:

> Ah, Monsieur, thank heavens there are still men like you.[258]

CHAPTER 27

ASCENSION

Have no fear of robbers or murderers. They are external dangers, petty dangers. We should fear ourselves. Prejudices are the real robbers; vices the real murderers. The great dangers are within us. Why worry about what threatens our heads or our purses? Let us think instead of what threatens our souls. [259]

—VICTOR HUGO

AS THE WAR RAGED ON Saint-Exupéry's writings became ever more salient and relevant. His accolades continued to mount, in France and in the United States. In 1940 the American Booksellers Association honored Tonio with the National Book Award. The French Ministère de l'Information recognized that Antoine de Saint-Exupéry had more clout with the Americans than any other Frenchman! Both the French Information Ministry and the French National Center of Scientific Research endeavored to suspend his aerial duties and enlist him under their banners. Antoine responded that he would be unable to write of the drama and sacrifice unless he personally sacrificed—"that he had to live in order to write, which naturally meant to risk not living." His friends, knowing of Tonio's fearless nature and disregard of danger, coupled with the extremely high mortality rate of reconnaissance pilots in general, sided wholeheartedly with government officials. What beauty, answered Antoine, was there in being safe in time of war? In *Wisdom of the Sands* he expressed these sentiments poetically from the mouth of the King:

> My Empire's civilization rests not on its material benefits but on men's obligations and the zeal they bring to their tasks. It derives not from owning but from giving. Civilized is that [man] who remakes himself in the thing he works on, and for his recompense, becomes eternal, no longer dreading death. . . . No love have I for the sluggards, the sedentaries of the heart; for those who barter nothing of themselves *become* nothing. Life will not have served to ripen them. . . . Here in the sand today you endure as the cedar tree endures, by reason of the enemies that beset and toughen you.
>
> Lest my camp should sleep and founder in unwariness, I girt it about with sentries who culled all the drifting echoes of the desert. Thus, as the cedar draws into itself the stony soil and changes it into cedarwood, likewise my camp was nourished by those threatening it from without. . . . Blessed are they who appear beside our camp fires so suddenly and with news so grave that in an instant all the fires are quenched with sand, the men fall flat, gun in hand, and a blue mist of powder smoke rings the camp![260]

By order of the French High Command, on May 23, 1940, Captain Saint-Exupéry took off from Orly to over fly Arras and ascertain if the French troops were holding the line against the German advance. He would fly two such missions which, fused into one, would become the basis for his masterpiece, *Flight to Arras.* He would be one of the few pilots to survive such missions, and was cited on June 2, 1940 for his bravery. The citation read:

> An officer uniting the best intellectual and moral qualities, he has constantly volunteered for the most dangerous missions. . . . He is for the personnel of the unit a model of duty and the spirit of sacrifice.[261]

Only the events of Pearl Harbor had a greater impact on the mindset of the American people towards involving our nation in World War II than Antoine's published accounts of the fall of

France, of which *Flight to Arras* is paramount.

The May 1940 German invasion of Holland, Luxembourg, Belgium and France was horrific. The lightening assault that had overwhelmed Poland, Norway and Denmark struck with such fury that Luxembourg capitulated immediately. Holland blew up her own bridges to slow the advance of Panzers, but nothing could prevent the aerial bombardment of the powerful Luftwaffe. In Rotterdam alone 80,000 were left homeless after only two days of bombing. By mid-May the self-exiled Dutch King surrendered his country to Hitler, desiring to spare his subjects a futile war that would destroy and kill all who resisted the German might. Belgium attempted to circumvent the war by declaring itself neutral, but to no avail. The paratroopers of the Third Reich descended on Belgian forces at Fort Eban Emael and with flamethrowers made short work of the defenders, forcing surrender.

Meanwhile France concentrated her forces along the Maginot Line, a chain of defensive fortifications built by France on its eastern border after World War I to prevent future invasions by Germany. However, the Germans flanked the Maginot Line, thrusting their infantry and tanks through the Ardennes, which the French believed impassible, crossing the Meuse River on May 13. Five German divisions rolled rapidly toward Paris. Churchill was shocked upon discovering that the French had mobilized their entire force against Hitler and that as of May 16, there remained no strategic reserves. The French High Command began losing control amidst the pandemonium. The supreme Allied commander, General Maxime Weygand, was forced down while flying to the front and completely lost contact with his officers for four critical days. When he emerged from obscurity he ordered his French Forces to join the British Expeditionary Force and to attack Rommel's 7th Panzer Division at the town of Arras.

The assault only slowed the German advance. Within several days over 300,000 British and French troops were cornered, with no retreat except to England. Every possible ship, civilian as well as military, was employed to save these forces from death or capture. Henri Philippe Pétain, a powerful leader in the French Government, began to realize that his country's plight was beyond redemption and, in meeting with Churchill, informed the English Prime Minister that France might be forced to make a separate peace with Hitler. As Italy had entered the war as an Axis power, allied to Germany, England faced the awful reality, that should France capitulate, they alone would face the pestilent storm of Nazism. On June 14, 1940 France surrendered to Germany and Pétain was installed as the head of the collaborationist Vichy French government. General De Gaulle made his escape, under the Vichy condemnation of death, and on June 18, over the BBC from England, bombastically declared that he was the rightful leader of the exiled Free French Forces.

It was during these final, desperate days that Saint-Exupéry flew his immeasurably dangerous reconnaissance flights to Arras, to gather aerial intelligence on the fight to stop Rommel's advance. There had been only fifty reconnaissance crews in the entire French Army, of which twenty-three crews comprised Antoine's 2-33 Group. Of the twenty-three crews of the 2-33rd, only six crews remained when Tonio took off for Arras.

> Crew after crew was being offered up as a sacrifice. It was as if you dashed glassfuls of water into a forest fire in the hope of putting it out.[262]

Antoine's assignment was to fly at thirty thousand feet photographing the region that surrounded Arras, then again at only two thousand feet. He departed Orly with his observer and camera man, Jean Dutertre, and a third crewman acting as his gunner. Initially he flew north to Meaux to pick up his fighter escorts, pilots of the 1-33 group. Two of the escort planes were shot down as they neared Arras. Dutertre reported the enemy was entrenched between Douai and Arras and that hundreds of Panzer's were within two miles of the city. Arras was in flames, bellowing mammoth clouds of smoke and waves of fire.

Six miles below Saint-Exupéry were villages that had stood for centuries. In the midst of each village the sentinel spires of ancient churches had risen high above age-old houses—homes that had sheltered generations upon generations of mothers, fathers, children, of the same surnames, holding fast to the same traditions, cherishing the same faith. Their homes had not been built, as so often our houses are, to be held for a mere decade, then sold—discarded for profit, and left for a finer, more prestigious dwelling. No—these homes were as old as the venerable trees that shaded their clay tile roofs; habitations also with roots as deep, with thick stout walls that held the warmth of the hearth and fortified the beloved within from the raging gale without, keeping still the air of comfort, sheltered from the storm's cold blast. In such an abode the light of lamps danced on shining hardwood floors, the scent of wax mingled with the aroma of the evening meal, cooked fresh from the fields that bordered the town. Lace, the art and love-gifts of matriarchs, wondrously wrought by aged hands, adorned their tables and pillows. Blossoms had cascaded from their window boxes, had twined the lattices that graced their vestibules, had spanned their arbors. In these homes there was a spirit greater than the sum of all its parts, composed not only of the lives of those who lived within, but of those long departed, who had walked the same polished floors, had tilled the same soil, whose hearts, though no longer beating, turned in love toward living descendants in whose veins coursed their own vital blood. In turn the living kept alive generations past in a thousand honored memories. And when the day was spent and the hearth aglow with embers only, a man could look through his window on a starlit night, could feel that on his mortal pilgrimage he had found love, the immortal guide, made real to him in the quiet breath of his slumbering wife and the peace of his children at rest. And this man knew that each man in his village was his brother, and each woman his sister, and each child was to him as his own. This, to Saint-Exupéry, was his civilization. It was the course lighted by the Lodestar marking the pathway to exalted manhood and glorious brotherhood. All that peace *was* but yesterday. On this day, as Antoine looked down, all was burning from "Alsace to the sea."

> Burning is a great word when you look down from thirty-three thousand feet; for over the villages and the forests there is nothing to be seen but a pall of motionless smoke . . . Below it the fires are at work like a secret digestion. At thirty-three thousand feet time slows down, for there is no movement here. There are no crackling flames, no crashing beams, no spirals of black smoke . . .
>
> When a war is on, a village ceases to be a cluster of traditions. . . .Things no longer mean the same. Here are trees three hundred years old that shade the home of your family. But they obstruct the field of fire of a twenty-two-year-old lieutenant. . . . In ten minutes time he destroys three hundred years of patience and sunlight, three hundred years of the religion of the home and of betrothals in the shadows round the grounds. . . .
>
> But how am I to quicken the sense of my language when all is confusion? When the trees round the house are at one and the same time a ship transporting the generations of family and a mere screen in the way of an artilleryman? When the press of the German bombers bearing down upon the villages has squeezed out a whole people and sent it flowing down the highways like a black syrup? When France displays the sordid disorder of a scattered anti-hill? . . . Jammed roads, flaming houses, tools lying where they were flung down, villages in ruins, muddle, endless muddle. . . .
>
> Looking down on those swarming highways I understood more clearly than ever what peace meant. In time of peace the world is self-contained. The villagers come home at dusk from their fields. The grain is stored up in the barns. The folded linen is piled up in the cupboards. In time of peace each thing is in its place, easily found. Each friend is where he belongs, easily reached. All men know where they will sleep when night comes. Ah, but peace dies when the framework is ripped apart. When there is no longer a place that is yours in the world . . . this is war.[263]

Bloch 174

Fortunately, on his reconnaissance flights to Arras, Saint-Exupéry was piloting the new Bloch 174. The Bloch 174 had a service ceiling of 36,000 feet and with a maximum speed of 329 miles per hour was, at the time, the fastest multi-engine airplane in the world. Unfortunately the aircraft's performance exceeded its systems. At high altitudes the rudder, throttles and guns would simply freeze. Antoine would repeatedly stomp on the rudder bar, trying to keep it free as long as possible. When completely frozen the only remedy was to descend into lower, warmer air where he could regain directional control and the use of his guns.

Saint-Exupéry wrote of his encounter with enemy fighters near Arras. Dutertre was first to spot six German Messerschmitts ME-109s fifteen hundred feet below them, portside. The Germans also saw Tonio and immediately banked their aircraft to intercept his Bloch. The speed of the Bloch 174, although slower than the ME-109, was nonetheless faster than most reconnaissance planes the agile Messerschmitt routinely encountered and shot down. To Antoine's advantage, the German fighters would have to climb to get into firing position, momentarily losing speed. Also Tonio's course was directly into the sun making him a more difficult target. However, the odds were still monumentally against him and his mind flashed back to a somber warning his comrades of the 2-33 had given him when he rejoined his old squadron—they told him he would be flying over enemy territory, with frozen guns and controls, but not to take it too hard, as when once spotted by German fighters they always shoot you down. This is not a fight, he thought—if they get us in their sights

Messerschmitt 109

it is simply murder. With all of his might he bore down on the rudder pedals, trying to break them free. If he could regain his controls, at least he could *attempt* to out maneuver the Germans if it came to it. But the steel was welded fast by the bitter cold.

At sixty degrees below zero he was sweating incredibly. Every energy he possessed was concentrated on that rudder bar. Then he realized that the instrument panel was blurring, his hands were losing their grip!—at this critical moment he was fainting as though his oxygen mask had stopped delivering its vital life saving gas. Sometimes ice formed in the tube, blocking the flow of oxygen. He pinched the tube and quickly released it; he was greeted by a fresh burst of oxygen proving that it was working as it should be. Still the hypoxia worsened—a rather pleasant feeling, he thought, slipping into unconsciousness. From somewhere in his lethargic mind came a sudden answer to his hypoxic dilemma. He was still bearing down on the rudder, straining like "a man trying to pick up a grand piano." In his extreme exertion he was expending his supply of oxygen faster than the system could deliver. He relaxed his muscles and slowly, ever so slowly, re-entered into life and the drama in which he played protagonist. Dutertre was speaking to him; like a convalescent Tonio replied so feebly that Dutertre was perplexed and concerned. Tonio would not waste the little energy he possessed attempting to explain what had caused his predicament. There was no time—the ME-109s were in hot pursuit. Should he attempt a dive or should he stay allied to the blinding sun? A bullet pierced one of his tanks. Saint-Exupéry knew now it was "God's business" whether they lived or died. Later he wrote:

> The fighters come down on you like lightning. Having spotted you . . . they take their time. They weave, they orient themselves, take careful aim. You know nothing of this. You are the mouse lying in the shadow of the bird of prey. The mouse fancies that it is alive. It goes on frisking in the wheat. But already it is the prisoner of the retina of the hawk . . .
>
> And thus you, continuing to pilot . . . to scan the earth, have already been flung outside the dimension of time because of a tiny black dot on the retina of a man.
>
> A bombing squadron possesses enough firing power to offer a chance for defense; but a reconnaissance crew, alone in the wide sky, has no chance against the seventy-two machine guns that make themselves known to it by the luminous spray of their bullets. At the very instant when you first learn of its existence, the fighter, having spat forth its venom like a cobra, is already neutral and inaccessible, swaying to and fro overhead. Thus the cobra sways, sends forth its lightning, and resumes its rhythmical swaying.
>
> The fighter has become a mere impartial onlooker when, from the severed carotid in the neck of the reconnaissance pilot, the first jets of blood spurt forth. When from the hood of the starboard engine the hesitant leak of the first tongue of flame rises out of the furnace fire. And the cobra has returned to its folds when the venom strikes the heart and the first muscle of the face twitches. The fighter group does not kill. It sows death. Death sprouts after it has passed.[264]

Saint-Exupéry droned on towards Arras while the suspense and dreadful expectations faded. The sky vacant; the ME-109s lost from view. Had the Germans crossed his path fifteen hundred feet above him *instead* of fifteen hundred feet below him the outcome would have surely been different. Unless, of course, you believe, as did Antoine, that our life's business is God's business, that our life's missions are appointed by Him—and if we do all that is in our power, we may leave the life and death outcome to Him.

What was the purpose of Saint-Exupéry's flight to Arras? If one says to gather essential intelligence he would be wrong—communication lines from the 2-33 to the general staff were severed even before he was airborne. The general staff itself was in a state of decomposition as was the entire population; a body torn by war, the arms detached from the torso, the feet severed brutally, the head decapitated. Tonio knew, as did those who still fought the enemy, that the fight was futile. They were dismembered "clusters of infantrymen" and isolated decimated aircrews "melting like wax flung into a fire." America, the only world power capable of intervening, refused to do so; instead choosing to arbitrate between France and the Luciferic Hitler. France, said Saint-Exupéry, had declared war in response to mass murders in democratic nations. But the French, in no position to take the offensive could now only observe their own destruction. Flying high above burning Arras, his craft frozen as if on a course leading only to annihilation, Saint-Exupéry asked himself why he and others continued the fight? Not accepting a certain mission only, or combat, or danger—but accepting death itself. Was it for democracy? He reasoned:

> If we die for democracy then we must be one of the democracies. Let the rest fight with us, if that is the case. But the most powerful of them, the only democracy that could save us, chooses to bide its time.[265]

He struggled for reasons, for answers. The thought came to him that there was a fundamental common cause. It was the cause of Poland as well as France. Those hundreds of thousands that had died in Norway, Holland, Belgium and England also had shed their blood for this common cause. It is a cause, he argued, that cannot be argued, "a verity that is higher than the pronouncements of the intelligence." To those who should understand it, there should be no need to explain it.

Not only was America withholding its resources, many Americans were extremely critical of the French. By this time most of France was already defeated. Tonio had absolute compassion for his countryman already in the Nazi grip, for it was a defeat they truly had not power to prevent. Yet the beaten soldier knew not whether he was a hero or one deserving a court-marital; for those nations who *talked* only, also *judged* harshly. As Saint-Exupéry put it:

> If the woman you loved were run over by a lorry, would you feel impelled to criticize her ugliness?[266]

Antoine fought for the fundamental cause—he had accepted that this cause would demand of him his very life. But that was not his only purpose in his flight to Arras. In the beginning he could not articulate the cause—could not define it, felt it in the depths of his heart, but could find no language to express it. If he, in the bowels of the battle, had difficulty in articulating the essential truths, how could his brothers in democracy, isolated by thousands of miles of seeming security from the horrors and putrefaction of war, understand that there can be no negotiations with evil that is fully ripe, that there is a cause fundamental to our mortal mission that is worth sacrificing life itself to defend. Out of these flights would come from Saint-Exupéry *a defense for the cause* greater than France, greater than democracy. He would emerge from these missions to Arras with a plainly spoken argument and would write such a compelling account of the truths he had learned that it would shake America from lethargy. His mission was to awaken the God-given powers of the United States in support of the fundamental *cause*. With the power of the pen Saint-Exupéry would vindicate the defeated innocent and would damn the guilty oppressor. His mission was one of testator.

Antoine de Saint-Exupéry would not live to see Germany

defeated and free France reestablished. Therefore, *what* he wrote in *Flight to Arras*, at the *time* he wrote it, is remarkable. Antoine wrote that France *would suffer defeat* before it obtained victory, that France *would* resurrect, but not until it had first been killed! He compared this death and resurrection of his nation to a seed that must be laid in the ground, "condemned to rot . . . buried for a time in silence." From that seed would spring forth a new life, an "awakening of resistance," and with the all important aid of America, France would grow from the ashes of death and destruction into a living tree. When these thoughts came to Tonio he was descending his frozen Bloch 174 from high altitude. He had no sooner reached these conclusions when he realized that his controls had thawed in the warm air of the low altitudes; his mobility was restored.

Antoine leveled his plane at two thousand three hundred feet above the terrain and just beneath a heavy overcast. He was now extremely vulnerable—in clear view and within range of numerous ground-based anti-aircraft guns. Jean Dutertre was busy photographing while Saint-Exupéry assumed a zigzag course, making his Bloch 174 a more difficult target. In a matter of moments he began to draw fire from the ground gunners. He could have taken himself out of harm's way instantly simply by pulling back on the control yoke, climbing and vanishing into the protective canopy of clouds overhead. Instead he pressed on, duty bound—for the surveillance photos garnered at two thousand feet are clear and focused, far superior to the hazy, smoke blurred images shot at thirty thousand feet. Ahead lay Arras, glowing crimson against the deepening blues of nightfall. As they rose to intercept the Bloch 174 the tracer-bullets clearly marked the path of the deadly projectiles. Dutertre would call out: "Captain! Firing very fast to port. Hard down!" Saint-Exupéry bore down with all of his might on the rudder bar, skidding his plane to the right, bending his course at near right-angles to his previous line of flight. The German gunners adjusted their aim accordingly and send forth a new volley of missiles and Antoine stomped on his left rudder, wrenching the plane in the opposite direction with incredible force. With each passing moment the firing intensified exceedingly. Saint-Exupéry described:

> We had been swaying heavily through this blue swamp already drowned in night. We had stirred up this silent slime; and now, in tens of thousands, it was sending towards us its golden bubbles. A nation of jugglers had burst into dance. A nation of jugglers was dribbling its projectiles in tens of thousands in our direction. Because they came straight at us, at first they appeared to be motionless. Like colored balls which jugglers seem not so much to fling into the air as to release upwards, they rose in lingering ascension. I could see those tears of light flowing towards me through a silence as of oil. . . . A thousand elastic rosaries strung themselves out towards the plain, drew themselves out to a breaking point, and burst at our height. When, missing us, the string went off at a tangent, its speed was dizzying. The bullets were transformed into lightening. And I flew drowned in a crop of trajectories as golden as stalks of wheat. I flew at the center of a thicket of lance strokes. I flew threatened by a vast and dizzying flutter of knitting needles. All the plain was now bound to me, woven and wound round me, a coruscating web of golden wire.[267]

The exploding shells from the large caliber guns shook the Bloch 174 so violently that it seemed impossible that the aircraft could hold together. Antoine could not indefinitely outmaneuver such a massive bombardment. Bullets and fragments of shells began to pierce his fuselage, fuel tanks, and oil tanks. He was hit so many times that the percussion seemed to his ears like a steady drum roll. Fortunately his tanks were coated with soft rubber that, contracting when pierced, sealed the punctures instantly, performing their designed task is if a living membrane. However, Dutertre exclaimed that there was no way they would ever get through such a gauntlet alive. All Tonio needed was a few more minutes and their mission would be accomplished. He could then cloak his ship in the safety of the clouds and turn for home. But minutes? How could they last so long when a realistic life expectancy in such a deluge of firepower would be ten seconds, twenty seconds at the most! It seemed as if the sky itself was rent, erupting as the earth is during an earthquake. Still Antoine flew on—his Bloch 174 taking hit after hit. With each metallic bang he queried his men: "Anybody hurt?" and was answered with "Not I," or "O.K., sir!" Saint-Exupéry wrote:

> How did it happen that we were still whole? I began to believe in us. . . . From that moment each explosion seemed to me not to threaten us but to temper us. Each time, for a fraction of a second, it seemed to me that my plane had been blown to bits; but each time it responded anew to the controls and I nursed it along like a coachman pulling hard on the reins. I began to relax, and a wave of jubilation went through me. . . .What I felt was the shock, then instantly the relief. Shock, relief. Fear, the intermediate step, was missing. . . . I was living. I was alive. I was still alive. I was thrilled through with the intoxication of living. "The heat of battle" is a familiar phrase; the heat of living is a truer one. "I wonder," I said to myself, "if those Germans below who are firing at us know that they are creating life within us?"[268]

At last the welcome words were heard from Dutertre: "First-rate, Captain. Two-Forty please"—meaning that he had finished his work and Tonio could turn the airplane to two hundred and forty degrees—the course home! The flames of Arras swiftly faded from view as Antoine ascended into the overcast. Never had he felt such emotions as now filled his heart. He realized, more than ever before, that there "is no growth except in the fulfillment of obligations." He was going home to the 2-33rd, to his friends, his comrades, his brothers, to his own kind. To men who saw the same truths that he saw, who fought as he fought, to those who had become a part of himself. That was it, he realized, the essence of the fundamental *cause*.

Finally he understood that he was part of Guillaumet, of Hochedé, of all of his comrades of the 2-33 Group and they were part of him. That he was part of France and France was part of Antoine. That he was inseparably joined to mankind and responsible for mankind. He wrote:

> Until I learned what I learned over Arras, I could feel no responsibility for this stream of refuges over which once more I fly. I can be bound to no men except those to whom I give. I understand no man except those to whom I am bound. I exist only to the degree that I am nourished by the springs at my roots. I am bound to that mob on the highways, and it is bound to me. . . . That mob is no longer a mob, it is a people.
>
> We dwell in the rot of defeat, yet I am filled with a solemn and abiding jubilation, as if I had just come from a sacrament. I am steeped in chaos, yet I have won a victory. . . . We had seen France in flames. We had seen the sun shining on the sea. We had grown old in the upper altitudes. We had bent our glance upon a distant earth . . . We had sported in the sunlight with the dust of enemy fighter planes. Thereafter we had dropped earthward again and flung ourselves into the holocaust. What we could offer up, we had sacrificed. . . .
>
> At a single bound we had leapt over the whole defeat. We were above and beyond it, *pilgrims* stronger than the desert through which they toil because already in their hearts they have reached the holy city that is their destination.[269]

Saint-Exupéry landed safely at Orly and relinquished his bullet-riddled Bloch 174 "made noble by her scars" to his ground crew. He had seen his beloved France in its death throes, hemorrhaging, but he had also seen in his soul that the mortal death of a nation, as well as a man, is not the end of its existence. That the outward body may be marred grotesquely, the material being may be literally severed from its members, its blood, the apparent life force, may flow copiously unchecked until the fragmented form lays still, the brain, the heart, the eye inanimate, ghastly features frozen, motionless. But the life was not in the blood or in the brain; nor even in the heart, but in the *spirit*, in the immortal intelligence. He thought back to that day in 1917 when François, his little brother, gasped his last breaths, and spoke his last words. Antoine, at his side, had seen the pain course through François emaciated body, robbing from him his ability to even speak until the agonizing wave subsided. Tonio thought François contracted in his fear of death; but François made it clear in the few words he could utter that he held no terror of dying. He whispered to Tonio:

> Don't worry, I'm all right. I can't help it. It's my body.[270]

François, himself, was fine. Tonio realized that his brother was telling him that the loss of his body had nothing to do with the end of anything. He could not save or help his outward form. The vital functions had nearly ceased and would soon fail completely. But he was fine. François, was in the final moments of his mortal pilgrimage. He knew death for what it was; it was nothing to fear. This world, with its corporeal attractions, had lost its luster for him. Said Antoine, "His body was already foreign territory, something not himself." The eyes of his spirit were now focused more acutely on the purpose of his being, a purpose as immortal as his intelligence. He was fine. Saint-Exupéry wrote:

> Man does not die. Man imagines that it is death he fears; but what he fears is the unforeseen, the explosion. . . .There is no death when you meet death. When the body sinks into death, the essence of man is revealed.[271]

It was in the very death of France that her true immortal essence was revealed to Antoine. His brother François would live in the spirit until his very body attained an immortal resurrection. France would also live in the spirit until she too, would walk in newness of life. An ancient prophet wrote:

> There is a space between the time of death and the resurrection . . . And when the time cometh when all shall rise, then shall they know that God knoweth all the times which are appointed unto man. . . .[272] The soul shall be restored to the body, and the body to the soul; yea, and every limb and joint shall be restored to its body; yea, even a hair of the head shall not be lost; but all things shall be restored to their proper and perfect frame.[273]

France would suffer death, as did François. But it would be the death of the body only and not the soul—both would live in the spirit until the times of restoration when all would be restored to their perfect frame. It is all part of the journey of man, the ascent of man. Already Antoine, his comrades of the 2-33rd, his brothers in France, were stronger than the desert of war through which they traveled, for they knew their true essence could not be slain, and that it was only through dying that they could continue to live. They were yet far from the holy city of their destination, but in their hearts they were already there.

These truths, now clear in his mind, drew back the curtains of sophistry which had obscured the fundamental cause. Saint-Exupéry stated:

> I reject non-being (death is not the end of being). My purpose is to be. And if I am to be, I must begin by assuming responsibility. Only a few hours ago I was blind. I was bitter. But now I am able to judge more clearly. . . . Each is responsible for all. France was responsible for all the world. Had France been France, she might have stood to the world as the common ideal round which the world would have rallied. She might have served as the keystone in the world's arch. . . . There was a time when my civilization proved its worth—when it inflamed its apostles, cast down the cruel, freed peoples enslaved.[274]

What had France lost? What had the other nations of the earth lost? Another ancient prophet wrote:

> We may see at the very time when [God] doth prosper his people, yea, in the increase of their fields, their flocks and their herds, and in gold, and in silver, and in all manner of precious things of every kind and art; sparing their lives, and delivering them out of the hands of their enemies; . . . yea, and in fine, doing all things for the welfare and happiness of his people; yea, then is the time that they do harden their hearts, and do forget the Lord their God, and do trample under their feet the Holy One—yea, and this because of their ease, and their exceedingly great prosperity.
>
> And thus we see that except . . . [they are visited] with death and with terror, and with famine and with all manner of pestilence, they will not remember [God].[275]

France, like the rest of the Christian world, had not *remembered* God, their Creator. Man can only be exalted when he recognizes his *son-ship* to the Almighty and renders to his Heavenly Father reverence through service to his fellow-man, his brothers—all children of the same Father. Paul wrote:

> Brethren, ye have been called unto liberty . . . by love serve one another.[276]

There is a definite link between freedom and liberty and our beliefs and actions toward each other. How we treat each other is dependent on how deeply our convictions are grounded in divine truth and our understanding of our literal relationship to God our Father. Our faith and knowledge of that relationship can only progress when we live our lives in harmony with His teachings. We cannot believe deeper than we live. God is a loving Father who delights in blessing his obedient children. However, history has shown repeatedly that we, His children, in our prosperous pride think ourselves self-sufficient. We begin to erect monuments to our own greatness and power. We begin to believe in the strength of our armaments and not in the strength of our character. We fancy that our prosperity results, not from heaven-sent blessings, but from our own intellect and superiority. Becoming, in our minds, superior to those we deem inferior we soon forget our accountability, to God and mankind. Once we no longer hold ourselves accountable we sear our conscience by denying God's very existence. Once we declare there is no *Father*, we deny, therefore, that we are brethren. If not brothers, then why should we serve and love each other. If not brothers, then those who suffer need not concern *we* who do not suffer. Just as those who *cause* the suffering believe themselves alienated from those whom they hurt, those who refuse to aid the sufferer likewise believe themselves alien. Nazi Germany had adopted Aryanism to only a higher degree than France and the rest of the world. Hitler had espoused that doctrine to horrific proportions; but in a lesser degree all the World had forgotten God and the commensurate relationship each man held to all men. Therefore, all the World would be chastened, visited with death, with terror, and with famine. All the world would be at war, because the world would not remember God. Saint-Exupéry wrote:

> There is in Man something more than the mere sum of the materials that went into his making. A cathedral is a good deal more than the sum of its stones. . . . But the significance of Man is not self-evident: it is a thing to be taught.
>
> For centuries my civilization contemplated God in the person of man. Man was created in the image of God. God was revered in Man. Men were brothers in God. It was this reflection of God that conferred an inalienable dignity upon every man. The duties of each towards himself and towards his kind were evident from the fact of the relations between God and man. My civilization was the inheritor of Christian values.
>
> It was in the contemplation of God that created men who were equal, for it was in God that they were equal. For we cannot be

> equal except we be equal *in* something. . . . As the manifestation of God, they were equal in their rights. As the servants of God, they were also equal in their duties . . .
>
> Men [are] brothers in God. One can only be a brother *in* something. Where there is no tie that binds men, men are not united but merely lined up. . . .
>
> However great one man may be, however insignificant another, no man may claim the power to enslave another. [Man is the ambassador of God.] One does not humble an ambassador. . . .
>
> I understand the profound meaning of the humility exacted from the individual. Humility did not cast down the individual, it raised him up. It made clear to him his role as ambassador. As it obliged him to respect the presence of God in others, so it obliged him to respect the presence of God in himself . . .
>
> I understand by this bright light the meaning of liberty. It is liberty to grow as the tree grows in the field of energy of its seed. It is the climate permitting the ascension of Man.[277]

Saint-Exupéry understood that as the seed is to the tree, we are to God. The babe compared to its father, although in his image, has little of the father's power and ability. Yet the child will grow, for it is of the same race; it is the offspring, the seed of the parent. If the child is obedient to the principles that made his father great, the child will be the inheritor of the father's powers and abilities. This, Saint-Exupéry finally understood was the *fundamental cause* for which he fought—the very purpose of our pilgrimage: *the ascension of Man.*

Our journey through life was designed to be traversed in freedom. God gave us agency, the power to choose the course of our odyssey. In liberty we may discover our purpose, our life's mission, and in faith may envision the holy city of our destination where we may become like Him who made us. As John wrote:

> Beloved, now are we the sons of God, and it doth not yet appear what we shall be: but we know that, when he shall appear, we shall be like him; for we shall see him as he is.[278]

C. S. Lewis wrote a great deal regarding the ascension of Man. He acknowledged the literal existence of a powerful intelligence who directly opposes our efforts to become like our Creator; that is to ascend from our present condition to a state of "perfect freedom." This Author of Evil is the true enemy to Man. It is he who entices the master dictators, the tyrants, the despots, the Hitler's of the world to subject mankind to totalitarianism. Said Lewis:

> There are two equal and opposite errors into which our race can fall about the devils. One is to disbelieve in their existence. The other is to believe, and to feel an excessive and unhealthy interest in them. They themselves are equally pleased by both errors and hail a materialist or a magician with the same delight.[279]

In his insightful book, *Screwtape Letters,* Lewis, has his antagonist, Screwtape by name, a ranking officer in the hierarchy of Hell, state:

> To us [devils] a human is primarily food; our aim is the absorption of its will into ours, the increase of our own selfhood at its expense. But the obedience which [God] demands of men is quite a different thing. One must face the fact that all the talk about His love for men, and His service being perfect freedom, is not (as one would gladly believe) mere propaganda, but . . . truth. He really *does* want to fill the universe with . . . replicas of Himself—creatures whose life will be qualitatively like His own, not because He has absorbed them but because their wills freely conform to His. We (the devils) want cattle who can finally become food; He (God) wants servants who can finally become sons.[280]

The enemy of Man has sought from the beginning to deny liberty, agency: the power to set one's own course. The enemy of Man seeks first to rob from man the knowledge of himself. He would take a prince, heir to a throne, and make the prince believe himself lower than a peasant. He would have him *forget* his Father, the King, and the dominion his Father would have him receive. He would have him forget that he is a Man, and would delude him into thinking that he is an animal; subject to no one, accountable to no one, coming from nowhere and destined to nothing. Again, Saint-Exupéry wrote:

> So long as my civilization leant upon God it was able to preserve the notion of sacrifice . . . Humanism neglected the essential role of sacrifice . . . little by little we lost our heritage. Instead of affirming the rights of Man present in the individual we had begun to talk about the rights of the collectivity (socialism, fascism, nazism, communism). . . . For want of an effective concept of humanity—which can rest only upon Man—we have been slipping gradually towards the ant-hill, whose definition is the mere sum of the [ants].
>
> What did we possess that we could set up against the religions of the State and of the Party? What had become of our great ideal of Man born of God? . . .[281]
>
> I believe that the primacy of Man founds the only equality and the only liberty that possess significance. I believe in the equality of the rights of Man inherent in every man. I believe that liberty signifies the ascension of Man.[282]

The ascension of Man—the fundamental cause. Moses quoted our Father when He said:

> Behold, this is my work and my glory—to bring to pass the immortality and eternal life of man.[283]

Wars are waged—wars within ourselves, wars in families, in cities, in nations and between nations—all with one purpose: to destroy the freedom of our pilgrimage and prevent Man's ascension.

Man comes a pilgrim of the universe,
Out of the mysteries that were before,
The world, out of the wonder of old stars.
Far roads have felt his feet, forgotten wells
Have glassed his beauty bending down to drink.
At altar-fires anterior to Earth
His soul was lighted, and it will burn on
After the suns have wasted in the void.
His feet have felt the pressure of old worlds,
And are to tread on others yet unnamed—
Worlds sleeping yet in some new dream of God. [284]

—EDWIN MARKHAM

At Orly Saint-Exupéry was billeted with a farmer and his family. When he returned from his flight to Arras he found them seated at their dinner table. He sat down next to the farmer's lovely young niece, modest and virtuous. She smiled at the weary aviator. This was the France that had been and would be. Her kind would live to see the rebirth of all that he loved. Soon the war would overtake this family as well, but for now they dwelt in an oasis of peace and Tonio basked in quiescence. Farmers have always dealt in the here and now. Their ongoing labor endows men of the earth with common sense and practicality. No doubt the farmer's tellurian manner brought Saint-Exupéry out of his soliloquy and back to the present moment. Tonio, a little prideful in the skill of his profession asked the farmer how many instruments did he think a pilot had to keep track of? The farmer answered:

> How should I know? Not my trade. Must be some missing, though, to my way of thinking. The ones you win a war with. Have some supper?[285]

CHAPTER 28

FLIGHT TO ETERNITY

He lifted me from the ground, and taking me by the hand, "Mirza," said he, "I have heard thee in thy soliloquies; follow me."

He then led me to the highest pinnacle of the rock, and placing me on the top of it, "Cast thy eyes eastward," said he "and tell me what thou seest." "I see," said I, "a huge valley and a prodigious tide of water rolling through it."

"The valley that thou seest," said he, "is the Vale of [Mortality], and the tide of water that thou seest is part of the great tide of eternity." "What is the reason," said I, "that the tide I see rises out of a thick mist at one end, and again loses itself in a thick mist at the other?" "What thou seest," said he, "is that portion of eternity which is called time." [286]

—THE VISION OF MIRZA, JOSEPH ADDISON

THE BLITZKRIEG SOON ENVELOPED ALL of eastern and northern France. The 2-33rd retreated from Orly to La Chapelle-Vendômoise, then to Bordeaux. Antoine arranged for Consuelo to be evacuated from Paris to Lyons. On June 14 Paris was largely deserted when the Germans officially took possession of the capital city and hung the red and black spider of the swastika from every notable monument. Raoul de Roussy de Sales remonstrated:

> France has fallen from the height of ten centuries of history in thirty-eight days.

The interdiction of Germany upon France read in part:

Franco-German Armistice, between the chief of the High Command of the armed forces, Col. Gen. [Wilhelm] Keitel, commissioned by the Fuehrer of the German Reich and Supreme Commander in Chief of the German Armed Forces, and the fully authorized plenipotentiaries of the French Government . . .

The French Government directs a cessation of fighting against the German Reich in France as well as in French possessions, colonies, protectorate territories, mandates as well as on the seas. It [the French Government] directs the immediate laying down of arms of French units already encircled by German troops.

In the occupied parts of France the German Reich exercises all rights of an occupying power. The French Government obligates itself to support with every means the regulations resulting from the exercise of these rights and to carry them out with the aid of French administration.

The French Government is permitted to select the seat of its government in unoccupied territory, or, if it wishes, to move to Paris.

French armed forces on land, on the sea, *and in the air* are to be demobilized and disarmed . . . These troops shall lay down their weapons and equipment at the places where they are stationed . . . They are responsible for orderly delivery to German troops.

Weapons, munitions, and war apparatus of every kind remaining in the unoccupied portion of France are to be stored and/or secured under German and/or Italian control.

French Government also will prevent members of its armed forces from leaving the country and prevent armaments of any sort, including ships, *planes,* etc., being taken to England or any other place abroad.

The French Government will forbid French citizens to fight against Germany in the service of States with which the German Reich is still at war. French citizens who violate this provision are to be treated by German troops as insurgents.

Flight by any airplane over French territory shall be prohibited. Every plane making a flight without German approval will be regarded as an enemy by the German Air Force and treated accordingly.[287]

At the airfield in Bordeaux airplanes were stacked wing tip to wing tip. Saint-Exupéry commandeered the largest plane he could lay hands on, a Farman 220. The 220 had four engines, mounted in tandem. It was a plane Antoine had never flown. Aboard this version of "Noah's Ark" he crammed 40 evacuees, along with a few pet animals. Through dense fog he lumbered into the air with his heavy load and set his course for Oran in North Africa. It is possible the fog could have been their salvation—for at a cruise speed of only 135 miles per hour the Farman 220 was a sitting duck for the Messerschmitts. He landed safely in Oran and the following day joined up with others of the 2-33rd in Algiers. However, he and his comrade aviators found themselves in no position to continue the battle. The airfield in Algiers was packed with some eight hundred aircraft, but there was little fuel, no funds, few munitions and no organization. Antoine was officially released from active service several weeks later, for officially France was no longer at war with Germany. Nearly overnight everything had changed. Letters received from the City of Lights were postmarked pitifully "Paris, Germany."

On August 4, 1940 he sailed to Marseilles where he began to formulate plans to travel to America where he hoped to be a persuasive unofficial ambassador for his defeated country. He also did what he could for Consuelo and his mother so that they would be provided for in his absence and in the event of his death. In Vichy,

Farman 220

the new capitol, he awaited the processing of his papers. One evening while dining at the Hôtel du Parc where Premier Pétain and Vice Premier Laval administered the new French government, Laval walked past Saint-Exupéry's table. Antoine spoke loud and derisively stating that there goes the collaborationist "who's giving France away." He was immediately cautioned to be careful of his speech to which he replied:

> Oh well, now that we've said enough to be shot at dawn let's go for a walk.[288]

Fortunately he obtained a visa authorizing his journey to the States. As he said his goodbyes to a friend he assured him that they would meet again—declaring with fervor that when the Americans landed in North Africa he would be with them! In Lisbon, a necessary stop enroute, he learned that Guillaumet had been killed flying over the Mediterranean. Guillaument was flying Chiappe, the French High Commissioner to Syria when, above the Gulf of Tunis, he unwittingly was caught in a dog-fight between British and Italian fighters and was shot down. During a speech Saint-Exupéry gave while in the city, he spoke of his friend from their days spent together in the service of Aéropostale. Guillaument, his old mentor, was his closest friend and he felt the loss terribly. Tears filled his eyes as he praised the man of valor. With Guillaument's death, Saint-Exupéry, although still relatively young, was the sole survivor of the "Casablanca/Dakar team."

The brief time Saint-Exupéry spent in Portugal was a surreal experience. It was a time of incongruity. Refugees poured into Lisbon, not only people in search of refuge, but expatriates who were there for the sole reason of preserving their wealth. It was a city of people who deluded themselves into happiness. In France his countrymen faced the threat of starvation, subjected to the Nazi overlords, slaves to the Führer. Lisbon, less than 500 miles from France, was yet well fed and possessed a countenance of gaiety; its citizens and guests alike, pretending neutrality. The deposed rich arrived nightly at the brightly lit casinos, "like a ballet of dolls," dressed in tuxedos and evening gowns, playing the roles of their former lives of privilege on a hallucinatory stage. They gambled with currency that was obsolete, filled the safe depositories of the hotels and banks with stocks of companies whose factories had been blown to bits. They dined with one another, in flighty conversation, claiming exemption from the effects of the ruinous assaults on their homelands, striving to believe that their fortunes, which circumscribed their life's meaning, were still whole—had not vaporized into the nothingness they most inwardly feared.

We have but one mortal life. Regardless of our allotted time here on earth, it is only a moment in eternity. We may, in that moment, grasp life's purpose, fight for the fundamental cause, complete our uniquely appointed mission, and successfully endure our pilgrimage. We thus qualify ourselves to continue our ascension, when mortality is spent, towards that perfect freedom prepared by God for his obedient children. Or we may abdicate eternity by investing *ourselves* in currency and stocks, which in our deaths will most certainly possess not one penny of value.

On December 21, 1940 Saint-Exupéry left Lisbon for New York aboard the *Siboney*. He gave his first press conference right on the pier as he arrived in the States. The renowned aviation pioneer, best selling author, journalist, and screen writer indeed held a fascination in the minds of Americans who were eager to learn more of his views of the war and the fall of France. Others were also anxious to engage Antoine de Saint-Exupéry—but not to acquire insight, but rather to exploit his fame in furthering their own agendas. There were three main French factions in New York: The first was a group who called themselves independents and were mainly an assemblage of writers and philosophers, most notably Jacques Maritain. The second group were Pétainists, lead by Vichy Ambassador, M. Henri Haye. Thirdly, there were the Gaullists, followers of Charles de Gaulle, the self-appointed leader of the movement known as "Free France" and "France Forever."

Saint-Exupéry could not find himself in sympathy with any of these factions and determined not to entangle himself in their politics. His mission was one of persuasion—to give the American people a true vision of the plight of Europe and persuade the U.S. to attack Hitler as the universal enemy. Since his prestige was unsurpassed the "Super-patriots," as Antoine called them, were more than anxious to recruit his name, if nothing else, to endorse and give validity to their aims. First Saint-Exupéry was appointed, without his consent of course, as a *Councillor of State* of the Vichy Government, by none other than the Premier of France, Marshal Pétain. Antoine immediately renounced the appointment, which made the headlines of the January 31, 1941 edition of the *Times.* The Pétainists reaction was predictable—a man of his stature, if not for them, must, of necessity, be discredited. Among other things the Pétainists labeled Saint-Exupéry as a philo-Semite, an insult, they said, to the powers of the occupation (as philo means *beloved,* were it not for the derisive nature of the accusation, Tonio would have readily agreed to this charge—for he loved many of the descendents of Shem, Arab and Jew alike). Ridiculously, after he published *The Little Prince* he was further branded as a Royalist.

From the moment de Gaulle had fled from France to England in the wake of Battle of Dunkirk, the Gaullists had sought Saint-Exupéry's allegiance. His refusal to back General de Gaulle was believed to be the primary reason why Washington would not recognize de Gaulle as the leader, in exile, of the Nation of France. However, Antoine regarded Charles de Gaulle as fascist and a proponent of belligerent nationalism; who, if given the opportunity, would rise from a military general to dictator. The Gaullists agents in New York, finding that he still refused them, started a rumor that Saint-Exupéry was a secret agent for the Nazis. He was also ridiculed by the "Free France" as an anti-Semite—a ridiculous charge in light of his close friendships with Jean Israël and Léon Werth, men whom he praised in his writings with unimpeachable character. Antoine wrote Dr. Pélissier:

> I have no very high opinion of physical bravery (in light of Antoine's life, where he constantly risked his life in the service of others, this itself is a statement of tremendous humility); but life has taught me that there is a real courage in standing up to blame and condemnation. I know that I have been more courageous in not deviating from the road set by my conscience, in spite of two years of insults and defamation, than when [flying reconnaissance missions over] Mainz or Essen.[289]

Antoine's health began to fail him. He had not completely recovered from his crash in Guatemala and yet had exposed himself to the riggers of warfare and high altitude flight. He would, without warning break out in terrible fevers. His bones, that he had broken and re-broken, caused him considerable pain. Certainly the stress of his antagonists contributed to these problems. At times when his body temperature rose above 104? he became delirious. Medical experts recommended surgery believing that his 1923 crash had left splinters in his perineum, and commensurate infections precipitated his fevers. His recovery from the operation was difficult, accompanied by hemorrhaging and agonizing spasms. Yet he continued to write prolifically. In this era he wrote *Letter to a Hostage*, *The Little Prince*, additions to his work-in-progress *The Wisdom of the Sands*, and most importantly for this precarious time of war, *Flight to Arras*. In the first eight months of 1941 he labored on this book that was to have such a dramatic impact on America. *Arras* was scheduled to be published in November of 1941. But Saint-Exupéry continued to re-write and revise this work, delaying publication. At one point, when his publisher demanded a reason for his delays he explained that had to set the project aside for a brief time, as he had been *visited by an angel* who instructed him to return for a time to another project, presumably *Wisdom of the Sands.* Whether he said this in jest or in sincerity can only be answered by Saint-Exupéry himself. However, the effect of these delays proved critical. *Flight to Arras* sold out its first printing before any critic had the opportunity of reviewing it. Stacy Shiff stated:

> Conceived as a volume on the fall of France, *Flight to Arras* was a war book by the time it was published. It won raves on both counts. It was universally thought to dwarf all other accounts of the French defeat; writing in the *Atlantic* Edward Weeks declared, 'This narrative and Churchill's speeches stand as the best answer the democracies have yet found to *Mein Kampf . . . Arras* was judged by many to be the single most redeeming piece [on the French cause] . . . the volume greatly influenced public opinion.[290]

One wonders what effect *Flight to Arras* would have had on the American public had it been released in November as planned. But Saint-Exupéry, although sharing most of its text with friends in the summer of 1941, would not allow publication to proceed on schedule. Then came December 7th and Peal Harbor. When *Arras* was released shortly thereafter, America read it with newly opened eyes.

Flight to Arras was also an instant success in France where the Vichy censors initially permitted its publication, editing only one statement: "Hitler is an idiot." However soon it was banned and condemned by the Pétainists as well as by the Gaullists. The French Resistance found that the book spoke to the hearts of their people—as later Roger Stéphane affirmed: "In those days Saint-Exupéry restored a meaning to our lives." Two clandestine editions were published by the Resistance, first at Lyons and then at Lille. The copies were secretly passed from hand to hand throughout all of France.

His purpose in coming to America had been achieved. Now the aviator, turned ambassador, desired more than anything else to return to the skies of war. His hope, his promise, his prophecy became a reality when on November 8, 1942, American forces invaded Vichy administered North Africa. The Vichy army was routed and the United States gained control of the airbases as well as essential port cities. General de Gaulle was not only a non-participant in the historic accomplishment; he was not even informed of the operation until after maneuvers commenced—the General was infuriated! When Saint-Exupéry learned of the invasion, with no political aspirations and only the welfare of France in his heart, he was, by contrast, ecstatic and offered up his services to American military authorities immediately. A dear friend, wife to a fellow aviator, Anne Lindbergh stated that she felt Saint-Exupéry was offering himself a sacrifice—a sacrifice even to death. Yet Antoine wrote Consuelo that he was off to war for he could no longer endure separation from the distressed, the hungry, the persecuted. He wrote:

> I only know one way to make peace with my conscience . . . I am not leaving in order to die. I am leaving in order to suffer and thereby be united with those who are dear to me.[291]

Saint-Exupéry was mobilized near the end of the following March. Prior to his departure for North Africa a friend gave him *a gold identification bracelet engraved with his name.* In Algiers he was happily assigned, once again, to his beloved 2-33rd reconnaissance group and promoted to the rank of Major. General de Gaulle had, by this time, usurped authority in the French provisional government and wielded considerable influence with the commander of the U.S. Air Force. Yet despite de Gaulle's opposition and despite Saint-Exupéry's age (ten years advanced of the age limit) Antoine secured an assignment to fly the most advanced aircraft then in the American fleet: the Lockheed P-38 Lightning. Powered by twin turbocharged 1,427 horse power Allison in-line piston engines, the P-38 had a maximum ceiling of 44,000 feet and a maximum speed of 414 miles per hour. Mostly the

Lightning was deployed as a fighter, but Antoine's was modified to be a superb platform for intelligence cameras. After ten hours of flight instruction Saint-Exupéry flew his first mission. Once again he was flying over his adored France and once again he was thrilled with the exuberance of living as the German anti-aircraft guns vainly attempted to bring him down.

For *Life* magazine Saint-Exupéry wrote an essay entitled *Letter to an American*. In this letter he explained the joy of returning to active service and gave thanks to our country for entering the war. However it was not published when written, but was read by Charles Boyer, one month before the war was over, in April of 1945 during a radio broadcast. In part Saint Exupéry declared:

> I left the United States in 1943 in order to rejoin my fellow flyers of *Flight to Arras.* I traveled on board an American convoy. This convoy of thirty ships was carrying fifty thousand of your soldiers from the Unites States to North Africa. . . . This convoy conveyed to me the joy of a crusade.
>
> I shall always bear witness . . . to your fundamental qualities. American mothers did not give their sons for the pursuit of material aims . . . it was a spiritual crusade that led you into the war.
>
> During this crossing in convoy, mingling as I did with your soldiers, I was inevitably a witness to the war propaganda they were fed. Any propaganda is by definition amoral, and in order to achieve its aim it makes use of any sentiment, whether noble, vulgar, or base. If the American soldiers had been sent to war merely in order to protect American interests, their propaganda would have insisted heavily on your oil wells, your rubber plantations, your threatened commercial markets. But such subjects were hardly mentioned. If war propaganda stressed other things, it was because your soldiers wanted to hear about other things. And what were they told to justify the sacrifice of their lives in their own eyes? They were told of the hostages hanged in Poland, the hostages shot in France. They were told of a new form of slavery that threatened to stifle part of humanity. Propaganda spoke to them not about themselves, but

about others. They were made to feel solidarity with all humanity. The fifty thousand soldiers of this convoy were going to war, not for the citizens of the United States, but for man, for human respect, for man's freedom and greatness. . . .

This war is honorable; may their spiritual faith make peace [when it comes] as honorable.

I am happy among my French and American comrades. After my first missions in P-38 Lightnings they discovered my age. Forty-three years! What a scandal! . . . At forty-three years of age one doesn't fly a fast plane like a Lightning. The long white beards might get entangled with the controls and cause accidents. . . .

I rejoined Gavoille, of *Flight to Arras* . . . I also met up again with Hochedé . . . I rejoined all those of whom I had said that under the jackboot of the invader they were not defeated, but were merely seed buried in the silent earth. After the long winter of the armistice, the seed sprouted. My squadron once again blossomed in the daylight like a tree. I once again experience the joy of those high-altitude missions . . . One flies in that light monster of a Lightning, in which one has the impression not of moving in space but of being present simultaneously everywhere on a whole continent. One brings back photographs that are analyzed by stereoscope like growing organisms under a microscope. Those analyzing your photographic material do the work of a bacteriologist. They seek on the surface of the body (France) the traces of the virus that is destroying it. The enemy forts, depots, convoys show up under the lens like minuscule bacilli. One can die of them.

And the poignant meditation while flying over France, so near and yet so far away![292]

Unfortunately a landing accident in the P-38 temporarily grounded Saint-Exupéry as a pilot. However, during the time he was not permitted to fly as pilot-in-command he still served the war effort by performing the duties of a radio operator or bombardier. There is an interesting parallel in how he served in these responsibilities compared to the assignments he accepted as a pilot.

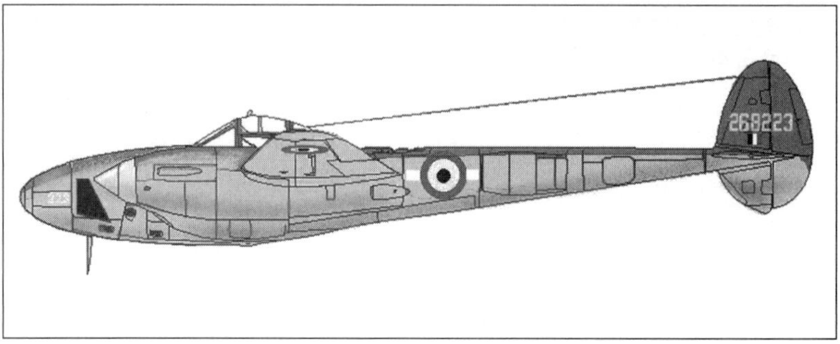

P-38 American built reconnaissance plane for the French 2-33rd Group

Saint-Exupéry possessed the skill to command the technologically advanced aircraft of each new generation of planes. Yet he never flew as a fighter pilot; instead he elected to fly reconnaissance missions. In like manner he did not participate in bomber flights that would take life—such as the bombing of towns or even factories. According to Richard Rumbold and Lady Margaret Stewart he "loathed the idea of dropping bombs on places where there were human beings"—hence he participated as a crewmember, working the radio or sighting bombs, on missions to take out bridges, rail lines or landing strips.

As the war progressed with ever accelerating horror and destruction, Saint-Exupéry felt, as he had described in *Flight to Arras*, a personal responsibility and an ever increasing sadness for the decline of culture and numinous values—in reverse correlation with the advance of technology. He abhorred this "civil war between civilized peoples." He wrote General Chambe:

> The Christian civilization of the West is responsible for the menace that hangs over it. What had it done in the last eighty years to bring its tenets alive in men's hearts? The only new ethic put forward was Guizot's "Prosper and amass riches" or the American idea of comfort. After 1918 what was there to exalt young men's hearts? My own generation played the stock exchange, discussed car models . . . made sordid business deals . . . with everyone looking

after his own interests. I wrote *Wind, Sand and Stars* in order to tell men passionately that they were all inhabitants of the same planet, passengers on the same ship.[293]

In another letter he wrote:

I am sad for my generation, empty as it is of all human content . . . a generation which thinks of . . . machines as forms of the spiritual life . . . Ah, General, there is only one problem, one alone in all the world: to awake in man a sense of spiritual values, of his spiritual significance.[294]

On the evening of April 23, 1944 Antoine dined with members of the 2-33rd in Pomigliano. His squadron was photographing eruptions of Mount Vesuvius. At his table was seated the eminent geologist, Professor Noetzlin, who was there, also, in connection with the volcano's upsurge. Saint-Exupéry had become skilled in many scientific fields, amazing his friends and experts alike. Here was a simple airman, who daily risked his life on the front lines of battle, yet who possessed an intellect that was suited for the universities, or the laboratories or the highest seats of governmental power. Noetzlin and Saint-Exupéry discussed both science and philosophy. Antoine related both to the war then raging. In speaking with the professor he displayed an incredible knowledge of molecular physics! Furthermore he explained that man was discovering the power to disintegrate matter—a frightful power for men to possess, one that could forever alter relationships within mankind and one that could dramatically impact our relationship with God. Stacy Shiff stated:

He stunned his colleagues with the news that an atomic bomb was in the making and with the prediction that it would be deployed before the end of the war.[295]

Antoine continued his work on *Citadelle* (the French title for

The Wisdom of the Sands) which occupied most of the time that could be considered his own.

Saint-Exupéry was restored to flying status, it is reported, by none other than Eisenhower himself. On one flight in June of 1944 he departed from Alghero on the island of Sardinia to shoot reconnaissance photographs over his homeland. While overflying France Antoine's port engine began to fail, requiring that he shut it down and feather the propeller. When he radioed his difficulties he was directed to fly to Borgo, Italy. His route took him down the Po Valley; an area concentrated with German bases. Of course flying much slower and lower on one engine he was more vulnerable to enemy fighters and anti-aircraft guns but it is assumed they did not fire at him thinking that no single allied aircraft would venture so near their strongholds. Nonetheless his cameras were rolling and produced astonishing sequential photographs that detailed the enemy's fortifications. Also on this flight he photographed the area around Agay, where his sister's home had been before being destroyed by the Germans. This, of course was impudent, as it was not an authorized recon target. Nonetheless, had he flown the mission without difficulty and as planned, he would have never captured on film the intelligence that would prove vital, and would posthumously earn him the Croix de Guerre avec Palme.

In July of 1944 the 2-33rd Group was relocated to Corsica. Since D-Day, June 6, 1944, Allied Forces had been in constant preparation for the impending invasion of Southern France. Reconnaissance was vital to the success of the forthcoming action—a tremendous contrast for Saint-Exupéry compared to his aerial intelligence work over France in May of 1940. Then he risked his life to obtain photographs that no matter how revealing and detailed could never reach a disintegrating high command, retreating in chaos and defeat. Now, four years later, his photographs were an integral part of the planned operations that would succeed! However, his missions were just as dangerous—and perhaps more so; for now he flew as a crew of one—without the aid of another pair of eyes in the person of the cameraman or without the defense of the tail gunner. Saint-Exupéry was well aware of the significance of his roll in the drama then unfolding and despite increasing pressures to moderate his personal efforts he insisted on flying every sortie he could gets his hands on. He bargained with other pilots, argued with his superiors, determined to remain in the thick of the war. He would contend that to others, "one mission more or less makes no difference." But to himself, aging as he was and who had been so long from the front, each mission was imperative.

Much has been written regarding Antoine's final flight. Certainly Saint-Exupéry, at times, felt it was unlikely that he would survive the war. Accordingly he made various arrangements with his friends to see to his affairs should he fail to return from a mission. For a man who thought deeply, as did he, this would altogether be the natural thing to do. Some have suggested, however, that his despair with the war and the calumny he continued to suffer at the hands of the Gaullists might have led him to seek death as a relief from life. This author finds it hard to believe that anyone who has read his writings and understands, in the least degree, his philosophy of life could accept such a notion. Saint-Exupéry believed in *endurance.* He believed in selflessness. Never did he accept a mission that would provide an easy way out. To put ones' self in harm's way with the intent of needlessly forfeiting life is cravenly and completely beneath a man of honor. Saint-Exupéry believed in responsibility and accountability. He believed, and he proved his belief with his actions, that duty, honor, integrity and sacrifice were more important than personal considerations. It is true that he put his life on the line, again and again, proving his *willingness* to make the ultimate sacrifice on the altar of the fundamental cause for which wars are fought. But this he had done since his earliest days in aviation and was nothing new. What is more, he made his intentions clear, in writing, to his good friend Georges Pélissier. Shortly before his flight to eternity, in mid July, he wrote saying:

> I've chosen the most wearing profession, and *as one must always carry things through, I won't give up.* I hope this sinister war will be over before I've meted away completely, like a candle burning in oxygen. I have other work to do later on.[296]

Also, there has been much speculation regarding how and where Saint-Exupéry's last flight ended. This author agrees with the editor of *Wartime Writings* who states that the most credible reports of his death are the corroborated narratives of Claude-Alain Jaeger, Leopold Böhm and Robert Heichele. In the years 1998 and 2000 additional evidence was discovered that further validates these accounts.

On July 30, 1944 Saint-Exupéry dined at a restaurant in Miomo where he again captivated friends with his talent for card tricks. He left alone before midnight. On the morning of July 31 he boarded P-38 Number 223, and according to the interrogation report, departed at precisely 8:45 a.m. for Annecy. It was a beautiful day, clear and warm. In less than a half hour radar showed his plane crossing the coast into Southern France.

Also on July 31, 1944 German Flying Officer, Robert Heichele, departed Orange, France, in his Messerschmitt, at 11:02 a.m.; assigned to observe enemy aircraft between Marseilles and Menton. He was accompanied by another flyer named Högel. Near the coast Heichele encountered a P-38 Lightning, one thousand feet above him, descending swiftly. It is probable that Saint-Exupéry's oxygen system had again failed, as it had on a recent mission. On that occurrence he had nearly passed out. In such a situation the only relief is to make an emergency descent to lower altitude. Below him, Heichele's camouflaged aircraft was no doubt unseen by Antoine, whose mental alacrity would still be in question. Heichele, seeing the P-38 dropping directly towards him thought he was under attack by the formidable Lightning and quickly maneuvered his plane in a "spiraling ascent" to gain the advantage. It was an easy advantage as his opponent was a reconnaissance pilot who had no intention or capability of engaging in a dog-fight. Amazingly reminiscent of the indelible description he wrote in *Flight to Arras* Saint-Exupéry may not have even been aware that "already [he was] the prisoner of the retina of the hawk . . . continuing to pilot . . . to scan the earth . . . already flung outside the dimension of time because of a tiny black dot on the retina of a man." Heichele closed the distance between them to approximately 150 meters, well within firing range. He let go with his first burst of gunfire then closed within 60 meters and fired again. A trail of smoke extended from the wounded P-38.[297]

> The fighter comes down on me like lightning. Having spotted me . . . he takes his time. He weaves, he orients himself, takes careful aim. I know nothing of this. I am the mouse lying in the shadow of the bird of prey. The mouse fancies that it is alive. It goes on frisking in the wheat. At the very instant when I first learn of its existence, the fighter, having spat forth its venom like a cobra, is already neutral and inaccessible, swaying to and fro overhead. Thus the cobra sways, sends forth its lightning, and resumes its rhythmical swaying.
>
> The fighter has become a mere impartial onlooker when, from the severed carotid in my neck, the first jets of blood spurt forth. When from the hood of my *starboard* engine the hesitant leak of the first tongue of flame rises out of the furnace fire. And the cobra has returned to its folds when the venom strikes the heart and the first muscle of my face twitches. The fighter group does not kill. It sows death. Death sprouts after it has passed.[298]

In the early days of his aviation career Antoine had lost power over an audience at an air show and was going down fast. He could have kept control by landing amidst the bystanders, with little damage to his plane and no injury to himself. But he did not. He extended his flight beyond the ragged edge of a stall, clearing the crowd—but in doing so, he lost control of his aircraft and tumbled to earth—preferring death over the possibility of harming others. Now nearing the densely populated city of Marseille he would reenact the same drama. To bail out would mean relinquishing control of his P-38 which would then plunge headlong into his beloved country, exploding on impact, killing many. No—he still had power. Despite whatever torture he most certainly at that moment faced—smoke pouring from his plane, flames quickly traversing the close confines of his cockpit, licking flesh from his agonized body, blood flowing from the bullet wounds—no, despite all that he suffered he would not abandon his Lightning to wreak havoc in Marseille. Heichele followed at a distance while Saint-Exupéry piloted his dying plane and body across the coast line and out to sea. He was losing altitude quickly and was either too low to attempt to bail or, by that time, was too badly injured. Flight Officer Heichele *saw flames shoot out from Tonio's "starboard engine.* The right wing dipped, plowing into the sea. [His] plane somersaulted several times and sank." Heichele reported that the P-38 disappeared from his sight at 12:05 p.m.

Before noon, in the village of Biot, Claude-Alain Jaeger saw a "completely silver plane with a double fuselage . . . flying at great speed toward the sea."[299] The plane was close enough that he clearly saw the "French tricolor insignia." Others in Biot saw the P-38 including M. Marcel Carmatte and Roger Léone, pursued by two German aircraft. Nearby a wounded officer, German Major Leopold Böhm, lay convalescing on a veranda at a villa in Tête de Chien. As there was a great deal of aerial action in the skies overhead, Böhm kept field glasses on hand, ready at the first drone of an aircraft engine. Suddenly Böhm saw "three dots appear on the horizon—three planes flying toward Monte Carlo . . . skimming above the sea. . . . The two pursuers forced the first one to crash-land on the waves, then they pulled out and disappeared."[300]

Back at the base, at 1:00 p.m. Gavoille asked the American

liaison officer, Vernon Robison if he would attempt to contact Saint-Exupéry by radio. The airwaves were silent as the grave. The scene that followed could well have been taken from *Night Flight*:

> The radio station looked like a laboratory with its nickel and its copper, manometers and sheaves of wires. The operators . . . touched their instruments, exploring the magnetic sky, dowsers in quest of hidden gold.
>
> No answer.
>
> The seconds flowed away, like ebbing blood. [Was he] still in flight? Each second killed a hope. The stream of time was wearing life away. As for twenty centuries it beats against a temple, seeping through the granite, and spreads the fane in ruin, so centuries of wear and tear were thronging in each second, menacing . . . Silence was gaining ground. Heavy and heavier silence . . . *like a heavy sea.*[301]

When asked back in the 1930s by a *Marianne* reporter, having survived so many accidents that could have proved fatal, what type of death he would "prefer," Saint-Exupéry said decisively that he would elect to die by water. He explained that it didn't feel like death, but was more like "falling asleep and beginning to dream." Who knows how badly he was burned while in flames, pursued by his enemies? We can, however, imagine how cool the Mediterranean waters felt as their waves embraced him and gently eased him into eternal sleep.

> Man does not die. Man imagines that it is death he fears; but what he fears is the unforeseen, the explosion. . . .There is no death when you meet death. *When the body sinks* into death, the essence of man is revealed.[302]

Years later, Jean-Marc Matalon of the Associated Press, reported from Marseille that on September 26, 1998 a fisherman, named Jean-Claude Bianco "netted" a bracelet inscribed with the names of Antoine de Saint-Exupéry, Consuelo and his publishers. Bianco was reported as saying: "I told myself, You're dreaming you're dreaming. The sea is vast and the bracelet was so small." On May 27, 2000 ABC News reported that diver Luc Vanrell had "found and photographed" the remains of Saint-Exupéry's P-38 in the "immediate vicinity" where Bianco had discovered Antoine's bracelet. Then on April 7, 2004 the New York Times, CNN, USA Today, and scores of other major news agencies reported that Vanrell had finally obtained permission from France's Culture Ministry to have pieces of the wreckage "brought up for analysis." "One of them bore a manufacturer's number, 2734, that researchers finally confirmed corresponded to the military number given to Saint-Exupéry's plane – 42-68223." Vanrell said the crash sight covers a large area—three thousand three hundred feet long by thirteen hundred feet wide.

On June 29, 1900 Antoine de Saint-Exupéry began his pilgrimage upon this earth. As a traveler he had just embarked from our Father's home in heaven, literally his son. As such, Antoine was born a nobleman, possessing a heritage far greater than his earthly aristocracy, for he was a prince, a son of the King of Heaven. As he left our Father's presence he was given a life's mission to perform. He was given rudimentary gifts that he was expected to develop and magnify through hard work and great adversity. Among these heavenly gifts were the abilities of thinking and feeling deeply, the desire to be an adventurer, a pilot, an ambassador of goodwill and industry; the recognition that he was a "wayfarer" on this planet filled not with strangers, but with his own kindred relations, literally brothers and sisters of the same *family*—and most importantly he was given the crowning gift to express in his writings the spiritual values of *our* pilgrimage and its *purpose*. Antoine said these were truths that must be *taught*, and his calling was to be one of the great teachers of the last century.

He was to do all in his power to awaken in Man the memory of Man's true origin—that all mankind were as he, elite members of the aristocracy of Heaven, sons and daughters of the same Heavenly Father.

Antoine's purpose was to fight, not so much against the political tyrants, but against the *doctrinal* tyrants who proclaimed that man is an animal. These dictators, whom Tonio fought to his last breath, falsely dictated (and enforced their edicts with the sword!) that Man is *not* related to a Superior being, a Superior Being who created all things. These despots abhorred the truth; for the truth is the Creator *is* a Superior Man who places His own *offspring* amidst his creation, to prove them, try them, and desires to exalt the obedient to an eternal life, as C. S. Lewis said, "qualitatively like His own." Saint-Exupéry's mission was to wage war against secularism and doctrines of devils, at a time in our history when Hell itself waged war throughout the entire world—when millions of our brothers and sisters were killed in battle—and fiendishly worse, were humiliated, molested, incarcerated, enslaved, and annihilated.

Saint-Exupéry completed his earthly pilgrimage and was released from battle on July 31, 1944. His life did not end as he sank beneath the waves of the Mediterranean. Antoine, like all of us, is immortal. "Man does not die," he said, "When the body sinks into death, the essence of man is revealed."[303] Antoine's spirit, his intelligence, at the moment of death, separated from his physical body, but *continued* alive. Once again, he could fly, at the speed of thought, without the artifice of wings. No doubt he soon reported back to his Superior, that he had successfully completed his mortal mission and eagerly awaited his next assignment, where next he would *fly*. He had proven himself a man and had fought valiantly for the liberty that provides the opportunity for Man's ascension—the great cause and purpose of Life.

One of his last letters was written to his mother.

My dearest Mama,

I would like so much to reassure you about me and to be sure that my letter reaches you. I'm well, very well. But I'm sad not to have seen you for so long and I'm worried about you, my darling Mama.[304]

Tonio was well. His body, although still young in years, was worn and exhausted. He was so stiff and racked with pain that it took him forty-five minutes, with the help of an aid, just to dress for flight. But Tonio knew that *he* was well, very well. His mind was not resigned to any form of retirement, which was his way of saying, resigned to uselessness. He had "other work to do."[305] He may have felt some harbinger of his death, but continued literally and figuratively to fly at full speed. To the last, his concern was not for his suffering, but for others, and in particular for his mother. Madame Marie de Saint-Exupéry outlived her son by many years, dying at the age of ninety-seven.

Bibliography – Book 3

Primary Sources

Rumbold, Richard: *The Winged Life—A Portrait of Antoine de Saint-Exupéry* (George Weidenfeld & Nicolson, London)

Schiff, Stacy: *Saint-Exupéry* (Alfred A. Knopf, Inc., New York)

de Saint-Exupéry, Antoine: *Airman's Odyssey*—a Trilogy Comprising *Wind, Sand and Stars, Night Flight, and Flight to Arras* (Harcourt Brace Jovanovich, New York)

de Saint-Exupéry, Antoine: *The Wisdom of the Sands*—Translated by Stuart Gilbert from the French *Citadelle* (Harcourt, Brace and Company, New York)

de Saint-Exupéry, Antoine: *Letter to a Hostage* as found in *New Writing and Daylight* (The Hogarth Press, London)

de Saint-Exupéry, Antoine: *Wartime Writings*—Translated by Norah Purcell (Harcourt Brace Jovanovich, New York)

The Columbia World of Quotations

The Scriptures

The Avalon Project at Yale Law School—World War II Documents. (New Haven, Connecticut)

CHAPTER 29

EPILOGUE

Everything that is great in life is the product of slow growth; the newer, and greater, and higher, and nobler the work, the slower is the growth, the surer is its lasting success. Mushrooms attain their full power in a night; oaks require decades. A fad lives its life in a few weeks; a philosophy lives through generations and centuries. If you are sure you are right, do not let the voice of the world, or of friends, or of family swerve you for a moment from your purpose. Accept slow growth if it must be slow, and know the results must come, as you would accept the long, lonely hours of the night,—with absolute assurance that the heavy-leaded moments must bring the morning. [306]

—WILLIAM GEORGE JORDAN

IT WAS MID-WINTER IN THE ANDES. Always the Andean great walls are massive barriers to the traveler, with towering peaks that rise twenty-two thousand feet. In this region when autumn dies it is always with violence and the extreme elevations are left to the elements alone. The malignant sky literally heaves snow, encrusting the vertical landscape. Ominous gale force winds sculpt phantasms of ice, solid apparitions, ever changing, shrouded in bitter mists—Death Reapers. Not even for a king's ransom will smugglers traverse the Andes when its lifeless slopes are gripped by unimaginable cold; for they say, "The Andes never give up a man in winter."

For five days Antoine de Saint-Exupéry had scoured these great mountains in his aircraft, probing where he could in the voids between clouds and cliffs. There was really no hope. Chilean officials had told him to cease his frantic search for, they said, only *one* night was sufficient to transform a man into a still hoary statue and it had now been *seven.* Somewhere in the frigid white wasteland below was Henri Guillaumet. Guillaumet was not only considered the best pilot on the Aéropostale line, but he was Tonio's mentor and dear friend. As a fledgling Latécoère pilot Saint-Exupéry had flown his first route familiarization flights between Toulouse and Alicante with this veteran aviator. Prior to Tonio's first flight on this same route as pilot-in-command, Guillaumet spent hours briefing him. Not even Daurat, commander of the line, was capable of instilling such confidence as this man who now had crashed in the eternal Andean chain. Without success, Antoine maneuvered his plane between colossal columns of granite, four miles in height, and returned to the landing field near Mendoza.

Seven days earlier fifteen feet of snow had fallen from a single storm. Through a narrow rift of blue sky, at twenty thousand feet, Henri Guillaumet flew his aircraft, bound for Argentina. The winter tempest was jealous that anything should escape its wrath. A downdraft seized Guillaumet and with far greater power than his aircraft could counter, pulled him violently earthward into vortices of wind shear that far exceeded his control capabilities. His aircraft tumbled over and over, like an ocean ship caught in the crest of a tsunami. So great was the turbulence that his shoulder harnesses cut into his torso. Temperatures inside the cabin plunged as the great clouds swallowed him whole, glazing over his artificial horizon with instant frost. Working flight controls was futile, and with no indication of aircraft attitude, Guillaumet released control to the wind's fury and gripped his seat for "fear of being flung out" of his airplane. In horrific gyrations he plunged eight thousand feet.

At ten thousand feet above sea level and only a few hundred feet above the ground, Guillaumet fell free beneath the overcast; his plane was miraculously intact. With visual reference restored he righted his aircraft. Amazingly, he also recognized his position—in the bottom of a huge volcanic funnel! Below him was Lake Laguna Diamante, flanking him were the mammoth walls of the volcano Maipu. Whirling snows obscured what little sky remained. Desperately Guillaumet held to a single point of reference—the frozen lake below. For two hours he circled, hoping the storm would ease, opening an escape route. To climb back into the overcast would be suicide; it would be impossible to navigate out of the throat of Maipu into which he had fallen. With fuel reserves depleted Guillaumet was forced to crash land in the deep snow fields. He no sooner touched down than his aircraft went over on its nose. Crawling from the broken ship, he tried to stand erect and stretch his aching muscles but the howling wind blew him down. Beneath his cockpit Guillaumet dug a snow cave and placing mail sacks around for additional insulation, waited out the storm. After two days and two nights the skies cleared.

Without the benefit of an ice-axe, snow shoes, ice cleats, ropes, or tent, Guillaumet began hiking out of the Maipu funnel. The outside air temperature was twenty degrees below zero. "With the obstinacy of an ant" he made his way around deep abysses, and in agony crawled with bleeding hands up walls fifteen thousand feet high. He could take no rest—for to sleep but a moment would be to slumber forever. After two days of excruciating walking, climbing, descending, falling, only one pervasive thought occupied Guillaumet's mind—sleep. Never had he experienced such temptation! His instinct for self-preservation was gone. Oh, just to close his eyes and slip into the warmth of sleep. And why stay awake? Why prolong inevitable death? Then a thought pushed away the horrible allurement. The image of his wife came into his mind. "If my wife still believes I am alive, she must believe that I am on my feet." With that he trudged on.

Another night and another day; passion was gone; hope was gone—yet Guillaumet continued, one unbearable step at a time. Then he slipped and fell hard, coming to rest face down in the snow. It was only one of many such blows he had endured, but this time he admitted to himself that he had done the very best he could and simply could not take any more. Of this moment Saint-Exupéry wrote:

> So little was needed to blot out that world of crags and ice and snow. Let drop those miraculous eyelids and there was an end of blows, of stumbling falls, of torn muscles and burning ice, of that burden of life [Guillaumet was] dragging along like a worn-out ox . . . Already [he was] beginning to taste the relief of this snow that had now become an insidious poison . . . Life crept out of [his] extremities and fled to collect round [his] heart . . . [307]

Slowly unconsciousness anesthetized Guillaumet's emaciated, sunburned, frost-blackened body. Delusional happiness was the only remaining emotion of the small portion of his mind that still flickered with life. Now he could see himself advancing with great "dream-strides" down from the cold Andes to the warm plains below. He was at rest. All was well.

Then a thought pushed its unwelcome way into his thinking. Again it was of his wife. He reassured himself that she would collect his life insurance. Something answered—yes, in four years time! He then envisioned his body being washed with the spring runoff into a deep crevasse where it never could be found. The words penetrated his mind, "When a man vanishes, his legal death is postponed for four years." He saw a rock fifty yards from where he lay. If only he could make it to that rock, perhaps he could position himself firmly against it where searchers would find his remains the next summer. Guillaumet arose and staggered one step at time. By the time he reached the rock he had forgotten its purpose. In fact he had lost his memory. He could think of nothing but the one step he was about to take. He said:

> What saves a man is to take a step. Then another step. It is always the same step, but you have to take it.[308]

From the moment Guillaumet crashed it was seven days and six nights, of which he hiked five days and four nights, enduring indescribable privation, when finally he staggered into the village of San Rafael! It was inconceivable that any living creature could survive such a trek, in sub-zero cold, without equipment, without so much as a trail marked in the trackless mountains—yet Guillaumet was alive! When Saint-Exupéry landed at Mendoza he received the joyous news. Less than one hour later Tonio landed his plane on a road not far from San Rafael, there a car had driven Guillaumet to meet him. Both men wept as they embraced—Antoine was astonished at the miracle he held in his arms. Gently he assisted the bruised and frost-bitten man aboard and flew him safely to Mendoza. Guillaumet would live for many more years until at last, flying transport in WWII, he gave his life in battle.

How can manhood be measured? Rickenbacker, Hall and Saint-Exupéry, like Guillaumet, endured extreme adversity—never giving way to self-abandonment. All of these men were of the fiber of hardwood. Rickenbacker and Saint-Exupéry lost their fathers at an early age. Yet in their formative years, with the help of loving mothers, they developed slow-growth strength of character. Hall scorned the mediocre opportunities of early ease and comfort of minding an established business. Instead Jimmy enlisted in a war that his own country had not yet recognized. In the trenches of France his virtues matured into tough oak, yet his heart was ever kind, and never did Hall allow the bitterness of war to cumber his soul.

Man-making is indelibly intertwined with responsibility. Ideally a boy first learns this lesson at home, as did Eddie Rickenbacker. But regardless of background, regardless of circumstance, one commences his journey in becoming a man when he begins to comprehend responsibility—first for self, then for ever increasing *others*. Every step of the journey to manhood will be met with opposition. It is man's responsibility to endure every opposing force that is placed in his path. Again William George Jordan wrote:

> [One] who is not self-reliant is weak, hesitating and doubting in all he does. He fears to take a decisive step, because he dreads failure . . . In his cowardice and his conceit he sees all his non-success due to others. He is "not appreciated," "not recognized," he is "kept down." He feels that in some subtle way "society is conspiring against him." He grows almost vain as he thinks that no one has had such poverty, such sorrow, such affliction, such failure as have come to him.
>
> The man who is self-reliant seeks ever to discover and conquer the weakness within him that keeps him from the attainment of what he holds dearest; he seeks within himself the power to battle against all outside influences. He realized that all the greatest men in history, in every phase of human effort, have been those who have had to fight against the odds of sickness, suffering, sorrow. To him, defeat is no more than passing through a tunnel is to a traveler—he knows he must emerge again into the sunlight . . . This self-reliance is not the self-sufficiency of conceit. It is daring to stand alone. Be an oak, not a vine.[309]

A true man builds his life on that which is greater than himself. A man is a maker and keeper of righteous covenants, regarding self, family, country and God. Never will he take an oath in darkness, but always in light. At times opposition can be met with reason and words. However, there are times when evil is so threatening that a man must bodily fight and be willing to sacrifice his own blood to keep the covenants he has made to posterity, his nation and to his Creator. The cost of Liberty is high, for in any conflict there is great danger. However, the real menace is never to the body, but to the soul. In the thick and tumult of combat a man can retain his manhood only if he retains sight of the Lodestar of Life. If a warrior loses his spiritual bearings in the confusion of hostilities, he will be destroyed.

Manhood is fatherhood. To every thing there is a season. Rickenbacker and Hall strove mightily for peace, not war. Peace to establish a profession, and security to raise a family. Both men valued heritage, and both established a family legacy between the wars. Saint-Exupéry was too young to fight in WWI, yet lost his life in the second global conflict. Like Antoine, many men are taken in battle before they are blessed with sons and daughters. The only solace to this tragedy is the truth that man is not a mortal being only, but is eternal in nature.

Like Guillaumet's Andean ordeal, Rickenbacker languished in a life raft, Saint-Exupéry suffered in the desert sun, and Hall endured captivity at Schloss Trausnitz as a prisoner of war. Through endurance they conquered the privations into which they were cast, not through self-sufficiency, but through self-reliance—enabled by faith in a power infinitely greater than their own strength.

A man despises self-limitations. He desires ever increasing freedom, but in his wisdom a man knows that *freedom of flight* is attained by governing law, not by foolish rebellion against nature. His first efforts may be no more than attempting to maneuver a clipped wing Blériot. However, with patience and determination the groundling may become a captain of the skies. When a man takes flight in any noble profession, having acquired the skills to push back his former claustrophobic horizons, he has learned to love learning. Ever he may climb, beyond any atmosphere into the very depths of space. No man flies, as did Hall, Rickenbacker and Saint-Exupéry unless they have acquired a passion for knowledge and an understanding that intelligence is never fixed, but is as expandable as the heavens.

No man is an accident of the cosmos. No man is independent of other men. Man is a traveler among his brethren, not a predator among other animals. A man does not believe in the survival of the fittest—rather he believes in the condescension of the Powerful to aid and nourish the weak. When man does this he most emulates his Creator. Man did not spring into existence at birth, nor will he suffer annihilation with death. Although his origins are cloaked in the mystery of the veil and his eternal destiny shrouded by the darkness of death, man is eternal. He possesses a heritage that makes the linage of earthly kings pale in comparison, for man is a son of God. Recognizing the fatherhood of God, man welcomes all men, regardless of race, as his brothers. It is true that envy and malice exist in some families, but not in families of love. True brotherhood eclipses jealousy, unkindness, hate, and retribution with understanding, tolerance, affection and goodness. A stronger brother will, without regret or thought of compensation, gladly assist his less able siblings, as did Rickenbacker to his family, as did Hall to his brothers and sisters in Polynesia.

A man finds security in faith—faith in himself, faith in his comrades, his family, his nation and his God. He does not suffer from the illusion of the security offered by material things. This understanding is the key to taking appropriate *risk*. A true man will risk his gold, he may even risk his life, but never will he risk his integrity. Faith enables a man to build and rebuild. Faith allows a man to trust. Faith allows a man to believe in the unseen. Faith always precedes accomplishment.

Wisdom is often used as a synonym for knowledge. It is not. A physician may know that smoking tobacco increases the risk of heart and lung disease, and yet lack the wisdom to refrain from smoking. Men of knowledge should ever seek to be wise.

Especially in our youth we desire to emulate the characteristics we admire in others. However, nature's principle of slow growth often frustrates these desires, particularly as we age. True this frustration can stifle the very young, but only if they are left without guidance. For example, a child may hear a great pianist perform and dream of becoming himself a virtuoso. When he sits down at the keyboard and attempts to emulate what he has heard he discovers it is *then* impossible. However, with opportunity, instruction, motivation, practice, continued desire and praise, *over time* the skill is acquired. The older a person is when this process is begun, the less likely it is that he will stick with the process and realize the goal. Why? Some may argue the young have more disposable time. Rather, the truth is the young have great faith in their ability to learn or *change,* and are more apt to accept the reality of slow growth. Certainly the young do possess greater flexibility than the old. However, age often brings cynicism, which is always a choice rather than a prerequisite. This is particularly true when it comes to acquiring the *skills* of high character. We know we must study, practice, and sacrifice a great deal of our time if we are to learn to play an instrument well, knowing that of course we will blunder and make errors as we learn. Yet if the acquisition of a virtue frustrates us, we often abandon the effort with a shrug and an excuse such as: "That's just the way I am." Character development is far more demanding than the lesser skills of music and art. There are no short cuts in learning self-mastery. These skills are always the product of slow growth.

This does not mean one cannot decide immediately upon a course of action. It does mean we understand that to emulate a quality is to practice it, again and again, until it is part of us. Benjamin Franklin stated that we may acquire virtues by no other way. In his own efforts to attain character traits of manhood Franklin found that *habit overpowered reason.* He therefore concluded that he must *practice* virtue until it became habitual. He then made a list of thirteen qualities of manhood and wrote them in his journal. Franklin realized that to attempt mastery over all these virtues simultaneously would be unrealistic and discouraging. Therefore he determined to focus on one virtue each week, beginning the list anew after thirteen weeks. In this manner he *exercised* each virtue and daily examined his progress. After a long period of time, and many thirteen week rotations, he found to his joy that twelve of the virtues on the list had become a part of his character.

To recognize great qualities is not enough. Like Franklin, Rickenbacker set down in writing the virtues he wanted to maintain and attain. Eddie not only practiced aerial maneuvers, he practiced, with even greater diligence, the virtues that make a great son, a great brother, a great leader, a great father—and he imbued them into every fiber of his being. These skills were at his disposal when the crises of life came upon him. Young men, you too can acquire the skills to serve and save others!

What greater demonstration of moral authority can be found than the true life story of the *seven who came through*? For twenty-four days, in three tiny life rafts, on a vast and dangerous sea, with no weapons to enforce his will, no stores of supplies to coerce behavior, no superior rank to command his brothers, yet using all the skills of manhood that were his, Eddie Rickenbacker saved the lives of seven of his friends and completed a vital mission. Opposing the elements took great skill and courage, but opposing the weaknesses of his fellow castaways and motivating these sufferers to faith and incredible *endurance* was a far superior achievement.

How can manhood be measured? The answer is found in this single word: *Endurance*. A pilot may admirably perform all the duties of an arduous flight enroute, but if he loses control at the *end* of flight, no matter how weary he may have become, he cannot be judged a success. Of all the ignominious epitaphs recorded at craters of crash sites is the two word inscription: "pilot error." British Aviator, Captain A. G. Lamplugh said: "To an even greater degree than the sea, Aviation is terribly unforgiving of any carelessness, incapacity or neglect." At the fatal scene of an aircraft accident you will never hear anyone praise the dead pilot for his excellent takeoff. Yet to captain your soul's journey is infinitely more critical than commanding a flight deck and how you finish *life* is all important. Therefore, upon the ruler of endurance all the virtues of manhood are gauged. If in dire circumstances one abandons his responsibilities, or renounces his covenants, compromises his morals, betrays his liberty, succumbs to adversity or forsakes his faith, manhood is lost; the end ruin overwhelms the record of his goodness. However, when a man holds his course, regardless of misfortune, temptation or peril and *endures* to the end of life, as did Rickenbacker, Hall and Saint-Exupéry that man *is* a man.

Young men, recognize your commission from the Almighty. You are *sent* to earth with tremendous purpose. There are many aspects to your mission, many things you are to master—the greatest of these is to master self. All males begin the journey to manhood weak and faulted. However, remember the lessons taught by Rickenbacker, Hall and Saint-Exupéry—remember that greatness is a matter of *becoming*. Rise above injury, sin, error and ignorance. Leave the dirt and grime of this world far below. Mount as with wings of eagles and ride the high places. Achieve what you were sent here to achieve. Remember that *nothing flies as fast as time*. When you end the days of your pilgrimage it will seem to you as if you only began a few hours before—like a pilot who leaves one continent and spanning oceans, lands in a far country the same morning of his departure. As Captain of your own voyage, leave fear to the groundlings, relish the storms through which you must navigate, overcome your adversaries (though it be in fierce combat), appreciate the immense beauty of flight, safeguard those entrusted to your care, and when you arrive at your final destination you will find it glorious beyond imagination. Never have you been to *the far land* to which you fly on this marvelous expedition of life. It is a singular crossing, never to be repeated. Everything you hold dear is at risk. The stakes of flight are always high. Determine then, to be a *MAN!*

APPENDIX

WISDOM

Doth not wisdom cry? and understanding put forth her voice? Unto you, O men, I call; and my voice [is] to the sons of man. Receive my instruction, and not silver; and knowledge rather than choice gold. I love them that love me; and those that seek me early shall find me.

The LORD possessed me in the beginning of his way, before his works of old. I was set up from everlasting, from the beginning, or ever the earth was. When [there were] no depths, I was brought forth; when [there were] no fountains abounding with water. Before the mountains were settled, before the hills was I brought forth: While as yet he had not made the earth, nor the fields, nor the highest part of the dust of the world. When he prepared the heavens, I [was] there: when he set a compass upon the face of the depth: When he established the clouds above: when he strengthened the fountains of the deep: When he gave to the sea his decree, that the waters should not pass his commandment: when he appointed the foundations of the earth: Then I was by him, [as] one brought up [with him]: and I was daily [his] delight, rejoicing always before him;

Rejoicing in the habitable part of his earth; and my delights [were] with the sons of men.

—PROVERBS 8

OF ALL SAINT-EXUPÉRY'S WORKS, *The Little Prince* is the most widely known. It has been translated into over seventy languages and still sells more than four hundred thousand copies annually. Apparently the least read of his writings is his book *The Wisdom of the Sands.* Perhaps the reason for this is that it is an unfinished work and was not published until after his death. In fact, Antoine had no intention of publishing this book during his lifetime; for it was to be an ever expanding compilation of the wisdom he acquired as he lived. He referred to it as his poem and his *oeuvre posthume*, or his posthumous masterpiece. This represents the purest of motives for he could not personally *profit* monetarily from *Wisdom of the Sands.* It is an extraordinary book, replete with second meanings; an inspired weapon, forged in the mind of a staunch defender of spiritual values, a sword of truth to be wielded in the war for the minds of men. Although it certainly is *not* scripture, it has been compared to biblical writings. All truth comes from the same source—from God. His revealed word is holy writ, scribed by His authorized prophets and apostles. Yet others are commissioned by our Father to spend their lives composing marvelous works, designed to ennoble, uplift and exalt mankind. It is in this latter category we would place *Wisdom of the Sands.* Little wonder that humanistic critics have denigrated the work, labeling it "archaic;" calling it Saint-Exupéry's "least lucid" writing. The battle against truth is a continual one. Our enemies, who would prevent the ascension of Man, are sophists and pseudo-intellectuals. They would label all spiritual truth as foolishness, subject to ridicule.

The other works of Antoine quoted in this book are still in print, while *Wisdom of the Sands* has long been out of print and is difficult to obtain. In the final years of his life, Saint-Exupéry labored on this manuscript whenever time allowed; in France before traveling to the States, in New York while simultaneously composing *Flight to Arras*, later in North Africa, Sardinia and Italy. Its pages were always in his protective custody—wherever he went. Before his death, he left instructions for his manuscript to be delivered safely to Pélissier. However, the fundamental reason for including quotations from *Wisdom of the Sands* in the conclusion of this biography is not because they are scarce, but because they contribute powerfully to the theme of Saint-Exupéry's life mission—the making of Man.

Stuart Gilbert, credited primarily with its English Translation, states:

> [*The Wisdom of the Sands*] abounds in vivid pictures of desert life, forays and sandstorms, mirage-born madness, beleaguered oases and cities, caravans going through perilous ways to safety or disaster. The narrator, ruler of a great empire in the desert, is no mere lay figure . . . but a poignantly human personality. . . . Aware that a change is coming over the world he governs, that essential values are being lost . . . he seeks to fix his subject's gaze on that "divine knot binding things together" which alone bestows meaning . . . he bids them, too, to be givers . . . not "sedentaries" placidly enjoying a hoard they have amassed.
>
> It may be that the near-biblical tone and language of Saint-Exupéry's message to the world of today, whose divided aims, animosities, and incoherences must dismay all who have not fallen back on a barren fatalism, will take aback some readers, . . . Yet it is but the immemorial language of a voice crying in the wilderness, the voice of a man of action, no mere Utopian dreamer, a poet who faced death not once but often, and a great lover of his kind whose constant aim was to rebuild man . . . [310]

Occidental authors tend to write in one plane, they direct the reader to think horizontally. Oriental writers would have readers awaken their mental and spiritual facilities to not only perceive what is ahead, behind or about them—but what is above and below them; they would have us search out the truths, that for the present, are unseen. Inspired writings are rich in layers. First there is the obvious—that which is plainly spoken, perhaps the facts of the story line. Subsequent layers of truth may be perceived by the reader only as he spiritually matures and learns to see beyond the obvious. Also, as C. S. Lewis observed, the writer himself may surpass his original intent and exceed his own understanding—for second meanings may be embedded in his text by heaven's inspiration. If the author leaves no added explanation it is left to the reader to discern whether the truths he sees in these second meanings are what the author intended for him to discover, as in allegory, or not. In the end it makes little difference, if the truths so gleaned benefit our understanding.

In *Wisdom of the Sands* the Prince states:

> There came a fool to me and said: "Do but free us from your constraints, and then we shall wax great." But I knew what my people stood to lose thereby. . . . So I resolved to enrich them, despite their unwillingness. For they were now proposing to me to lay low the walls of my father's palace, wherein every footstep had a meaning, so that they might roam at greater ease within it.[311]

Our Father, our Heavenly King, did not send us forth on our pilgrimages blind. True, he created temporary amnesia in our minds, so that, for a time, we would forget our divine origins. Nonetheless, he has revealed Himself periodically to eyewitnesses. For example the scripture plainly states that Moses spoke with God "face to face, as a man speaketh unto his friend." To such men, our Father laid out His plan for Man's ascension—*requirements* for his sons and daughters to complete while traveling across the *time* of mortal life. Call these requirements what you like; biblically they are referred to as commandments. However, they are given coincidentally with free agency. These prerequisites to attain the quality of life which our Father enjoys are very demanding and so are regarded by the foolish as "constraints." One cannot achieve anything that is great without discipline, but there are always dreamers who wish to fly without enduring the rigors of acquiring the skills of a pilot. They imagine that if only they could be freed from constraints they "could wax great." They strive to pull down the walls of the palace, pull down the strength of the King's fortress, lay his commandments in ruin, and freely trample on sacred ground—and by so doing *think* themselves more free. The King of Man would exalt us, give meaning and order to each step we take as we ascend in his Kingdom; from the gates of his palace, to his towered high places. Conversely, the Enemy of Man would lay us low; he fights continually to destroy the Kingdom of Man and replace it with anarchy, where in misery we climb not, but stumble through the rubble of walls that we, of our own agency, have pulled down upon us.

> Vast was my father's palace, with one wing set apart for the women and a secret inner garden where a fountain sang. (And I ordain that every house shall have just such a heart within it, where a man may draw near to something and whereto he may retreat from something.) A focal place of goings out and of comings in . . . You cannot love a house which has no visage, and where footsteps have no meaning.
>
> Also there was a Hall of Audience, reserved for great embassies alone. It was thrown open to the light only on those days when horsemen could be seen approaching in a golden cloud of dust and on the horizon great banners billowed in the wind. That hall was left unused when lesser chieftains came. Then there was the hall where justice was administered; and another where the dead were laid. And there was an empty room, whose use none knew—and which perchance truly served no purpose but to teach men that there are things secret, that never may they reach (in this life) the core of knowledge.
>
> As they hastened down the corridors, bearing their burdens, the [servants] thrust aside heavy curtains that lapped their shoulders. They climbed steps, opened doors, and went down other flights of stairs; and always, according as they were farther from or nearer to the central fountain, they raised or lowered their voices, growing still as death and moving on tiptoes when they were in the precincts of the women's chambers, to have entered which unwittingly would have cost them their lives.[312]

To enter a woman's chamber unwittingly, taken obviously, would mean to enter by mistake. In a desert citadel to be found in the women's quarters was a capital offense. No excuse of the offender could justify his trespass. As in the case of a sentinel who is found asleep while ordered to guard the gates—and who pleads for mercy as he didn't *intend* to betray his trust, the gravity of his "mistake" requires his life to be forfeit. To indulge such behavior, in both circumstances, would give license to others to regard their duty with sloth. A sentinel asleep could permit the enemy to enter the citadel in stealth, causing the death of many. Also, the very knowledge of the severity of the penalty imposed would work upon the minds of all men to hold the chastity of women in greater esteem than their very lives.

Unfortunately the standards held today think it no transgression for a man to enter a woman's bedroom, especially if he *intends* nothing but harmless sociality. But many a good man and many a good woman can sadly relate that such impropriety has led to actions that neither foresaw, resulting in the loss of virtue. If both are single, a partial restoration can be made through marriage. However, if either or both are married, immorality severs vows so sacred that scarcely no greater harm can be done, except the shedding of innocent blood.

Why is chastity, according to Christian values, so vital? Man's ascension is ultimately designed for one purpose—to make us like God. What makes God, God, is that He is our Father—our Creator. What other gift has He given His children, here and now, that more closely emulates Him than the creation of life? Literally, chastity guards the very fountain of life. Life is governed by law. When a new life is conceived, by law, a spirit son or daughter of God is called forth from our heavenly home, across the immensity of space and miraculously enters the womb of his mother. No longer belonging to the pre-mortal world—now a traveler, a pilgrim, with a mortal mission to complete, trials to endure, testing his selflessness, faith and perseverance. His eternal future weighs heavily on the balance of the few short years of his sojourn upon the earth. At home with God a man cannot prove his manhood; no more than an earthly son can prove his merit if he stays coddled at home, or is controlled by his parents. Such a person fails to develop his own core structure. One who leans solely and continually upon the emotional and physical maintenance of parents is robbed of necessary internal framework. He cannot stand against the fury if he has not developed the strength to stand. Hence we are called to leave our home in heaven and are sent to earth where our character may be truly tried and manifested.

With such import fixed to this life, every person would have, if given the *choice*, the advantage of beginning his pilgrimage with the guidance of a noble mother *and* father. But when life is called forth outside of marriage, the choice is denied and that soul's task is made incredibly more difficult. It is for this reason that true Christianity guards the portal to mortality with the *Law of Chastity*. Man's ascension requires that he honors virtue, womanhood, and family.

> I can hear the voice of the fool, saying: See how much space is wasted here, what wealth left unexploited, what conveniences lost through inadvertence! Far better were it to lay low those useless walls and level out those short flights of steps, which merely hinder progress. Then men will be free.
>
> But I make answer: Then men will become like cattle in the marketplace and to beguile the tedium of their days they will invent new, foolish pastimes, which likewise will be hedged about with rules, but they will be rules devoid of grandeur. For the palace may give birth to poems, but what poem could be made about such pastimes as their games of dice?
>
> Thus is it with the man without an hierarchy, who envies his neighbor if his neighbor excels him and fain would pull him down to his own level. But when all are leveled out into the flatness of a stagnant lake, what joy will they have of it?[313]

It is not our prerogative to decide what is right and what is wrong. We are not the law-givers! The King of Heaven decrees right from wrong. It is our prerogative to *choose* His right, or in defiance, choose wrong. If we believe there is no Hierarchy of

Heaven, no rules but self-justification, no merit in excellence, we will be ruled by envy and animal baseness. God will cease to be our Father, Men will cease to be our brothers, and we will have lost our humanity and our manhood. Life will be void of joy, and in the end we will find nothing but disillusionment and misery.

> My task is to set up rallying-points of power. I build dams in the mountains to hold in the water, and thus I set myself up—unjustly, if you will—against natural inclinations. Where men are becoming clotted together in a morass of uniformity I re-establish hierarchies . . . I renew directives where men have settled tamely down, each in his pothole, calling stagnation happiness. I scorn the shallow puddles of their justice, and release him whom a noble injustice has founded in his manhood.
>
> Men destroy their best possession, the *meaning of things*: on feast days they pride themselves on standing out against old custom, and betraying their traditions, and toasting their enemy. True, they may feel some qualms as they go about their deeds of sacrilege. So long as there is sacrilege. So long as there still is something against which they revolt. Thus for a while they continue trading on the fact that their foe still breathes, and the ghostly presence of the laws still hampers them enough for them to feel like outlaws. But presently the very ghost dissolves into thin air, and then the rapture of revolt is gone, even the zest of victory forgotten. And now they yawn. On the ruins of the palace they have laid out a public square; but once the pleasure of trampling its stones with upstart arrogance has lost its zest, they begin to wonder what they are doing here, on this noisy fairground. And now, lo and behold, they fall to picturing, dimly as yet, a great house with a thousand doors, with curtains that billow and slumberous anterooms. Perchance they dream even of a secret room, whose secrecy pervades the whole vast dwelling. Thus, though they know it not, they are pining for my father's palace where every footstep had a meaning.[314]

The world at the time when Saint-Exupéry lived had largely

pulled down the conventions of faith, selflessness, conviction, integrity, fidelity, service, sacrifice—in short, his world abandoned the truths of religion. Much of mankind had gone beyond rebelliousness, for if you rebel against God you must still *believe* in Him. They had reached a state where they denied His existence—they were Arians, either to the extent of the Nazi, or to a lesser degree, fascists or humanists. Proud, arrogant, regarding not mankind as members of their own family, but rather as objects to despoil, enslave or destroy. In the wreckage of war many began to wonder what they were doing, what purpose remained to life amid the din of destruction? Chastened severely by world war, mankind began to pine for what it had lost, for *meanings* forgotten. Man began to envision once again the majesty of brotherhood, religious faith, and the beauty of commandments that constrain baseness and evil only—a vision of a palace of a thousand rooms, mansions awaiting pilgrims who fulfilled their life's missions. After six years of bloodshed, and seeing they had not power to save or exalt themselves, they appealed to their King, once again believing that He *was* their King—their Father. The Usurpers were, at the cost of millions of lives, cast down. The debris was painfully cleared, and stone by stone, the protective walls of Manliness re-erected. That generation of Saint-Exupéry is dying away. Whatever the personal cost, we must not be among the fools who *again* strive to destroy the *meaning of things*.

In far space there are undoubtedly worlds like ours, worlds without number. But in near space there is no other habitable planet. Earth is surrounded by an immense desert—regions of permanent cold or intense heat, dry wastelands or frozen oceans, toxic atmospheres with wild skies, void of verdure and of life as we understand it. Earth is an oasis in the midst of this desert, built and constructed by God, the Creator, as the land of our pilgrimage. Here he directed the resources of the universe, took of eternal matter and organized a sphere of incredible *balance*; all of the elements combined in perfect synergy. He did not design the earth solely for functionality, for this was *not* to be a place of mere existence, but rather a province of erudition. It is here we are to learn the principles of manhood, the governing values of eternal truth. Here we are schooled, and although a great part of schooling is *testing*, the greater part is *acquiring*. In the short time of one mortal life we are to acquire knowledge, understanding, skills, wisdom and intelligence. The Schoolmaster designed our school grounds in such a manner that literally everything *teaches—if* we have eyes to see, ears to hear, a mind to think, a heart to feel. Again in *Wisdom of the Sands*, the Prince states:

> Behind all seen things lies something vaster; everything is but a path, a portal, or a window opening on something other than itself.

Albert Einstein said:

> A human being is part of a whole, called by us the "Universe". . . . He experiences himself, his thoughts and feelings, as something separated from the rest—a kind of optical delusion of his consciousness. This delusion is a kind of prison for us, restricting us . . . Our task must be to free ourselves from this prison . . . [315]

To be a man one must rise above spiritual myopia. He must see beyond the purely physical and rid himself of the "optical delusion of his consciousness." To aid us in this quest God has immersed us in a corporeal world where *everything* has meaning. A man must look around himself and begin to see the truths manifested in the grandest and most minute features of life. An ancient prophet wrote these words of God:

> All things have their likeness, and all things are created and made to bear record of me, both things which are temporal, and things which are spiritual; things which are in the heavens above, and things which are on the earth, and things which are in the earth, and things which are under the earth, both above and beneath: all things bear record of me. [316]

The air we breathe is not just air, but a symbol of the spirit that animates our body. You cannot see air nor can you see the spirit. Take away the unseen breath, we stifle, suffocate and die. Remove the unseen spirit from the body and our bodies likewise perish. Deciduous trees are symbolic of the four seasons of mortality. In spring tender leaves bud forth, the symbol of new life. Next comes the maturity of summer beauty, vibrant in deep and abundant green, a time of growth and expansion, a representation of virile maturity. The autumn tree withdraws the vital sap from its leaves and branches. It is a time of gradual decay coexistent with incredible beauty, a symbol of aged man. Winter comes and the tree is barren and to all outward appearances, dead. But never was there a winter eternal, for spring returns, emblematic of the resurrection from the grave. Although the seasons come and go in rounds of mortality, for man there are but four seasons. Therefore God has given us the evergreen tree to witness to our understanding that there is life that alters not, but lives green eternally. Layers upon layers of *meaning* are manifest to the man who sees beyond the obvious. And at the summit of his understanding he sees the hand of the Creator in every breath he takes, in every tree's leaf, in every soft and delicate flake of snow. With this understanding comes an appreciation of the beauty, complexity and importance of the entities of creation, *other than himself.* Donald Culross Peattie stated:

> As the brain of man is the speck of dust in the universe that thinks, so the leaves—the fern and the needled pine and the latticed frond and the seaweed ribbon—perceive the light in a fundamental and constructive sense. The flowers looking in from the walled garden through my window do not, it is true, see me. But their leaves see the light, as my eyes can never do. They take it, as it forever spills away radiant into space in a golden waste, to a primal purpose. They impound its stellar energy, and with that force they make life out of the elements. They breathe upon the dust, and it is a rose. Say that this is done with neither thought nor passion,

> and by something other than will. True that a plant may not think; neither will the profoundest of men ever put forth a flower. Of the use and the beauty of flowering there can be no shade of doubt. It is a rare thought of which as much can be said.[317]

A true man labors for treasure that endures. The Prince declared:

> If they build houses but to live in, why should they barter their lives for these houses? For then each man's house is made to serve his own life and nothing else, and he calls his house "useful" and esteems it not for itself but for its utility alone. It serves him, and he busies himself therein, amassing wealth. But such an one dies barren, for he leaves nought of himself . . . Called on to barter himself, he preferred being provided for. And when such men depart, nothing remains . . . *Place no hope in man if he works for his own lifetime and not for his eternity.*
>
> [Real men toil] all their lives, building up a treasure not for daily use and bartering themselves for things of beauty incorruptible.[318]

The Son of Man said:

> Lay not up for yourselves treasures upon earth, where moth and rust doth corrupt, and where thieves break through and steal. But lay up for yourselves treasures in heaven, where neither moth nor rust doth corrupt, and where thieves do not break through nor steal.[319]

The Enemy of Man is the author of babel. He desires our lives to be complicated, confused. His call is a thousand voices urging us to misuse our God-given agency, imagination, passions, appetites and intelligence. Our Enemy would have us search for happiness where it cannot be found—in the false hope of seeking for joy after the manner of *his* economy. The Adversary labors to pull us in scores of conflicting directions—leading us away from the strait and narrow way of our pilgrimage. From *Wisdom of the Sands* we read:

> I can enforce my will when I *simplify,* when I constrain each man to become different, clearer visioned, more generous and more fervent—in a word, at one with himself.[320]

James taught that if a man was not at one with himself, he would surely flounder.

> He that wavereth is like a wave of the sea driven with the wind and tossed . . . A double minded man is unstable in all his ways.

Edward Sanford Martin wrote a poem entitled *My Name is Legion:*

> Within my earthly temple there's a crowd;
> There's one of us that's humble, one that's proud.
> There's one that's broken-hearted for his sins,
> There's one that unrepentant sits and grins;
> There's one that loves his neighbor as himself,
> And one that cares for naught but fame and pelf.
> From much corroding care I should be free
> If I could once determine which is me.[321]

For a person to rid himself of his many faces and become one man, unvarying in the course of life, that will ascend to his divine potential, he must prioritize his efforts. Saint-Exupéry, through the Prince, admonishes:

> I have long learned to distinguish that which is important from that which is urgent. True, it is urgent that man should eat, for else he cannot live . . . Yet love, the sense of life and the quest of God are more important.[322]

No one begins his pilgrimage the finished product of what he will become. We are all faulted and need a great deal of abrasion to sand away our imperfections. A man, therefore, must not be resistant to *change*. To help us understand the necessity and meaning of change, God has given us powerful symbols. The Prince taught:

> The caterpillar dies when it has made its chrysalis; the plant, when it has run to seed. Thus all that is changing its condition travails and suffers. . . . No renewing is there for the caterpillar, nor the plant once it has run to seed, nor for the stripling whose childhood has left him, though fain would he recapture its carefree joys and still delight in toys whose colors have faded, and relish his mother's fond embrace and the sweet flow of milk. But from those childish things the glamour has departed; there is no refuge in his mother's arms, the milk has lost its savor. . . .
>
> None has ever undergone a change of heart without suffering. Thus it is and must be when I raise you up out of your old selves, enabling you to slough your past and, like the snake, don a new skin.[323]

We call the transformation of a crawling insect into a flying butterfly metamorphosis. The transformation of bad conduct to good we call *repentance*, which comes from the Greek word *metanoia*—which literally means *change of mind and heart*. There is no ascension of man without repentance. There are those who say they have not power to change and rationalize their sins and mediocrity; they justify with words their grimy behavior. The truth is they will not suffer the pain of being scrubbed. The Prince states:

> Why should I listen to him who pleads the cause of his disease?
>
> Rather, I shall make shift to save him, for this I owe to God. In that man, too, God dwells. But I shall not deal with the man accord-

> ing to his desire, for his desire is but the mouthpiece of the disease gnawing his flesh.
>
> After I have cleansed and washed and taught him, then his desire will be changed; he will disown the man he was. So why should I play ally to the man whom he himself will soon abhor?[324]

The nature of life is constant movement. A pilgrim is a traveler who moves along a path, following a course that he has never trod before. On every hand obstacles arise to oppose him. This opposition creates absolute *necessity.* Our success will always be won while confronting powers that would destroy us mercilessly. Every flight that Saint-Exupéry flew involved the risk of crashing. The Prince declared:

> Salvation lies in necessity. You cannot play with dice that bear no values. You cannot satisfy yourself with dreams, because dreams offer no resistance. Even thus it is with youth's callow flights of fancy, which bring but disillusion. That alone is useful which resists you.[325]

Water, the very life-source, needs resistance to fulfill its vital mission. When it is flanked by higher ground, when it is destined to travel great distances, when it receives abundantly from tributaries—then it is a mighty river, giving until its course is complete and it is received home in the ocean of heaven. But if water is encompassed with lowlands, if it has no course but moves with sloth towards a hazy destination, its freshness turns foul and it becomes elemental in quagmire, insouciant, nothing more than a swamp. Even worse, if a body of water receives not and goes nowhither, it desiccates into the nothingness of a lifeless dry lake. If a lake receives copiously, yet gives nothing, then it becomes a dead sea, barren and fetid. So it is with man's pilgrimage. Unfortunately, there are multitudes that waste away the days of their pilgrimage and become like swamps, dry lakes or dead seas. However, there are many men who choose to become mighty rivers—whose adventurous life-long course is fraught with danger and beauty. These men are made powerful through contributions given them and as freely they nourish all whom they touch—until at last their quest is complete and they are received by their Creator into the celestial sea of home.

Man's ascension, therefore, requires that he understand the meaning and purpose of his earthly journey. Man must learn to value work, and must labor, not for this life only, but for eternity. He must simplify his direction with single-mindedness. He cannot progress on his quest save he suffer the change of heart called repentance. His strength will be forged by the resistance of the forces that oppose him. He may begin his travels so sinful and faulted that he can scarce be called a man—yet destined, if he will but answer the call of the Prince, to ascend to such greatness that his former self could never imagine! Saint-Exupéry gives these words to the Prince:

> When I wish to found a city I gather together the thieves and the lowest of the low, and I uplift them by the grant of power, offering them joys far other than the squalid thrills of plundering, ravishing, money-snatching. Then you will see them fall to building manfully, their pride becoming towers, battlements and temples, and their cruelty [becoming] grandeur and discipline. They are serving a city of their own begetting, for which they barter themselves wholeheartedly. They will die on the battlements in its defense. And now you will find them the gold of virtue without dross.[326]

Men labor to build towers, where upon are set watchmen to warn of the enemies advance. Men build battlements to defend their loved ones. And finally, men build temples to protect the sacred from the profane and to receive the inner guidance necessary to fulfill their assigned missions. What are temples and how do they differ from the other buildings of the citadel? The first type of temple is one a man cannot create himself, but only inhabit and clean. It is the temple of his body.

There is a second temple a man *may* build; it is the temple of the home, wherein he shelters his family. To reiterate the suffering required to change from boyhood to manhood, the Prince further explains:

> No renewing is there . . . for the stripling whose childhood has left him . . . The boy who has grown up and no longer needs his mother's care will know no rest until he has found the woman of his choice. She alone will reassemble his scattered selfhood.[327]

This temple of home is formed when a man chooses a wife, and together they welcome into life new pilgrims, their children, whom they protect, teach, and nourish. It is within the temple of the home that manhood is most revealed—for in the family a man literally serves sons and daughters of his own begetting.

The final temple built by man is a literal building, such as was built by Solomon, at God's command, and is known as His house. Regarding this holy edifice, the Prince states:

> There is beauty in those temples only which are born of God's behest and are made over to Him as men's ransom. . . . [Their purpose is to bring peace]. As for peace, I impose it not by force . . . The better part is to convert; and to convert is to welcome in. It is the offering to each man of a garment to his measure, in which he feels at ease. The same garment for all . . .
>
> Building peace is building the palace vast enough for all men to gather within it . . .
>
> Building peace is persuading God to lend his shepherd's cloak so that all may be enfolded under it . . .
>
> Without love nothing can be achieved . . . The harder the task wherein you consume yourself for love's sake, the more it will exalt you. The more you give, the greater you become . . .
>
> The Temple does not serve for rest, or cooking, or gatherings of the notables, or the storage of water, but solely for the greatening of men's hearts and the tranquillizing of the senses . . . [a place

> where] man can retire to steep his soul for some hours in the peace that comes of comprehension, when passions are lulled and justice rules without reprisal . . . where the sufferings of the body are transformed into hymns and offerings and where death's imminence seems like a tranquil haven, glimpsed through the murk of the storm . . .
>
> [The Temple is] a harbor of still, shining waters, where the waves are at rest and there is no more strain or struggle and Time itself seems sleepbound, where there is an all pervading silence hardly broken by the low sound of ripples as the ship glides to her moorings . . . Sweet it is to men, this landlocked harbor, after the foam-fringed breakers, the white manes of the coursers of the sea . . .
>
> [Into this] harbor of silence, and of immortal hopes . . . the temple will draw them to it like a magnet and in its silence they will search their souls—and find themselves! . . . Temples . . . transmute them, like the chrysalis, into a nobler race. . . .
>
> The deep forest is good for men; good too, the Milky Way and the blue plain seen from the mountain-top. And yet—what are those vastnesses . . . compared with the pregnant darkness of the stones of the temple . . . [that] will lift you up above yourselves . . . pedestals, stairways, ships, that bring Man nearer God.[328]

Who is the Prince in Saint-Exupéry's book, *The Wisdom of the Sands?* The obvious answer is simply that he is the protagonist of his work who serves as the mouthpiece for the wisdom acquired by Antoine throughout his life. But there is an underlying answer—that, although not applicable throughout the entire manuscript, parallels the motif found in Psalms surfacing in some of these writings. The psalmist mostly speaks as a wise man—yet there are passages that are un-mistakenly spoken in the first person of Deity. In this same manner, Saint-Exupéry in the character of his protagonist emulates the only perfect Man who ever lived; the great exemplar of true Manhood. He it was who called himself the Son of Man. Uniquely different from other men, for not only was his spirit sired by our Heavenly Father, but his physical body was likewise begotten of God. The parallels between certain truths espoused by Saint-Exupéry's Prince and the absolute truths taught by Christ are no doubt intentional. For as Antoine saw the fundamental purpose of life's pilgrimage to be the ascension of Man, there was only One to whom he could look to show the way—the One Man who had indeed ascended to the right hand of the Father and who declared:

> And I, if I be lifted up from the earth, will draw all **men** unto me.[329]

Copyrights and Permissions

***Valiant Young Men, Heroes of Flight,* 1st Edition.**

From FIGHTING THE FLYING CIRCUS by Captain Eddie Rickenbacker, copyright © 1965 by Doubleday, a division of Random House, Inc. Used by permission of Doubleday, a division of Random House, Inc.

From SEVEN CAME THROUGH by Edward V. Rickenbacker, copyright 1943 by Doubleday, a division of Random House, Inc. Used by permission of Doubleday, a division of Random House, Inc.

All works by Edward V. Rickenbacker cited and quoted herein, as held by the family estate, used by permission of David Brian Rickenbacker, Nancy (Rickenbacker) Schindler, James Rickenbacker, Thomas Rickenbacker, and Marcie Rickenbacker.

From FATHER TO SON: THE LETTERS OF CAPTAIN EDDIE RICKENBACKER TO HIS SON WILLIAM, published by Walker and Company 1970. Used by permission of Walker Publishing Co., Inc.

Quotations from the works of James Norman Hall, including HIGH ADVENTURE, KITCHENER'S MOB, MY ISLAND HOME and THE FORGOTTEN ONE, used by permission of Nicholas and Nancy (Hall) Rutgers.

Excerpts from THE WISDOM OF THE SANDS by Antoine de Saint-Exupéry, English translation copyright 1950 and renewed 1978 by Harcourt, Inc., reprinted by permission of the publisher.

Excerpts from WARTIME WRITINGS 1939-1944 by Antoine de Saint-Exupéry, copyright © 1982 by Editions Gallimard, English translation copyright © 1986 by Harcourt, Inc. reprinted by permission of Harcourt, Inc.

Excerpts from NIGHT FLIGHT by Antoine de Saint-Exupéry, English translation copyright 1932 by Harcourt, Inc. and renewed 1960 by Stuart Gilbert, reprinted by permission of the publisher.

Excerpts from FLIGHT TO ARRAS by Antoine de Saint-Exupéry, English translation copyright 1942 by Harcourt, Inc., and renewed 1970 by Lewis Galantiere, reprinted by permission of the publisher.

Excerpts from WIND, SAND AND STARS, copyright 1939 by Antoine de Saint-Exupéry and renewed 1976 by Lewis Galantiere, reprinted by permission of Harcourt, Inc.

Reprinted with the permission of Simon & Schuster Adult Publishing Group, from RICKENBACKER: AN AUTOBIOGRAPHY by Edward V. Rickenbacker. Copyright © 1967 by Edward V. Rickenbacker.

Paintings by Stan Stokes, GOTCHA, THE KAISER'S BATTLE, THE FOKKER SCOURGE, and BALLOON BUSTER EXTRAORDINARE, used by permission of The Stokes Collection. Originals paintings by Stan Stokes are in the collections of most of the prestigious aviation museums such as the Smithsonian Air and Space Museum, the Museum of Naval Aviation at Pensacola, and the Air Force Museum at Wright Patterson Field. Additional fine art by Stan Stokes may be seen at www.stokescollection.com.

Paintings by Herb Kawainui Kane, JIMMY HALL GUIDES EDDIE RICKENBACKER TO HIS FIRST VICTORY and JIMMY HALL'S FIRST VICTORY, used by permission of Herb Kawainui Kane. Herb

Kawainui Kane is an artist-historian and author with special interest in Hawaii and the South Pacific. Additional fine art by Herb Kawainui may be seen at www.herbkaneart.com.

Paintings by Rich Thistle, FINAL VICTORY and ENCOUNTER WITH A LEGEND, used by permission of Rich Thistle. Rich Thistle is a Canadian artist respected for his military and general aviation images as well as Canadian watercolor landscapes. Rich's online gallery at www.richthistle.com offers a full selection of originals and prints as well as his published aviation articles.

Photographs and reproductions of photographs by Bryan Cox, used by permission of Bryan Cox. Bryan is a highly acclaimed international photographer whose celebrity style imaging is featured at www.BryCox.com.

Paintings by James Dietz, BETWEEN HEAVEN AND HELL, CIRCUS ROLLS AT DAWN, and MUD IN YOUR EYE, used by permission of James Dietz. James Dietz is an internationally acclaimed artist whose clientele includes Boeing, the 101st Airborne Division, Flying Tigers, and The US Air Force Museum at Wright Patterson Air Force Base. Additional fine art by James Dietz may be seen at www.jamesdietz.com.

Painting by Jim Laurier, THE 13TH AERO SQUADRON, used by permission of Jim Laurier. Jim Laurier's work has received international accolades from such hallmark institutions as the Experimental Aircraft Association and the U.S. Naval Air Museum. Additional fine art by Jim Laurier may be seen at www.jimlaurier.com

Paintings by Robert Taylor—BALLOON BUSTER, DAWN PATROL, and COMING IN OVER THE ESTUARY © The Military Gallery, Ojai, California. Images used by permission of The Military Gallery. Robert Taylor is one of the world's foremost aviation artists—additional images may be viewed at www.militarygallery.com.

From SAINT-EXUPERY by Stacy Schiff, Copyright (c) 1994 by Stacy Schiff. Used by permission of Alfred A. Knopf, a division of Random House, Inc.

References – Book 1

1. Morrison, James Dalton, Editor: *Masterpieces of Religious Verse, Man-Making by Markham, Edwin* (Harper & Brothers Publishers, New York and London), 1948, p.419

2. Jordan, William George: *The Kingship of Self-Control* (Fleming H. Revell, USA), 1899

3. Lewis, C.S., *Learning in Wartime*

4. de Saint-Exupéry, Antoine: *The Wisdom of the Sands*—Translated by Stuart Gilbert from the French *Citadelle* (Harcourt, Brace and Company, New York), 1950, p. 101

5. Emerson, Ralph Waldo: *Essays and English Traits, The Harvard Classics* (P. F. Collier & Son Corporation, New York), 1937

6. Rickenbacker, Edward V: *Fighting the Flying Circus* (Doubleday and Company, Inc., New York), 1967, p. 82

7. Rickenbacker, Edward V: *Fighting the Flying Circus* (Doubleday and Company, Inc., New York, 1967, p. 85

8. Rickenbacker, Edward V.: *Rickenbacker—An Autobiography* (Prentice-Hall, Inc., Englewood Cliffs, New Jersey), 1967, p. 111

9. Rickenbacker, Edward V: *Fighting the Flying Circus* (Doubleday and Company, Inc., New York, 1967, p. 87

10. Rickenbacker, Edward V.: *Rickenbacker—An Autobiography* (Prentice-Hall, Inc., Englewood Cliffs, New Jersey), 1967, p. 112

11. Morrison, James Dalton, Editor: *Masterpieces of Religious Verse, The Present Crisis by Lowell, James Russell* (Harper & Brothers Publishers, New York and London), 1948, p.523

12. Rickenbacker, Edward V.: *Rickenbacker—An Autobiography* (Prentice-Hall, Inc., Englewood Cliffs, New Jersey), 1967, p. 5

13. Rickenbacker, Edward V.: *Rickenbacker—An Autobiography* (Prentice-Hall, Inc., Englewood Cliffs, New Jersey), 1967, p. 2

14. Rickenbacker, Edward V.: *Rickenbacker—An Autobiography* (Prentice-Hall, Inc., Englewood Cliffs, New Jersey), 1967, p. 3

15. Rickenbacker, Edward V.: *Rickenbacker—An Autobiography* (Prentice-Hall, Inc., Englewood Cliffs, New Jersey), 1967, p. 7

16. Rickenbacker, Edward V.: *Rickenbacker—An Autobiography* (Prentice-Hall, Inc., Englewood Cliffs, New Jersey), 1967, p. 12

17. Rickenbacker, Edward V.: *Rickenbacker—An Autobiography* (Prentice-Hall, Inc., Englewood Cliffs, New Jersey), 1967, p. 13

18. Rickenbacker, Edward V.: *Rickenbacker—An Autobiography* (Prentice-Hall, Inc., Englewood Cliffs, New Jersey), 1967, p. 18

19. Rickenbacker, Edward V.: *Rickenbacker—An Autobiography* (Prentice-Hall, Inc., Englewood Cliffs, New Jersey), 1967, p. 31

20. Rickenbacker, Edward V.: *Rickenbacker—An Autobiography* (Prentice-Hall, Inc., Englewood Cliffs, New Jersey), 1967, p. 47

21. Rickenbacker, Edward V.: *Rickenbacker—An Autobiography* (Prentice-Hall, Inc., Englewood Cliffs, New Jersey), 1967, p. 67-68

22. Hillhouse, James Abraham: *Hadad* (E. Bliss & E. White, New York) 1825, p. 72-73

23. Ether 8:18-19, 22

24. http://www.spartacus.schoolnet.co.uk/FWWapis.htm, 2004

25. Duffy, Michael:
http://www.firstworldwar.com/origins/causes.htm, 2000-2005

26. Levine, Isaac Don, editor: *The Kaiser's Letters to the Tsar*, copied from the government archives in Petrograd, and brought from Russia, (Hodder and Stoughton), London, 1920

27. Numbers 30:2

28. Alma 48:13

29. Helaman 6:26

30. Alma 37:29

31. Ephesians 6:12

32. Ephesians 6:11

33. Hall, James Norman: *High Adventure* (Arno Press, A New York Times Company, New York), 1980, p. 82-86

34. *The New York Times Current History*, **Volume II, Number 3,** *The European War*, June, 1915

35. Rickenbacker, Edward V: *Fighting the Flying Circus* (Doubleday and Company, Inc., New York, 1967, p. 24

36. Rickenbacker, Edward V.: *Fighting the Flying Circus* (Doubleday and Company, Inc., New York, 1967, p. 55

37. Rickenbacker, Edward V.: *Rickenbacker—An Autobiography* (Prentice-Hall, Inc., Englewood Cliffs, New Jersey), 1967, p. 107

38. Rickenbacker, Edward V.: *Rickenbacker—An Autobiography* (Prentice-Hall, Inc., Englewood Cliffs, New Jersey), 1967, p. 114

39. Rickenbacker, Edward V.: *Rickenbacker—An Autobiography* (Prentice-Hall, Inc., Englewood Cliffs, New Jersey), 1967, p. 114

40. Rickenbacker, Edward V.: *Rickenbacker—An Autobiography* (Prentice-Hall, Inc., Englewood Cliffs, New Jersey), 1967, p. 121

41. Pierpont, John: *The Fugitive Slave's Apostrophe to the North Star, An American Anthology* edited by Edmund Clarence Stedman, 1900

42. Rickenbacker, Edward V.: *Fighting the Flying Circus* (Doubleday and Company, Inc., New York, 1967, p. 237

43. Rickenbacker, Edward V.: *Fighting the Flying Circus* (Doubleday and Company, Inc., New York, 1967, p. 261

44. Rickenbacker, Edward V.: *Fighting the Flying Circus* (Doubleday and Company, Inc., New York, 1967, p. 262

45. Rickenbacker, Edward V.: *Rickenbacker—An Autobiography* (Prentice-Hall, Inc., Englewood Cliffs, New Jersey), 1967, p. 124

46. Rickenbacker, Edward V: *Fighting the Flying Circus* (Doubleday and Company, Inc., New York, 1967, p. 286

47. Rickenbacker, Edward V: *Fighting the Flying Circus* (Doubleday and Company, Inc., New York, 1967, p. 310

48. Mark 8:36

49. Rickenbacker, Edward V.: *Rickenbacker—An Autobiography* (Prentice-Hall, Inc., Englewood Cliffs, New Jersey), 1967, p. 134

50. Rickenbacker, Edward V.: *Rickenbacker—An Autobiography* (Prentice-Hall, Inc., Englewood Cliffs, New Jersey), 1967, p. 135

51. Dryden, John: *Aurengzebe.* Act iv. Scene 1., 1676

52. Rickenbacker, Edward V.: *Seven Came Through* (Doubleday, Doran and Company, Inc., Garden City, New York), 1943, p. 104

53. Rickenbacker, Edward V.: *Seven Came Through* (Doubleday, Doran and Company, Inc., Garden City, New York), 1943, p. 103

54. Rickenbacker, Edward V.: *Rickenbacker—An Autobiography* (Prentice-Hall, Inc., Englewood Cliffs, New Jersey), 1967, p. 164

55. Rickenbacker, Edward V.: *Seven Came Through* (Doubleday, Doran and Company, Inc., Garden City, New York), 1943, p. 106-107

56. Epictetus (A.D. 50–A.D. 138): *The Golden Sayings of Epictetus, CLVII, The Harvard Classics, Volume 2* (P. F. Collier & Son Corporation, New York), 1938

57. Rickenbacker, Edward V.: *Rickenbacker—An Autobiography* (Prentice-Hall, Inc., Englewood Cliffs, New Jersey), 1967, p. 244

58. Rickenbacker, Edward V.: *Rickenbacker—An Autobiography* (Prentice-Hall, Inc., Englewood Cliffs, New Jersey), 1967, p. 249

59. Rickenbacker, Edward V.: *Seven Came Through* (Doubleday, Doran and Company, Inc., Garden City, New York), 1943, p. 14

60. Rickenbacker, Edward V.: *Seven Came Through* (Doubleday, Doran and Company, Inc., Garden City, New York), 1943, p. 25

61. Rickenbacker, Edward V.: *Rickenbacker—An Autobiography* (Prentice-Hall, Inc., Englewood Cliffs, New Jersey), 1967, p. 316

62. Rickenbacker, Edward V.: *Rickenbacker—An Autobiography* (Prentice-Hall, Inc., Englewood Cliffs, New Jersey), 1967, p. 317

63. Rickenbacker, Edward V.: *Rickenbacker—An Autobiography* (Prentice-Hall, Inc., Englewood Cliffs, New Jersey), 1967, p. 318

64. Rickenbacker, Edward V.: *Rickenbacker—An Autobiography* (Prentice-Hall, Inc., Englewood Cliffs, New Jersey), 1967, p. 323

65. Kipling, Rudyard: *The Choice, A Treasury of War Poetry*, edited by George Herbert Clarke (Houghton Mifflin, Boston), 1917

66. Rickenbacker, Edward V.: *Rickenbacker—An Autobiography* (Prentice-Hall, Inc., Englewood Cliffs, New Jersey), 1967, p. 332

67. Benson, Ezra Taft: *Teachings of Ezra Taft Benson*, (Bookcraft, Salt Lake City) p.704-705

68. Rickenbacker, Edward V.: *Rickenbacker—An Autobiography* (Prentice-Hall, Inc., Englewood Cliffs, New Jersey), 1967, Appendix

69. Rickenbacker, William F.: *From Father to Son: the letters of Captain Eddie Rickenbacker to his son William, from boyhood to manhood* (Walker and Company, New York), 1970, p. 18

70. Rickenbacker, William F.: *From Father to Son: the letters of Captain Eddie Rickenbacker to his son William, from boyhood to manhood* (Walker and Company, New York), 1970, p. 81

71. Rickenbacker, William F.: *From Father to Son: the letters of Captain Eddie Rickenbacker to his son William, from boyhood to manhood* (Walker and Company, New York), 1970, p. 85-91

72. Rickenbacker, William F.: *From Father to Son: the letters of Captain Eddie Rickenbacker to his son William, from boyhood to manhood* (Walker and Company, New York), 1970, p. 109-110

73. Rickenbacker, William F.: *From Father to Son: the letters of Captain Eddie Rickenbacker to his son William, from boyhood to manhood* (Walker and Company, New York), 1970, p. 177-122

74. Rickenbacker, William F.: *From Father to Son: the letters of Captain Eddie Rickenbacker to his son William, from boyhood to manhood* (Walker and Company, New York), 1970, p. 173-174

75. Rickenbacker, William F.: *From Father to Son: the letters of Captain Eddie Rickenbacker to his son William, from boyhood to manhood* (Walker and Company, New York), 1970, p. 193-198

76. Rickenbacker, William F.: *From Father to Son: the letters of Captain Eddie Rickenbacker to his son William, from boyhood to manhood* (Walker and Company, New York), 1970, p. 199-200

77. Rickenbacker, Edward V.: *Rickenbacker—An Autobiography* (Prentice-Hall, Inc., Englewood Cliffs, New Jersey), 1967, p. 442-443

References – Book 2

78. Hall, James Norman: *High Adventure* (Arno Press, A New York Times Company, New York), 1980

79. Hall, James Norman: *High Adventure* (Arno Press, A New York Times Company, New York), 1980, p. 32

80. Hall, James Norman: *High Adventure* (Arno Press, A New York Times Company, New York), 1980, p. 30-31

81. Hall, James Norman: *High Adventure* (Arno Press, A New York Times Company, New York), 1980, p. 53

82. Hall, James Norman: *High Adventure* (Arno Press, A New York Times Company, New York), 1980, p. 37

83. Hall, James Norman: *High Adventure* (Arno Press, A New York Times Company, New York), 1980, p. 38-40

84. Hall, James Norman: *High Adventure* (Arno Press, A New York Times Company, New York), 1980, p. 42-44

85. Hall, James Norman: *High Adventure* (Arno Press, A New York Times Company, New York), 1980, p. 58

86. Hall, James Norman: *High Adventure* (Arno Press, A New York Times Company, New York), 1980, p. 60-61

87. Hall, James Norman: *High Adventure* (Arno Press, A New York Times Company, New York), 1980, p. 67

88. Hall, James Norman: *High Adventure* (Arno Press, A New York Times Company, New York), 1980, p. 70

89. Pope, Alexander: *An Essay on Criticism*, 1744

90. Hall, James Norman: *High Adventure* (Arno Press, A New York Times Company, New York), 1980, p. 77-78

91. Hall, James Norman: *High Adventure* (Arno Press, A New York Times Company, New York), 1980, p. 78, 81-82

92. Hall, James Norman: *High Adventure* (Arno Press, A New York Times Company, New York), 1980, p. 85-86

93. Hall, James Norman: *High Adventure* (Arno Press, A New York Times Company, New York), 1980, p. 87

94. Hall, James Norman: *My Island Home, an Autobiography* (Mutual Publishing, Australia), 2001, p. 236

95. Hall, James Norman: *My Island Home, an Autobiography* (Mutual Publishing, Australia), 2001, p. 241

96. Hall, James Norman: *My Island Home, an Autobiography* (Mutual Publishing, Australia), 2001, p. 4-5

97. Hall, James Norman: *My Island Home, an Autobiography* (Mutual Publishing, Australia), 2001, p. 8

98. Hall, James Norman: *My Island Home, an Autobiography* (Mutual Publishing, Australia), 2001, p. 17

99. Hall, James Norman: *My Island Home, an Autobiography* (Mutual Publishing, Australia), 2001, p. 3

100. Hall, James Norman: *My Island Home, an Autobiography* (Mutual Publishing, Australia), 2001, p. 22

101. Tennyson, Alfred Lord: *The Works of Alfred Lord Tennyson—Morte d'Arthur* (Wordsworth Poetry Library, Denmark) 1994, p. 111

102. Ruskin, John: *Sesame and Lilies, Lecture I.—Sesame: of King's Treasuries, The Harvard Classics, Volume 28* (P. F. Collier & Son Corporation, New York), 1938, p. 99-100

103. Hall, James Norman: *My Island Home, an Autobiography* (Mutual Publishing, Australia), 2001, p. 69

104. Longfellow, Henry Wadsworth: *The Works of Henry Wadsworth Longfellow—The Golden Legend* (Wordsworth Poetry Library, Denmark) 1994, p. 474

105. Romans 8:28

106. Hall, James Norman: *My Island Home, an Autobiography* (Mutual Publishing, Australia), 2001, p. 65

107. Hall, James Norman: *My Island Home, an Autobiography* (Mutual Publishing, Australia), 2001, p. 100

108. Hall, James Norman: *My Island Home, an Autobiography* (Mutual Publishing, Australia), 2001, p. 98

109. Hall, James Norman: *My Island Home, an Autobiography* (Mutual Publishing, Australia), 2001, p. 99

110. Hall, James Norman: *My Island Home, an Autobiography* (Mutual Publishing, Australia), 2001, p. 101

111. Hall, James Norman: *My Island Home, an Autobiography* (Mutual Publishing, Australia), 2001, p. 107

112. Hall, James Norman: *My Island Home, an Autobiography* (Mutual Publishing, Australia), 2001, p. 117

113. Hall, James Norman: *Kitchener's Mob* (Grosset & Dunlap Publishers, New York), 1916. p. 67-68

114. Hall, James Norman: *My Island Home, an Autobiography* (Mutual Publishing, Australia), 2001, p. 133

115. Hall, James Norman: *My Island Home, an Autobiography* (Mutual Publishing, Australia), 2001, p. 134

116. Hall, James Norman: *Kitchener's Mob* (Grosset & Dunlap Publishers, New York), 1916. p. 3

117. Hall, James Norman: *Kitchener's Mob* (Grosset & Dunlap Publishers, New York), 1916. p. 14

118. Hall, James Norman: *Kitchener's Mob* (Grosset & Dunlap Publishers, New York), 1916. p. 30

119. Hall, James Norman: *My Island Home, an Autobiography* (Mutual Publishing, Australia), 2001, p. 140

120. Hall, James Norman: *Kitchener's Mob* (Grosset & Dunlap Publishers, New York), 1916. p. 31

121. Hall, James Norman: *Kitchener's Mob* (Grosset & Dunlap Publishers, New York), 1916. p. 41-42

122. Hall, James Norman: *Kitchener's Mob* (Grosset & Dunlap Publishers, New York), 1916

123. John 1:6-7, 9

124. Moroni 7:18-19

125. Hall, James Norman: *Kitchener's Mob* (Grosset & Dunlap Publishers, New York), 1916. p. 49

126. Hall, James Norman: *Kitchener's Mob* (Grosset & Dunlap Publishers, New York), 1916. p. 60

127. Hall, James Norman: *Kitchener's Mob* (Grosset & Dunlap Publishers, New York), 1916. p. 140-141

128. Hall, James Norman: *My Island Home, an Autobiography* (Mutual Publishing, Australia), 2001, p. 151

129. Hall, James Norman: *My Island Home, an Autobiography* (Mutual Publishing, Australia), 2001, p. 151

130. Hall, James Norman: *Kitchener's Mob* (Grosset & Dunlap Publishers, New York), 1916. p. 169-170

131. Hall, James Norman: *Kitchener's Mob* (Grosset & Dunlap Publishers, New York), 1916. p. 136

132. Hall, James Norman: *Kitchener's Mob* (Grosset & Dunlap Publishers, New York), 1916. p. 138-139

133. Hall, James Norman: *Kitchener's Mob* (Grosset & Dunlap Publishers, New York), 1916. p. 187

134. Hall, James Norman: *Kitchener's Mob* (Grosset & Dunlap Publishers, New York), 1916. p. 180, 183, 190

135. Hall, James Norman: *Kitchener's Mob* (Grosset & Dunlap Publishers, New York), 1916. p. 193

136. Whitney, Orson Ferguson: *Love and the Light—An Idyl of the Westland* (J. F. Smith, Salt Lake City), 1918, p. 109

137. Hall, James Norman: *My Island Home, an Autobiography* (Mutual Publishing, Australia), 2001, p. 159

138. Hall, James Norman: *My Island Home, an Autobiography* (Mutual Publishing, Australia), 2001, p. 161

139. Hall, James Norman: *My Island Home, an Autobiography* (Mutual Publishing, Australia), 2001, p. 163

140. Hall, James Norman: *My Island Home, an Autobiography* (Mutual Publishing, Australia), 2001, p. 165-166

141. Hall, James Norman: *My Island Home, an Autobiography* (Mutual Publishing, Australia), 2001, p. 169

142. Hall, James Norman: *My Island Home, an Autobiography* (Mutual Publishing, Australia), 2001, p. 173-174

143. Hall, James Norman: *High Adventure* (Arno Press, A New York Times Company, New York), 1980, p. 103

144. Hall, James Norman: *High Adventure* (Arno Press, A New York Times Company, New York), 1980, p. 104-106

145. Hall, James Norman: *High Adventure* (Arno Press, A New York Times Company, New York), 1980, p. 132

146. Hall, James Norman: *High Adventure* (Arno Press, A New York Times Company, New York), 1980, p. 138

147. Hall, James Norman: *High Adventure* (Arno Press, A New York Times Company, New York), 1980, p. 141

148. Hall, James Norman: *High Adventure* (Arno Press, A New York Times Company, New York), 1980, p. 156

149. Hall, James Norman: *My Island Home, an Autobiography* (Mutual Publishing, Australia), 2001, p. 180

150. Hall, James Norman: *High Adventure* (Arno Press, A New York Times Company, New York), 1980, p. 172-173

151. Hall, James Norman: *High Adventure* (Arno Press, A New York Times Company, New York), 1980, p. 174

152. Hall, James Norman: *High Adventure* (Arno Press, A New York Times Company, New York), 1980, p. 175

153. Hall, James Norman: *High Adventure* (Arno Press, A New York Times Company, New York), 1980, p. 223

154. Hall, James Norman: *My Island Home, an Autobiography* (Mutual Publishing, Australia), 2001, p. 195

155. Alma 44:1-2,5-7

156. Rickenbacker, Eddie: *Fighting the Flying Circus* (Avon Book, New York), 1967, p. 54

157. Dyer, Sir Edward: *My Mind to Me a Kingdom Is, The Harvard Classics, English Poetry I: From Chaucer to Gray* (P. F. Collier & Son Corporation, New York), 1938

158. Hall, James Norman: *My Island Home, an Autobiography* (Mutual Publishing, Australia), 2001, p. 204-205

159. Hall, James Norman: *My Island Home, an Autobiography* (Mutual Publishing, Australia), 2001, p. 211

160. Hall, James Norman: *High Adventure* (Arno Press, A New York Times Company, New York), 1980, p. 236-237

161. Hall, James Norman: *My Island Home, an Autobiography* (Mutual Publishing, Australia), 2001, p. 213-214

162. Hall, James Norman: *My Island Home, an Autobiography* (Mutual Publishing, Australia), 2001, p. 215-216

163. Hall, James Norman: *My Island Home, an Autobiography* (Mutual Publishing, Australia), 2001, p. 217

164. Doane, William Croswell: *Ancient of Days, An American Anthology* edited by Edmund Clarence Stedman, 1900

165. Hall, James Norman: *My Island Home, an Autobiography* (Mutual Publishing, Australia), 2001, p. 222

166. Hall, James Norman: *My Island Home, an Autobiography* (Mutual Publishing, Australia), 2001, p. 225

167. Guest, Edgar A.: *The Package of Seeds—Collected Verse of Edgar A. Guest* (Reilly & Lee Co, Chicago), 1934

168. Hall, James Norman: *The Forgotten One* (Little, Brown and Company in association with The Atlantic Monthly Press, U.S.A.), 1952, p. 84

169. Hall, James Norman: *The Forgotten One* (Little, Brown and Company in association with The Atlantic Monthly Press, U.S.A.), 1952, p. 85-86

170. Hall, James Norman: *The Forgotten One* (Little, Brown and Company in association with The Atlantic Monthly Press, U.S.A.), 1952, p. 87

171. Hall, James Norman: *The Forgotten One* (Little, Brown and Company in association with The Atlantic Monthly Press, U.S.A.), 1952, p. 93

172. Hall, James Norman: *The Forgotten One* (Little, Brown and Company in association with The Atlantic Monthly Press, U.S.A.), 1952, p. 95

173. Hall, James Norman: *The Forgotten One* (Little, Brown and Company in association with The Atlantic Monthly Press, U.S.A.), 1952, p. 96-97

174. Hope, Bob: *Don't Shoot, It's Only Me* (G. P. Putnam's Sons, New York), 1990, p. 13

175. Hall, James Norman: *The Forgotten One* (Little, Brown and Company in association with The Atlantic Monthly Press, U.S.A.), 1952, p. 4

176. Hall, James Norman: *The Forgotten One* (Little, Brown and Company in association with The Atlantic Monthly Press, U.S.A.), 1952, p.28

177. Hall, James Norman: *The Forgotten One* (Little, Brown and Company in association with The Atlantic Monthly Press, U.S.A.), 1952, p. 28, 31

178. Hall, James Norman: *The Forgotten One* (Little, Brown and Company in association with The Atlantic Monthly Press, U.S.A.), 1952, p.46

179. Hall, James Norman: *The Forgotten One* (Little, Brown and Company in association with The Atlantic Monthly Press, U.S.A.), 1952, p. 51

180. Hall, James Norman: *The Memories of Chaucer,* written while a prisoner in Landshut, Germany as quoted: http://www.jamesnorman-hallhome.pf/indexen.html

181. Hall, James Norman: *Her Daddy's Best Ice Cream* (Advertiser Publishing Co., Ltd., Hawaii) 1952, (Pacific Greetings, Hawaii), 2003, p. 9

182. Hall, James Norman: *Her Daddy's Best Ice Cream* (Advertiser Publishing Co., Ltd., Hawaii) 1952, (Pacific Greetings, Hawaii), 2003, p. 18-20

183. Hall, James Norman: *Her Daddy's Best Ice Cream* (Advertiser Publishing Co., Ltd., Hawaii) 1952, (Pacific Greetings, Hawaii), 2003, p. 21-22

184. Durant, Will: *Caesar and Christ—The Story of Civilization: Part III* (Simon and Schuster, New York), 1944, p. 58-59

185. Durant, Will: *Caesar and Christ—The Story of Civilization: Part III* (Simon and Schuster, New York), 1944, p. 90

186. Hall, James Norman: *My Island Home, an Autobiography* (Mutual Publishing, Australia), 2001, p. 330

187. Hall, James Norman: *My Island Home, an Autobiography* (Mutual Publishing, Australia), 2001, p. 337

188. Hall, James Norman: *My Island Home, an Autobiography* (Mutual Publishing, Australia), 2001, p. 341

189. Hall, James Norman: *My Island Home, an Autobiography* (Mutual Publishing, Australia), 2001, p. 347-348

190. Hall, James Norman: *My Island Home, an Autobiography* (Mutual Publishing, Australia), 2001, p. 355

191. Hall, James Norman: *My Island Home, an Autobiography* (Mutual Publishing, Australia), 2001, p. 358

192. Hall, James Norman: *My Island Home, an Autobiography* (Mutual Publishing, Australia), 2001, p. 359

References – Book 3

193. de Saint-Exupéry, Antoine: *Airman's Odyssey*—a Trilogy Comprising *Wind, Sand and Stars, Night Flight, and Flight to Arras* (Harcourt Brace Jovanovich, New York), 1984, p. 47-49

194. de Saint-Exupéry, Antoine: *Airman's Odyssey*—a Trilogy Comprising *Wind, Sand and Stars, Night Flight, and Flight to Arras* (Harcourt Brace Jovanovich, New York), 1984, p. 50

195. Wordsworth, William: *Intimations of Immortality from Recollections of Early Childhood— The Works of William Wordsworth* (Wordsworth Editions Ltd, Cumberland House, Crib Street, Ware Hertfordshire) 1994, p. 588

196. Hebrews 11:13

197. Morrison, James Dalton, Editor: *Masterpieces of Religious Verse, Festus by Bailey, Philip James* (Harper & Brothers Publishers, New York and London), 1948, p.358

198. Schiff, Stacy: *Saint-Exupéry* (Alfred A. Knopf, Inc., New York), 1994, p. 42

199. Rumbold, Richard: *The Winged Life—A Portrait of Antoine de Saint-Exupéry* (George Weidenfeld & Nicolson, London), 1953, p. 22

200. de Saint-Exupéry, Antoine: *Airman's Odyssey*—a Trilogy Comprising *Wind, Sand and Stars, Night Flight, and Flight to Arras* (Harcourt Brace Jovanovich, New York), 1984, p. 389

201. Rumbold, Richard: *The Winged Life—A Portrait of Antoine de Saint-Exupéry* (George Weidenfeld & Nicolson, London), 1953, p. 23

202. Russell, George William: *Hope in Failure, Collected Poems by A.E.*, 1913

203. Schiff, Stacy: *Saint-Exupéry* (Alfred A. Knopf, Inc., New York), 1994, p. 67

204. Schiff, Stacy: *Saint-Exupéry* (Alfred A. Knopf, Inc., New York), 1994, p. 71

205. de Saint-Exupéry, Antoine: *The Wisdom of the Sands*—Translated by Stuart Gilbert from the French *Citadelle* (Harcourt, Brace and Company, New York), 1950, p. 41

206. Ruskin, John: *Sesame and Lilies, Lecture II.—Lilies: of Queens' Gardens, The Harvard Classics, Volume 28* (P. F. Collier & Son Corporation, New York), 1938, p. 144

207. Hugo, Victor: *Les Misérables,* translated by Lee Fahnestock and Norman MacAfee, based on the classic C. E. Wilbour translation (New American Library, a Division of Penguin Books, New York), 1987

208. D&C 124:99

209. Schiff, Stacy: *Saint-Exupéry* (Alfred A. Knopf, Inc., New York), 1994, p.117

210. Isaiah 40:31

211. Schiff, Stacy: *Saint-Exupéry* (Alfred A. Knopf, Inc., New York), 1994, p.132

212. de Saint-Exupéry, Antoine: *Airman's Odyssey*—a Trilogy Comprising *Wind, Sand and Stars, Night Flight, and Flight to Arras* (Harcourt Brace Jovanovich, New York), 1984, p. 11

213. de Saint-Exupéry, Antoine: *Airman's Odyssey*—a Trilogy Comprising *Wind, Sand and Stars, Night Flight, and Flight to Arras* (Harcourt Brace Jovanovich, New York), 1984, p. 5

214. de Saint-Exupéry, Antoine: *Airman's Odyssey*—a Trilogy Comprising *Wind, Sand and Stars, Night Flight, and Flight to Arras* (Harcourt Brace Jovanovich, New York), 1984, p. 6-7

215. de Saint-Exupéry, Antoine: *Airman's Odyssey*—a Trilogy Comprising *Wind, Sand and Stars, Night Flight, and Flight to Arras* (Harcourt Brace Jovanovich, New York), 1984, p. 8

216. de Saint-Exupéry, Antoine: *Airman's Odyssey*—a Trilogy Comprising *Wind, Sand and Stars, Night Flight, and Flight to Arras* (Harcourt Brace Jovanovich, New York), 1984, p. 85

217. de Saint-Exupéry, Antoine: *Airman's Odyssey*—a Trilogy Comprising *Wind, Sand and Stars, Night Flight, and Flight to Arras* (Harcourt Brace Jovanovich, New York), 1984, p. 85

218. de Saint-Exupéry, Antoine: *Airman's Odyssey*—a Trilogy Comprising *Wind, Sand and Stars, Night Flight, and Flight to Arras* (Harcourt Brace Jovanovich, New York), 1984, p. 87

219. de Saint-Exupéry, Antoine: *Airman's Odyssey*—a Trilogy Comprising *Wind, Sand and Stars, Night Flight, and Flight to Arras* (Harcourt Brace Jovanovich, New York), 1984, p. 87-88

220. Schiff, Stacy: *Saint-Exupéry* (Alfred A. Knopf, Inc., New York), 1994, p. 226

221. Schiff, Stacy: *Saint-Exupéry* (Alfred A. Knopf, Inc., New York), 1994, p. 25

222. Epictetus (A.D. 50–A.D. 138): *The Golden Sayings of Epictetus, CLVII, The Harvard Classics, Volume 2* (P. F. Collier & Son Corporation, New York), 1938

223. Schiff, Stacy: *Saint-Exupéry* (Alfred A. Knopf, Inc., New York), 1994, p. 182

224. de Saint-Exupéry, Antoine: *Airman's Odyssey*—a Trilogy Comprising *Wind, Sand and Stars, Night Flight, and Flight to Arras* (Harcourt Brace Jovanovich, New York), 1984, p. 59

225. de Saint-Exupéry, Antoine: *Airman's Odyssey*—a Trilogy Comprising *Wind, Sand and Stars, Night Flight, and Flight to Arras* (Harcourt Brace Jovanovich, New York), 1984, p. 61-62

226. Morrison, James Dalton, Editor: *Masterpieces of Religious Verse, My Orders by Wetherald, Ethelwyn* (Harper & Brothers Publishers, New York and London), 1948, p.971

227. de Saint-Exupéry, Antoine: *Airman's Odyssey*—a Trilogy Comprising *Wind, Sand and Stars, Night Flight, and Flight to Arras* (Harcourt Brace Jovanovich, New York), 1984, p. 263-264

228. de Saint-Exupéry, Antoine: *Airman's Odyssey*—a Trilogy Comprising *Wind, Sand and Stars, Night Flight, and Flight to Arras* (Harcourt Brace Jovanovich, New York), 1984, p. 265

229. Whitman, Walt: *Leaves of Grass.* (David McKay, Philadelphia), 1900

230. de Saint-Exupéry, Antoine: *Airman's Odyssey*—a Trilogy Comprising *Wind, Sand and Stars, Night Flight, and Flight to Arras* (Harcourt Brace Jovanovich, New York), 1984, p. 109

231. de Saint-Exupéry, Antoine: *Airman's Odyssey*—a Trilogy Comprising *Wind, Sand and Stars, Night Flight, and Flight to Arras* (Harcourt Brace Jovanovich, New York), 1984, p. 115-116

232. de Saint-Exupéry, Antoine: *Airman's Odyssey*—a Trilogy Comprising *Wind, Sand and Stars, Night Flight, and Flight to Arras* (Harcourt Brace Jovanovich, New York), 1984, p. 117

233. de Saint-Exupéry, Antoine: *Airman's Odyssey*—a Trilogy Comprising *Wind, Sand and Stars, Night Flight, and Flight to Arras* (Harcourt Brace Jovanovich, New York), 1984, p. 126

234. de Saint-Exupéry, Antoine: *Airman's Odyssey*—a Trilogy Comprising *Wind, Sand and Stars, Night Flight, and Flight to Arras* (Harcourt Brace Jovanovich, New York), 1984, p. 128

235. de Saint-Exupéry, Antoine: *Airman's Odyssey*—a Trilogy Comprising *Wind, Sand and Stars, Night Flight, and Flight to Arras* (Harcourt Brace Jovanovich, New York), 1984, p. 132-133

236. de Saint-Exupéry, Antoine: *Airman's Odyssey*—a Trilogy Comprising *Wind, Sand and Stars, Night Flight, and Flight to Arras* (Harcourt Brace Jovanovich, New York), 1984, p. 141

237. Hebrews 13:2-3

238. 1 Corinthians 10:13

239. de Saint-Exupéry, Antoine: *Airman's Odyssey*—a Trilogy Comprising *Wind, Sand and Stars, Night Flight, and Flight to Arras* (Harcourt Brace Jovanovich, New York), 1984, p. 142

240. Schiff, Stacy: *Saint-Exupéry* (Alfred A. Knopf, Inc., New York), 1994, p. 259

241. de Saint-Exupéry, Antoine: *Airman's Odyssey*—a Trilogy Comprising *Wind, Sand and Stars, Night Flight, and Flight to Arras* (Harcourt Brace Jovanovich, New York), 1984, p. 146

242. de Saint-Exupéry, Antoine: *Airman's Odyssey*—a Trilogy Comprising *Wind, Sand and Stars, Night Flight, and Flight to Arras* (Harcourt Brace Jovanovich, New York), 1984, p. 150

243. John 15:6

244. de Saint-Exupéry, Antoine: *Airman's Odyssey*—a Trilogy Comprising *Wind, Sand and Stars, Night Flight, and Flight to Arras* (Harcourt Brace Jovanovich, New York), 1984, p. 150

245. de Saint-Exupéry, Antoine: *Airman's Odyssey*—a Trilogy Comprising *Wind, Sand and Stars, Night Flight, and Flight to Arras* (Harcourt Brace Jovanovich, New York), 1984, p. 154-155

246. Schiff, Stacy: *Saint-Exupéry* (Alfred A. Knopf, Inc., New York), 1994, p. 260

247. Schiff, Stacy: *Saint-Exupéry* (Alfred A. Knopf, Inc., New York), 1994, p. 264

248. Rumbold, Richard: *The Winged Life—A Portrait of Antoine de Saint-Exupéry* (George Weidenfeld & Nicolson, London), 1953, p. 133

249. Hugo, Victor: *Les Misérables,* translated by Lee Fahnestock and Norman MacAfee, based on the classic C. E. Wilbour translation (New American Library, a Division of Penguin Books, New York), 1987, p. 169-170

250. de Saint-Exupéry, Antoine: *Airman's Odyssey*—a Trilogy Comprising *Wind, Sand and Stars, Night Flight, and Flight to Arras* (Harcourt Brace Jovanovich, New York), 1984, p. 192

251. Job 38:7

252. Acts 17:24, 26, 28

253. Rumbold, Richard: *The Winged Life—A Portrait of Antoine de Saint-Exupéry* (George Weidenfeld & Nicolson, London), 1953, p. 160

254. *Avalon Project : The French Yellow Book : No. 368* - M. Georges Bonnet, Minister for Foreign Affairs, to all the Heads of Diplomatic Missions accredited to Paris. Paris, September 3, 1939. URL : http://www.yale.edu/lawweb/avalon/wwii/yellow/ylbk368.htm

255. Rumbold, Richard: *The Winged Life—A Portrait of Antoine de Saint-Exupéry* (George Weidenfeld & Nicolson, London), 1953, p. 165-166

256. Rumbold, Richard: *The Winged Life—A Portrait of Antoine de Saint-Exupéry* (George Weidenfeld & Nicolson, London), 1953, p. 156

257. Rumbold, Richard: *The Winged Life—A Portrait of Antoine de Saint-Exupéry* (George Weidenfeld & Nicolson, London), 1953, p. 156

258. Schiff, Stacy: *Saint-Exupéry* (Alfred A. Knopf, Inc., New York), 1994, p. 326

259. Hugo, Victor: *Les Misérables,* translated by Lee Fahnestock and Norman MacAfee, based on the classic C. E. Wilbour translation (New American Library, a Division of Penguin Books, New York), 1987, p. 27

260. de Saint-Exupéry, Antoine: *The Wisdom of the Sands*—Translated by Stuart Gilbert from the French *Citadelle* (Harcourt, Brace and Company, New York), 1950, p. 30, 35-36

261. Rumbold, Richard: *The Winged Life—A Portrait of Antoine de Saint-Exupéry* (George Weidenfeld & Nicolson, London), 1953, p.170

262. de Saint-Exupéry, Antoine: *Airman's Odyssey*—a Trilogy Comprising *Wind, Sand and Stars, Night Flight, and Flight to Arras* (Harcourt Brace Jovanovich, New York), 1984, p. 285

263. de Saint-Exupéry, Antoine: *Airman's Odyssey*—a Trilogy Comprising *Wind, Sand and Stars, Night Flight, and Flight to Arras* (Harcourt Brace Jovanovich, New York), 1984, p. 337, 347-349

264. de Saint-Exupéry, Antoine: *Airman's Odyssey*—a Trilogy Comprising *Wind, Sand and Stars, Night Flight, and Flight to Arras* (Harcourt Brace Jovanovich, New York), 1984, p. 324-326

265. de Saint-Exupéry, Antoine: *Airman's Odyssey*—a Trilogy Comprising *Wind, Sand and Stars, Night Flight, and Flight to Arras* (Harcourt Brace Jovanovich, New York), 1984, p. 373

266. de Saint-Exupéry, Antoine: *Airman's Odyssey*—a Trilogy Comprising *Wind, Sand and Stars, Night Flight, and Flight to Arras* (Harcourt Brace Jovanovich, New York), 1984, p. 368

267. de Saint-Exupéry, Antoine: *Airman's Odyssey*—a Trilogy Comprising *Wind, Sand and Stars, Night Flight, and Flight to Arras* (Harcourt Brace Jovanovich, New York), 1984, p. 383

268. de Saint-Exupéry, Antoine: *Airman's Odyssey*—a Trilogy Comprising *Wind, Sand and Stars, Night Flight, and Flight to Arras* (Harcourt Brace Jovanovich, New York), 1984, p. 391

269. de Saint-Exupéry, Antoine: *Airman's Odyssey*—a Trilogy Comprising *Wind, Sand and Stars, Night Flight, and Flight to Arras* (Harcourt Brace Jovanovich, New York), 1984, p. 403, 405-406

270. de Saint-Exupéry, Antoine: *Airman's Odyssey*—a Trilogy Comprising *Wind, Sand and Stars, Night Flight, and Flight to Arras* (Harcourt Brace Jovanovich, New York), 1984, p. 389

271. de Saint-Exupéry, Antoine: *Airman's Odyssey*—a Trilogy Comprising *Wind, Sand and Stars, Night Flight, and Flight to Arras* (Harcourt Brace Jovanovich, New York), 1984, p. 389

272. Alma 40:9-10

273. Alma 40:23

274. de Saint-Exupéry, Antoine: *Airman's Odyssey*—a Trilogy Comprising *Wind, Sand and Stars, Night Flight, and Flight to Arras* (Harcourt Brace Jovanovich, New York), 1984, p. 415, 417

275. Helaman 12:2-3

276. Galatians 5:13

277. de Saint-Exupéry, Antoine: *Airman's Odyssey*—a Trilogy Comprising *Wind, Sand and Stars, Night Flight, and Flight to Arras* (Harcourt Brace Jovanovich, New York), 1984, p. 421, 423-426

278. 1 John 3:2

279. Lewis, C. S.: *The Screwtape Letters* (Bantam Books, New York), 1982, p. xiii

280. Lewis, C. S.: *The Screwtape Letters* (Bantam Books, New York), 1982, p. 23

281. de Saint-Exupéry, Antoine: *Airman's Odyssey*—a Trilogy Comprising *Wind, Sand and Stars, Night Flight, and Flight to Arras* (Harcourt Brace Jovanovich, New York), 1984, p. 428-429

282. de Saint-Exupéry, Antoine: *Airman's Odyssey*—a Trilogy Comprising *Wind, Sand and Stars, Night Flight, and Flight to Arras* (Harcourt Brace Jovanovich, New York), 1984, p. 434

283. Moses 1:39

284. Morrison, James Dalton, Editor: *Masterpieces of Religious Verse, The Pilgrim by Markham, Edwin* (Harper & Brothers Publishers, New York and London), 1948, p. 269

285. de Saint-Exupéry, Antoine: *Airman's Odyssey*—a Trilogy Comprising *Wind, Sand and Stars, Night Flight, and Flight to Arras* (Harcourt Brace Jovanovich, New York), 1984, p. 407

286. Addison, Joseph: *The Vision of Mirza, The Harvard Classics, Volume 27* (P. F. Collier & Son Corporation, New York), 1937, p. 74

287. ARMISTICE AGREEMENT BETWEEN THE GERMAN HIGH COMMAND OF THE ARMED FORCES AND FRENCH PLENIPOTENTIARIES, COMPIÈGNE, JUNE 22, 1940. Source: United States, Department of State, Publication No. 6312, Documents on German Foreign Policy 1918-1945 Series D, IX, 671-676. Washington, DC : Government Printing Office, 1956.

288. Schiff, Stacy: *Saint-Exupéry* (Alfred A. Knopf, Inc., New York), 1994, p. 339

289. Rumbold, Richard: *The Winged Life—A Portrait of Antoine de Saint-Exupéry* (George Weidenfeld & Nicolson, London), 1953, p. 176

290. Schiff, Stacy: *Saint-Exupéry* (Alfred A. Knopf, Inc., New York), 1994, p. 363-364

291. Schiff, Stacy: *Saint-Exupéry* (Alfred A. Knopf, Inc., New York), 1994, p. 397

292. de Saint-Exupéry, Antoine: *Wartime Writings*—Translated by Norah Purcell (Harcourt Brace Jovanovich, New York), 1990, p. 195-199

293. de Saint-Exupéry, Antoine: *Wartime Writings*—Translated by Norah Purcell (Harcourt Brace Jovanovich, New York), 1990, p. 204-205

294. Rumbold, Richard: *The Winged Life—A Portrait of Antoine de Saint-Exupéry* (George Weidenfeld & Nicolson, London), 1953, p. 194

295. Schiff, Stacy: *Saint-Exupéry* (Alfred A. Knopf, Inc., New York), 1994, p.422

296. de Saint-Exupéry, Antoine: *Wartime Writings*—Translated by Norah Purcell (Harcourt Brace Jovanovich, New York), 1990, p. 207

297. de Saint-Exupéry, Antoine: *Wartime Writings*—Translated by Norah Purcell (Harcourt Brace Jovanovich, New York), 1990, p. 213-214

298. Paraphrase of quotation used earlier in this work—de Saint-Exupéry, Antoine: *Airman's Odyssey*—a Trilogy Comprising *Wind, Sand and Stars, Night Flight, and Flight to Arras* (Harcourt Brace Jovanovich, New York), 1984, p. 324-326

299. de Saint-Exupéry, Antoine: *Wartime Writings*—Translated by Norah Purcell (Harcourt Brace Jovanovich, New York), 1990, p.215

300. de Saint-Exupéry, Antoine: *Wartime Writings*—Translated by Norah Purcell (Harcourt Brace Jovanovich, New York), 1990, p. 216-217

301. de Saint-Exupéry, Antoine: *Airman's Odyssey*—a Trilogy Comprising *Wind, Sand and Stars, Night Flight, and Flight to Arras* (Harcourt Brace Jovanovich, New York), 1984, p. 274

302. de Saint-Exupéry, Antoine: *Airman's Odyssey*—a Trilogy Comprising *Wind, Sand and Stars, Night Flight, and Flight to Arras* (Harcourt Brace Jovanovich, New York), 1984, p. 389

303. de Saint-Exupéry, Antoine: *Airman's Odyssey*—a Trilogy Comprising *Wind, Sand and Stars, Night Flight, and Flight to Arras* (Harcourt Brace Jovanovich, New York), 1984, p. 389

304. de Saint-Exupéry, Antoine: *Wartime Writings*—Translated by Norah Purcell (Harcourt Brace Jovanovich, New York), 1990, p. 207

305. de Saint-Exupéry, Antoine: *Wartime Writings*—Translated by Norah Purcell (Harcourt Brace Jovanovich, New York), 1990, p. 207

306. Jordan, William George: *The Majesty of Calmness* (Kessinger Publishing, USA), p. 8

307. Saint-Exupéry, Antoine: *Airman's Odyssey*—a Trilogy Comprising *Wind, Sand and Stars, Night Flight, and Flight to Arras* (Harcourt Brace Jovanovich, New York), 1984, p. 34

308. Saint-Exupéry, Antoine: *Airman's Odyssey*—a Trilogy Comprising *Wind, Sand and Stars, Night Flight, and Flight to Arras* (Harcourt Brace Jovanovich, New York), 1984, p. 35

309. Jordan, William George: *The Majesty of Calmness* (Kessinger Publishing, USA), p. 14

310. de Saint-Exupéry, Antoine: *The Wisdom of the Sands*—Translated by Stuart Gilbert from the French *Citadelle* (Harcourt, Brace and Company, New York), 1950, p. IX, XII

311. de Saint-Exupéry, Antoine: *The Wisdom of the Sands*—Translated by Stuart Gilbert from the French *Citadelle* (Harcourt, Brace and Company, New York), 1950, p. 16

312. de Saint-Exupéry, Antoine: *The Wisdom of the Sands*—Translated by Stuart Gilbert from the French *Citadelle* (Harcourt, Brace and Company, New York), 1950, p. 16-17

313. de Saint-Exupéry, Antoine: *The Wisdom of the Sands*—Translated by Stuart Gilbert from the French *Citadelle* (Harcourt, Brace and Company, New York), 1950, p. 17-18

314. de Saint-Exupéry, Antoine: *The Wisdom of the Sands*—Translated by Stuart Gilbert from the French *Citadelle* (Harcourt, Brace and Company, New York), 1950, p. 18-19

315. Einstein, Albert: 1950 Letter (quoted in H Eves Mathematical Circles Adieu, Boston), 1977

316. Moses 6:63

317. Peattie, Donald Culross: (Flowering Earth, Chapter 1, Putnam), 1939

318. de Saint-Exupéry, Antoine: *The Wisdom of the Sands*—Translated by Stuart Gilbert from the French *Citadelle* (Harcourt, Brace and Company, New York), 1950, p. 28-29

319. Matthew 6:19-20

320. de Saint-Exupéry, Antoine: *The Wisdom of the Sands*—Translated by Stuart Gilbert from the French *Citadelle* (Harcourt, Brace and Company, New York), 1950, p. 60

321. Morrison, James Dalton, Editor: *Masterpieces of Religious Verse, My Name is Legion by Edward Sanford Martin* (Harper & Brothers Publishers, New York and London), 1948, p. 274

322. de Saint-Exupéry, Antoine: *The Wisdom of the Sands*—Translated by Stuart Gilbert from the French *Citadelle* (Harcourt, Brace and Company, New York), 1950, p. 76

323. de Saint-Exupéry, Antoine: *The Wisdom of the Sands*—Translated by Stuart Gilbert from the French *Citadelle* (Harcourt, Brace and Company, New York), 1950, p. 75, 93

324. de Saint-Exupéry, Antoine: *The Wisdom of the Sands*—Translated by Stuart Gilbert from the French *Citadelle* (Harcourt, Brace and Company, New York), 1950, p. 38

325. de Saint-Exupéry, Antoine: *The Wisdom of the Sands*—Translated by Stuart Gilbert from the French *Citadelle* (Harcourt, Brace and Company, New York), 1950, p. 97

326. de Saint-Exupéry, Antoine: *The Wisdom of the Sands*—Translated by Stuart Gilbert from the French *Citadelle* (Harcourt, Brace and Company, New York), 1950, p. 68-69

327. de Saint-Exupéry, Antoine: *The Wisdom of the Sands*—Translated by Stuart Gilbert from the French *Citadelle* (Harcourt, Brace and Company, New York), 1950, p. 75

328. de Saint-Exupéry, Antoine: *The Wisdom of the Sands*—Translated by Stuart Gilbert from the French *Citadelle* (Harcourt, Brace and Company, New York), 1950, p. 71-72, 74, 78-80

329. John 12:32

Albatros combat aircraft of Jasta 2

Chaudun Airfield

The 99th Observation Squadron at Luxeuil in 1918

German Observation Balloon

Eddie Rickenbacker, Doug Campbell and Ken Marr

Eddie Rickenbacker with SPAD Number One

Eddie Rickenbacker with his SPAD

Major Raoul Lufbery

Fifty Horsepower Bleriot Trainer such as Jimmy Hall flew

Jimmy Hall learning to fly at Ecole d' Aviation

Combat Pilot Jimmy Hall

Jimmy Hall's Nieuport brought down by German Anti-aircraft Fire

An injured Hall after crash landing behind German lines

Hall, shown respect by his enemies, is being transported in a German staff car

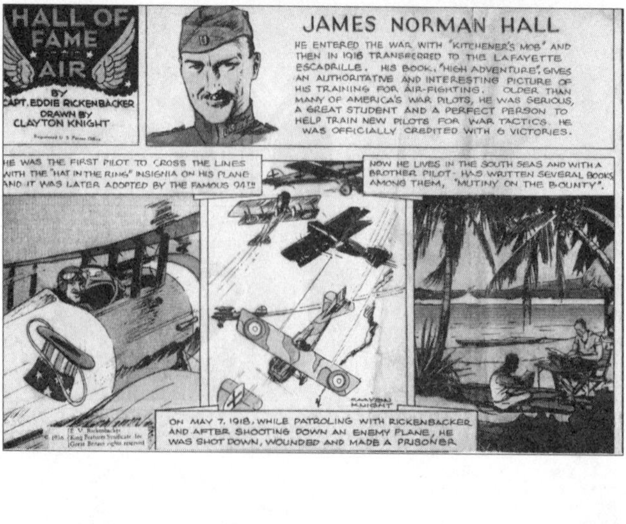

Chief Saint-Exupéry, third from left, at Cape Juby, Africa

Reconnaissance Pilot Antoine de Saint-Exupéry

Henri Guillaumet and his Potez 25

Guillaumet's Potez 25, recovered after the winter snow melt

Antoine de Saint-Exupéry (center) and Henri Guillaumet (right) during WWII

A P-38, possibly flown by Saint-Exupéry

The Author when he flew for Rickenbacker's Airline